W9-BCV-946

DEFENDERS OF GOD

Defenders of God

THE FUNDAMENTALIST REVOLT AGAINST THE MODERN AGE

Bruce B. Lawrence

1817

Harper & Row, Publishers, San Francisco

New York, Grand Rapids, Philadelphia, St. Louis
London, Singapore, Sydney, Tokyo, Toronto

Unless otherwise noted, Scripture quotations contained herein are from the Revised Standard Version of the Bible, copyrighted 1946, 1952, 1971 by the Division of Christian Education of the National Council of the Churches of Christ in the U.S.A., and are used by permission. All rights reserved.

DEFENDERS OF GOD: *The Fundamentalist Revolt Against the Modern Age.* Copyright © 1989 by Bruce B. Lawrence. All rights reserved. Printed in the United States of America. No part of this book may be used or reproduced in any manner whatsoever without written permission except in the case of brief quotations embodied in critical articles and reviews. For information address Harper & Row, Publishers, Inc., 10 East 53rd Street, New York, NY 10022.

FIRST EDITION

Library of Congress Cataloging-in-Publication Data

Lawrence, Bruce B.
    Defenders of God: The fundamentalist revolt against the modern age.
    Bibliography: p.
    1. Fundamentalism—Comparative studies.   I. Title.
BL238.L38   1989   291′.09′048   89-45394
ISBN 0-06-250509-2

89 90 91 92 93 RRD(H) 10 9 8 7 6 5 4 3 2 1

To Marshall G. S. Hodgson,
an American Islamicist,
a global visionary.

Contents

Preface

I would never have thought about writing such a book without the shock of the 1978–79 revolution in Iran. I have written about that revolution elsewhere but in this study I attempt to come to terms with the Khomeini phenomenon as but one expression of the global reactivation of traditional religious symbolism and values often called "fundamentalism." Whether one considers the Salman Rushdie affair or the protests against the movie *The Last Temptation of Christ* or the emergence of religious parties as potential power brokers in the last Israeli elections, the salience of scriptural absolutism is inescapable. It is also modern. Fundamentalists do not deny or disregard modernity; they protest as moderns against the heresies of the modern age. In the Salman Rushdie affair they confronted freedom of speech with loyalty to age-old cultural norms. To the makers of *The Last Temptation of Christ* they posed blasphemy as a higher standard than artistic freedom, while in Israel they favored occupying *all* the Land of Israel *(Eretz Yisrael)* rather than pursuing pragmatic policies dictated by the secular state of Israel.

These recent events have surprised many observers. They will continue to surprise, until we understand the global context of fundamentalism. It is not one revolt but a series of revolts by those who uphold deep-seated religious values against what they perceive to be the shallow indeterminacy of modern ideologies. Rationalism or relativism, pluralism or secularism—each undermines the Divine Transcendent, challenging his revelations, denying his prophets, ignoring his morally guided community. Without certitude the world is doomed. With it salvation (for some) is assured. The righteous remnant are emissaries of an All-Powerful, All-Knowing Being who has been betrayed by the freedom he granted the modern age. Who are the fundamentalists? They are the last-ditch defenders of God.

In a preface I have only to account for intellectual motivation and personal indebtedness. Trained as a historian of religions, I have devoted much of my academic life to the study of cross-cultural debates, theoretical mysticism, and institutional Sufism, mostly in the region of South Asia but more recently also in North Africa. Preoccupation with fundamentalism would seem an aberration from my demonstrated interests and major publications. Yet I have also resisted every effort to channel my own thinking into ever narrower subdisciplinary specialties. I have frequently taught and written about Islam as one of the major categories of comparative analysis in civilizational studies. It is to comparison that the deeper urges of my research have tended, from my first book examining Hindu and Muslim doctrines . . . to the present work. I concur with another historian of religions, Jonathan Z. Smith, that "comparison is, at base, never identity"; rather, "comparison requires the postulation of difference as the grounds of being interesting (rather than tautological) and a methodical manipulation of difference, a playing across the gap in the service of some useful end."[1]

The useful end for me is to make sense of fundamentalism as something more than journalistic banter, while also not ignoring that such banter plays a powerful mediating role in today's world. One may disagree with Marshall McLuhan that the medium *is* the message, but so intertwined is fundamentalism with the print and electronic media that it becomes fatuous to discuss its content apart from its packaging. Fundamentalism is an ideology; the press is an instrument of ideologies. Fundamentalists not only want a platform for their ideas; they need outlets to enhance their influence and to register their success. Reporters, on the other hand, need stories, and fundamentalists provide lively headlines: threats from them or fears about their influence help to sustain both viewer ratings and magazine subscriptions.

Fundamentalism is as modern as the media and as novel as ideology. Fundamentalism is the aggressive advocacy through print and picture media of scriptural mandates that provide—or at least fundamentalists believe they provide—the only panacea for a corrupt age. Fundamentalism is an ideology rather than a theology. Just as no theologian ever rose to new heights of fame through the press, so no ideology ever succeeded in being viable without the press or, more recently, the press and the television. Underlying both the puzzle of fundamentalism and the prevalence of the media is the emergence of the modern world. The contradictions it embodies have been cogently set forth by the premier American Islamicist, Marshall G. S. Hodgson. Though never privileged to meet him, I have used his *magnum opus, The Venture of Islam; Conscience and History in a World Civilization* for over a decade in the classroom. It was his insights in volume 3 of *The Venture of Islam* that prepared me for the Iranian Revolution and also for the emergence of fundamentalism as a global phenomenon. In coining the term the Great Western Transmutation (which I frequently abbreviate to the GWT), Hodgson reconceived the most recent phase in human history. It was no longer a clash between superstition and reason, tradition and modernity. It was rather an accidental process that happened in one place, at one time, due to a cluster of factors. It is subject to rational inquiry and discourse without privileging reason or excluding the discourse of others. The juggling of antinomies characterized Hodgson's lively imagination; it resonates with my own experience that mysticism and fundamentalism, which at first seem like polar extremes, hold in common a suspicion of untrammeled reason. Since Imam Khomeini was a student of 'irfan or Islamic mysticism, it seems fitting to dedicate this book to a Quaker quietist whose life was absorbed with the intricacies of Islam but who also tried to relate Muslim happenings to world history.

Several people with uncommon perspectives and disparate talents have contributed to the making of this book. Among colleagues, Kalman Bland, Emmanuel Sivan, Ehud Sprinzak, Gideon Aran, Jerrold Green, Henry Munson, Albert Hourani, Charles Adams, AbdulAziz Sachedina, Mahmoud Ayoub, Richard Martin, and Marilyn Waldman have been forthright in offering critiques some of which I have tried to refute but all of which have helped to reshape my ideas. Students also instruct, and I learned about some of the stubborn perplexities clustered around the concept fundamentalism through interaction with members of a Master of Arts in Liberal Studies course which I taught at Duke University during the final stages of writing this book. To colleagues and students as well as to support staff, especially Wanda Camp and Becky Hayes, I am grateful. They are not responsible for what has eventuated, but without them my vision would have long since been dulled, my patience spent in wrestling with the issue of fundamentalism.

My best critic has also been my strongest supporter. Miriam Cooke has spent hours stretching into days on multiple chores—rethinking, revising, and finally proofreading parts of this manuscript. Her help has been inestimable. She is my wife and more, the mainstay through eight years of research and writing on fundamentalism. To her, as also to her parents, Edit and Hedley Cooke, who read *in toto* the penultimate draft of what follows and offered valuable suggestions, I owe a special debt of gratitude.

And I would be remiss if I did not also thank two institutions as splendid as they are recent. The Fundamentalism Project of the University of Chicago, begun in 1988 under the direction of Martin Marty and Scott Appleby, provided a forum through which I refined some of the thoughts in this study, especially concerning Jewish Fundamentalism (chapter 6). The Dartmouth College Institute of the Humanities convened its first group of fellows in Spring 1989. Directed by Robert Oden and enlivened by Albert Hourani, it stimulated me to reflect further on the recurring traits of fundamentalism (enumerated at the end of chapter 4). For the multiple generosities of both institutions I am a better scholar, although no one in Hyde Park or Hanover should be held responsible for what I have construed about religion in the modern age.

Introduction

So pervasive have been generalizations about fundamentalism, so strident denunciations of fundamentalists themselves that at the outset it is essential to state what fundamentalism is not. Fundamentalism is not a political gambit, to seize public power through appeal to aggrieved parties. Nor is it an economic ploy, to take resources from the privileged few and redistribute them among the disadvantaged and dispossessed. Nor is it a social strategy, to gain visibility and prestige for upwardly mobile malcontents. Fundamentalists *do* relate to the public sphere. They *do* care about political power, economic justice, and social status. But they are above all religiously motivated individuals, drawn together into ideologically structured groups, for the purpose of promoting a vision of divine restoration.

Divine restoration does not imply blind reaction against all features of the contemporary era. Fundamentalists are not atavistic Luddites opposed to the instrumentalities of modern media, transport, or warfare. Fundamentalists relate fully to the infrastructures that have produced the unprecedented options for communication and mobility that today's world offers. Fundamentalists are moderns.

And they are moderns in the sense that Marshall Berman explicates in his magnificent study, *All That Is Solid Melts Into Air: The Experience of Modernity.* Trying to expose the facile, often flippant use of "postmodern," Berman argues that "to be modern is to experience personal and social life as a maelstrom, to find one's world and oneself in perpetual disintegration and renewal, trouble and anguish, ambiguity and contradiction: to be part of a universe in which all that is solid melts into air."[1] Fundamentalists, like other moderns, recognize that the world in which they strive to locate their deepest identity is constantly shifting, that there is an unbridgeable gap between who they are and where they want to be.

Fundamentalists are moderns but they are not modernists. Again, Berman provides a definitional framework that clarifies the difference. "To be a modernist is to make oneself somehow at home in the maelstrom, to make its rhythms one's own, to move within its currents in search of the forms of reality, of beauty, of freedom, of justice, that its fervid and perilous flow allows."[2] While moderns recognize a collective past that informs their individual presents, modernists see only a single thread tracing their particular instincts, needs, and desires. If moderns are conflicted universalists, modernists are unabashed relativists.

Fundamentalists oppose modernism and its proponents. They have been catalysed by their unremitting opposition to all those who equate modernity as an index of material potentials with modernism as the sole value orientation appropriate to citizens of the "modern" world. Fundamentalists divide modern consciousness into two categories: objective givens and ideological variables. They posit a constant tension between the former and the latter, between modernization and modernism. Modernization may be epitomized as that complex of material structures, derived from technological innovations and abetted by capitalist initiatives, that launches a process sustained by its own momentum, but is its inevitable sequel and companion an ideology that usurps its name, to wit, modernism? To those who espouse it, modernism connotes simply "a species of pure spirit, evolving in accord with its own autonomous artistic and intellectual imperatives."[3] Modernity, *not* modernism, does complement modernization, as effect to cause, and together modernization and modernity aggregate the range of objective, structural givens to which every modernist ideology must relate either explicitly or implicitly.

Modernity has to be reduced to be comprehended. It is the cipher symbolizing the technological surplus of our era. As such, it is the key category to consider when interpreting fundamentalism. It becomes and remains the enveloping context. Without modernity there are no fundamentalists, just as there are no modernists. The identity of fundamentalism, both as a psychological mindset and a historical movement, is shaped by the modern world. Fundamentalists seem bifurcated between their cause and their outcome; they are at once the consequence of modernity and the antithesis of modernism.

Either way, one cannot speak of premodern fundamentalists. In the premodern era there were not the material conditions that made the coherence and communication of fundamentalist ideology possible. The premodern era also lacked the exponents of that form of radical individualism now known as modernism. To speak about fundamentalism and to trace the lineage of any cadre of fundamentalists one must begin with the specific points of connectedness to, and interaction with, the processes that heralded the global material transformation of our world that we call modernization, the result of which was modernity. It follows that the moment when fundamentalists first appear differs within each religious tradition. It is earlier for *haredi* and quasi-Hasidic Jews, later for Protestant Christians, still later for Sunni and Shi'i Muslims, but in each instance the time line for discovering, describing, assessing, and perhaps explaining fundamentalists depends on modernity. The context frames the text; fundamentalists are products of modernity.

Because modernity is global, so is fundamentalism. Fundamentalists are not the privileged offspring of one modernizing religious tradition. The name in English is linked to turn-of-the-century Protestant Christianity, yet fundamentalism, like other reactions to modernity, has been at once cross-creedal and multicultural. Fundamentalism is as intrinsic and inevitable to Israeli *haredim* and Sunni or Shi'i Muslims as it is to American Protestants.

Finally, fundamentalism is not an intellectual isolate, a datum to be discussed, deciphered, and contained by armchair scholarly inquiry. One cannot rest content with the analysis of fundamentalism as someone else's problem. It is more than an unexpected or unwelcome social movement injecting scriptural shibboleths into public discourse. What the academy studies, others have created and also sustain. Fundamentalism is a blue-chip stock in that massive industry of symbol production known as journalism. Fundamentalists are marketable symbols. They are, before all else, the quarry of journalists, mined for the combination of fear, awe, and ridicule that they evoke in the minds of modern readers.

It was not always so. Both the print and TV media have, in the words of one observer, woken up to that which they had almost forgotten. "When the cosmopolitan journalists 'rediscovered' fundamentalism, they over-reacted."[4] Their overreaction has produced a contagion of concern with fundamentalism that shows no signs of ebbing or disappearing. The result is that no single study, however comprehensive, nor prime-time TV documentary, however graphic, will exhaust the myriad dimensions of fundamentalism. Fundamentalism is coextensive with our world. It will change, adapting to new circumstances, but it will not disappear.

Up till now fundamentalism has been a multicultural phenomenon attracting notoriety chiefly through negative media attention. Journalists have seized on fundamentalism without quite understanding their prey. In creating that which they proceed to criticize, journalists have pluralized fundamentalism. They recognize it as a social malaise in multiple religious guises. Protestant Christian fundamentalists have surfaced not only in the United States of America but also in Canada, England, and Europe, Jewish fundamentalists in the United States and Israel, Sunni and Shi'i fundamentalists[5] throughout parts of Africa and Asia. American journalists have tended to downplay the widely divergent cultural contexts within which fundamentalist movements have emerged. Far too often, they have linked all expressions of fundamentalist fervor to Protestant Christianity. Indulging in instant comparisons of seeming lookalikes, they relate every religious protest to the implicit model of domestic fundamentalism.

Consider the CBS "Evening News" program aired on 23 January 1986. It was titled "A Fundamental Dispute." The immediate pretext was a State Department warning that ultraorthodox Jews in Jerusalem were challenging the secular tone of contemporary Israeli society. There followed a string of images. First, hordes of veiled Muslim women were shown with this commentary: "the first wave of fundamentalist fervor flooded Tehran, then another wave blackened Beirut." Next, Jewish men, dressed in black coats and hats, with their long earlocks flying as they crowded into a Jerusalem market: "And now," intoned the reporter, "the Jewish fundamentalists, as passionate, extreme, and uncompromising as their Arab counterparts. They want to refashion Israel in their own image, closing Saturday matinees, cable cars, even El-Al (the national airline). They have burned bus stops covered with provocative advertising. They have tried to stop the Mormons from building an American university in Jerusalem." He goes on to decry them as "an organized, vocal minority pitted against a disorganized, silent majority. They seek to exercise power through the Knesset, where the minority religious parties are a swing voting bloc. They even want a law banning pig farming in Israel. They oppose compromise." The focus then shifts to the notorious Arab hater, Rabbi Meir Kahane. His face lingers on the screen longer than any other. "Alas," bemoans the fiery rabbi from Brooklyn, "Israel is heading toward a civil war between religious Israelis and their secular compatriots." "Smart betting money," adds the commentator, "is against the moderates. The ultraorthodox want to make Israel into a real Jewish state. They want to make the laws of Judaism into the laws of Israel, just as the laws of Islam have become the laws of Iran. The Israelis are caught between angry Palestinians (the screen flashes with a mob of thousands, fists held high) and fanatic Jews (a few black hats and bearded faces bobbing up and down at the Wailing Wall)."

The entire report lasted about two minutes. It vividly conveyed a sense of strife within Israel directly linked to a group labeled fundamentalist. The reference to "an organized, vocal minority against an unorganized, silent majority" could only trigger familiar, if reverse, associations in an American audience: here was a minor foreign instance of our own religious zealots, though ours were more fearsome because they claimed to be a "moral majority," at once organized and vocal.

All moderns pay attention to the news, even if they refuse to watch the nightly programs that the major networks orchestrate. The sociologist Robert Wuthnow correctly observed that "the national press has come to play a major role not only in the making of political and religious movements, but in setting the agenda for scholarly discussion as well."[6] For numerous reasons, not the least of which is the academic presumption that only scholars know the truth and can advance understanding, few have been willing to admit the inflated role that journalistic issues have assumed in the modern academy. Whatever else derives from our protracted inquiry into fundamentalism, we hope to demonstrate that the interface between the yellow press and the ivory tower has become more intricate than either reporters or professors have acknowledged.

Like journalists, EuroAmerican scholars of global religiosity tend to acknowledge Protestant fundamentalist cadres as the norm but with a difference. Unlike the popularizers, most academics either avoid mention of non-Christian varieties of fundamentalism or else minimize their importance by comparing and contrasting them with Christianity. All discourse is pegged to the American context. It is assumed that the potential for scriptural absolutism has been realized in only one religion, at one place, at one time. The epitome of fundamentalism is Protestant Christianity in early twentieth-century America. All others are epigones.

In his extended study of Christian fundamentalism, the biblical scholar James Barr illustrates the prevalent disposition among academics. Though insightful and suggestive, his study is limited to the aspirations, and also the declamations, of his Christian subjects. About other fundamentalisms, Barr wryly comments:

Some kinds of Judaism . . . are very conservative about the Bible. . . . [Yet] one cannot handle conservatism about the Bible within Judaism as if it was of one piece with the phenomenon within Christianity. Islam also can be said to be 'fundamentalist' [since] Muslims believe that the Qur'an was verbally revealed to the Prophet [Muhammad] in its Arabic words, and the exact form of the text was divinely inspired, its purity [being] above question.[7]

In his view, Protestant Christian fundamentalism remains distinct from its monotheistic counterparts. Despite a certain similarity in attitude that extends to Roman Catholicism, Greek Orthodoxy, Judaism, and Islam, "in none did these built-in features of the Biblical tradition and its interpretation go on to produce a *full fundamentalism of the Protestant type.*"[8] Why is Protestant fundamentalism deemed to be the norm? Because other traditions pose inhibiting correctives: in Roman Catholicism, the presence of the papacy as well as a developed and explicit philosophical theology; in Greek Orthodoxy, the use of allegorizing exegesis; in Judaism and Islam, the acceptance of the authority of tradition.

Barr's analysis falters on two questionable assumptions: first, that "attitude toward scripture" can be isolated from other motives for espousing a fundamentalist posture, and second, that only Protestant Christians give unqualified priority to scripturalism in their religious outlook. The pivotal question reverts to a definition that Barr never offers, the meaning of scripture.

Scripture is more than sacred books and canonical judgments. It is also an appeal to one community as authoritative interpreters of the pure, the sole, the "inerrant" sense of scripture. Only if Christian scriptures are identified with the King James Version of the Bible is Barr's evaluation of fundamentalism correct. His reasoning might be justified with respect to Roman Catholicism and Greek Orthodoxy, since in both traditions ecclesiastical, as well as scriptural, authority is invoked. Yet the case is different with Islam and Judaism. Despite variant notions of cultural authenticity, the potential for scriptural absolutism among both Muslims and Jews is at least as high as it is among Protestant Christians. The appeal to scripture is firmly embedded in sections of Jerusalem, Cairo, and Tehran that yield nothing to the choirs of Lynchburg, Virginia, in their fervor for inerrancy.

The major conceptual problem goes beyond both the academy and the media. Neither scholars nor journalists to date have grasped the larger context within which fundamentalism must be viewed. It is a series of parallel socioreligious movements in the *modern* world that accept the instrumental benefits of modernity but not its value reorientations. All fundamentalists, whether quasi-Hasidic Jews, Sunni or Shi'i Muslims, or Protestant Christians, embrace the canon of scriptural authority as self-conscious advocates of anti-modernist values. In each instance, despite varying creedal loyalties and contrasting cultural settings, the catalyst for fundamentalist loyalty is hatred of the modernist value agenda.

To study fundamentalism one must engage in comparative analysis. Comparison alone reveals what is common, and also what is unique, in each fundamentalist cadre. The comparative study of fundamentalism requires the tandem pursuit of two goals. First, one must displace the biblicist, Eurocentric notion that fundamentalism is, by nature as well as by origin, the special preserve of Protestant Christianity. Second, one must demonstrate, rather than merely catalog,[9] which forces converge under which circumstances to shape various fundamentalist groups. The single, most consistent denominator is opposition to all those individuals or institutions that advocate Enlightenment values and wave the banner of secularism or modernism.

Within this book we have delineated our subject matter in relation to these twin goals. Fundamentalist challenges have arisen in several traditions. One could locate fundamentalist cadres that are Sikh or Buddhist, Baha'i or Hindu.[10] We limit our investigation to Judaism, Christianity, and Islam because in each of these traditions a fundamentalist protest was raised *explicitly* against modernism. Although other issues were at stake in each setting, none defined the tone of fundamentalist rhetoric as much as the hatred, which is also the fear, of modernism.

Modernism is more than a class ideology; it has become a paradigmatic way of viewing the world. In its formative phase, as Marshall Berman has convincingly argued, it could only be sustained by a dialectical interplay between the modernizing, specifically urban, environment of

EuroAmerica and imaginative modernist thinkers as well as artists. Whether or not Berman is correct that modernism has atrophied in the spiritual impoverishment of post–World War II EuroAmerican society,[11] it continues to inform not only the outlook of the privileged but also the study of the underprivileged or marginalized.

It is important to understand in what sense fundamentalists are underprivileged or marginalized. They are reacting against a notion of intellectual hegemony as well as sociopolitical privilege. They are not studying others; they are being studied. They are not granted access to the circles of the dominant ruling group; they are challenging their exclusion from such echelons of power. Fundamentalists may be viewed as either social malcontents in religious disguise or religious dissidents embracing social activism. Either way they are ideologues who look in from the margins. They demur from the modernist vision of a homogeneous global community ruled by an enlightened, which is to say secular, elite.

In promoting individual autonomy and de facto relativism, the modernist paradigm claims to be universal. It envelops its dissidents as well as its advocates. Fundamentalists may protest, but their modernist adversaries, by domesticating their protests whether through the media or the academy, try to reduce the autonomous power they project. Domestication takes place at many levels. Perhaps nowhere is it more glaringly evident than in scholarly efforts to discount the fundamentalist retort to those dispositions and actions that reflect a modernist mindset. If fundamentalism is inimical to the modern world, it is anathema to the modern university. Professors are or should be above creedal claims. Fundamentalists challenge the claim of value-free research or teaching. They throw down the gauntlet not only to secular society but also to those who would defuse their threat by including them as simply one more datum in the secular study of religion.

Until recently, fundamentalism did not even have the status of a datum. While Protestant Christian fundamentalism received more attention than any other, it, too, was understudied.[12] Why? Because most academics implicitly downplay the threat of fundamentalism; it is a brand of religious behavior peculiarly uncongenial to their own worldview. The sociologist Robert Bellah has observed that

the ethos of the modern university was dominated by an Enlightenment tradition that viewed religion as a negative influence on human culture and one destined to be replaced by science. Even today university professors are among the least religious people in American society, although, ironically, natural scientists are somewhat more apt to be religious than their humanist and social scientist colleagues.[13]

Whatever the truth of Bellah's assertions, they point to a malaise that academics feel in dealing with religion as a field of study. Contemporary religious movements pose an especially acute problem. They force themselves on public awareness. They are grist for network programmers in charge of providing action footage for the evening news. How can they not be taken seriously when they seem to be omnipresent?

Many social scientists as well as humanists would like to see the fundamentalist threat evaporate, becoming a bad dream limited to the eighties just as the civil rights movement was to the sixties. Assuming that it will persist, the larger question becomes, how is fundamentalism to be assessed within the academy? As Bellah noted, it is the Enlightenment that defines the ethos of the modern university. In the name of equality, it establishes a hierarchy of values. Despite recurrent demurrals from concerned administrators, the "hard" sciences dominate curricular as well as personal canons of judgment in the American academy. Social sciences are less powerful but still favored, while the "softest" sciences, the humanities or human sciences, including religious studies, rank as a distant, poor relation.[14]

Fundamentalists, in challenging secular society, also call into question the adequacy of the secular study of religion. Social scientists have repeatedly failed to take account of the autonomous nature of the religious impulse. Can humanists fare better? Are they disposed to focus on the constitutive elements of fundamentalism? Can they acknowledge the Enlightenment influence on them as participants in the modern university while at the same time remaining wary of Enlightenment presuppositions and categories? That is a subsidiary concern of our investigation. It pertains to the methodology of religious studies rather than the interpretation of fundamentalism as a discrete religious phenomenon. It may well be that those defiant antimodernists labeled fundamentalists will help to shape questions that go beyond their own immediate historical and social impact.

Whatever the outcome of the fundamentalist challenge, its origins are inseparable from the specter of its declared enemy: the Enlightenment. To study fundamentalism is to assess the Enlightenment as at once the precursor and the foil of all fundamentalist thought. The Enlightenment undergirds the modern world. It also launches the modern study of religion. It looks at everything human, yet considers its own viewpoint as observer and interpreter to be superior. It is that implicit assumption of superiority that offends. We will try to unravel its complex formation in what follows. Its impact has been so diffuse that we must grasp at diachronic notations, many of them biographical. We will briefly reflect on the contribution of founding fathers, particularly Kant and Comte, before assessing how different branches within the academy have appropriated Enlightenment attitudes toward religion.

"What is religion?" That should be the simplest, and also the most basic, of all questions. Whether they be Jews, Christians, or Muslims,

Sikhs, Parsees, or Arya Samajis, all monotheists would assent that religion requires belief *and* participation, that is, belief in God, prophets, and scripture, along with participation in a like-minded community of others faithful to the same belief pattern.

But such a "simple" definition of religion does not take into account its radical reassessment under the impact of the Enlightenment. Among Enlightenment spokesmen, few rival in importance the German philosopher, Immanuel Kant. By enlarging the role of practical reason and defining the categorical or moral imperative as equivalent to belief in God, Kant spurred the modern quest for the autonomy of man. Kant contrasted the limitless horizons of human potential with the lowered horizons, the "blinders," of institutional religious life. The former was available through the untrammeled exercise of reason, the latter sustained by reliance on age-old superstitions. Churches and synagogues, mosques and temples, were lumped together. All typified the physical edifices of institutional religiosity. They, as well as the professional classes who staffed and operated them, became, in Kant's view, barriers to the Enlightenment mandate: awaken the spark of practical reason and utilize it fully. His was not a clarion call to antinomianism. Indeed, in the hand of clever ideologues it could be, and was, used to justify the extensive power of newly industrializing, centripetal military patronage states. Yet Kant's arguments changed forever traditional religious structures, undermining the belief systems that supported them while also superannuating the clergy who served them.

Kant was not the sole exponent of Enlightenment thought. However universal the thrust of his challenging treatises, they would have had but a limited impact had not other intellectuals of his time concerned themselves with similar issues. Among these others, Schleiermacher, Hegel, Feuerbach, Comte, and later, Nietzsche, Marx, and Freud helped to shape a new view of religion in the post-Kantian period of European history. Even when they disagreed with Kant to the extent of refuting him, later thinkers were influenced by his categories, above all, by his idea of an internalized (i.e., rational and immanentist) sense of duty as the foundation of ethical conduct. In effect, Kant did what few thinkers of any age or place have ever done: he reversed the analytical referents of his contemporaries. The eighteenth century Königsberg philosopher did not prove but eloquently argued and repeatedly demonstrated that "ethics do not rest on religion [i.e., metaphysics] but the other way round—religion rests on ethics." [15]

Kant's bold demotion of religious authority, despite its appeal to other Continental intellectuals, might still have been rejected had he not lived in an age when change had begun to accelerate in several spheres, lending credibility to Enlightenment attacks on theistic presumptions. The theocratic basis of pre-Enlightenment society seemed threatened by numerous events: the political revolution in France, with its ideologues propounding a new era in civil religion; the industrial revolution in England portending an unforeseen expansion of regional and overseas commerce for all of North Europe; and the sudden succession of wars, which seemed at once larger and more destructive than those of preceding eras.

More than God-talk was at work in eighteenth century Europe. Major segments of North European society were probably never as wedded to a religious worldview, nor as loyal to ecclesiastical institutions, as has often been suggested. Yet in reducing the claims of metaphysics as a category (and also theology as a discipline), Kant laid the foundation for a new tradition of rationalist authority. Even though the subsequent Kantian tradition did not always remain loyal to Kant, it was the philosophical legacy bearing his name that colored the history of Roman Catholic and Protestant theological reflection in succeeding centuries. Branches of Jewish sectarian loyalty also became nuanced with reference to Kant,[16] and his impact on Islam has been evident in the Egyptian and South Asian contexts at least since the time of the modern pioneers in Islamic rationalism, Muhammad 'Abduh and Sayyid Ahmad Khan.[17]

Beyond *individual* responses to the Enlightenment derogation of religion is the *systemic* redistribution of religion as a field of study. The range of approaches to the investigation of religious beliefs, rituals, structures, and outcomes has expanded rather than contracted, as one might have expected, in the modern academy. Religion remains a topic of keen interest and sustained investigation in the most "enlightened" universities of Western Europe and North America. No longer the monopoly of scripturalists, theologians, ethicists, philosophers, or historians of religion, the study of religion has been broadened, and also reshaped, by approaches from the social sciences (now sometimes called, with beguiling imprecision, the human sciences). The novelty of this development is still relatively unappreciated. Until the first quarter of the present century, there was almost no perception of religion as a legitimate field of inquiry for any but those creedally as well as professionally committed to it. The emergence of the social or human sciences since that time has had an enormous impact on all studies of religion. It also has direct, immediate, and profound relevance for considering the role of fundamentalism in contemporary society.

The sociology of religion, like sociology, was founded in Europe. The shadow of Kant fell on sociology as it did on all the intellectual enterprises of the Enlightenment. Though too often accused of being an ethical reductionist, Kant did not fully abandon religion; he merely tried to frame the basic construct of human consciousness in such a way that religion became dependent on ethics, not the other way around. While eager to downgrade the authority of institutional religion, Kant never denied the value of religion as an inner compulsion, "the recognition of all our duties as divine commands."[18]

The decisive contrast is between Kant, who wanted to redefine religious values while retaining duties as *divine* commands, and Auguste Comte, the putative founder of sociology, who sought to *displace* religion as the source of values. Comte's views are sometimes labeled "positivist." From a religious perspective, they are nihilist. Comte advocated an interpretation of history that was at once evolutionary and deterministic. He equated religion with childhood, philosophy and science with adulthood. Since science is the highest stage of evolution in the human cycle, according to Comte, can science then fulfill the function of religion? In Comte's view, yes. It is, in fact, the special task of sociology to play an ersatz religious role, a role not unlike that which Marxists and psychoanalysts, in keeping with the vision of their respective faiths, have projected for humankind in this century.

Humanists as well as social scientists construe a buffer between the creedal affirmations of the believer and the religious probings of the academic. The buffer is designed to permit the latter an approach to his or her subject that is authentic but not indulgent; slippage into overt sympathy or advocacy or particular beliefs is the cardinal "sin" never to be committed by a scholar of religion. Yet excessive vigilance also introduces a danger; it may cause the buffer to become a chasm. At what point does distance turn into disdain and produce a guileless distortion instead of a privileged communication about the religion and its practitioners? Humanists and social scientists alike face these central issues. Though they differ in their strategy for resolving them, both stand apart from Marxists for whom religion has still another valuation, at once sharper and more negative.

The social scientific appropriation of the Enlightenment legacy requires close scrutiny. Most social scientists, especially sociologists, mirror the Enlightenment categories in a manner that precludes, even while seeming to permit, self-criticism. The study of religion, problematic for the humanist, becomes paradoxical for the social scientist.

A bold few sociologists and anthropologists are beginning to attempt the comparative study of fundamentalism.[19] Layered within the cultural construction of reality, fundamentalism looms as a new frontier, at once inviting and dangerous. Social scientists, confronting the literary antecedents and historical variables of fundamentalism, do not ignore such evidence, yet they also do not accept it as primary. It has to be ratcheted into two other kinds of evidence deemed to be foundational: first, field data gathered from taped interviews with fundamentalist subjects, or first-hand observations on the structure of fundamentalist groups, their rituals, social interactions, preferred occupations and modes of political expression; together with, second, sociological theories about the significance of all data, especially the field data at hand. Even if the investigator does argue for the relative autonomy of the religious sphere, as did, for instance, Max Weber, the argument would be couched in terms and categories that subordinate faith to the multiple expressions of religious behavior.

While this approach has often been hailed as a "value-free" methodology, it is laced with epistemological assumptions. First, it assumes that objectivity is possible, and second, that objectivity is the core of a scientific metavalue system.

Sociologists are aware of the ambiguity involved in their own professed canon of investigation. According to one theorist, an attitude of sympathetic detachment requires living on the "frontier of tension" between sympathy and detachment:

The sociologist can, and indeed must, seek to acquire an empathetic understanding of his subjects' commitment and their beliefs. Only if he can gain some apprehension of what it means to be a believer can he say anything useful about the religious movements he studies; and yet, in gaining that understanding, he must not actually become a believer.[20]

But the distance required for objectivity in the sociological investigation of religion has *two* poles. One has been aptly described above, distance from the subject being studied. The other, however, is distance from one's own religious presuppositions or antireligious prejudices.

Numerous are the attempts to face this problem. The decisive question is as recurrent as it is inexhaustible. It concerns the role of the interpreter vis-a-vis the data being interpreted. Social scientists, in pursuit of value-free, objective analysis, tend to focus on the need for "sympathetic detachment" from their subject(s). Yet sympathetic detachment has to be balanced by equally strict attention to hidden values, implicit preconceptions or predispositions in the interpreter. Less apparent but no less important than the value field of intended subjects, hidden values are also more difficult to admit, to confront, and to neutralize.

The strategies devised to solve the problem of "how to interpret" are manifold. Among the most exhaustive efforts to break this methodological logjam is George Devereux, *From Anxiety to Method in the Behavioral Sciences* (1967); yet the effort is compromised at the outset by Weston LaBarre's preface declaring that

self-designated "social sciences," yearning for the prestige of exact physical sciences from the seventeenth century onward, solemnly continue to pattern themselves on a seventeenth century mechanistic Newtonian model, quite as if Einstein and Heisenberg had not revolutionized physics in the three-century interim.[21]

While LaBarre criticizes his colleagues, he himself retains an implied allegiance to the standard of the exact sciences. If only social scientists would update their conceptions of physics, he seems to suggest, they would obtain a correct, that is to say, objective and defensible method.

Some stress that the only way to understand the religious experience of others is to suspend or bracket one's own beliefs, judgments, and religious dispositions. First advocated by the Dutch scholar Gerardus van der Leeuw more than fifty years ago (1933), this approach had been marred by its own historical bias in favor of Protestant Christianity. Van der Leeuw was above all a theologian. He designated three categories of religious life as universal: dynamism, animism, and deism. Yet all three accorded too narrowly with his own beliefs, and they never gained wide acceptance.[22]

Still another approach has come from linguistics. Projecting the distinction between phonetic and phonemic onto the mental world of the researcher, the anthropologist Kenneth Pike argued that a truly scientific approach distinguishes emic from etic knowledge. Emic knowledge derives from the subjective insider, etic from the objective outsider. Implicit in this demarcation, however, is the superiority of etic over emic, since it is outsiders who define insiders for their own benefit. Unsuccessful attempts have been made to demonstrate that those who invoke the emic/etic distinction do not claim epistemological superiority for the researcher over his or her subject(s). Yet to anthropologists such as Marvin Harris, the validity of etic descriptions is the cornerstone of social science research. To deny their validity, in his view, is "to deny the possibility of a social science capable of explaining sociocultural similarities and differences," which is tantamount to urging "the surrender of our intellects to the supreme mystification of total relativism."[23]

The anthropological theorist Clifford Geertz is more constrained in his assessment of this issue. Conceding that "the ethnographer does not, and, in my opinion, largely cannot, perceive what his informants perceive,"[24] he tries to sidestep the emic/etic dilemma. In its stead he recreates and, of course, justifies the hermeneutic circle, "a continuous dialectical tacking between the most local of local detail and the most global of global structure in such a way as to bring them into simultaneous view."[25] The end result? To apprehend symbol systems and to study them apart from those engaged by them. It is as if, to cite one critic, "we observe what the natives think is true, i.e., what they take seriously. We construct an account of their universe, their frames of meaning, and then we converse with it. We bring it into our conversation. The anthropologist thus succeeds in studying what is serious and truthful to others without it being serious or truthful to him."[26] Authority inheres in the individual researcher. It is not subject to objective verification, nor does it claim universal validity.

Perhaps the most crucial issue of interpretation turns not on the evaluation of data but on the data selected for evaluation. Apart from symbolic and interpretive anthropologists, most social scientists seek hard data, evidence capable of observation and measurement in models or graphs; it derives from behavior, especially interactive behavior between groups. Apart from cultural historians and historians of religion, most humanists seek soft data, evidence capable of mediation through literary texts and biographical compilations; it relates to beliefs, especially among elites or leaders who are assumed to exemplify the groups that they represent.

The cleavage between social scientists and humanists goes deeper still. If there is a difference in data selected, there is also a different weighting of the meaning of history in general and socioreligious movements in particular. Almost all social scientists tend to share Durkheim's fascination with "primitives," and Weber's propensity for schematization. The anthropologist A. F. C. Wallace, for instance, derives a "universal" model for revitalization movements based on his study of one such movement among the Seneca Indians. Despite his designation of the Senecans as "primitive" (i.e., preliterate and homogeneous), he claims the applicability of his model to other religious communities, Muslim, Christian, and Buddhist. Adopting the general outline of Wallace's model, a historian of American Christianity has tried to apply its categories to the five major awakenings that, in his view, have punctuated public religion in the United States. The tidy periodization that results is too uniform and seamless, as the author himself seems to recognize when he demurs that Wallace's model may not be "totally applicable to the complex, pluralistic and highly literate people of the United States."[27]

What is at question here is more than a choice of research strategies. It is a presumption about the commonality of human existence. Wallace and his admirers presume that once an effective model has been located one can apply it with equal validity to both primitive and civilized societies. They further presume that the gradient of explanation will also move in predictable evolutionary patterns.[28]

While reliance on primitive models and evolutionary stages emphasizes the need for hard data, that is, recurrent behavioral evidence in the public sphere, it also minimizes the significance of soft data, such as scriptural references, creedal assertions, and biographical analyses, all of which are messy, admit of a thousand exceptions, and, of course, preponderate in the private sphere.

Though taking account of the social sciences, I opt to locate my own work in the humanities or human sciences. At every instance of investigation, I find it necessary to challenge the presumption of superiority for the observer over "natives," the advocacy of primitive over civilized as primary data, and the preference of observation over textual evidence of the human condition. In my view, there are four formative elements in the study of any tradition or socioreligious movement. First, there is a reciprocal reinforcement between creedal belief and ritual action. Second, the tradition they articulate claims legitimacy from a scriptural authority that may or may not match socioeconomic needs. Third, the eruption of charismatic leadership may lead to institutional formation, but it also may challenge or even change that process. And finally, fourth, an ideology coalesces, binding various groups, often for disparate motives, to the charismatic leader; they accept not only the leader's affirmation of tradition but also his or her interpretation of scripture. What results is a religious ideology.

In this approach to the study of fundamentalism, scripture becomes a crucial, defining element. Remove scripture, and you no longer have fundamentalism but some other, nonreligious social movement. Intimately linked to the authority of scripture is the penchant of fundamentalists for particular selections of scripture: all scripture is invoked, but not all is cited with equal relevance to the actual outlook of particular fundamentalist cadres. Intertwined with a select reading of scripture is a partial loyalty to the past and a selective recall of its importance: not all moments, persons, or events are recalled with equal fervor, not all crystallize the point of crisis that provokes action. Charismatic leaders choose; they choose enemies from their contemporaries, scripture from scripture, focal points from the past. For the humanist it is impossible to study fundamentalism without making sense of all three: the invocation of scripture, the reference to the past, the reliance on charismatic mediaries. But the point of departure rests with scripture.

Looking at scripture as primary data, one also is compelled to see ideology, politics, and psychology in a different light. Religious ideology arises out of scripture. It entails a specific plan of action that translates the "clear" teaching of scripture, the "honest" memory of the past, and the "inspired" role of the charismatic leader into a collective ethos that sets those who understand apart from others who remain in ignorance. Religious ideology is textually based before it is contextually elaborated and enacted.

The actual consequence of the new reading of scripture by the leader inspired with a fresh vision of the past impacts society at numerous levels, one of which is psychological. At a personal level the new belief-action pattern meets socially embedded needs for satisfaction. Whether such needs are due to deep-seated deprivation or surface unrest, the new belief-action pattern provides moral guidelines where they may have been lacking or in need of restatement. *Anomie* is replaced with purposefulness, a purposefulness that is, however, directed inward to the "emboldened" group and not outward to the "distracted" or "misguided" masses.

Another level of impact is political. The transformation of existing political structures provides one but only one index of socioreligious movements. Even when it is the major consequence, its achievements have to be framed in a larger, transpolitical perspective. It is at this juncture, namely, evaluating the significance of political motives in scripturalist protests against the existing social order, that humanists part company from social scientists. For the latter, the observable instances of behavior or action modified by religious belief is the crucial index, whether at the psychological level or in the political realm. But for the former the consequence is less significant finally than the cause, and the cause derives from the complex interaction of scripture, tradition, and charisma.

A case instance that seems to have little to do with fundamentalism reveals the demarcation of humanist from social scientist. Those preoccupied with the fate of Islam in the Asian subcontinent have had to examine several explanations for the emergence of Pakistan as a modern nation-state independent from its neighbor, India. Paul Brass, an American political scientist, and Francis Robinson, a British historian of culture, have carried on a lengthy debate on which of two views ought to be embraced. Paul Brass defends an instrumentalist or materialist view. He focuses on "the specific interests of religious and political elites and their skills in symbol selection and manipulation."[29] Francis Robinson, on the other hand, advances the primordialist or idealist position. He traces the origin of Pakistan, as do Pakistanis themselves, to "the religio-political ideas of Islam." Robinson argues from *textual* evidence that Muslims require "a separate political order,"[30] while Brass maintains that what is most significant is "the [diverse] ways in which new religious and political elites deal with the written texts of a tradition, interpret and transform them from generation to generation."[31] Brass finally cannot admit that textual authority, even when manipulated or misconstrued, remains the major motivating force for Pakistani separatism. Still, he is forced to conclude that the alternative to an appeal to textual authority, "the Social Science explanation of a particular historical movement," is also "never quite satisfactory."[32]

What underscores the inadequacy of Brass's approach is the frequency of the indigenous appeal to scripture. Whether one approaches the formation of a religious state, or the reclamation of a religious legacy, the appeal to scripture is too recurrent and too central to be ignored. Humanists, whatever their disciplinary base in the academy, must adopt the strategy of prioritizing textual evidence even while admitting and examining a wide variety of textual interpretations. They still face major interpretive hurdles: how to decide on what bases particular groups mobilize around one interpretation of scripture rather than another? and how to match social reality with rhetorical strategies? But the point of departure remains the primacy of scripture as a marking of collective identity and cultural authenticity.

Primitive vs. civilized, public vs. private, hard vs. soft, scientist vs. humanist are frequently invoked as exclusive opposites, irreconcilable one with the other. While the larger purpose of this book is to call into question the viability of such binary *logic*, its immediate strategy is to nuance binary *classification*. Philosophers frequently speak of the distinction between contraries and contradictories. Contraries pose sharp differences, for example, between plants and animals, men and women, Americans and Canadians, students and teachers, but they never allow the contrast to exclude the possibility of rapprochement and even, from time to time, inversion. Contradictories, however, are incommensurate opposites. They allow no dialectical or sympathetic interaction but only stark juxtaposition: male chauvinists stand apart from and over against radical feminists, as do capitalists to communists, generals to pacifists. Every instance where we invoke binary contrasts in this study is predicated on classificatory distinctions, yet our purpose is to register contraries rather than to perpetuate contradictories. At the same time, we acknowledge that many others, those for whom we write as well as those about whom we write, may tend to view the world in terms of binary logic. Seeing only contradictions, they posit irresolvable opposites. Though black and white are dominant color tones, we argue that gray also has its value. We will try to accent gray in what follows.

The major division of this book is itself shaped by two equally significant parts: *context* and *countertexts*. Part one depicts the emergence of the modern world. We frame it as *context*. In it we explore a subset of pairs: modernity—the constituent material elements of the modern world—and modernism—the contingent ideological reshaping of human experience in response to the modern world. Both modernity and modernism determine the context of the High Tech Era in world history, but their relationship is ambiguous. In part two we examine the religious responses to modernity and modernism labeled "fundamentalist." They are labeled "fundamentalist" because those who articulate them try to recuperate what is authentic from their past to counter what they find objectionable in the present as they prepare for a future that they hope will vindicate their choice.

We examine Jewish, Christian, and Islamic fundamentalists. What each offers is *countertexts* to the modernist vision of our world. These countertexts will strike variant responses in different groups of readers depending on how closely the readers identify either their lives or their studies with one of the three groups we examine.

At the outset, though, we must stress the necessary conjunction of context and countertexts in all instances. The argument is simple and straightforward: the context of the modern world has to be defined, explored, and narrated before *any* religious movement can be studied in the latter part of the twentieth century. The fundamentalists with whom we concern ourselves are caught in a peculiar tension: they accept implicitly the benefits of modernity, often thriving through their use of technology, while explicitly rejecting modernism as a holistic ideological framework. They are moderns but not modernists.[33]

Too often the barrage of images that portray fundamentalists conflate their stated opposition to modernism with their presumed rejection of modernity. To disentangle that confusion we choose to present all fundamentalisms, Jewish, Christian, and Islamic, as countertexts to *modernism*. Reluctant heirs of modernity, fundamentalists challenge the ideological implications of the transition to the Technical Age that have been most graphically posed as modernism, while at the same time they eschew the chimera of retreat to a "golden era" that would erase the modern world as both a material structure (modernity) and a spiritual disease (modernism).

The *context* is treated in four chapters. Chapter one outlines the dialectical affinity between modernism and fundamentalism, related to the familiar antinomy between universalism and monadism or relativism. Chapter two surveys the historical process that produced both the modern world and the ascendancy of certain strata of Western society within it. Among those not privileged by the emergence of modernity were marginal groups that retained a strong adherence to traditional values. Chapter three assesses the role of religious ideology in mobilizing and sustaining their protest to multiple modernisms. Chapter four serves as a methodological excursus, reviewing quasi-philosophical arguments against the viability of fundamentalism as an analytical category. It points up not only the inadequacy of such arguments but also the benefit of a qualified use of fundamentalism to explore religious protest in several societies. It concludes with a listing of those properties and traits that continue to characterize fundamentalists while also differentiating them from their coreligionists.

In part two the focus shifts to a close reading of the multiple rejections of modernism. Because modernists project an aura of inevitability and invincibility, their movement provides the *context* for our study. The negative response to that context, claiming eternal validity as well as divine providence, results in the several *countertexts* of fundamentalists. To the extent that modernism entails ontological indifference and/or moral relativism, fundamentalists have tried to resist its influence. They have produced alternative visions to the modernist utopia, visions that reflect scriptural antecedents, creedal moorings, and corporate loyalties.

It is the scriptural and creedal legacy of the monotheistic tradition that authorizes the fundamentalist worldview. It links fundamentalists to their coreligionists but also separates them from one another. Chapter five looks at the fundamentalist interpretation of monotheism. That interpretation is selective. It draws attention only to certain passages of scripture. It highlights the biographies of its own seminal figures. Though invoking the authority of the past, fundamentalists do not indulge in nostalgia or sentimentalism. Their outlook has been shaped by monotheism, which branched into sectarianism, which was reshaped by modernity, which gave rise to revivalism. The cumulative force of these developments may be reduced to the serialized slogan: one God, one moral universe, one law, one scripture. While most revivalists draw on scripture to reclaim what they perceive to be a now lost golden age, fundamentalists do not; they uphold ideals from the past while accommodating to the realities, including the material and technological benefits, of the contemporary era.

The next three chapters (chapters six, seven, and eight) examine the three major antimodernist movements that have emerged as expressions of fundamentalist fervor: *haredi* and quasi-Hasidic Jewish, Protestant Christian, and Sunni-Shi'i Muslim. Among the cluster of issues that have stamped their corporate identity, none looms larger than the modern nation-state, the companion and pacesetter of the Technical Age and now the High Tech Era. Although the nation-state impinges unevenly on each of the fundamentalist groups in our study, it is ideologically crucial to all three in ways that are often implied but seldom stated.

Chapter six looks at both Neturei Karta and Gush Emunim as Jewish fundamentalists who relate to one another at sharp angles. It also evaluates the Kach party as a pseudo-fundamentalist, quasi-fascist movement inseparable from the personality of Meir Kahane. Though they embrace divergent political views, Jewish fundamentalists nonetheless share a religious malaise about the secular presuppositions of the modern state of Israel. They commonly project a closely defined group identity in sparring with the values of the dominant culture. Above all, it is from contemporary reinterpretations of religious charisma, traceable to the Hasidic legacy, that they derive their distinctive worldview.

Chapter seven places American Protestant fundamentalists within a comparative perspective for the first time. Unlike other fundamentalists, they are preoccupied with social issues, issues that involve constitutionally mandated and legally defended rights for the majority of a state's citizens. Their vision of a "pure" past relates to the supposed virtues of a Christian civilization that flourished only in first-century Roman Palestine and nineteenth-century Victorian England. It leads them to marshal public, issue-specific protests against abortion, pornography, and homosexuality. Although they seem unconcerned about intellectual issues, the creationist controversy embodies a host of cognitive moves and countermoves. If explored as a de facto metaphysical contest in the Technical Age, creationism may offer the sharpest ideological litmus test for the elusive identity as well as the persistent influence of Protestant Christian fundamentalists.

Chapter eight shifts the focus to the group of fundamentalists with the most at risk and also with the deepest urge for political confrontation: Sunni and Shi'i Muslims. Islamic fundamentalists are not the only Muslims who wrestle with the dilemma of being both religious and modern. They must be painstakingly differentiated from other Muslim activists, whether Sunni or Shi'i. The resulting profile leaves no doubt that, in comparison to their fundamentalist counterparts, Jewish or Christian, the Sunni Muslim fundamentalists are the embodiment of a publicly oriented, politically frustrated opposition group. Iranian Shi'i Muslim

fundamentalists, by contrast, represent that group of religious ideologues who have unexpectedly yet convincingly achieved the greatest
measure of political success.

The conclusion reconsiders the future of fundamentalism in the light
of its origins and subsequent development. We ponder the long-term
consequences for fundamentalism as a religious ideology differentiated
but not separated from that which it opposes, namely, the modernist
worldview. While fundamentalists challenge the hegemonic presuppositions of scientific positivism, they are willing adepts of contemporary
technology, especially as it applies to mass communications and the media. Distancing themselves from the embrace of moral relativism, they
accept technical efficiency as an instrumental good. They are tenaciously
ambivalent. They require continuous and broad evaluation. Even when
they affront, they attest to the persistent human quest for religious absolutes, and that may be not only their challenge but also their contribution to the twenty-first century.

Part 1

CONTEXT

CHAPTER 1

The Making of a Construct: Modernism and Fundamentalism

Now the whole earth had one language and few words. And as men migrated from the east, they found a plain in the land of Shinar and settled there. And they said to one another, "Come, let us make bricks, and burn them thoroughly." And they had brick for stone, and bitumen for mortar. Then they said, "Come, let us build ourselves a city, and a tower with its top in the heavens, and let us make a name for ourselves, lest we be scattered abroad upon the face of the whole earth." And the Lord came down to see the city and the tower, which the sons of men had built. And the Lord said, "Behold, they are one people, and they have all one language; and this is only the beginning of what they will do; and nothing that they propose to do will now be impossible for them. Come, let us go down, and there confuse their language, that they may not understand one another's speech." So the Lord scattered them abroad from there over the face of all the earth, and they left off building the city. Therefore its name was called Babel, because there the Lord confused the language of all the earth; and from there the Lord scattered them abroad over the face of all the earth.

—GENESIS 11:1–9

Counting is innate to man, the measure of a thing becomes knowable in comparison with another thing which belongs to the same species and is assumed as a unit by general consensus.

—ABU RAYHAN AL-BIRUNI

Tribal and scribal are "the fire/ice-like golden extremes of anthropology."

—JAMES BOON

The modern world has at least permitted and perhaps accelerated the displacement of the religious idiom in public discourse. Too often modernism vs. fundamentalism has been seen as an intrareligious squabble. It may be fueled by the introduction of critical methods to the study of the Bible. It may derive from accommodation to scientific discoveries in the outlook of mainline Protestant denominations. But in both instances, it is deemed to be a private struggle. It is off-stage rather than center-stage for citizens of the twentieth century. The nature of fundamentalism as a reaction to modernism can only be broached if religion is reconsidered in its premodern temper and scope.

A drastic change has been transforming the entire world during the Technical Age. Its manifestations are physical and material, but its undercurrents are spiritual and psychological. Begun in the public sphere of commercial activity, political control, and military prowess, it has also pervaded and transformed the private sphere of family life and religious loyalty. Public and private may be descriptively separated, but they remain intrinsically, inexorably conjoined.

We need to begin by tracing the pattern of change that characterizes the modernist outlook as it pervades every aspect of contemporary life. We need to examine its linguistic markings and its interlocking identity with Western culture. Since religion continues to be a crucial index of change, we can, through its prism, discern two opposite templates of the world in which we live: one is modernist, the other fundamentalist.

The greatest threat to humankind is nuclear disaster, whether accidental or as the outcome of a Star Wars conflagration. Yet even without a nuclear nightmare to haunt us, the metamorphosis of human life itself has become so rapid that we instinctively think of the future as past.

While the lingering delight of the present, or the nostalgic recollection of the past, still suggests orientations of equal weight for some people, for "fundamentalists" the future is *now.* The future presents itself through the otherness of a divine contingency challenging our day-to-day expectation of continuity in the natural and social order: to live in faith is to live in anticipation of the "end of time," the last days of what one Protestant evangelist called "the late great planet earth."[1] There is no escape or reprieve from an imminent, cataclysmic judgment. It will be beyond human control. Only a few humans will be spared punishment or surprise because they have been watchful. They are the believing remnant vouchsafed eternal salvation.

It matters not whether one takes sides as a premillennial or postmillennial dispensationalist—that is, whether believers will be saved before or after the final tribulation on earth—in the debate among Protestant fundamentalists. What does matter is that the presentness of the future for all fundamentalists looms as a cataclysmic judgment. This contrasts with the modernist perspective of future dates as expedient signposts for noting portentous change. Third world economic planners grapple with five-year plans. United Nations demographers project the effects of birth explosion on ten-, fifteen-, and twenty-year curves. Club of Rome forecasters chart the spectrum of disparities that will characterize tomorrow's world, while communications experts devise the technology for new patterns of learning, patterns that are visual as much as auditory, patterns that are accessible to illiterate as well as literate, patterns that will prevail in the twenty-first century.

Fundamentalists and modernists may seem to disagree on how to interpret the future in the light of the present, yet both share a propensity to live as if that future were already stripped of any meaning other than that which they singularly ascribe to it. Both accept the axiom that time is a function of language. To think in the future is to presuppose a tense sequence of past-present-future. That, however, is an Indo-European (traceable back to a Greek) framework of temporality. It has no counterpart in Semitic conventions of tense. Consider Hebrew. The tense system of the Hebrew verb does not distinguish between past, present, and future. Tense in Hebrew conveys the aspects of action (incomplete or completed), not the periodization of time as discrete units of measurement implying discontinuity as well as continuity. The latter was a Greek "invention," or at least it has been so closely associated with Greece that the metahistorian Arnold Toynbee typologized two worldviews: the Greek, which extends to the Indian, he deemed to be cyclical, philosophical, and teleological; and the Hebrew, which extends to the Iranian, he viewed as linear, religious, and eschatological.[2]

Toynbee's typology remains speculative. It is subject to neither verification nor falsification. It can only hint at what is at once unknown and unknowable: the relationship of language to culture at the point of origin or formative development within a civilizational worldview. Was it, for instance, preexilic Israelite culture that determined the grammar of Hebrew, or did language shape Israelite culture, including its religious thought forms? Could it have been the "defect" of Hebrew that allowed for the postulation of an inscrutable but also inescapable God? Or was it a reverse process—in George Steiner's words "the axiom of an immeasurable, inconceivable yet omnipresent God"—that informed the development of Hebrew grammar?[3]

We are face-to-face with a major dilemma of historical inquiry. Whether we search for empirical facts or pursue intuitive hunches, we are left in the dark. The descendants of Isaac and Ishmael did not know that their language lacked any grammatical capacity, nor did the God of Abraham tell them. While we can observe the coincidence between Hebrew grammar and the emergence of monotheism, its source remains a mystery, a cipher inaccessible to both the skein of reason and the light of faith.

What we can ask are ancillary questions: Do the Hebrew and Greek worldviews remain incommensurable? Does grammar not only shape thought forms but also limit the possibility of interaction and accommodation between custodians of different cultural norms? That line of inquiry touches on the capacity of language to go beyond its surface qualities. Time, a function of language, can also be its adversary. Both

Hebrew and Greek have been used to express a human revolt against the givenness of the factual present. Whatever their linguistic differences, Judaism and Hellenism alike affirm the recurrent urge to free oneself from time through language, to "overcome momentarily (in the comfort of the written word) the presence and presentness of one's own punctual death."[4] The desire to postpone mortality lies at the heart of Western literature. It also informs the spectrum of religious reflection for all of us, whether we be fundamentalists, modernists, or straddlers.

The urge to survive is at the same time the wish to extend dominion through the word. For the "we" who brush up against the future by winking at death do not speak only for ourselves. We also presume to speak for unnamed, unknown others; if not for all others, then we speak at least for the educated few who, in stretching their vision beyond their own cultural confines, try to scan the future that all humankind is destined to live. Between the literate and illiterate, the conscious and the unconscious, we presume a hierarchy of destiny. We attach others to us. It is they who become part of our destiny.

We also make a further, temporal presumption about the era in which we live. We shut out the past from active memory while relegating the *actual* future to a distant echo not heard. Our template of the present focuses on the potential for annihilation: something so momentous has occurred *now,* or is in the process of occurring *now,* that no one can escape its impact. So imminent is the prospect of cataclysmic disaster in the material world that the sole delight, if it can be called that, lies in the possibility of acquiring advance knowledge of our own destruction. Jonathan Schell's *The Fate of the Earth* is suffused with the promise that we who know the horrors of a nuclear holocaust are somehow better off. In its voyeuristic depiction of nuclear doom and disaster, his book becomes the environmentalist-ecologist's mirror response to the evangelical-fundamentalist's Armageddon depicted in the *The Late Great Planet Earth.*[5]

Few non-Westerners can relate to either scenario of the earth or to the crisis-catastrophe cycle predicted for its inhabitants. This is not due to ignorance or insensitivity but to preoccupation with a different set of problems. Afro-Asian elites live in societies that generate neither the physical power for hemispheric destruction nor the theological impetus welcoming spiritual intervention to achieve the same end. A major question confronting us in this book is, how does Western society harbor simultaneously *both* potentialities for a discontinuous future without surrendering to either?

An exploration of language provides part of the answer. Language is words, but it is also the codification of unconscious patterns of thought, feeling, and shared perception.

At the unconscious level, two features of language recur again and again, with powerful liminal influence on all human exchange. *Aggregation* and *referentiality* are the cloak and dagger of discourse. They conceal yet shape much of what we present as our thoughts, to ourselves as well as to others. Aggregation is horizontal, synchronic. It is the tendency of words, especially abstract or technical terms, to envelop multiple connotations. Referentiality is vertical, diachronic. It is the capacity of all words to presuppose a discrete set of antecedents, implicit or explicit, without which their own coherence would be diminished, if not lost.

Aggregation is needed for useful analysis, but it can also impede understanding. The audience is "we," and "we" too often becomes an appeal to the few disguised as a message for the many. Literary critics, philosophers, and historians frequently invoke the authority of "we," but the "we" may actually refer to only a handful of others in their own profession. This rather slippery pronoun, by inflating the boundaries of audience, implies that the writer speaks on behalf of at least most educated citizens of Western culture.

Almost all flag words in common discourse have multiple meanings, a quality that is scarcely controllable. The present study is also replete with aggregation. We face it at every turn, whether we look back to terms we have just discussed, such as language, time, and culture, or we look ahead to the most persistent catchall categories: fundamentalism, modernity, and modernism. While we cannot eliminate aggregation, we can try to curtail its limitless expansion. We will briefly define the primary sense of each of our three major terms. Their further connotations will be explored at length in subsequent chapters.

Fundamentalism is the affirmation of religious authority as holistic and absolute, admitting of neither criticism nor reduction; it is expressed through the collective demand that specific creedal and ethical dictates derived from scripture be publicly recognized and legally enforced.

Modernity is the emergence of a new index of human life shaped, above all, by increasing bureaucratization and rationalization as well as technical capacities and global exchange unthinkable in the premodern era.

Modernism is the search for individual autonomy driven by a set of socially encoded values emphasizing change over continuity; quantity over quality; efficient production, power, and profit over sympathy for traditional values or vocations, in both the public and private spheres. At its utopian extreme, it enthrones one economic strategy, consumer-oriented capitalism, as the surest means to technological progress that will also eliminate social unrest and physical discomfort.

Let us look more closely at the term fundamentalism. Having defined it, we also need to describe it. It encompasses a spectrum of discrete institutional groups, whether Protestant Christian sectaries in twentieth century America or marginalized protest cadres in Israel and the Muslim world. The toughest questions concern the force and also the scope of fundamentalism. How is it to be differentiated from other religiously motivated protest movements, such as Gandhian pacifism or liberation theology? And does it adequately express all the diversity within its ranks, especially when one speaks not only of American but also Middle Eastern and Asian fundamentalisms? In other words, how does one justify a common designation of such diverse social groups? And, assuming that there is a nonapocalyptic future toward which we all can look, what will be the further, interpretive yield of our investigation of fundamentalism? Can it assist us in evaluating the patterns of religious loyalty and social expression that will continue to characterize the Technical Age?

All these questions will be explored in the pages that follow. Each presupposes the intelligibility of language as an instrument of communication reflecting both its culture of origin and external influences on that culture.

That may sound like a simple proposition. It becomes less simple when we begin to explore the shifts in thought and twists of history that shape and reshape language, often at an unconscious level. Then we come face to face with *referentiality*. Benjamin Whorf, the engineer turned linguist, tried to explain the disposition to rely on particular referents (while excluding others) as "the unperceived intricate systematizations of (each person's) language." George Steiner, Whorf's admirer and sometime critic, describes the process in detail:

It . . . [consists of] a manifold reciprocity between grammar and concept, between speech form and cultural pressure. Intricate grooves of possibility and of limitation, neurophysiological potentialities of many-branched but not unbounded realization, prepare . . . for a grammar and *system* of symbolic reference. Presumably the dialectic of interaction is persistent, between linguistic "spaces" and the trajectories of thought and feeling within them, between such trajectories and the unfolding or mapping of new spaces.[6]

Unfortunately, Steiner never goes beyond Whorf in mapping out first principles for a science of interpretation that would situate symbolic reference in its *modernist* context. Internalized, that context may be seen as the subliminal elements that frame our current way of thinking, leading us to choose words, express feelings, and pursue actions that conform to the social expectation of what is modern. Their distinction from premodern coordinates can be traced with reference to three crucial elements: *counting, comparing,* and *systematizing.* Each needs brief elaboration before we can examine the historical context out of which fundamentalism emerges, and against which it revolts.

Counting is the basic premise of all science, including the cosmological soundings of religious traditions. Yet its use in the modern period is stamped by the utilitarian or instrumentalist outlook:

Precise measurement and mathematical statement [are] the major methods in scientific inquiry. . . . Before the genesis of industrial civilization, counting and calculation in numbers were matters of convenience, carried on to satisfy other ends than the maximization of scarce means or the statement of scientific laws. The use of figures derived from quantitative surveys as guides to economic and political action or on behalf of what may perhaps be called social purposes is a modern phenomenon.[7]

And as a modern phenomenon, the art of counting, or applied mathematics, infuses all forms of life and all fields of intellectual endeavor, including literary criticism. It is no accident, for instance, that George Steiner's choice of words reflects a disposition to mathematics and, above all, to mathematical analogues: branches are subproofs of theorems, boundedness and unboundedness represent finitude and infinity, while trajectories describe geometric projections. To speak in the modern idiom is to genuflect toward mathematical references. How else could we speak of complex, diffuse terms except as "aggregates"? In the modern period, mathematical analogues suggest a precision that orders *all* language.[8]

Implicit in counting is *comparison,* the comparison of one set of numbers to another, the comparison of all numbers to the two antipodes of zero and infinity. Comparing for the purpose of contrasting is a feature of the classical mind, traceable back to the ancient Greeks. It is also present in the paired idioms of biblical imagery. Note how light/darkness, order/chaos, crooked/blameless, become especially powerful in the compressed antinomies of proverbs or poetry.[9] In the nineteenth century, however, a trio of German idealist philosophers, Hegel, Nietzsche, and Marx, turned comparing and contrasting into a cornerstone of intellectual discourse. The form remained the same: to measure one thing by its like or opposite, but the doubles were no longer moieties. Instead of being spliced halves of a single whole, as they had been in Greek and biblical as well as Indian and Chinese literature, they became disengaged others, pitted in deadly combat as incommensurate opposites. Dialectical sparring proved to be an analytical tool of tremendous didactic power; it could be applied to an infinite range of data, especially in the social sciences. Thought/action, tradition/modernity, continuity/change, nature/culture, primitive/civilized—the list is seemingly endless. Yet the doubling or pairing no longer originates in the given order of things but rather in the analytical eye of the observer. The privilege, as also the challenge, is to conjoin two disparate, often irreconcilable categories, weigh them, rank them, and finally choose between them or somehow reconcile them.

To ponder the chasm between premodern and modern dabbling in doubles is instructive. Paul of Tarsus was perhaps the most persistent dialectician in the biblical canon. He wrestled with distinctions like male/female, Jew/Greek, free/slave, and despite the complexity of his thought, the basic dyads were recognizable to his audience, since they echoed gender, ethnic, or social distinctions familiar to educated citizens of the western Roman Empire. By contrast, a modernist such as Freud worked out his elaborate therapeutic strategy with an almost obsessive reference to antinomies that he himself defined and he alone understood: demand/remission, interdictory/counterinterdictory, neurotic/healthy, control/release, instinct/intelligence.[10] To the extent that some of these and other Freudian constructs are familiar to the modern reader, they reflect the influence that Freud enjoys in the public at large. They still lack the immediate recognition of intrinsic contrasts.

While Freud may have been exceptional in the rigor and influence of his dialectical dueling, the formulation and exposition of intuitively conceived, implicitly held dyadic constructs is the grist of modern thinking. It prevails in the social sciences and also in every branch of the human sciences.[11] For anthropologists of the structuralist school, not only Claude Levi-Strauss but those who honor him by opposing him, "cultures are at base dialectical."[12] Despite its inevitable excesses, dialectical dichotimization is secure as an element of contemporary social scientific theory.

The symbolic anthropologist James Boon reveals both the current propensity for dialectical reasoning and also its shortcomings. Though he describes the tribal and the scribal as "the fire/ice-like golden extremes of anthropology," Boon challenges the notion that they are incommensurate opposites. Dual moieties, he argues, are not "reciprocally opposed as sacred and profane," but rather "each is both, vis-à-vis the other. Dualism's dialectical basis ensures balance, differentiation, holism: anything they are to us, we are to them." Perhaps it does, but the biblical tribal is not on the same continuum of human experience as the aborigine tribal, and even Boon must admit that despite attempts at transformation or complementary juxtaposition, the distinctions between them remain more evident and significant than their similarities:

(1) Aboriginal tribal cosmology [defining the limits of humankind quite narrowly] organizes its system of differences as mutual necessities; [while] (2) biblical tribal cosmology [desiring to propagate a universalistic ethic] organizes its system of differences as mutual exclusions, at least until the Apocalypse.[13]

The demarcation of biblical from aboriginal tribal cosmologies has to do with more than different moieties. It serves as a crucial example of the struggle between self-conscious universalism (growing out of a reciprocal exchange between the tribal deity who becomes the global deity and the tribe who deified that god) and unacknowledged relativism (continued maintenance of local values and myriad deities without strategies for competition or expansion beyond accepted boundaries).

Anthropologists, however, seldom examine the metaphysical import of their dyads. It is considered bad science to ask *why* the ancient Israelites "desired to propagate a universalistic ethic." The true scientist instead explores *how* that desire to be universalist was expressed, with what outcome, and for what duration, but never *why*. Method is the enduring challenge, even when it goes against the grain of the modern world. Nietzsche forged an antipositivist methodology at a time when confidence in reason ran high. Among his latter-day disciples, Michel Foucault shares Nietzsche's fervent commitment to antiscientism. He has tried to lay bare the doubling propensity of what he calls the Western episteme, in order to transcend both it and its parent, Kantian rationalism. Although he is especially critical of anthropology, Foucault himself seems to wind up inventing contrasting doublets at least as complex and obscure as those that he seeks to excise from the human sciences.[14]

Despite its inescapable problematic, the propensity to double will not go away. It may derive from the process of speech acquisition. In surveying human discourse, Jakobsen located twelve binary oppositions that, in his view, accounted for all the contrasts found in all the languages of the world.[15] It could also be that the binary function of the brain, with the mystery of right and left hemispheres, secures an internal, biological basis for complementarity that corresponds to the external gender distinction between male and female. Some would argue that the inner/outer dyads are intrinsically complementary and that only social conditions makes them conflictual. Either way, our brains, like our bodies, seem to predestine us as women and men to think in terms of doubles and therefore to compare as well as contrast. But the questions remain: Which doubles do we choose? With what preconceptions do we compare? Toward what ends do we invoke contrasts? And how do we acknowledge the critical distinction between contrasts and contradictories? In answering these questions, we show how far we have moved from the syzygy of ancient thinkers to the dialectical dances of their modern successors.

Nor is there a neat progression from counting and comparing to the showcase of modernist thought, *systematizing*. The latter presupposes the existence of the other two. Only the numbers differ. If comparing presupposes counting, at least to two, then systematizing or classifying extends the abacus to infinity. Systematizing depends on both counting and comparing yet goes beyond them. Its goal is to attempt a holistic reordering of diversity, channeling randomness into a visual, palpable framework that serves the group or groups to which the system applies, and at the same time advances their interests. Reflexively, social scientists who struggle to make sense of complexly nuanced terms like religion or ideology revert to the word "system" as the linchpin symbol signifying order, reason, function, structure.[16] Steiner exhibits the modernist instinct when he depicts linguistic complexity as "a grammar and *system* of symbolic reference."[17]

Though seldom recognized, a related feature of systematizing and classifying is to summarize, reduce, compress. Again, the mathematical analogue comes to mind: numbers are but symbols of larger complexities reduced to manageable, manipulable form by "counters," i.e., mathematicians and their surrogates (accountants, brokers, actuarial scientists, economic planners, and now computer scientists). It is hardly accidental that the founder of modern day structuralism, Claude Levi-Strauss, "endeavored to establish the rudiments of a semantic algebra."[18]

Symbols, like stereotypes, too often suppress or alter meaning. Both perform a similar function in literary code. By abstracting, generalizing, and reducing a range of untidy, indigestible particulars, they offer the possibility of control through assimilation. But in stereotyping something is lost, not only from the object(s) perceived but also from the subject who perceives through the prism of stereotypes. The cultural historian Owen Chadwick explains:

What stands out [in molding public opinion] is the necessity for symbols or, as they have been called, stereotypes: easily identifiable names or persons or pictures or issues. . . . The most experienced of journalists tell us that "at the level of social life, what is called the adjustment of man to his environs takes place through the medium of fictions." By fictions he does not mean lies. These symbols might be false, but they might be as true as the molecular models which scientists construct in laboratories to explain their observations. We act like men who see through a glass darkly. *Our world is too big and complex to be understood.* Yet we cannot move in it without trying to see what cannot be seen, and so we move with the aid of symbols or stereotypes, names or slogans.[19]

Chadwick, like Steiner, has accepted the modernist perspective even while offering a critique of its acceptance and application by others. He echoes the paradoxical theme of human supremacy and helplessness. On the one hand, there is no universal consensus about absolute, eternal Truth. All truth, whether scientific or journalistic, is provisional, resting on the decision and actions of human agents. The philosopher of science Thomas Kuhn makes a similar argument in *The Structure of Scientific Revolutions.*[20] It is the inevitable consequence of what Michel Foucault once called "the Kantian moment," i.e., "the discovery that the subject, insofar as he is reasonable, applies to himself his own law, which is the universal law."[21] Yet at the same time Chadwick projects a modern malaise, the attitude of existential bewilderment that laments the manifoldness and diversity of our world. That is a frequent rejoinder of doomsday soothsayers. Chadwick differs from them in combining an explicit monadist perspective with an implicit universalist hope. At the epistemological level, he opts for the part (what we know is limited and inadequate), while still trying to retrieve at the ontological level a failsafe whole (the cosmic order is somehow coherent, despite our unthinking and unknowing).

Part of the problem that Chadwick and others face is disagreement over what is meant by universal. Many universals are construed not as given and discoverable but as changing and evolving, whether due to forces that operate within individuals, groups, or societies, or due to other forces that are outside their control but still impinge on them. The sociologist Talcott Parsons, for instance, has tried to systematize all social action on a fivefold continuum that he calls "pattern variables." They are:

> Universalism–particularism
> Performance–quality
> Affective neutrality–affectivity
> Specificity–diffuseness
> Self-orientation–collectivity orientation.[22]

While recognizing the importance of universals, he situates them on a complex gradient of change that draws more attention to change than to universals. The goal, thoroughly modernist, is to subordinate even the broadest definitional aggregate ("universal") to an instrumentalist function: one can and must systematize everything, even universals, in this case by constructing a comprehensive model for social action. In effect, Parsons tries to transpose his goal into the foundation of his methodology, but he cannot secure universalism merely by invoking it. Contradictions abound, despite the elegant simplicity of the initial model.

Both the relativist and the evolutionary approaches to human society deny universalism. They deny it on different grounds. The distinction is clarified by the anthropologists Richard Shweder and Edmund Bourne. In their article—provocatively titled, "Does the Concept of the Person Vary Cross-Culturally?"—they state that there are three interpretive models which all social scientists implicitly or explicitly choose in processing information about alien idea systems. They categorize the three as follows:

The universalist opts for homogeneity. "Apparently different but really the same" is his slogan. Diversity is sacrificed to equality; equal because not different! The evolutionist, however, opts for hierarchy. Diversity is not only tolerated, it is expected, *and it is ranked.* "Different but unequal" is the slogan of the evolutionist. The relativist, in contrast, is a pluralist. "Different but equal" is his slogan; equality *and* diversity is his "democratic" aspiration.[23]

By comparing the three positions and reducing their characteristic emphases to slogans, Shweder and Bourne are suggesting that they merit equal consideration as valid methodological stances. In this scheme, as in Parsons' pattern variables, universalism is finessed by being considered first. It is presumed that once the limitations of universalism have been exposed, alternative approaches can claim equal validity. The alternatives, however, are really variations or subclasses of a single outlook that we have called monadism. The evolutionist invokes *hierarchy* as his ultimate authority: other people's worldviews are valued as incipient and less adequate stages in the development of our own understandings. The relativist invokes *isolation* as his authority: self-contained, incommensurate views are independently considered and separately validated; it is deemed impossible either to bridge their differences or to provide a rational criticism of their salient features. What the evolutionist does through hierarchy, the relativist does with isolation: deny the common, shared humanity of those who have different cultural legacies, either by presuming a privileged status for the present (the evolutionist) or the equivalence of all periods and all viewpoints (the relativist).

Ignored in each instance is the primacy of universalism as the defining context. Both evolutionism and relativism are responding not to one another but to universalism. As the catalyst for all discussion, universalism merits reconsideration at the conclusion, not at the beginning, of any review of interpretive principles. Universalism alone vouchsafes the coherence of both human experience and historical enquiry.

The crucial question remains: can universals ever be freed from the web of self-interests that inform not only participants-performers in a given social context but also observers-analysts of that context? That is a question which we shall explore at length in chapter three. It needs to be noted here that some skilled analysts see the entire endeavor of comparison as already flawed by the implicit desire of the comparer to classify and rank all data in accordance with his or her own undisclosed interests. The historian of religions Jonathan Z. Smith, for instance, gives a long list of the most frequently invoked dichotomies, including true/false, natural/revealed, collective/individual, cosmic/historical as well as ethnic/universal. In his view they are all crude, jingoistic slogans that subordinate one group as negative "they" to another as positive "we." Since every listing implies a value judgment and a ranking, none are the objective, scientific classifications they claim to be. They are instead impressionistic divisions reflecting a misguided search for essence. Rather than indulging in further lists or taking scriptural pronouncements at face value, he recommends a polythetic mode of classification, a scientific model derived not from the physical but from the biological sciences, since the latter, unlike the former, "must take the historical into account."[24]

While Smith's diagnosis poses a healthy counterweight to facile generalization and overdependence on mathematical models, it also contains its own prejudgments. By debunking *all* higher level generalizations, he is demoting "universal." "Universal" becomes but one more slogan. Parsons, Bourne, and Shweder at least gave it first consideration in their analyses before moving to other options. They also contrasted "universal" with "particular" or with "relative" and "evolutionary," while Smith brackets it with "ethnic," implying my group against the world. In actuality, however, the most frequent usage of universal is to parade my group *as* the world, for the universalist impulse arises out of a collective effort at self-transcendence, as Boon's discussion of aborigine and biblical tribalism indicated with telling clarity.

There is a larger problem with Smith's refusal to allow any generalization and his dismissal of all pairing as prejudicial. What alternative conceptual tools make it possible to assess enormous ranges of data? Fernand Braudel's study of late medieval Europe would have to be rewritten by someone other than Braudel. Smith himself is hard pressed to find much in ancient Judaism other than human circumcision rites and epigraphic data to illustrate the concrete, context-specific elements that provide walnuts (his metaphor for "hard" data) rather than artichoke hearts ("soft" data).[25]

It seems preferable to recognize recurrent traits that, when clustered together, delineate one context from others without presupposing the superiority of one to others or the isolation of each from its equivalents. Those traits which in combination characterize the contemporary era are *counting, comparing, systematizing.* They have produced a distinctive brand of thought which we choose to call, by way of shorthand, the modernist mindset. It is never possible, even for the most sophisticated of moderns, to be fully conscious of the influence that their context has on their patterns of thought, feeling, and action. Yet the more one investigates the modernist mindset the more the crucial contrast demanding an either/or choice seems to be between universalism and monadism, between holism and relativism.

Universalists are modernists swimming against the tide. They maintain that beyond seeming opposites, there is a tacitly holistic structure, that irreducible differences do not preclude an underlying unity. To "rescue" universalism, it is necessary to insist on its conjunction with two other principles. One is the distinction between *latent* and *manifest.* It refers not only to motives but also to feeling-patterns. What is latent informs what is manifest, but often it is unknown to the individual or group and, therefore, unrecoverable, except through the eyes of others. In linguistic theory the construct of latent/manifest or implicit/explicit boasts a distinguished lineage, from Alexander von Humboldt to Ferdinand de Saussure to Roman Jakobsen (and then to Levi-Strauss). At the beginning of the nineteenth century, long before Freud, Humboldt was probing the interface between interior consciousness and the empirical world. He hypothesized language as the distinctly human instrument that bridges who we are with what we observe. In his view, language mediates the first antinomy outer/inner, and also its correlates: objective/subjective, public/private and past/future. De Saussure, developing this insight, distinguished the external sign from the internal object signified, paralleled linguistically by the distinction of the manifest *parole* (word) from the latent *langue.* Roman Jakobsen, in turn, specified the range of expressed phonemic dyads that characterize all linguistic/ conceptual patterns, prompting Levi-Strauss to develop binary oppositions as the structural basis not only for human language but also for social exchange.

In short, modern linguistic theory, along with cultural anthropology, depended on a sophisticated, protracted development of the latent/manifest construct to sustain the argument for universals. Those who challenge the argument attack the "unscientific" connection between unconscious and universal. Of Levi-Strauss, the anthropologist Edmund Leach writes: "I am ready to concede that the structures which he displays are products of an unconscious mental process but I can see no reason to believe that they are human universals."[26] The issue is more complex, however, and Levi-Strauss illustrates both the promise of universalism in general and the difficulty of structuralism as its academic midwife. He separates humankind from all other animals and justifies human uniqueness with reference to a theory of symbols that relies on the Saussurian distinction between the sign and what is signified. One recognizes a sign as different only after first recognizing its relatedness to other signs. It is the ability to do both things simultaneously that, in Levi-Strauss's view, distinguishes humankind from animals. Only humans can "distinguish A from B while at the same time recognizing that A and B are somehow interdependent."[27]

Levi-Strauss seems to have rescued universalism. By postulating ambivalence as not only an objective condition but a subjective choice of human beings, he makes it possible to hypothesize a spectrum analysis of symbols; there is a range of relatedness (contiguity, metonym) as well as distinction (contrast, metaphor) that characterizes human thought. He eliminates an either/or incommensurate opposition. Even humans are related to animals by biological functions though separated from them by symbolic capabilities. There is nothing, human or otherwise, that is not universal in some degree.

Yet not all groups have equal power or motivation to assert their universality. In expanding the domain of universals, Levi-Strauss overlooks the possibility that one group could arrogate to itself the prerogative of asserting its values or interests as an excluding universal norm. It is not logic but history that confounds his acrobatic synthesis. The universalism of Levi-Strauss becomes problematic because it does not disentangle his theory of universals from the historical development of universalism. He is confounded by the recurrent anthropological proclivity to ahistoricism, drawing "a sharp (though arbitrary) line between primitive societies, which are grist for anthropologists because they are timeless and static, and advanced societies, which elude anthropological analysis because they are 'in history.'"[28]

To preserve or rescue universalism from rampant subjectivism, it is necessary to accept Levi-Strauss's insights but move beyond his conclusions. A further principle demands our attention: the conjunction of *truth* and *power* in their relationship to universalism. It is easy to make the case that truth is essential to universalism. Among the Continental philosophers, Paul Ricoeur and Jürgen Habermas have tried to salvage universalism by reintroducing truth either as the *outcome* of validity claims in a system of universal pragmatics (Habermas) or as the positive *condition* of historical understanding achieved through distanciation (Ricoeur). In both cases, truth is an incidental rather than a primary component of what is claimed as universal,[29] but even more importantly, universals are not distinguished from universalist norms. It is a distinction worth making. While universals are given, existing either within humans or in their social-cultural exchanges and awaiting only the proper scientific insight to be discovered, universalist norms are actively advocated, often through the use of force, by particular groups. If history has any enduring lesson, it is to underscore the vital distinction between the innate model of universals and the conquest model of universalism. The former has influenced the development of social scientific thought, but the latter has shaped the political birthing of the modern world.

Marxists make the further presumption that every exercise of power conjoined with truth is inevitably a deception or lie since it promotes inequality and oppression while laying claim to a higher principle. That amounts to a blanket negation of power as a valid social force. However, since power relations exist at every level in every human grouping, it is not the use but the abuse of power that has to be criticized. Nor do we have to concur with Foucault that power flaws all systems of knowledge, or epistemes, since their proponents reflect, above all, the urge to dominate or exclude others. Rather, knowledge, like power, can be disciplined and channeled to different ends. It is, above all, the public exercise of power that is required when universalist norms are advocated as truth claims, irrespective of the advocates' motives, whether they represent a worldview that is biblical, Hellenistic, or Western.

The universalist/monadist construct must be reconceived. First, it is a process with latent as well as manifest dimensions, and second, its instrumental core, more latent that manifest, is the projection of power through truth and vice versa. Viewed in this light, universalism is no longer an analytical category alternative to monadism. It is an operative ideology that denies the contingent validity of separate, self-sustaining units, i.e., monads.

The conquest model of universalism does not become less dependent on linguistic factors once its further consequences are projected beyond the academic arena. The overlap between the ideal and the real, the theoretical and the practical becomes clear in examining George Steiner's arguments on universalism versus monadism. Steiner is equivocal. He allows for the prevalence of monadism while advocating the potential of universalism. On the one hand, he declares that "every language structures and organizes reality in its own manner and thereby determines the components of reality that are peculiar to this given language" and hence "universalist models are at best irrelevant and at worst misleading." Yet he hesitates before the threshold of monadism. He backs away from his own conclusion, noting that "the similarities between men are finally much greater than their differences" and hence "the ancient controversy between relativist and universalist philosophies of language is not yet over."[30]

Steiner is pinned between two incommensurates only to the extent that he restricts himself to lexical meanings and syntactic rules. Monadists, relying on such surface distinctions, deny all other evidence. But there is an alternative and opposite view. It holds that despite the bewildering variety of languages, their underlying structure remains universal, its properties shared by all human discourse. Linguistic theorists such as Roman Jakobsen, Benjamin Whorf, and Noam Chomsky, together with cultural anthropologists like Claude Levi-Strauss and more recently Melford Spiro, all have tried to demonstrate that there is a primal level of language. It may not be recoverable, but it is identifiable.

Steiner knows full well these theories and also the scripturalist, mystical premise that before Babel, the human race spoke a now lost paradigmatic speech. In writing *After Babel,* he at first highlights the diversity bordering on mutual unintelligibility that characterizes linguistic patterns and cross-cultural codes, but finally he hints at a mediating position. Once Steiner has acknowledged and demonstrated the pervasiveness of monadism he is ready to broker a modified universalism. He invents another -*ism.* He calls it biculturalism. By this he means that there is a kind of Manichean faultline separating Western from non-Western worldviews.

Given our common neurophysiological build, archetypal images and sign systems ought to be demonstrably universal. Those stylizations and continuities of coding which we can verify are, however, *cultural specific.* Our western feeling-patterns, as they have come down to us through thematic development, are "ours," taking this possessive to delimit the Graeco-Latin and Hebraic circumference.[31]

Numerous others besides Steiner have debated about what is contained within "the Graeco-Latin and Hebraic circumference." Usually it is taken to mean that the Greek contribution to art, philosophy, and literature has been conjoined with the Jewish gift of God as One—absolute, transcendent yet omnipresent. Together they have shaped the resources, the achievements, and also the limits, of Western civilization. But that conjunction has also produced an internal tension. Two contemporary Continental philosophers quarrel over the serial antinomies, Greek/Jew, Hebraism/Hellenism, Jerusalem/Athens. Their dialectical sparring could be seen as an extended commentary on the suggestive line from *Ulysses:* "Jewgreek is greekjew. Extremes meet."[32]

Yet it is an internal meeting. It takes place within Western culture, and therefore one is constrained to marvel at both its achievements and its limits simultaneously. They apply to science as well as to nonscience:

Even as the history of religion in the West has been one of variations on and accretions to the Judaic-Hellenistic canon, so our metaphysics, visual arts, humanities, scientific criteria, have reproduced, more or less designedly, the Platonic, Aristotelian, Homeric or Sophoclean paradigm.[33]

As clear as this statement may sound, it leaves open the question of defining precise temporal as well as spatial boundaries for the "Judaic-Hellenistic canon." Are the Amerindians excluded because they inhabited the American continents before the advent of the European legatees of the Judaic-Hellenistic canon? Are Muslims discounted because their genetic contiguity through Abrahamic stock and philosophical custodianship of the Hellenistic classics proved less significant than their geographical location on the perimeter of the "greekjew" synthesis?

Steiner's postulation of biculturalism poses a danger. In reclaiming universalism as two-tiered, he is also redefining monadism as dyadic. Either way, he is advocating truth through power. The Western worldview is ranked above the other to which it is linked but from which it is differentiated. In drawing attention to the referential oddities of the Western intellectual-linguistic paradigm, he places those outside the Western sphere on a lower rung of humanity. Western culture becomes a cause for hubris rather than a neutral marking.

The dominant strain in the Enlightenment has reinforced just this myopia. Few were the philosophers, like Kant's student J. G. Herder, who rebelled against the ascendant order. Even in his rebellion, Herder was forced to embrace a variant to monadism, conceding that "the cultural manifestations of the human are myriad, unpredictable, and discontinuous." In his view, each people, despite its equivalent status with every other, "remains a self-contained Leibnizian monad."[34]

Steiner's biculturalist hypothesis needs to be qualified. Modernism may be identified with Western cultural markings, but it can also be interpreted by criteria external to the Western worldview and its peculiar language. This is a frequent approach in much of the literature on modernization theory. Modern is implicitly bracketed with and differentiated from tradition. Modernism is all the things that traditionalism is not. Modernism entails competition, specialization, equality, the rebellion against hierarchy, advocacy of change. It is a process that focuses on, and is spearheaded by, the individual, who is usually male. His domain is the public sphere. There he is cast in a contractual and voluntary rather than a covenantal and "obedient" relationship vis-à-vis the groups and institutions of his society.

The argument hinges on two valent terms: "change" and "growth." In the words of a prominent sociologist, modernization has three salient characteristics:

(1) continuous change on the scale of various indices of social mobilization; (2) change in types of structural social organization (i.e., growing differentiation and specialization and universalistic and achievement criteria), and (3) the development of institutional frameworks capable of self-sustained growth.[35]

The cumbersome abstractness of this definition should not blunt its double emphasis. First, change is decisive yet never defined. It alone is absolute. The only certainty becomes the certainty of change. Second, growth is pervasive. Not only do vocational options expand but so, too, do social options or lifestyles. The goal, in the words of another sociologist, is to maximize "the emporium of life-styles, identities *and* religious preferences." [36]

Modernism, by the abstraction of its defining goals, escapes geographical boundaries. Yet, in shifting the ideological context of contemporary life, modernism has not escaped the bonds of language. The modernist "apostasy," in all its ramifications, begins with the opaquely paradoxical power of language. No matter what changes or how it changes, there must be an attempt at explanation. One can justify, one may advocate, one may even reject, but in each instance one must also try to explain.

We are now in a position to understand why modernism/fundamentalism is such a complex interaction. It is not the first antinomy of the present era. Rather it is one of several contraries that have been inflated into contradictions, because the modernist mind thinks dialectically. It frames and counterposes antinomies. It sets the stage and then compels the choice between incommensurable, hostile, exclusive opposites.

Modernism/fundamentalism is best understood when viewed as a subset of the larger, longer battle between universalism and monadism. Universalism claims all as ultimately one. Monadism sees all as provisionally many. They are engaged in a multileveled, varied combat. The weapons, like the goals, are not totally visible above the ground. Some are concealed from both protagonists. And the outcome depends on more than the assertion of truth. It also requires the exercise of instrumental power.

Both modernists and fundamentalists claim the mantle of universalism. They differ in their interpretations of what is meant by universalism. The modernists, invoking scientific method, posit it as the discovery of universal principles that operate throughout all periods in all human societies. They also agree to argue among themselves about which category is ascendant: is it universals, or is it self-contained isolates, i.e., monads? But in the debate only empirically observable and testable data count. The fundamentalists, by contrast, declare themselves to be advocates of universalist norms. Their norms are not discoverable. They have been revealed once and for all. They are codified in Holy Writ.

They require assent not debate. They are understood by faith not by reason.

Each claim and counterclaim depend on tacit presuppositions. If the interpretations of universalism and the rules of combat differ, so do the subsurface (the unspoken) aspects of each side's agenda. The modernist goal is objective truth. To paraphrase Parsons, objective truth is supposed to be marked by affective neutrality or dispassionate unconcern with the consequences of truth. In fact, however, every major scientific discovery suggests the replacement of one paradigm by another, and also one group of "orthodox" by another. Though they may not have a Holy Writ, scientists do have their heroes who match prophets in popular folklore. Einstein is a Moses, Carl Sagan, an Ecclesiasticus, the seven astronauts of *Challenger*, martyrs to a new faith. For fundamentalists, the advocacy of universalist norms supplants the search for universals. Humankind, in their view, has not created the doubles of good and evil, faith and reason, or heaven and hell. They are evident in the nature of things. According to the Scottish Enlightenment, which latently influenced many fundamentalists, they are "common sense." Hence, fundamentalism, despite claims about revelational authority, involves a process of discovery, change, and growth in one's perception of the material world.

And the struggle between fundamentalism and modernism could not take place did not both sides have the power to mobilize resources, each on its behalf. Modernists, self-styled defenders of science, depend on the enormous prestige of EuroAmerican and now Asian technology. Technology works at increasingly effective levels in people's lives. No one wants to grant it ultimate power, but neither does anyone want to be bereft of its instrumental benefits. Moreover, technology provides some of the most lucrative and challenging jobs in the private as well as the public sector of EuroAmerican societies. The expanding frontier of space exploration, even with temporary setbacks, continues to give the general populace a sense of limitless horizons. What greater truth can there be than the discovery of new galaxies? What greater power than the ability to harness their potentialities to existence on planet earth? For modernists the truth of discovery is inextricably conjoined with the power to implement and to impress.

Fundamentalists have a reduced but still potent arsenal. The truth that they claim is more publicly accessible. Everyone knows of the Bible in North America, the Torah in Israel, the Qur'an in Dar al-Islam. Everyone can read or be told about the Holy Writ. Everyone can work out his or her understanding of its message. Also, that message, now as never before, is carefully packaged to accord with the expectations and possibilities of electronic media TV preachers. In Protestant America and in parts of the Muslim world, such media manipulators use the instrumentalities of modern technology to proclaim an antimodernist message. The modern system permits the flourishing of antimodernism. Insofar as it converges with democratic ideals and the separation of church and state, the modern state allows religious groups to congregate, even when they compete with the cherished ideals of a secular state, even when they can mobilize followers on moral issues that proclaim the rebirth of a Christian or Jewish or Muslim civilization to replace the secular model that now prevails.

To begin to analyze modernism and fundamentalism is to acknowledge that they interact one with the other at multiple levels. It is not enough to repeat tired slogans and say that modernism embraces change, fundamentalism opposes it, or to claim that the dispute between them is an internal squabble, limited to Protestant America in the twentieth century. Instead, it is a battle that has been in the offing for at least two centuries. Its impact reverberates throughout Africa and Asia as well as Europe and America. The current phase of the conflict has a long prologue, inseparable from the historical emergence of the West. Yet the West was itself an accident of time and geography. Without attention to that accident we cannot interpret the modernist/fundamentalist controversy in our own era. Only when we have reconstructed the coming into being of our world can we hope to understand how and why some of its determinative forces provoked the fundamentalist response.

CHAPTER 2

Reinterpeting the Rise of the West

Suffering has been the lot of a very large portion of humanity for nearly all of recorded history. The inarticulateness of the victims, very few of whom have left any records, has to a great extent masked its extent. Furthermore, before the scientific, industrial, and democratic revolutions of the last four centuries it could hardly occur to the victims of any social order that human societies might take a different form. In other words, a secular diagnosis and remedy of social evils were out of the question except as an intellectual exercise for a few philosophers. The mass of the population had to make the best of it, seeking solace in religion, asceticism, and its opposite, intermittent festivals. Since human beings do display an extraordinary capacity for feeling happy under oppressive circumstances, and do at times become attached to their chains, it would probably be a mistake to paint the general picture in dramatically dark lines.

—BARRINGTON MOORE, JR.

Among the more powerful aggregates of contemporary vocabulary is the West. It evokes an image of strength and superiority. It presupposes the notion of a uniform geographic entity, encompassing numerous ethnic and social substrata. Privileged by historical development, it created and then dominated the modern era. It is ranked over and above but also over against all others who are labeled, and also libeled, as "non-Western."

The exclusionary emphasis of the West was integral to the self-definition of its exponents. The world was arrayed into three groups: primitives, the Orient, and the ascendant West. The first had no history, because it had produced no texts and built no monuments. The second could boast both texts and monuments yet lacked social mobility and representative government. "Only the ascendant West, reclaiming the ancient Greek heritage through the catalyst of the Reformation and the Enlightenment, could espouse Truth, Liberty and Progress and hence achieve Modernity and, with it, world domination."[1]

This bifurcation of the world into winners and losers amounts to a reductionist stereotype, a kind of collective cultural slur on all "others."

It has had insidious consequences for both winners and losers. The harm to the losers has been analyzed at length, for instance in Edward Said's *Orientalism* and the multiple responses that it occasioned.[2] What has not often been done is to examine the problems created for the winners.

To understand who were the winners, and also the limits of what they won, we need to ask two separate but related questions: Which countries became the driving forces propelling the West into the modern era? And also, how were different socioeconomic groups within these dominant countries affected by the modernizing process?

These may not sound like religious questions, yet their answer, in part, depends on evaluating the mediation to modernity that religion effected. The most controversial thesis derives from Max Weber's *Protestant Ethic and the Spirit of Capitalism*, published in 1904.[3] Weber argues that Protestant merchants in Northern Europe fostered a changed outlook toward the material world and modes of production. It was in the period after the Reformation that a burgeoning economy, fueled by the capitalist spirit, provided a this-worldly outlet for certain Protestant elites, thereby assisting Europe's transformation from a feudal to a modern society. Weber's thesis broke new ground. It deflected attention away from the biographical approach to the development of Protestantism that had focused on individual leaders, stressing their role as scriptural, doctrinal, and ecclesiastical protesters against the monopolistic rigidity of Roman Catholicism. Weber instead saw the primary value of Protestantism not in its theological appeal nor in the success of its founding figures but rather in its shaping of a new way of viewing the world. He called this new outlook "disenchanted," distinguishing it from the Catholic view which he labeled "enchanted."

Weber may have been partially mistaken on both sides of his analytical construct. For Calvinists there was more to asceticism than acquisitiveness,[4] and the Reformation was not limited to economic, specifically capitalist, consequences.[5] Yet many social scientists, following Weber's lead, have ascribed to religious variables a major role in the modernization of northern Europe. The anthropologist Atwood Gaines, for instance, differentiates the impact of modernization by tracing not one but two great traditions in the West: the Northern European cultural area and its Mediterranean counterpart. The basic differences between them, in his view, are due not to ethnic, linguistic, or economic factors but rather to "religion and its impact upon social organization." Why? Because

Northern Europe is home to the world view which Weber referred to as "disenchanted" and heir to the Magisterial Protestant Reform which symbolized a practical, empiricist, non-magical approach to the social and natural world. The goals of this world are to be achieved by action in the world, not by intercession of preternatural forces and beings into this life. Action in this world is caused by physical factors, not by fate, immaterial saints, genies (as in Islamic lands), devils or miracles (which are the touch of divinity itself).

The disenchanted world view deriving from the Protestant Reformation in Europe is found in Northern Europe, . . . (while) Latin Europe, a species of Mediterranean tradition, is that of the enchanted world view and evidences the dualistic cosmology (the City of God is contrasted with and opposed to the City of Man) which contrasts with the monistic cosmology of Protestant Reformers (e.g., God's world is this world, all work is God's work, God is omnipresent).[6]

Nor is the religious bifurcation of disenchanted and enchanted, Northern European and Mediterranean worldviews limited to Europe. It persists in the New World since Continental adherents to both world-views emigrated to America:

Evangelical, Pentecostal, Southern Baptist and other forms of fundamentalist religiosity termed "Protestant" in America may be seen as returns to traditional Mediterranean *ideology*, one form of which is Roman Catholicism. The Bible, the major source of inspiration for these groups, serves as a vehicle for the trans-portation of *ideology* to an ostensibly other culture, time and place. Since these groups use (what they construe to be) literalist interpretations of Scripture, the sacred text becomes, in essence, a sacred ethnography. Exegesis of the sacred ethnography serves as a model of and for social behavior and morality. In this way role relations (patriarchy, patripotestality, matrifocality, familial and person-al honor) become highly similar in fundamentalist and Catholic Christian soci-eties.[7]

Ideology is the pivotal term in Gaines's argument. It refers not simply to public posture but to the most basic moral orientation. As such, it undergirds and connects seemingly disparate churches—Catholic and Protestant. Gaines's is a bold effort to locate structural similarities be-neath surface differences, yet its success depends on a prior judgment that what Mediterranean Catholics and American fundamentalists hold in common (a reverence for "traditional" social values vs. an expectation of change) is more important than what divides them (their view of *all* authority, ecclesiastical, scriptural, and personal).

Even if one agrees with Gaines, a basic question looms large: Can the spectrum of Western thought be delimited to two outlooks, implying that all evidence may be sorted out neatly into two groupings viewed as discrete ideologies reflecting antithetical views of continuity and change? While ascetic Protestantism did stress disenchantment from this world and affirmation of individual change, it itself "was only one factor in a constellation of the factors" that led to the transformation of European society, the hegemony of certain Western countries and the emergence of the modernist mindset.[8]

Weber never claimed that Protestantism was *the* source of capitalism, only that there was a strange coincidence and common ground between the Puritan ethic and modern life. Yet his redolent antinomies seem to embody the cognitive parallel to the world domination they describe. Weber epitomizes the nineteenth century idealist fascination with abstract categories, upscaling differences among human societies to such a level of generalization that they run the risk of "not accounting for the actual pluralism of functions and properties" that characterize social exchange and human experience.[9]

Present-day historians tracing the parameters of modernity seldom invoke religion. The Weberian thesis, despite its structural symmetry and rational appeal, has become a sidelight to the major theses on the origins of the modern West. Like Durkheim, Weber may have presumed too much about the givenness of religion. Indeed, he may have been drawn to analyze religion precisely because its pervasiveness as a general human condition was matched only by its malleability as a contextual variant open to limitless interpretation.

In one aspect Weber's contribution is secure: the investigation of origins that occupied him continues to dominate historical inquiry. Weber would have applauded Marc Bloch's caveat that in the search for origins "there lurks the danger of confusing ancestry with explanation."[10] Origins do not explain beginnings, and what Weber, Gaines, and other social science theorists have underscored is the need to differentiate the multiple groups caught up in that process too glibly recalled as the rise of the West. The seventeenth, eighteenth, and nineteenth centuries did not augur a sweeping transformation of *all* European societies and *all* religious parties into a utopia of capitalist triumphs over feudal lethargy. There were pivotal decisions rather than an inevitable process. There were stops and starts, not an inexorable acceleration. In the previous chapter we posited fundamentalism as a religious rejection of modernism that continued to be shaped by modernity. To make sense of that seeming paradox we, too, have to particularize the process by which the modern West came into being. Our analysis has to be less abstract and more concrete. We may not agree with Fernand Braudel that "total society can only be a sum of living realities, *whether or not* these are related to each other, like several containers and their contents,"[11] but we do need to look at the content of that one large container out of which spilled the modern world. Without declaring ourselves as monadists or universalists, we have to get back behind social scientific theory and look at tough diachronic, structural questions: Where did it begin? In which countries, among which groups, by what strategies, and with what results?

In the emergence of the modern West *religion* plays a doubly important role, first by its absence from the technological process decisive for modernization and secondly by its postulation as the enemy against which both the new math and the new science are defined.

What every investigator strives to find is a turning point, some moment or series of moments that, when isolated, contextualized, and integrated with other factors, explain what happened. The shorthand term most often invoked for that switch that illumines the mystery of modernity is *revolution*. Some would prefer to see several stages of accelerated *evolution*, less glowing in their semantic appeal than one, giant *revolution* but perhaps more reflective of the actual pattern of change in human societies.[12]

Still others recoil from the burdensome connotations of both words, evolution because of its Darwinian legacy, revolution, its Marxist appropriation. The sociologist Barrington Moore, like Marshall Hodgson, calls attention to the concatenation of several revolutions rather than the decisive effect of one. The emergence of the modern world, in Moore's view, was due to the combined effect of three revolutions: the scientific, the industrial, and the democratic. He sees their combined force as the catalyst that shaped the destiny of Northern Europe and eventually the rest of Europe, the rest of the West, and the whole world.[13]

Yet Moore sidesteps the central analytical problem: How do scientific discoveries shape patterns of commercial investment that lead, over time, to large scale, irrevocable industrialization? It is a knotty question. Britain, for instance, was able to pioneer the industrial revolution due to internal developments dating back to the mid-sixteenth century. The interaction and mutual stimulation of industry and commerce which preceded the Elizabethan age made possible the further discoveries of that period. Of decisive importance was a new industrial outlook emphasizing *quantity*. "This change was as revolutionary as the new scientific outlook. Between them these two revolutions made almost inevitable the eventual triumph of industrialism."[14]

Only in hindsight, however, does the triumph of industrialism seem inevitable. At first none but Holland followed the British example. It wasn't till the middle of the eighteenth century that the attraction of industrialization became irresistible for the other Continental countries.

How does one explain what almost didn't happen as something that had to happen? The historian Marshall Hodgson calls attention to the accidental character of what appeared to be the irreversible occurrence of industrialization in the West. He also stresses the decisive role of technicalization. For Hodgson correct historical analysis depends on the cautious, often revisionist, choice of terminology. It is the word "transmutation" that in his view best evokes the momentous, glacial-like shift which produced the modern world. The biologist Jean Baptist de Lamarck had used "transmutation" to explain his pre-Darwinian evolutionary theories. The linguistic theorist Roman Jakobsen had also used "transmutation" to elaborate the philosopher Charles Peirce's theory of signs and meaning. Hodgson follows Jakobsen rather than de Lamarck. He sees "transmutation" as a word that speaks through its silence. It is a signifier akin to the linguistic shift that takes place in the nonverbal realm when moving from one language to another. The ambiguity, both tonal and contextual, of "transmutation" mirrors the gradient of change in premodern Europe signaling the ascent of the West. For Hodgson, as for Fernand Braudel, it was the shift in investment patterns and cumulative buildup of social power that finally achieved a critical mass in certain sectors of Northern European society and, being irreversible, produced the "takeoff" into a new historical era.

The resulting process, ever changing, was not perceptible even to its agents and beneficiaries. More than a mere regional transmutation, it became the Great Western Transmutation (often abbreviated hereafter as GWT). The Great Western Transmutation is said to have begun at the end of the eighteenth century, but pegging its inception to any century is a convenient fiction since "the Modern pattern of development [was] already established in nucleo by about the year 1800. It was the transformations of the seventeenth and eighteenth centuries that served to set off decisively westerners from the rest of mankind." [15]

Hodgson labeled this new stage in world history the Technical Age, contrasting it with the preceding Agrarianate Age. Once again his choice of nomenclature reflects his indebtedness to intellectual forebears. It was the philosopher Karl Jaspers who delineated periods within the Agrarianate Age, tracing its greatness back to the seminal or axial period, from 800–200 B.C. It is a grand scale of reckoning, too distant and vague for many. More palpable is the reckoning of centuries as distinctive brackets of time. To some, the eighteenth century stands out as "the age of enlightenment," followed by "the age of revolution" (till mid-nineteenth century), then "the age of ideology" (till the early twentieth), and finally "the age of analysis" (till now). [16] The problem, of course, is that patterns of thought persist beyond the time in which they dominate, and their domination does not extend to all sectors of society in any age. Moreover, "age" has a lingering association with the ternary division of history into dark, middle, and modern. "Era," less sweeping in its temporal claims, seems a preferable category to refer to the characteristic emphases and new directions of the present period in world history. And the era in which we live no longer posits the mere presence of technology. It also strives for the perfectability of technical skills. Among scientists, whether it be the microbiologist examining the smallest particles of matter or the astrophysicist scanning the edge of outer space, the optimal goal is to surpass current technological frontiers. And so the time span in which we find ourselves since World War II is best designated as the High Tech Era.

The High Tech Era qualifies but does not refute the essential thrust of Hodgson's argument. The denotation of this or any future era goes back to the Great Western Transmutation which ushered in the Technical Age. For the emphasis of the new investment patterns, as also the direction of the new social forces, was technical rather than industrial. To recognize that the modern world came into being first in Northern

Europe prior to the nineteenth century is to look for the interaction of numerous discrete factors that collectively augured change. The term "technicalization" better describes the process than "industrialization." Hodgson's definition of technicalization still satisfies: "a condition of calculative (and hence innovative) technical specialization, in which several specialties become interdependent on a large enough scale to determine patterns of expectation in the key sectors of a society, especially overseas commerce." [17]

Technicalization did not occur everywhere at the same time with the same force. Isolated as the denotative key of the modern era, it must still be related to its many faceted appropriation. It was the upstart Reformation countries of Northern Europe that overtook the established Catholic countries of Mediterranean Christendom. For a time religion did play a positive role, cohering trade alliances between England and Holland against their southern competitors, Portugal and Spain, but it also played a negative role in fostering the Wars of Religion, leading to the breakdown of Protestant trade networks in favor of overriding national interests. The Wars of Religion, in turn, provided fertile ground for the Counter-Reformation.

More determinative than the seesaw of religious and creedal allegiances was the incipient hierarchy of power relations that characterized the new world system. Two countries, England and France, dominated the early centuries of the Technical Age. Their open and bitter rivalry often masked their underlying complementarity, nowhere more clearly seen than in the contest between pure math and new math. It pitted the qualitative elegance but nonutilitarian mathematics of Descartes against the pragmatic instrumentality of Newton's quantitative proofs of Kepler's theorems. Yet both aspects of modern mathematics were crucial to the success of the technological and industrial revolutions.

The implicit elitism of the French-British rivalry is also evident in their development of commercial networks. At the center of their growing influence was their coexistence as the two greatest sea powers of the eighteenth century. They surpassed and supplanted the Spanish, the Dutch, and the Portuguese. The external overseas holdings of the latter dwindled before the onslaught of French and/or British traders. Naval superiority made possible both competition in overseas trading activity and market expansion. The process was neatly integrated into a new pattern that took maximal advantage of the irreversible modernist emphasis on technical specialization. Merchants and politicians, capitalists and rulers cooperated at home and abroad, to their mutual advantage, and with the added buffer of a vastly superior system of military organization. [18]

The nature of British-French rivalry also determined modern war as a great power struggle of technically proficient giants. By the end of the eighteenth century, the expansion of technical proficiency had led to the bureaucratization of violence, nowhere more dramatically than in Northern Europe. The watershed event is often said to be the French Revolution. Prior to 1789 all wars, including the Wars of Religion, had been games engaging only the elites of Northern Europe. British superiority in mining and manufacturing had been matched by French superiority in military experimentation and technical innovation on the battlefield. The resulting contests had been limited to a royal contest in which most British and most French had no stake.[19]

Precisely because it came at the juncture of a sustained buildup to the modern world, the French Revolution had a pivotal impact on subsequent history. It finally matters little whether or not the ancient regime was really replaced, for the revolution did have a fatal effect on subsequent warfare. It injected politically motivated crowd violence into the arena of international conflict. It enhanced the scope of warfare but also made the stakes too high for some players to keep in the game. That may sound like faint praise for a process that has now produced numerous bloodlettings, including the horror of two world wars and the ongoing Great Power struggle. But consider that the prize of technicalization for the winners is to separate the Great Powers from the lesser powers. If one uses a single yardstick to record the players and nonplayers, the big players and little players, the winners and the "also rans" in the Great Western Transmutation, that single yardstick might be called modern warfare: the ability to prepare for war, wage war, and win war on a transregional scale. By that standard only ten players existed before the French Revolution. All of them, except the Ottoman Empire, were European. But by the time of World War I, four of those players, including the Ottoman Empire, had already forfeited their right to be a "Great Power." In their stead came four more, only one of whom was European (Italy). The other three were the United States, Japan, and China.[20]

The canon of military might makes clear, first, that the genesis of modern warfare was Eurocentric and, second, non-Europeans were increasingly able to play the game. The ability to participate in the deadliest of all games was determined by the edge of technical superiority that was introduced, and set in place as irreversible, by the Great Western Transmutation. In elevating the few, it destroyed the rough social parity that had existed within the agrarianate societies of Afro-Eurasia prior to 1800.[21]

The results were disastrous. They were disastrous not only for those European countries that could not compete on equal terms with their advanced neighbors but also for those members of the advanced countries who did not share in the mechanisms that produced or exercised economic, military, political, and social power. But they were most disastrous for those countries that became increasingly peripheral to the emergent world power system. Labeled as non-Western, such countries were also denigrated as backward. They came to be ranked at the bottom of the Great Power scale; they were third world.[22]

All these groups became losers before the unstoppable *golem*[23] of intractable change that Hodgson calls the GWT, and their loss has to be considered before we can assess the social roots for the emergence of fundamentalism on a global scale. What is loss? How does one reckon loss for a group, a nation, a region? To characterize loss on a military, economic, or political scale is to miss the point. There is also a religious disorientation that is global in scope yet differentiated in its temporal occurrence and perceptual force. By this criterion even the winners became losers to the extent that their orientation to the world, their ethos and outlook, were radically displaced. For emphasis on the quantitative, the calculative, the specialized seemed to induce speculations that went a long way toward undermining the cosmological presuppositions of the medieval world and the privileged social role of the institutional church.

Many observers register the force of change from the philosophical or metaphysical past. Hodgson goes so far as to declare that

the result [of technicalization] was to place in jeopardy any sense of a cosmic whole. The natural science traditions had maintained also in the Occident that degree of intellectual autonomy they had early won from commitment to the intellectual predispositions of overall life-orientational tradition [i.e., they could exercise effective agnosticism!]. . . . But now, *with intensive speculation*, the autonomy of the natural-science traditions was pushed much further, and the accompanying empiricism became almost routine. Every major scientist found himself forced to try to work out for himself (if he cared) his own sense of the cosmic whole; and alert laymen were left "with all coherence gone." By 1800 the technicalistic spirit had spread from astronomy and physics to chemistry, geology, and biology. From Descartes to its culmination in Kant, the new epistemological philosophy was inspired by the new technicalistic science and *by its very disengagement from ultimate questions.*[24]

Hodgson implies that the metaphysical *angst* engendered by the new empiricism touched only a small, albeit elite, group of Europeans, primarily mathematicians, natural scientists, and "alert laymen." Many others continued to find in traditional beliefs a recourse for age-old human problems. An index of popular sentiment is provided by the printing industry. The mass production of books was begun in Europe in 1447. From the mid-fifteenth till the nineteenth century, the most popular and profitable topic for books continued to be religion. Clearly, even the GWT and its Enlightenment ideology had not dislodged God from His universe for the masses. One sociologist has gone so far as to argue that the Enlightenment legacy could only have been preserved because it did *not* achieve universal acceptance:

Once religious beliefs were discredited and religious and neighborly communities shaken—which occurred to some extent through the successful prosecution of the ideals of the Enlightenment . . . societies became endangered. [Yet] the rational consensus which was anticipated did not come about over as wide a radius as had been desired. [In the nineteenth century class conflicts became openly acute but] they did not endanger society because they were still very confined in scale and intensity; traditions of authority [including religious beliefs and rituals] were still strong enough to contain them.[25]

A shift in metaphysical paradigms, therefore, did not solve the riddle of modernity. The GWT may have been great in its definitional force for those in its vanguard; it was not great in its scope. The majority of Northern Europeans and others remained outside its arc.

To differentiate the impact of the GWT, we need to look at the groups excluded from its "progress." The landed aristocracy, agriculturalists, and even the intellectual elite benefited only in limited degrees compared to the new mercantile and entrepreneurial classes. Racial minorities and women were marginalized and often suppressed.

Because the French Revolution only partially changed the condition of the masses, its historical reality does not match its legendary image. While it suggested the opening of a democratic era of mass participation, there were limits imposed on the degree of actual participation since the other two revolutions with which it has been linked fostered rather than reduced elitism. As Nef has explained, "the new emphasis which . . . distinguished the science of early modern Europe from earlier science was confined to a very few. The scientific revolution was even less a mass movement than the industrial revolution."[26]

Relative to the rest of the world it still seemed that increasingly after 1500 popular participation in economic, cultural, and political life was far greater in Western Europe than in the other civilizations of the world.[27] For what the ideals of the French Revolution had set in motion was a tidal wave of rising expectations that led all social groups within the dominant European states to compare themselves not with "those others" but with the improved condition of the best among themselves.

And so a social contradiction was launched. On the one hand, the extensive world trade network[28] had set the stage for the GWT, but on the other hand, the interdependence it ensured reinforced the hierarchy of its participants. At the top of the scale were the chief beneficiaries, merchants and bankers, just below them were the politicians with whom they were in tacit, if not explicit, alliance. It became increasingly more difficult for other groups within society to be isolated from their influence. By the end of the eighteenth century any real autonomy was no longer possible.

The scope of the new world system often concealed the fact that its beneficiaries were few and their power enormous. For "the world market of the eighteenth and nineteenth centuries was . . . managed in an important degree by a small number of bankers, merchants, politicians, officials, nearly all of whom were based in western Europe. Indeed, the price of complete personal freedom is to consume only what one can produce for oneself in a place where risk of armed attack by outsiders has somehow been effectually exorcised. Such places are far and few in our world."[29]

The establishment of a pervasive set of market relations on a global scale was the spur to colonialism and also its most enduring consequence. The newly empowered economies of Northern Europe began an expansion of overseas commercial networks that imposed on the rest of the world a form of hydraulic relations that sustained the exploiter at the expense of those exploited. Its wider impact can be assessed in vague terms, with reference to indices of power that apply mainly to the public sphere. As McNeill explains,

the really important result of the balance between superior armed force and most untrammeled commercial self-seeking that characterized European ventures overseas in the nineteenth century was the fact that the daily lives of hundreds of thousands, and by the end of the century of millions, of Asians, Africans and Americans were transformed by the activity of European entrepreneurs. Market-regulated activity, managed and controlled by a handful of Europeans, began to eat into and break down older social structures in nearly all parts of the earth that were easily accessible by sea.[30]

What began on the coastal regions of Asia, Africa, and America extended inland, with the rapid improvement of transportation and communication, especially the advent of railroad and telegraph after the middle of nineteenth century. Those millions who were peripheral to the West yet shaped by its impingement on their lives had not even the venue to voice their protest prior to World War I. Many fought their European masters, sometimes in the name of religion, but they were compelled to stage desperate uprisings on a limited scale with a predictable outcome: the defeat of the nativist leaders and their followers, often followed by the killing of families, friends, and any suspected sympathizers.[31] In the marketplace of global power, Asians and Africans had no voice. The Technical Age conferred on nationalism the major marking of corporate identity in the public sphere. Improved communications bolstered the prestige of the Great Powers, at the same time confirming the loss of the losers, i.e, those who ranked at the bottom of the Great Power hierarchy or who were excluded from it altogether.

Up till World War I, politics was dominated by the European Great Power game. It seemed as natural, and as interminable, as the American-Soviet rivalry today. Trade-offs between France and England, and increasingly also Germany and Russia, controlled all aspects of military confrontation and intercontinental diplomacy. But the outburst of World War I brought an era to an end. The large-scale slaughter of trench warfare led to the deaths of 2.5 million French and British soldiers, although 10.5 million peasants drafted into the rival armies were the real victims of slaughter. Peasants elsewhere seemed to be victors rather than victims. The Bolshevik Revolution dramatized the possibility that aristocratic society could be overturned by the underprivileged, that those out of power could come into power. Even more dramatically than the French Revolution, it signified the potential of political violence to change directions in the public order. And beyond the Western fold, also as a result of World War I, there emerged new nations, hardly more than crippled diminutions of colonial avarice. Yet they did appear and they were crowned as nations. Among them were Egypt, Turkey, Iran, and the Kingdom of Saudi Arabia.

Following World War II, there occurred a still more dramatic dismembering of European empires. Former colonies were sorted out into newly independent states, though with uneven leverage between those countries and the former powers controlling them, as well as unequal power for the social groups within these countries. Women, ethnic, and religious minorities, with few exceptions, were marginalized still further from the center of political and economic influence in the public sphere.

So rapid and far-reaching have been the changes since World War II that some have argued that we now ought to think of a threefold instead of a twofold classification of world history. What used to be medieval and modern periods, should be redesignated as medieval, modern, and contemporary, with the following time frames: the medieval (1450–1890), the modern (1890–1955), and the contemporary (1955–) eras of world history.[32] Even if one were to accept these new calendrical sightings, they would not change the major emphasis of Jaspers and later Hodgson. It was the Technical Age, followed by the High Tech Era, that separated premodern from modern man, and the GWT was the instrument affecting that change.

There are three points at which we need to assess the impact of the GWT on *homo religiosus*—i.e., on the creed of outlook, the liturgical practices, and the socioreligious institutions of humankind. First, the GWT had no allegiance to a specific place, race, or religion. Because it occurred in Northern Europe among Anglo-Saxon Protestants, it is called "Western," but it could and did spread to Catholic Europe and later to the New World of the Americas and, most recently, to the Pacific Basin, beginning with Japan. Although the first reaction it produced has been among cultures imbued with monotheistic legacies, it can also challenge a Confucian or Shinto ethos. Second, the GWT was tangential to the moral plane. Its impact there was indirect and secondary. It grew out of, adapted to, and claimed the material world. It ignored ultimate questions; the God-talk of theologians, philosophers, metaphysical poets, and artists did not affect the driving edge of change. Third, and least recognized, the rate of change was *ad hoc* and sporadic. Growth was sometimes rapid within a decade, then planed off for a longer period, even spanning decades (or centuries) till 1800. It is at the cusp of the nineteenth century that the GWT took off, creating a new class of explorers, technocrats, and rulers who did not concern themselves with the spirit or even the mind apart from its functional use. The philosopher David Hume perhaps best summarized the zeal of scientific exclusivism when he recommended to his contemporaries that they browse through their libraries and ask of each book of religion: "Does it contain any abstract reasoning concerning quantity or number? No. Does it contain any experimental reasoning concerning matters of fact or existence? No. Commit it then to the flames; for it can contain nothing but sophistry and illusion."[33]

It should not be surprising, therefore, that reflection on the modernist hegemony everywhere produced an attenuation of specific referents and an unconscious upward displacement of loyalty. Among European Jewry it was by explicit appeal to the symbols of the Enlightenment as a pretext for noncompliance with the *mitzvoth*. In African and Asian Islam it was by a similar appeal to nationalist and socialist slogans as the fulfillment of age-old aspirations, whether the *pancasila* in Sukarno's Indonesia or the three circles in Nasser's Egypt. In the United States the dislocation came through a uniquely American amalgam of church-state loyalties, the framing of a new national religion, a civil religion that has been aptly labeled Progressive Protestant Patriotism.[34]

Did organized religion prepare for its own marginalization in the modern world? Among the theses advanced to explain the dilemma of modern believers, one of the most speculative declares that the churches did contribute to their own destruction by accommodating to those religious forces that were responsible for shaping the distinctive directions of the modern world. The same could be said of certain groups of Jews in premodern Europe and of Muslims in twentieth-century Africa and Asia.

But the thesis is constructed on a false premise, that religions in general and their adherents in particular had an independent, voluntary role in the Technical Age. The very nature of the GWT is to deny both its participants and its victims any decisive identity. The key word is "decisive." Whatever role Christians, Jews, and Muslims played in the emergence of modern culture, they acted as agents of the technical spirit. In his novel *The Chosen* Chaim Potok has caught the mood of fear and anger that the GWT engendered in Hasidic Jews. To them, Judaism was inseparable from Diaspora culture. Those Jews who took advantage of the professional and educational opportunities increasingly available in the urban centers of modernizing Europe participated as members of the dominant culture. They did not participate as Jews. The same was true of overseas Christian missionaries working as nonconversionary agents in distant parts of Africa and Asia. In their self-understanding, they were bearing witness to the gospel by performing good deeds, but the deeds they performed were in fact modern deeds, effected through medical and educational outposts in still "heathen" lands that were "heathen" precisely because they were untouched by the technical spirit.

Even before the separation of church and state in late eighteenth-century America, there was the separation of technical people from their nontechnical forebears and contemporaries. It is the implicit link of "technical" skills to the possession and use of "rational" faculties that has led to confusion, anger, and outright misunderstanding about the relation of the Technical Age to other periods of history. The sociologist Edward Shils, for instance, summarizes the Enlightenment view of religion, and in so doing suggests the extent to which Comte's bias persists:

Religious knowledge . . . has been regarded as the very epitome of all that reason refuses. Prejudice, dogmatism, superstition, taboos against rational thought, and plain error have been regarded as the marks of religious belief. The learned believers as well as the simple, unlettered believers have equally come under this charge. The transmitted unchanging religious dogma has been made into the prototype of traditionality and is one of the main constituents in the established rationalistic view [read: critique] of tradition. The rationalistic rejection of religious knowledge has given the word belief a bad name.[35]

Shils goes on to try and refute this view of tradition as unjustified, but he fails to note that the force of the rationalist critique has been magnified by the technical achievements linked to the scientific use of reason. What needs to be uncovered is, first, the narrow appropriation of reason underlying this claim and, second, the confirmatory role of technological achievements in justifying "reason" as its source.

The exuberance of scientific culture in the Technical Age provides its own blinders. Technological discoveries, with their accent on commercial use of discovery and quantitative (not qualitative) output, emphasize reliance on only one kind of reason. A limited appropriation of reason was not common to all scientists, but it became the popular understanding of the reason = common sense = usefulness = science seriatim equation that was popularized by the Scottish Enlightenment and later became influential in America.

The constraints and benefits of "enlightened" reason need to be equally stressed. The appeal to common sense is itself a reversion of what most people take to be common sense. Because the new math and the new science limited reason to "only what is positively verifiable, there is a sense in which the scientific revolution focused the minds of men on an unreal world which is of little concern in their lives, which has little to do with their nature and destiny."[36]

Despite the unreality of the modern scientist's world, the scientist's work has yielded practical results which are at once tangible and prized. Though we may qualify the grandiose universalist claims of the GWT, it has been proven that modern science does succeed "in lengthening lives, lightening labor, and multiplying output."[37] It has also maximized profit as an incentive and capital accumulation as a reward in modern society. The communist challenge, drawing attention to the limits of capitalism, seeks to harness the instrumentalities of science to its own ends. Both systems, capitalist and communist, accept the premise that technology is the engine driving the Great Powers into the twenty-first century.

The modernist hegemony, by its very nature, is also the modernist apostasy. It does not explicitly identify with ultimate values, even those which its proponents themselves espouse. As Thomas Kuhn, among others, has demonstrated, the prevalent tone of scientific inquiry is puzzle solving rather than truth seeking. Truth is an absent or unattainable or unspeakable category; hence religion is a diversion, churches useless fossils of another era, offering solace or amusement to the superstitious. What we do have in place of religious truths are motivating ideologies and counterideologies. It would be more accurate to describe the modernist hegemony as the universe of possibility, the fulcrum within which ideologues of all sorts must be situated, whether they claim to be religious or, renouncing religion, espouse secular causes.

The elements that comprise the modernist apostasy may be briefly summarized. First, change alone is absolute. Second, change elevates quantity over quality, pragmatism over truth, efficiency over aesthetics. All the high-handed Weberian discourse about rationalization and bureaucratization is a Germanic way of pointing to the basic value shift indicated more simply and directly by Anglo-Saxon thinkers like Nef and Whitehead. Third, change increases options and maximizes benefits. The more options the better is the potential for all groups within a given society to achieve happiness. Fourth, pluralism is the standard of social exchange. There ought to be a pluralism of groups sharing equal access to the public sphere and deriving equal benefits from it. There ought also to be a pluralism of discourse at two modes, literary and technological. Everyone should be both conversant with cultural artifacts and competent in scientific lore, but if there is only time, energy, or commitment to master one skill, then it should be technologically related. It is better to function well in today's world than to understand yesterday's worlds at the cost of being scientifically illiterate. Fifth, the new "universal" language will be pictorial instead of textual. It will elicit more auditory than reflective responses. It will engage persons in the public sphere rather than encouraging them to pursue eccentric diversions or lapse into solitude.

Since modernism is *not* synonymous with modernity, we need to distinguish the structure of the High Tech Era from interpretations of reality and projections of meaning that claim to derive from it. The GWT has changed even the way in which we conceive of change. We need a mediating category that permits us to examine change without reifying it. Among EuroAmerican analytical terms ideology seems preferable, and in the next chapter we will explore the debate about ideology before moving to the consideration of fundamentalism as a religious ideology.

CHAPTER 3

Ideology Between Religion, Philosophy, and Science

> The possibility that rhetoric can be integrative and not necessarily distortive leads us to a nonpejorative concept of ideology. If we follow this path, we may then say that there is something irreducible in the concept of ideology. Even if we separate off the other two layers of ideology—ideology as distortion and as the legitimation of a system of order or power—the integrative function of ideology, the function of preserving an identity remains. It may be that our regressive analysis can go no further, because *no group and no individual are possible without this integrative function.*
>
> —PAUL RICOEUR

In order to contextualize our case-by-case study of particular fundamentalist movements, we must first complete four additional tasks: first, set forth a nonprejudicial depiction of ideology; second, establish fundamentalism as a religious ideology distinct from, and oppositional to, secular ideologies; third, refute arguments against the cross-cultural use of the term fundamentalism; and fourth, delineate the major characteristics of fundamentalists as religious ideologues. The first two tasks are the most difficult. We will concern ourselves with them in this chapter. The other two will occupy us in chapter four.

Ideology is a significant analytical category meriting separate treatment on several counts. First, it is a crucial topic in contemporary philosophical discourse, much of which has been framed with reference to the pervasive authority of science but without consensual agreement on what constitutes science. Second, ideology is invoked by sociologists and sometimes anthropologists of religion in order to explain how the sociology of knowledge is superior to all ideologies, including secularism, on the assumption that only a social scientist can establish the proper "scientific" framework prerequisite to objective analysis. Third, ideology straddles philosophy and science. Though rejected by some philosophers and nearly all scientists as a term of reference to what they do, ideology mediates the conflicting claims of disparate fields, at the same time that it denotes the cluster of motivating concepts crucial to specialists in every discipline.

Ideology has a fourth and decisive value: it is integral to the study of religion in the contemporary era. Too often social scientists mistakenly separate religion from ideology.[1] Religion and ideology must be conjoined in examining fundamentalists: we need to understand how as well as why fundamentalist groups select particular scriptural texts and accord them decisive authority, thus empowering action in the public sphere for moral ends.

In this chapter we will demonstrate the analytic viability of ideology despite the critiques mounted against it.[2] The major desideratum is to set forth the defining characteristics of fundamentalism as a religious phenomenon apart from its manifestation in specific historical contexts. Unless ideology is located on the spectrum of competing terms of reference, even the most exhaustive efforts to describe it will fail.[3]

Ideology is related, above all, to the modernist context. It is that context which shapes all our attitudes to ideology and to related concepts. The previous chapter indicated how the world in which we live broke the chain of filiation with its own past through the Great Western Transmutation (GWT). While a number of factors combined to create the Technical Age, scientific discovery was the fuel that drove the engine of modernity. The natural sciences gained a prestige that they have never relinquished, despite the confusion between their truth-claims and those of other sciences.

The social sciences experienced a conflict that has yet to be resolved. The source of conflict becomes clear once we reverse the defining noun and the qualifying adjective: What is scientific about society? That question goes to the heart of what is meant by social sciences. It stretches the definitional parameters of science and at the same time displaces society from its human constituents. Fernand Braudel was correct when he observed that "sociology, unlike economics which is in a way a science, has not completely succeeded in defining its subject."[4] A prominent sociologist has tried to deflect the definitional question, suggesting that "most of the social sciences are more like philosophy and theology than like the natural sciences."[5] But the question persists: do the social sciences take the experimental method as their model, or, despite their nominal link to science, do they stand closer to the humanities? The latter identity seems more plausible because of the human factor. Unlike the natural sciences, social sciences cannot bracket out the dialectic of subject/object. They must explain its condition. They also must interpret its function.

Explanation. Interpretation. These two words have informed discussion of the problem facing social sciences *qua* sciences for the past several decades. The discussion has mushroomed into a major controversy since 1971, when a philosophical essay of that title appeared in German.

The controversy retains much of the idealist character of German phil-osophical discourse, despite the fact that translations and the frequent exchange between Anglo-American and Continental philosophers have made it an international debate. It focuses on the concept of science. Is it unified or fissiparous? Are the social sciences included or excluded? If included, on what criteria? The translator's preface to a recent Ger-man book on the subject frames the debate, even while trying to smoth-er its participants in a still more abstract level of Teutonic rhetoric. On the one hand, there are advocates of a "unified science." They stress the methodological unity of the natural and social sciences, claiming that progress in the social sciences requires adoption of the methods and standards of the natural sciences. On the other hand, there are repre-sentatives of the *"verstehende* social sciences." They emphasize the affini-ties between the social sciences and the humanities. The latter argue that the social sciences, because of the nature of the objects they study, cannot conform to the logic of the natural sciences. They must entail an interpretive dimension. Rather than relying only on observation and explanation, their practioners are required to "explore (and interpret, i.e., come to terms with) the complex of 'meanings' that form the context of the actions and practices of a given social group (and all social groups)."[6]

The distinction between explanation and interpretation, between nat-ural sciences and social sciences, quickly expands into a spate of quali-fications. The crucial term of reference is values. In social scientific terms, values come very near to being "prejudice." The natural sciences try to exclude them, the social sciences to suspend them. The bench-mark for objectivity is said to be the absence of values. Since total ab-sence is impossible, conscious recognition, we are told, will at least expose them and so reduce their influence.

It ought to be a simple procedure to monitor the factors determina-tive of one's own outlook, but the testing of internal consistency runs aground on its own linguistic-philosophical premises: where does one draw the line between explaining data (the natural sciences) and under-standing action and thought (the social sciences)?[7]

The standard position against which contemporary philosophers react is termed positivism, although from time to time it has also been labeled "scientism." Positivism or scientism privileges the natural sciences as the only valid model for *all* human knowledge. Other fields of knowledge, to the extent that they seek validity and claim to be "scientific," must derive some model from natural sciences and then apply it to their own realm of research. False knowledge is generated in those disciplines of human inquiry that reflect moral or other value judgments, such as metaphysics and theology (although literature, art, and philosophy itself also become suspect, if this linear logic is applied unrestrictively). Ob-jectivity is thought to exist "out there," beyond human beings or human institutions. Value-free is the only way to be scientific, and hence those sciences that take human society as their object of study have to free themselves not only from the values of those whom they study but also from their own values as students.

Since Weber, most of the debate has tried to avoid the paradoxical ambiguity that characterizes his formulation of value-freeness. Social scientists have shifted the debate to weighing the viability of alternate strategies for approximating value-freeness. Ideology has received prominent attention in the debate because in "the age of ideology," i.e., the nineteenth century, Marx and his followers despised ideologues and condemned ideologies as deceptive lies. The analytical knife proved to be a polemical boomerang. Marx's opponents labeled his and related systems of thought "ideological," giving the term a connotation even more pejorative than the one he had condemned. The Marxist and post-Marxist distortions of ideology persist. We must situate them in the intellectual context of the Technical Age before speaking of fundamentalism as religious ideology.

A preliminary task is to broaden the spectrum of analysis and to look at particular -*isms* that are identifiably ideological. One of the most controversial is secularism. In the social sciences, it has been studied as a process called "secularization."

Secularization takes on added importance in our study of fundamentalism since it abounds in that attribute of polysemy that George Steiner identified with ideology.[8] "Secularization" is a term coined in the nineteenth century. It means one thing to fundamentalists, something else to sociologists. For fundamentalists, it is the most pejorative term of abuse that they can hurl at their opponents. To call others "secularist" is to charge them with emptying the divine dimension out of human experience. It is to collapse the world that God made into the arena of rival material interests. It is tantamount to unbelief.

Some social scientists share the fundamentalist scorn for secularism but with opposite motives. In their view, the defect of secularization is its inadequacy as an analytical category of explanatory value. They deem it to be neither a scientific worldview nor a natural consequence of the GWT but rather just one more groping ideology. David Martin, surveying other studies on the subject, reaches the conclusion that secularization, far from being an objective description of modern society with scientific validity, is itself a "a tool of counter-religious ideologies."[9] It is not so much *for* something as *against* other things. According to Martin, secularization, because it is value-laden rather than value-free, because it is ideological rather than scientific, should be abandoned in social scientific analyses of modern society.

Yet most sociologists have taken the opposite view, arguing that secularization is a genuine, verifiable process, that its followers either reject religion or adapt to it or at the least provoke a powerful negative reaction from threatened believers. Each response to secularization is determined by group interest and ideologies, and since it is secularists who pose the challenge, they are the ideologues to be reckoned with.[10]

While the latter position has more viability than the former, it still begs the basic question: how does secularization function as an ideology, especially if one lacks criteria by which to measure its diffusion? That is to say, how does it mobilize its advocates, encouraging and enabling them to oppose religious influence on behalf of their own group interests? To answer that question one must not only define the criteria of ideology but also relate ideology to sociology.

The secularization debate leaves little doubt that sociologists have difficulty disentangling their own "values" and group interests from their study of secularization. Advocates of the posttraditional world want to believe in "secularization" (Peter Berger, Bryan Wilson). Those who retain a sense of the tenacious durability of religious beliefs and practices, despite changing structures and competing influences, want to be rid of "secularization," or at least to reduce its scope if not its force (Mary Douglas, Robert Bellah).

Even if one ignores the verbal duels between sociologists, it is now clear that secularization did not sweep the masses of late nineteenth century European society. The historian Eric Hobsbawm feels that there was a definite secularization of masses as well as elites,[11] but others demur. Owen Chadwick, for instance, offers a comprehensive delineation of secularizing trends among British, French, and German bourgeoisie, yet he stops short of postulating mass secularization. The evidence for it, he allows, has never been assembled. At best it can be inferred retrospectively.[12]

If sociologists have not been value-free in their wrestling with secularization, it is perhaps because, as Alvin Gouldner noted,

sociology has set itself up as the study of society, stressing the profound power and influence of the objects it studied—societies, groups, social structures—and then it proceeded to claim that its own researches were free of biases derived from these same powerful influences. . . . The more one believed the claims of sociology, the more one had to concede that it, too, must necessarily embody social limits on its cognition, which gave it no clear cognitive superiority to ideologies.[13]

In sum, sociology elides with ideology. It is a portentous elision, not just for the social sciences but for the natural sciences and even more, for science as the authoritative referent of the modernist hegemony. What is at stake is nothing less than the foundational scientific claim to be both universal and objective.[14] Once bracketed with ideology, instead of outside or against it, any branch of science runs the risk of being just another interest group or cluster of groups advocating some priorities over against others. It becomes just one among several competing ideologies.[15]

The history of ideology, therefore, brings into sharp focus the linguistic debate between universalism and relativism. Science can not be both universal and ideological. Philosophy claims to find the limits of science as ideology even while escaping counterclaims that it too advocates self-interests that are inherently ideological.

A powerful current within German philosophy wants to retain the negative sense of ideology as normative for all philosophical discourse. The Frankfurt school has unremittingly deprecated both ideology and ideologists. It has tended to evolve a neo-Kantian, post-Marxist perspective on knowledge, science, and the sciences.[16] Its members criticize Max Weber and also Karl Popper, claiming that in different ways each espoused conservative ideologies of bureaucratic capitalism. Why? Because the net result of the speculative theories of Weber and Popper is to "help sustain the power of the capitalist ruling class over the rest of society. As ideologies they are, crudely, both false and immoral."[17]

The Frankfurt school fails to see, however, that the Marxist, revolutionary tone of their own critical formulations is at least as ideological as that of their opponents.[18] What level of violence is justified in a revolutionary transfer of power? What are the "rational" criteria of individual revolutionaries or revolutionary causes? Whose exercise of power becomes "true" and "moral?" The questions and counterquestions go on and on. The debate about who or what is or is not ideological becomes a dead-end exercise in chasing puffs of air unless the parameters of that debate can be framed with reference to defensible criteria of what is or what is not ideological.

The major opponent to the Frankfurt school has been Hans-Georg Gadamer. On the one hand, he challenges the claim of its members to be the true successors and legitimate heirs to the neo-Enlightenment, post-Marxist quest for a universal ontology that takes account of science but goes beyond it by subsuming it. At the same time, he shares the implicit assumption of the Frankfurt school that modern science has become so powerful that no recovery of universalist norms is possible without encompassing science in all its branches, despite the fact that science itself has been separated off from philosophy since before the turn of the century.

If the debate sounds reminiscent of the theme that predominated in *After Babel,* it is because it partially touches on the same linguistic issues that preoccupied Steiner. To grapple with the central issue of universal meanings versus relative values, we need to look at the language of contemporary philosophical discourse, but we also have to survey more closely notable participants in the debate on science and ideology.

While Hans-Georg Gadamer is among the most rigorous German philosophers to take seriously the crisis of philosophy in its isolation from the ongoing work and influence of the scientific community, his American counterpart is Alvin Gouldner.[19] Though differing in the tone and topics of their discourse, they share a common concern. Both adhere to the strategy of seeing the part vis-à-vis the whole. Both question every presumption of atomism or positivism. Gadamer stretches for a linguistic, logical whole that goes back to the Aristotelian tradition, while Gouldner encompasses the actuality of the technological world, especially its powerful network of multimedia communication. Both project an awareness of the inadequacy of their own efforts to universalize. Even in trying to account for the whole, they are constrained to admit the limits of what they can achieve. Yet both contribute to the study of the modernist mindset as the precursor and also the adversary of fundamentalism.

The pivotal role of Gadamer in contemporary philosophy can be seen by the fact that the two outstanding proponents of the Frankfurt school, Jürgen Habermas and Karl-Otto Apel, jointly wage their debate against him. The issues they raise point up the broad range of Gadamer's stance on the question of ideology and science. The more important debate takes place with Habermas, but the more bitter debate is waged with Karl-Otto Apel. Both debates merit a brief review.

Gadamer provokes Apel's attack through his own attack on the cornerstone of social scientific methodology, which is also the linchpin to its self-validation: objectivity. In *Truth and Method,* Gadamer argues that "it is precisely a concern with objectivity that blocks an adequate account of the structure of understanding." In Gadamer's view, prejudice informs all human knowledge, for "one apprehends meaning in terms of one's own prejudices and at the same time is forced to reconsider these prejudices in light of the questions provoked by confrontation with the object of interpretation."[20]

How then can there then be any objectivity? For Gadamer, it is a restricted possibility, contingent on the extent to which "one is aware of one's participation in the unfolding of tradition."[21] Hence no interpretation can claim to be uniquely correct or to possess a privileged position of insight. All must be informed by a humility in the act of inquiry and a modesty in the advocacy of conclusions.

Apel, defending the Frankfurt school, sees in Gadamer's restriction of objectivity a "scientistic fallacy." Gadamer is restricted not because of what he says about the social and human sciences but because he ascribes to the natural sciences *alone* the possibility of objective scientific enquiry. Instead, Apel wants "an expanded conception of scientific rationality," and to this end he formulates his own "transcendental-pragmatic perspective." He attempts to combine understanding "with a form of theoretical explanation, or 'critique of ideology,' capable of appealing to a reference system outside the tradition's account of itself."[22]

If Apel and Gadamer debate about what is really "objective," the debate between Gadamer and Habermas takes on an explicitly historical dimension, framed by their attempt to occupy common ground. Both are trying to formulate "a more adequate and empirically verifiable theory of communicative practice." Their presuppositions diverge widely. Although Habermas expresses his commitment to the Enlightenment and Kantian values in trying to delineate a universal moral system, he also affirms the validity of Marxist materialism. Gadamer, on the other hand, tries to shift the argument back beyond Marx or Kant to the underlying assumptions of the Enlightenment itself. For him the decisive issue is the "prejudice against prejudice," which does not entail a willful embrace of antinomianism but rather a patient sorting out of "the positivist exaggerations of method and modern science."[23]

Ideology is a crucial category on both sides of the debate. In the view of Habermas and other members of the Frankfurt school, it is seen to be the embodiment of prejudgment, prejudice, masked self-interest amounting to self-deception. It is a lie, to which philosophy counterposes the truth. Gadamer, for his part, does not flinch from criticizing those who criticize ideology. In his view, those who advance the critique of ideology (including Habermas) are not aware of the context in which they themselves and their argument are situated. The hermeneutical circle needs to be enlarged. The critics of ideology must grasp the lingering positivism, which is also the Cartesian idealism, of their own position. After all, "the work of ideology critique has a dialectical structure. It is related to determinate social conditions upon which it has corrective and dismantling effects. It becomes itself, then, instrumental to the social process that it criticizes. That is the ineluctable presupposition that cannot be replaced by any scientific pretension."[24]

In effect, Gadamer throws down the gauntlet to all Enlightenment boasts of objectivity. Just as the so-called critique of ideology called scientific neutrality into doubt, advancing the Marxist claim that the theoretical teachings of the sciences necessarily reflected the interests of the dominant social class, especially that of the entrepreneurs and capitalists, so the new concept of interpretation looks at the postulation of perfect self-understanding, authorized with reference to Hegel but failing to grasp his epistemological ambiguity, and says, "Never." Never can human beings lay claim to "the total sum of our knowledge of the world" as something we objectively grasp. Never can we assert that our knowing, our "science" is objective. Why? Because "self-understanding is always on the way; it is on a path whose completion is an entire dimension of unilluminated unconscious. . . . One has to ask oneself whether the dynamic law of human life can be conceived adequately in terms of *progress,* of a continual advance from the unknown into the known, and whether the course of human culture is actually a linear progression *from mythology to enlightenment.* . . . Is [not] the notion of an ever-mounting and self-perfecting enlightenment finally ambiguous?"[25]

If it is ambiguous, if interpretation, like self-understanding, must always be provisional, "always on the way," then how can philosophy relate to science? How can the self-critical insights of Aristotle and his Enlightenment successors be brought to bear on the exclusionary, unreflective emphasis of modern science? Gadamer suggests a two-staged approach: first, to recognize that a disjuncture has taken place and to acknowledge its enormity; and second, to nudge scientists back toward an attempt at self-reflection.

The disjuncture was not inevitable. From Leibniz to Kant to Hegel, the early giants of Enlightenment thought strove to posit the unity of the philosophic sciences as the unity of all knowledge. But the Hegelian synthesis of philosophy and science broke down in the nineteenth century when the age of science (or what Jaspers calls the Technical Age) came into being and philosophy proper suffered an eclipse in the public eye. What resulted was the pluralization of consciousness and the relativization of historical moments: many eyes, many turning points, with no shield of continuity, no ground of unity.

The fissive trend continued into the twentieth century. Not only did philosophy and science become estranged, but *"the sciences* [now pluralized] were allowed to stand on their own in their compelling correctness and were removed from the foundational claim of philosophy."[26] To the extent that the situation is now reversible, it is not because scientists are showing a new respect for the self-critical reflection of philosophers but rather because scientists themselves have begun to ask questions that push them against the frontier zones of inquiry that have been the traditional preserve of philosophers. Whenever or wherever science yields part of its privileged isolation, it inches toward questions of self-reflection about the nature of its task, all of which come back to the ambiguity of language. The philosopher of science Thomas Kuhn illustrates the problem, both in what he said about "paradigms" and in the response of others to his novel evaluation of the scientific enterprise. In Gadamer's view, "his [Kuhn's] theory of revolution in science rightly criticizes the false linear stylization supposedly connected with the progress of science. It shows the discontinuity effected by the dominance at any given time of basic paradigmatic frameworks. The whole problem area of the relevance of questions depends on this [dominance], and that constitutes a hermeneutic dimension." At the same time, scientists are coming to appreciate and apply another "hermeneutical principle: that the way any given utterance, discourse, or text is to be understood depends upon its particular scope." In other words, if any declaration is to be understood correctly, one has to understand its scope.

Yet *within* the sciences themselves, Gadamer depicts the pattern of reflection as widely variant:

In the natural sciences it [the hermeneutic principle] appears as the dimension of paradigms and the relevance of one's frameworks of inquiry. In the social sciences a similar structure might be described as the self-transformation of the social engineer into a social partner. In the historical sciences, finally, it is at work in [the redefining of the historian's task as no longer the scientific mastery of an objective field of knowledge by a presuppositionless inquirer but rather as] the ongoing mediation of what was once before, what is now, and what will be tomorrow.[27]

If Gadamer is correct, there may emerge a unity of method but not a convergence of purpose in the scientific enterprise, for implicit even in the hopeful dimension of his discussion is the recognition that limitless change is matched by unchallenged doubt. The spiraling increase of pluralization and specialization allows, even encourages, the finessing of those cohesive metaphysical questions that go back to the early Enlightenment figures and also to their religious contemporaries.

Or does Gadamer rather suggest that such questions are not excluded but simply deferred? The strength of his method is its insistence on rigorous, explicit self-questioning. Together with his attention to defining scope, this may be his most significant contribution to the struggle for locating a universalist perspective in the High Tech Era. "One of the more fertile insights of modern hermeneutics," he observes, "is that every statement has to be seen as a response to a question and that the only way to understand a statement is to get hold of the question to which the statement is an answer." But the process becomes rapidly complicated since "the question to which each statement is an answer is itself motivated in turn, and so in a sense every question is itself an answer again. It responds to a challenge. Without an inner tension between our anticipations of meaning and the all-pervasive opinions and without a critical interest in the generally prevailing opinions, there would be no opinions at all." In effect, then, the first step of hermeneutic endeavor requires "going back to the motivating questions when understanding statements."[28]

It is, of course, just such a process of patterned questioning that requires further reflection on the not-so-simple critique of ideology. In reexamining the prejudice against prejudice, one begins to sense the soft edges of the pervasive rationalism that has cast all questions into a dialectical web of its own construction. There are recurrent constructs that may be preclusive opposites at one level, yet also interact and even correlate at other levels. One such construct is what Steiner called the Graeco-Latin and Hebraic circumference of thought, Foucault the Western episteme. Either term connotes the exclusive superiority of the ascendant West in the Technical Age, but in Gadamer's view the repository of universal wisdom does not lie exclusively between Jerusalem, Athens, and Rome. Even jewgreek/greekjew connotes an outlook that is framed by historical limits and ideological interests.

Once freed of its Marxist and positivist shackles, ideology can be reclaimed as a malleable category that allows us to look beyond seemingly incommensurate opposites. To understand how the semantic unbinding of ideology is possible, and also to evaluate the role that modern communications play in fostering but also limiting the role of ideology, we need to examine the contribution of Gadamer's American counterpart, Alvin Gouldner.

Alvin Gouldner engages in the philosophy of science with the same passion as Gadamer and Habermas. He quotes Habermas frequently, Gadamer hardly at all. Yet he stands closer to Gadamer in his skeptical disposition to the claims of rationality, whether couched in Marxist or sociological discourse. Like Gadamer, his approach is at once holistic and humble: he strives to make sense of all the data that can be labeled "ideological" while also recognizing the internalized impact of the modernist hegemony that preforms not only others' ideologies but also one's own statements about them.

Gouldner's views are set forth most cogently in the first volume of his intended trilogy on modern society, *The Dialectic of Ideology and Technology*. He offers the self-portrait of an intellectual straddling the two disciplines of academic sociology and Marxist philosophy. Gouldner ensembles Gadamer's putative outsider: a displaced participant now marginal observer. In his own words, he is a kind of intellectual mulatto; half-sociologist and half-Marxist, he rebels against both.[29]

The premise of Gouldner's book is prosaic, even pedestrian. Life is muddled. The task of the intellectual is to make sense out of what muddles modern humankind. Everywhere there are dyads, but the dialectical dance never consists of two constant partners. Like Eric Hobsbawm, whom he quotes approvingly,[30] Gouldner sees the contemporary West as emerging from a dual revolution, political and industrial. Each fostered and contributed to the other. Each also interacted with the other and limited its consequences. They produced distinct modalities. For the political revolution it was ideology, for the industrial, technology.

Yet the story of the West is more than "the dialectic of ideology and technology," and so is Gouldner's book by that title. For in addition to the "obvious" revolutions, there is a third, the communications revolution. A hybrid offspring of the other two, its hardware comes from technology, its software from ideology. Though a product of the modernist hegemony, accentuating the disjuncture between this era and earlier eras, it also provides seldom observed historical continuities that will persist into the future.

Gouldner arrives at his thesis through an exercise that is unremittingly dialectical. Challenging his "parents," sociology and Marxism, he still acknowledges, with an ironic fillip, that he is forever their child. Methodologically committed to Hegel, he nonetheless inveighs against "normal" Marxist dialectic. Its polarities are too stark:

The world is divided into two and only two conflicting parts. But this view freezes the world into an immobility behind the mask of a speciously radical dialectic. This view is based on a dialectic that only knows thesis and antithesis, but forgets that antithesis itself is the child of the very thing it opposes and therefore has certain of its parents' limits built into it. The very victory of an antithesis overthrows part, but ensures the continuance of at least another part, of what it had struggled against.[31]

The critique of Marxism extends to academic sociology. As a scientific endeavor, sociology fails on several counts. Blind to its beginnings, insular in its development, it has become myopic in its cultural outlook. At the outset, sociology succeeded principally due to the uncritical alliance of its founding figures with historically ascendant forces. As it developed, it disengaged itself from the subject of its study, and has persisted by identifying itself with a bourgeois Western mindset even while claiming universal validity for its theses.

In Gouldner's view, both academic sociology and normative Marxism parade as pseudosciences. And the shallowness of their assertions is nowhere more evident than in their critique of ideology. It is the ideology of others that they attack, while camouflaging or denying the existence of their own. Criticizing the critics (much as Gadamer attacks the prejudice against prejudice), Gouldner builds his own defense of ideology. Why should ideology be stigmatized as a pathological object, "as irrational cognition, defective discourse, false consciousness, or bad sociology?" What of ideologies like vegetarianism, prohibitionism, liberalism, the nonviolent movement for black rights, all versions of women's liberation? Can they be classified as identical with oppressive polities like totalitarianism or Nazism, or rival economic systems like capitalism and socialism?[32]

For Gouldner, the answer is an unequivocal "No!" He traces the self-deception of sociology to its paradoxical beginnings. Comte separated his new science of humanity from both metaphysics and epistemology. He wrapped himself in the mantle of science but never demonstrated how what he did was scientific. Nor was he ever challenged to provide a justification for his action. It sufficed that he identified himself with the prestige of science in the aftermath of the French Revolution. In effect, it was the seeming success of the French Revolution that secured both the "demise" of religion and its replacement by a new authority-referencing discourse, ideology. It was a triumph of circumstance not logic that secured a scientific footing for sociology as a science.[33]

If Gouldner accuses sociology of masking its historical origins, he also criticizes it for fostering institutional separation from the subject of its study. Like Marxists, sociologists failed to maintain the unity between their thought and practice. Marxists evolved theories of revolution while hoping themselves to be insulated from the consequences of real revolution. Sociologists analyzed the evils of proliferating ideologies, yet assumed that they would never be contaminated by them. In time sociology withdrew into the isolation of the university. Its proponents arrogated to themselves the exclusive right to study but never to defend the issues over which others fought and also died.[34]

In Gouldner's view, the final shortcoming of sociologists has been their failure to see the continuity between ideology and religion. To echo Ninian Smart's felicitous comment, one must locate "secular ideologies . . . along a spectrum another part of which is occupied by the traditional religions."[35] Both ideology and religion form part of a distinctly Western outlook. Traceable back to Plato and Hellenism, it has its most significant reference in what Gouldner calls the bifurcation between the ideal and the real within the Judeo-Christian tradition. He postulates a culture-specific disposition similar to Steiner's "western feeling-patterns within the Graeco-Latin and Hebraic circumference." But unlike Steiner, he projects the tragic dimension of Western sensibilities as a continuing element of ideology in the High Tech Era.

Gouldner helps lay the groundwork for our consideration of fundamentalism as a religious ideology. His basic argument is threefold: first, that there is a "distinctively western symbol system," second, that it is "ultimately grounded in the Judaic-Christian tradition that makes a sharp distinction between the ordinary way of the everyday world, and the extraordinary world of God that stands above it," ensuring a constant tension, but also a persistent mediation, between that other world and this world, with the result that, third, modern ideology becomes "a branch of that massive historical continuity in the West" since it "seeks the unity of the real and the ideal by transforming the world into some conformity with the good."[36]

However, Gouldner never goes so far as to collapse the distinction between the tragic vision of religion and the ideological vision of modernity. For "in the tragic vision . . . the word and the ideal have the power to help by reconciling men to what is, to an essentially unchanging fate, by giving men the capacity to *endure* the world's failures and disappointments." By contrast, "in the ideological vision, the word and the ideal are seen as having the power practically to *change* what is, here in this world, and it intimates that this world is all there is, thus making the outcome in it a matter of some urgency, if not of desperation." Because it is action oriented, ideology can never settle for passive compliance, even with a divinely prescribed fate. Hence Gouldner is forced to conclude that "ideology, although grounded ultimately in the Judaic-Christian tradition, always secularizes transcendence."[37]

Gouldner affirms religious values yet confers on ideology the mantle of modernity because it ceaselessly promotes change. Ideology wins, religion loses, in his view, because of the final revolution that shaped the contemporary world, the communications revolution. Since this third revolution is the linchpin of Gouldner's thesis, it must be examined before it can be qualified or refuted. It encompasses all the elements that are distinctively tragic in the Judeo-Christian-Western outlook yet it also discloses their tensions and resolutions at a new level of human experience.

Technology gave the communications revolution its hardware through "the development of printing, printing technologies, and the growing production of printed products."[38] It was the added emphasis on literacy that made printing and all its related industries commercially viable. Ideology came to depend on literacy at many levels. At the most basic level literacy offered a potential for ideological exploration. Even though literacy extolled the written over the spoken word, reading was never fully divorced from either listening or doing. The printed word could also be heard and enacted, its readers and listeners motivated to a purposive response. That perspectival shift was the key to ideology, and the mechanism that transformed the reader into the doer was the news.

For Gouldner news also became the pivotal instrumentality that moved EuroAmerica into the modern era. "The news" presupposed a paradoxical relationship of private to public. Since "the bourgeois public constituted one of the great historical advances in rationality"[39] its opponents, such as Marx, Engels, and Lenin, directed their attacks against its two core institutions: private property and patriarchy. Their attacks had the unintended opposite consequence. They entrenched *both* institutions as sacrosanct private values. Private property and patriarchy became topics exempt from censorship: whatever else one could question and criticize in public, these two were off-limits.

The news is, therefore, never the whole news. Although the avowed intent of journalists is to make the unknown known and the private public, in practice they can only generate selective, partial disclosures. Modern newsmaking "divides the social worlds into (1) the seen-but-unnoticed regularities of everyday life and (2) the 'news' which is the seen, noticed and publicly commented on accentings of or departures from these regularities." There is nothing rational about what is deemed regular. The social world of journalism is neither empirically evident nor universally accepted. All news reports become value-constructing. The news, in effect, "devalues, censors and represses certain aspects of everyday life, making these difficult to see and to accept even by the people living them."[40]

News reinforces ideologies by making them appear to be universally evident to common sense. Ideologues, for their part, want both to control and to challenge the media and newsmakers. They perceive news as the crucial public confirmation of their significance, even as it can also be a devastating weapon if directed against them by foes. They can be counterchallenged in the news or, worse, excluded altogether from news coverage.

Ideologies do more than confirm and develop background elements of the news. They also particularize the conceptual abstractions of social and political theorists. They reclaim the urgency of the present from those who live outside the realm of explicit partisanship.

In Gouldner's view, a crucial construct demonstrating the ambivalent function of news for ideologues is equality versus freedom. The French Revolution had held out the hope that liberty and equality (along with fraternity) could be simultaneously achieved, and the nineteenth century concept of progress had been founded on the hope of their eventual joint realization. Every democratic polity accordingly claimed allegiance to both ideals, and political philosophers since Hegel have seen in equality and freedom a test case of their own explanatory power, making them one more antinomy or set of contradictions to resolve.

Yet ideologues, because they are concerned to unite theory with practice, have seldom upheld freedom and equality as equivalent values, either to be jointly denied, as in fascism, or jointly affirmed, as in socialism. The most prevalent ideologies have been selective in their emphasis. Their proponents, sensing the irresolvable tension in the immediate context of the separate demands posed by freedom and equality, have opted for one or the other. Consider capitalism. It values freedom highly but equality less so. Communism, on the other hand, values equality much more than freedom. In each case, it is because of their innate sense of accommodation to practical exigencies that capitalism and communism have flourished in open competition for most of the twentieth century. Similarly, the news media of capitalist and communist nations alike accept the divergent applications of freedom and equality by their respective constituents without ever holding them accountable to the norm which they commonly violate.

Ideologies, therefore, remain dependent on the news-making profession, even when they oppose it. The ambivalence of their relationship is part of the muddle of life, for

the path from critical theory to the long march through institutions must go over the bridge of the mass media, and undertake the struggle for and critique of these media for what they are: a complex system of property interests, technologies, professionalizing skills, striving for domination and for autonomy, all swarming with the most profound inner contradictions.[41]

Among the most profound of these inner contradictions is the passage of the communications revolution into its second phase. Through the eighteenth and nineteenth centuries it emphasized literacy, but increasingly in the twentieth century, with the advent of radio and television, the relevance of literacy to the Technical Age has been attenuated. There has now come into being in the industrial West a new industry. It might be termed the consciousness industry. So pervasive has been its influence that some call our era "the postmodern information age." Those who spearhead it are profit-maximizing technicians. Aligned with political interests of the state, they have become the dominant force in public communications. They replace the old elites, residual ideologues of the printed word.

Will the last decade of the twentieth and the first decades of the twenty-first century witness an accelerated transition from print ideologues to image technologies? The expanded audience, the ease of access, and the paleosymbolic effect of multimodal communications all seem to favor visual technologies over their literary-fixated ideological forebears and contemporaries in the High Tech Era.

The modernist hegemony, which gave new emphasis and wide diffusion to the written word, may end by spelling its demise as anything but the cultural artifact of a bygone era. Yet words, even as visual, semiotic signposts, will continue to motivate people singly and collectively, on behalf of their own interests and also against the interests of others. For ideology has not only benefited from literacy, it has promoted its value and prolonged its life. The written word may be eclipsed, but it cannot be erased.

The triumph of technology will continue to promote some form of ideology, especially as it relates to modernism. Beyond the parameters of literacy or counterliteracy, there persists the need to see the part vis-à-vis the whole. The tension of parts to whole characterizes the critique of ideology. It also frames the limits of ideology of the modernist hegemony.

For modernism, like ideology, resides "in the one-sidedness and oursidedness of the part—in the fact that, whoever else it favors, it also favors itself, and is on its own side. There remains a conflict between the egoistic self-regard of the part and its desire to project an image of itself as being altruistically concerned for the welfare of the group as a whole."[42]

Gouldner and Gadamer combine to make possible a revaluation of ideology as both neutral and, in some cases, religious. It is too easy to criticize them, Gadamer for his quasi-scientific presuppositions, Gouldner for his archcaricature of the members of his own profession. Neo-Enlightenment proponents of the Frankfurt school oppose Gadamer, sociologists of almost every stripe, Gouldner. Together, however, Gadamer and Gouldner have resurrected ideology as an analytical category that is both viable and invaluable in the High Tech Era. A summary listing of their achievements is in order.

What Gadamer has done, with singular bluntness, is to challenge the phalanx of modernity, the scientific community, and the objective method on which it is predicated. On the one hand, he acknowledges the power of science as the determinative principle of knowledge and interpretation, to be explained or co-opted but never challenged in its basic premises. The content of what science is or the sciences do is beyond questioning. It represents what Ernst Cassirer once called the shift in indexical references to which all else must be related, but always on a lower, subordinate scale of valuation. Despite Gadamer's broad appeals to knowledge, truth does not intrude, and God is absent at the end, as at the beginning.

On the other hand, no one has explained the implicit ontological claims of science better than Gadamer. He credits Heidegger with the insight that "science originates from an understanding of being that compels it unilaterally to lay claim to every place and to leave no place unpossessed outside of itself."[43] To explore that claim, in all its ramifications, within the social as well as the natural sciences, is to begin to understand the challenge facing fundamentalist thought. For the alternative strategy (to sequester science as just another way of looking at the world and so ignore its universalist claim) is to surrender any metaphysical, cosmological, or ontological claims advanced by traditional religions. Gadamer forces even nonphilosophers to come to terms not just with single issues (like creation) on which the scientific view is contestable, but rather to look at the distinction between science as a cluster of ideologies and science as a holistic category, invoked explicitly or implicitly over against other holistic authorities, especially religion but also art, philosophy, literature, and poetry.[44]

Gouldner's virtues are the mirror reflection of his flaws. He opens himself up to even more criticism than Gadamer in trying self-consciously to bridge two volatile fields while at the same time challenging the reigning theories of each.[45] In depicting the origins of sociology, Gouldner overstates the historical defeat of traditional religion. While political circumstances may have secured Comte's "victory," they also limited the repercussions of defeat for his adversaries. It was not religion but certain advocates of a state religion in the capital of one European country who were defeated. Their defeat did not reverberate throughout all classes of Paris, all regions of France, all countries of Europe, or even all dioceses of the Catholic church. Moreover, even the restricted victory which ideology gained through its identification with science was short-lived. Napoleon, reacting to the ideologues' opposition to his imperial designs, later denigrated them as "impractical, unworldly and unrealistic theorists," i.e., not scientists at all. He won, and they lost. Following his lead, the classical German idealists (Kant, Hegel, Fichte, Schelling) and their successors (Marx, Nietzsche, and Engels)[46] completed the reversal, decrying ideology as the equivalent of "original sin" in the modernist mindset. It was something that affected everyone. It was indelibly bad yet insurmountable. The present study has to examine and explain ideology at length precisely in order to reclaim it from the Napoleonic curse.

Yet Gouldner makes historical mistakes precisely because he tries to use a historical approach to depict the generation of ideology within and beyond the social sciences. He takes seriously the limits of Mannheim's sociology of knowledge: to see the science of society as superior to all thought systems or ideologies is to ignore the egoistic or prejudicial element in the very presumption of superiority. The hubris of knowing extends to the problematic of German classical philosophy, including Marxism. Though it claimed to solve problems by correctly naming them, it absolved itself from the messiness of actual life and rival interest groups.[47]

Gouldner's distinctive contribution is to address the ongoing changes within the modernist process, represented above all by the communications revolution that began with, but did not limit itself, to the printed word. It is here that he offers the necessary complement to Gadamer. While Gadamer stresses the limits of the critique of ideology, calling attention to the prejudice against prejudice that it unreflectively perpetuated, Gouldner suggests that ideology persisted through the communications revolution, first as an extension of the printed word, and more recently as a visual reflex of media efforts to mold consciousness. In his view, the limit to ideology comes not from its armchair critics, who have in common their reliance on the nomological-deductive fallacy, but rather from the same modernist hegemony which it has fostered. We may not yet understand the ideological promptings of audio-visual imagery, but we do know that the technicians of consciousness who manipulate them think words that reflect Western feeling-patterns and purvey a sense of the tragic vision. That in itself is an advance over those who uphold technology as a utopian ideal or else dread it as a nightmare of apocalyptic proportions.

Both Gadamer and Gouldner discuss ideology as a dimension of the modernist mindset. They provide a helpful corrective to the negative connotations usually associated with ideology. These derive from its checkered history in the nineteenth century: Freudians linked it to the motive analysis of individuals, Marxists to the political power strategies of groups.[48] Rare is the political scientist like Paul Sigmund who can define ideology as "an action-oriented system of beliefs capable of explaining the world and of justifying decision, of limiting and identifying alternatives and of creating the most all-embracing and intensive social solidarity possible."[49] Few also are the anthropological theorists who, like Clifford Geertz, try to balance their assessment of ideology. Geertz concedes the negative implications of ideology but tries to deflect them by both qualifying his definition and giving opposite case instances of ideology:

Whatever else ideologies may be—projections of unacknowledged fears, disguises for ulterior motives, phatic expressions of group solidarity—they are, most distinctively, maps of problematic social reality and matrices for the creation of collective conscience. Whether, in any particular case, the map is accurate or the conscience creditable is a separate question to which one can hardly give the same answer for Nazism and Zionism, for the nationalisms of McCarthy and of Churchill, for the defenders of segregation and its opponents.[50]

Most attempts to define ideology, reflecting the legacy of Freud and Marx, are unremittingly negative. The German construction, not only in Habermas and Apel but also in their contemporaries, is the most severe. In this view,

ideologization is based on a conglomerate of deception and self-deception: pseudo-religious needs, idealism and perfection mania ultimately support even the "ideological self-authorization for power." Added to this religious-moral legitimation is a claim to "scientific character" and simultaneously to the elimination of all conflicts through the magic formula of dialectics. From the idea of possessing the ultimate truth there follows eventually not only the idea of justification but indeed the necessity of self-deceit and life, of persecution and terror, in order to make that idea finally prevail.[51]

Ideologies are finally ambivalent. They are neither abstract philosophies nor empirical facts. They are a bridge between the realm of thought and the theater of action. Both polarities of ideology need to be stressed before attempting a functional definition. To ask a Gadamerian question, what are the cluster of traits that characterize ideology and ideologues? Ideologues tend to be explicit in their cognitive claims, exclusionary in their membership, authoritarian in their leadership, rigorous in their ethical mandates, and insistent on the rightness of their causes.

Yet beyond discerning such traits, one must be able to clarify the difference and sharpen the contrast between ideological and nonideological statements, as the historian Karl Bracher has noted.[52] The sociologist Edward Shils makes an effort to distinguish ideologies from their apparent synonyms, namely, outlooks, creeds, systems of thoughts (or worldviews), and programs. Shils, like Geertz, focuses on the cognitive content of ideologies. They are explicitly and authoritatively systematized "around one or a few pre-eminent values." Outlooks are not explicitly promulgated nor are they deemed to be authoritative. Creeds demand verbal utterance but not ethical compliance on a wide spectrum of issues. Systems of thought, on the other hand, are indifferent to action, demanding reflection rather than risk taking. Programs, by nature, have limited objectives for limited time periods.[53]

Shils hints at the activist, ethical dimension of ideology even while stressing its cognitive focus. Both elements need to be highlighted, for the tension that they fuse in every ideology distinguishes ideology from philosophy but also from patterned action motivated by other values. The cognitive aspect is the easier of the two poles to define. Every ideology connotes a fixed and unquestioned set of beliefs, views, and assumptions that constitute the general framework within which all other questions take place. Consider, for instance, the assumptions of a feminist ideologue. They would be at least twofold: first, gender is a major, if not the most major, category in examining all social phenomena; and second, any social arrangement that fosters or perpetuates the oppression of women is wrong.

The second assumption contains an implicit mandate for action. If a social arrangement oppresses women, it must be opposed. It must be opposed not only in theory but also in practice, by deed as well as by word. There is an unequivocal pragmatism to feminist ideology. For numerous feminists, the immediate goals that promote the self-interests of feminists are more important than the ranking of feminism on a universal gradient of human values. The two interests are complementary, yet advocacy is preferable to reflection.

It is on the other pole, at the level of praxis, that Marxists mount their most telling critique of ideology. Through their deeds, ideologues promote one set of beliefs to engender solidarity within their group while at the same time claiming that promotion of their interests is conducive to the general benefit of all groups. Feminist ideology, for instance, promotes the expansion of women's role in the public sphere. If more political leaders were women, goes the argument, there would be less likelihood of war and the whole world would be better off. Therefore, as many political leaders as possible should be women. It is less important that one agrees or disagrees with this axiom than to note that it focuses on women's role in the public sphere. For those who espouse patriarchal values, whether due to capitalist pressures or religious sentiments, that expansion of opportunity for women threatens their own core identity, and they can perceive the newly public profile of certain women as nothing but the denial of their own cherished values.

On the spectrum of plausibilities, the concept of ideology needs grounding in both poles—the cognitive and the pragmatic—in a way that makes sense of its morphological variety. There are at least three indispensable characteristics, though arguably the third is so manifold that one could say there are six.

1. Ideology is explicit not implicit. As opposed to Althusser,[54] ideology is not something given, performed in the world, either genetically inherited or transmitted soon after birth. Nor on the other hand are ideologues, like farmers, stockbrokers, and insurance

salespeople, fully aware of the ambiguities and paradoxes intrinsic to their profession. Rather, "each ideology . . . takes itself as engaged in the analysis of an out-there objective reality," that is, it always reflects an explicit tension between the ideal and the real.[55]

2. Ideology is conscious and volitional (not subconscious or determined). Ideology must entail an act of will, which is not always tantamount to the exercise of free choice; consider, nazism and communism. Ideology differs from religion, nationality, race, or gender. You are born black, female, American. Your family may be Christian, Jewish, agnostic, but in the initial stages of life you have little opportunity to reject or modify parental preferences. Adulthood confers the possibility, and also the responsibility, to choose. To be feminist, ethnic, nationalist, Republican or Democrat, or atheist—each entails choice. It involves an adult commitment to ideology. There are no child ideologues.

3. Ideology is motivational to this world, not cognizant or reflective of the other world. It is on this point that the content of ideology and religion diverge most widely. Religions are marked by rites of passage for the individual,[56] while ideologies aim to mobilize energies toward achieving corporate goals. It could be said that religion focuses on maximizing individual benefit through group participation, while ideology is intent on maximizing group benefit through individual participation.

The this-worldly aspect of ideology should not be mistaken for crude materialism. Ideologies do appeal to deep-seated human instincts. In this sense they are quasi-religious. They complement as well as contrast with religions. The ambivalent relationship of ideology to religion has three aspects. Each needs to be acknowledged:

a. The claim on individual loyalty must be major (not minor or incidental or clustered with others). This is the most acute point of conflict between ideology and religion. They both stake out ultimacy, religion to multivalent truth, ideology to univalent expediency. "Ideologies are . . . partly legitimated by the fact that, focally or tacitly, they ground their discourse in the interests of the whole."[57] Like religions, they attempt to be all-inclusive. They demand verbal assent from individuals, but even more they claim total authority over thoughts, words, and deeds.

b. At the same time ideologues tend to exclude. Recognizing that not all can be wise enough to see the logic that applies to them and appeals for a change in thought or action, they mobilize a vanguard that acts on behalf of the whole but often against others, also claiming to represent the whole. Ideologies, because of their universalist appeals, become not only exclusive but also oppositional. Unlike religions, which claim comprehensive discourse eliciting universal compliance, ideologies advocate certain parts against other parts of the whole. Religions tend to support the existing social order, ideologies to oppose it, or else to claim it as the basis for opposing external enemies. Ideologies are not merely world-reflecting but world-constituting. Ideologues try to discover the meaning of the whole but they also recover the vitality of a component of the whole. In this disposition, ideologies have a "missionary" zeal to show others what they need to do, to correct and help them to that end.[58]

c. Ideologies are rational rather than mystical. In a sense they are quasi-scientific as well as quasi-religious. Geertz has pinpointed the difference in strategies between science and ideology. Ideology seeks identification with self-interests ("egoistic self-regards") rather than discovery of universal laws (natural sciences) or construction of valid theorems (social sciences). The scientist encourages disinterestedness, the ideologue commitment. While the scientist is diagnostic, the ideologue is apologetic.[59] The two become antagonistic to the extent that each claims that it is his or her approach that uniquely encompasses the truth.

All these characteristics of ideology presuppose that it is an activity at the individual level, eliciting and requiring participation in collective endeavors advocating group interests. In *History and Class Consciousness,* however, the Marxist revisionist Lukacs had asserted that the modernist hegemony (which he, following Weber, called rationalization) changed not only the economic and political but also the conceptual and communicative zones of human society. "All the qualitative and multifold dimensions of the precapitalist world are systematically reorganized by the new capitalist rationality on all levels, from those of sense perception to those of science and thought." This process of ineluctable modernization Lukács called "reification," and for him it embodied the most dire diagnostic outcome of Marx's concept of alienation.[60]

With its focus on the rupture between public and private spheres, and its emphasis on the significance of emergent consumerism, this approach parallels much of Gouldner. Unlike Gouldner, however, Lukacs postulates "ideology as objective process," i.e., as something that exists out there beyond the possibility of individuals to either embrace or reject it. Such an approach is radically deterministic. The mechanization of "consumer society" cannot be held in check or redirected. It alone charts the future direction of EuroAmerica; the group interests or creative promptings of its citizens are excluded. However, the instrumental structures of the High Tech Era have not precluded the human factor, as both Gouldner and Gadamer have demonstrated, and ideology rather than being just another name for technology is also its ambivalent antipode.

Even if ideology can be rescued from the iron cage of capitalist rationality, can there be such a category as religious ideology? Religious ideology?! For academic sociologists as for Marxist theorists, the phrase appears to be an oxymoron. Ideology arose against religion. By implication, therefore, all ideology is secular. But that argument fails to take account of the origins of ideology. It opposed religion not only as a metaphysical system but also as a social structure. It linked itself to science without explaining why science provided an epistemology more adequate than the metaphysical model which it, in the name of science, was rejecting.

To justify religious ideology we have to lay to rest the oversights of Marxists—whether they be historians, philosophers, or literary critics. Marx was not a consistent theorist. His life sorted out into two distinct phases. It was only in the first phase, pre-1848, that he was combating ideologies of a religious or metaphysical type. Marxism as materialism is opposed to the idealisms of religion and metaphysics, but that outlook originated in a circumstance where Germany had not yet experienced either a political or a scientific, intellectual revolution against the *ancien regime*. Once Marx located himself in a place (England) where the Great Western Transmutation had advanced and the modernist hegemony was evident, he shifted his attack from religion to society, from metaphysics to class consciousness. Yet Marx himself never integrated the two phases of his life.[61] Religion retained the negative evaluation of the young Marx. It was seen as an individual error that each person, exercising reason, could correct, while bourgeois consumerism, unrelated to religion, became projected as corporate error, a value system ensuring social domination of one group by another.

The task of integration which Marx neglected was taken up by others. For Comte and other pre–Marxist Enlightenment philosophers, religion, identified with the *ancien regime,* had been opposed to ideology, the new science of humanity. With early Marxists, ideology was discredited but its scope ironically enlarged. Religion was subsumed by ideology. It became but one form, a *lower* form of ideology. A disguised reflex of power, its superstition and error had to be exposed by reason and eliminated, in order that the masses could approach the core evil, which was also the principal ideology, of capitalist society: economic exploitation. Class consciousness was the remedy for the oppressed, revolution their sole recourse. Only that which related to economic grievances was deemed valid. Hence ideology in general and religious ideology in particular were seen to distort rather than project "true" class consciousness.

We propose an alternative approach. To talk about religious ideology is not only inherently possible, it is also advantageous. It has a double advantage for ideologues: first, it recovers for their discourse its pre-Lukács sense of volitional, explicit participation in an advocacy movement, and second, it broadens ideology beyond the political or social sphere, where it must always be seen as a substitute for religion, a quasi-religion rather than an expression of genuine religious belief and commitment.

Religious ideology as an analytical category also provides a double benefit to religious actors. First, religious ideology removes religion from the garbage heap of history to which early ideologues had consigned it. Religion is no longer separated from the modern world, as something to be linked to prescientific error, the opposite of rational truth. Second, religious ideology suggests the varied forms of expressiveness that are available to institutional religion in the modern world. Religion is not just individual commitment entailing personal piety nor group loyalty eliciting ecclesiastical membership. It can also be the corporate public action of religiously motivated individuals on behalf of what they perceive to be their deepest spiritual loyalties.

While sociologists have talked a lot about fundamentalism, they have seldom identified fundamentalism or any other church-related movement as religious ideology. The same cannot be said of historians. Eric Hobsbawm, in *The Age of Revolution,* does not hesitate to speak of two kinds of early nineteenth century ideologies: religious and secular. The two major expressions of the former, in his view, are Islam and sectarian Protestantism.[62] He never elaborates their relationship to nonideological expressions of religion, but he does infer what they hold in common with their secular counterparts: motivating people to act on behalf of their own perceived self-interests. Similarly, the historian of religions Charles Adams, in writing about the major proponent of an Islamic system in contemporary South Asia, titles his essay, "The Ideology of Mawlana Mawdudi." Adams, like Hobsbawm, focuses on the power of ideology, in this case Mawdudi's ideal Islamic system, to mobilize readers into followers and engage them in the public sphere.[63]

The intellectual historian Michael Walzer also embraces ideology in the non-Marxist sense. He advocates it as an analytical category uniquely suited to interpret Calvinism. In *The Revolution of the Saints,* Walzer argues that Calvin "as a practical man of ideas . . . is best explained by calling him not primarily a theologian or a philosopher but an ideologist." That distinction begs for an elaboration of the respective roles of theologian, philosopher, and ideologue. Walzer provides it:

The power of a theology lies in its capacity to offer believers a knowledge of God and so to make possible an escape from the corrupted earth and a transcendental communion. The power of a philosophy . . . lies in its capacity to explain to its students the world and human society as they are and must be and so to win for them that freedom which consists in an acknowledgement of necessity. The power of an ideology, on the other hand, lies in its capacity to activate its adherents and to change the world. Its content is necessarily a description of contemporary experience as unacceptable and unnecessary and a rejection of any merely personal transcendence or salvation. Its practical effect is to generate organization and cooperative activity.[64]

Like Calvinism, fundamentalism is best assessed as an ideology not a theology or philosophy or, for that matter, a social deprivation or historical recurrence. Paralleling Walzer's approach to Calvinism, we categorize fundamentalism as a religious ideology of protest. All fundamentalists are ideologues protesting the modernist hegemony in the High Tech Era. Numerous other features of fundamentalist cadres need to be assessed, and we will discuss their likely tactics, their organizational patterns, their scope and consequence, but unless we first locate fundamentalism on a spectrum of discourse that allows access to its innate character, our analysis will flounder and ultimately fail.

The distinctiveness of fundamentalism as a religious ideology emerges when we contrast it with that secular ideology which has become its principal nemesis. The archenemy of fundamentalism is not biculturalism à la Steiner. Nor is it Comtian positivism nor Darwinian evolutionary theory. It is nationalism. Nationalism preceded fundamentalism. It is also likely to survive it. They are incommensurate opposites: contradictories rather than contraries, both cannot occupy the same ideological space. Yet interaction between them will determine the fate of fundamentalist cadres in all three monotheistic traditions. In examining Judaism, we will draw attention to the countervailing appeal of Zionism. In surveying Protestant Christianity, we will assess the experience of American democracy. Both tangents of nationalism determined aspects of fundamentalist thought and behavior in the Technical Age, and in the case of Islam, nationalism also became the durable foil to fundamentalist fervor. Consideration of Afro-Asian nationalism informs, even as it qualifies, all reflection on Islamic fundamentalism.

Before exploring the complex interaction of fundamentalism and nationalism, we must try to make sense of nationalism. Does it cohere as an aggregate term, given the multiple contexts to which it must be applied? More than borders separate first from second from third world countries. Since nineteenth–twentieth-century nationalism has been inextricably linked to the Great Western Transmutation, can it have the same function in the European countries where it originated as in Asian, African, and also Latin American countries where it was later adopted?

The relation of nationalism to religion raises a host of questions about the latter. Has religion played any role in the reception or dissemination of nationalism? Has each of the three monotheistic traditions had a similar experience with nationalism? If not, how, where, and why have nationalist movements elicited a different response from Christian, Jewish, and Islamic fundamentalists?

Nationalism, in the view of many, is restricted to those countries that have achieved a certain level of socioeconomic power. As a modernist ideology it may be generically unsuited to the non-European world. George Steiner has drawn attention to the Judaic-Hellenistic canon that epitomizes Western civilization. Does the GWT then extend that canon, dividing the whole world into those who are competent to compete commercially, technologically, and militarily and those who are not? Ernest Gellner, though an archstructuralist, seems to reflect the prevalent view when he limits nationalism to both the Technical Age and to the West. He goes so far as to make a trait analysis of nationalism, claiming that such traits could only occur in the modern era and, by implication, only in those societies that encouraged a modernist outlook:

Nationalism is a very distinctive species of patriotism, . . . which in fact prevail[s] *in the modern world, and nowhere else.* Nationalism is a species of patriotism distinguished by a few very important features: the units which this kind of patriotism, namely nationalism, favors with its loyalty, are culturally homogeneous, based on a culture striving to be a high [literate] culture; they are large enough to sustain the hope of supporting the educational system which can keep a literate culture going; they are poorly endowed with rigid internal sub-groupings; their populations are anonymous, fluid and mobile, and they are unmediated; the individual belongs to them directly, in virtue of his cultural style, and not in virtue of membership in nested sub-groups. Homogeneity, literacy, anonymity are the key traits.[65]

And all these traits cluster in an industrial high culture that is coextensive with the state and not subordinated to a faith or a church, i.e., it is a polity that is explicitly non- or antireligious. This same polity strives to be universalist in scope, each nation being limited only by the counterforce of another nation-state. The "reality-shaping power [of each nation-state] is exercised in multiple ways,"[66] among them the patterning of acceptable moral discourse, giving rise to what Kenneth Cragg has called "the state as an obedience context."[67]

Institutional religion relates to the modern nation-state through circumstantial coincidence, not political planning. Protestantism may have foreshadowed both the emergence of the industrial world and the coming of nationalism, yet it did not retain its own privileged position as public authority.[68] Anthony Smith makes a strong case for modern nationalism as an *anti*religious ideology. Contrasting it with "the supernaturalist pessimism of millennial movements," he argues that twentieth-century nationalism "is revealed as an optimistic, secular and practical ideology." It succeeds in incorporating elements from the prenationalist religious culture yet transforms them to its own ends. The nationalist movement finally "seeks to create a world in its own image, a world of theoretically independent and equal nation-states."[69]

The ideology of the nation-state sometimes takes on an explicitly religious aura. Many nationalists believe that the messianic age "will arrive only when men and women come to share common values and sentiments, as in a close-knit family." [70] Such an ersatz religious appeal has deep-seated Enlightenment roots. Fueling modern-day nationalism were the same antitraditional forces that gave rise to the French Revolution; hence it is inherently as antireligious and secular as the earliest Enlightenment theorists (chief among them Comte, Kant, and Marx). Whenever nationalists have accommodated to religious interests, it has been due to pragmatic motives. Negatively, they have wanted to prevent a reversion to theocracy. Positively, they have hoped to provide the social cohesion that makes the state an effective instrument of power against both internal and external challenges to its authority. However, it has been the retention of political power, not the assertion of religious truth, that has loomed as their ultimate goal.

The incommensurability of political and religious priorities is seldom clear-cut. Nationalism can be modulated into a liminal outlook that rejects ethnic chauvinism as well as state religion. That outlook is called patriotism. Despite Gellner's attempt to conflate the two, nationalism and patriotism are not identical. True patriotism, in fact, offers an ideal that contrasts with jingoistic nationalism. It is the ideal of civic republicanism. It retains the moral but not the metaphysical *élan* of religion. It eschews the obsession with territorial sovereignty that too often besets nationalist ideologues. In its stead it offers a cosmopolitan embrace of compassion and justice, the ideal of a pluralist world organized on counteruniversalist norms. [71]

Like nationalism and unlike patriotism, all the monotheistic traditions are universalists; they not only incorporate universal norms, but they strain for universalist compliance with those norms. Hence the historic triumph of nationalist statism has required each monotheistic tradition to weigh its survival in the public arena. The very success of the modern nation-state has politicized religious responses. Separation of church and state might be better termed the preservation of church (or synagogue or mosque) from state, because the power of the latter is as universalist in intent today as the former was in the pre–Technical or Axial Age. Nationalism, even in religious guise, pushes up against the limits of religious norms. Nationalists, whatever their private loyalties, are inevitably pitted against religionists. Among the custodians of institutional religion only fundamentalists have intuited the high stakes in this protracted struggle.

Vis-à-vis nationalism all three monotheistic traditions face the same question: how can believers preserve their symbolic identity within a public order that is structurally antireligious? To reduce the struggle to a war of material interests is to miss the crucial level of conflict. It is above all ideological, weighted toward religion for fundamentalists, toward nationalism for secularists. The two are incommensurate. They are not mere contraries; they are genuine contradictions. The outcome of their conflict has not been decided, though the markings are different for each monotheistic tradition.

The position of Protestant Christianity is at once the most moderate and the most ambivalent. It has been argued that Protestant Christian fundamentalists succeeded in America because of the elective affinity between them and their fellow citizens. There remains a tacit congruity between the scripturally mandated faith of fundamentalists and the constitutionally sanctioned ethos of the majority of Americans. Together they forged the dominant value system of middle America, one best described by Henry May as Progressive Protestant Patriotism (PPP). To be American you had to be all three: progressive because you believed in the forward march of history towards some shadowy utopia; Protestant because you accepted the separation of church and state, with the right to practice one's own faith or even to deny all faith as a "God-given right"; and patriotic because it was only in the United States that the optimal expression of innate human dispositions could flourish. "America—love it or leave it" is the bumpersticker slogan echoing the most extreme version of Progressive Protestant Patriotism.[72] Even though PPP reflects the notion of a civil religion, PPP could also be the fundamentalist slogan, if one but reversed the last two words and accented protestantism rather than patriotism. American fundamentalists would readily define themselves as Progressive Patriotic *Protestants,* especially if one limited patriotism to nationalism and exalted territorial aspirations to the level of a universalist mandate, for instance on foreign policy issues that involve Israel.[73]

Yet that shift of emphasis from Protestant Patriotism to Patriotic Protestantism puts American fundamentalists at odds with their fellow citizens. Fundamentalists see a point of tension between the demands of faith and the exercise of public authority. They would like to compel all Americans to adopt their interpretation of the Constitution. They have often tried, notably in the form of the constitutional amendment that produced Prohibition.[74] They have also advocated changing juridical decrees that oppose their outlook. But they have never tried to undermine the peculiarly American system of governance. While they have enjoyed only slight success in reshaping the public sphere of American life, all their efforts are exerted *within,* rather than against, the framework of democratic institutions. They want to replace one set of laws with another, one policy with another. They have not opted to abandon the political arena or to subvert it, only to redirect it.

Hence, despite their ambivalence, American Protestants remain both progressive and patriotic. In comparison to other fundamentalists Progressive Patriotic Protestants stand out for their moderation with respect to the political process. Unlike them, Jewish and Islamic fundamentalists have not experienced the development of their communities in tandem with the GWT. Their situation reflects the growing disparity between the monotheistic traditions as the Technical Age advances. Equally displaced, they have not been equally privileged in finding a subordinate place within the new order symbolized above all by the power of the nation-state. Jewish fundamentalists have to grapple with modernism in the form of one of the most successful of all nationalist ideologies, Zionism. One group, Neturei Karta, has accommodated to it by remaining in the heart of the state and opposing its persistent efforts to develop a civil religion. Instead of compliance with the requirements of a modern nation-state, they have proposed a strict attention to traditional observances (*mitzvoth*) within the physical confines of one district of Jerusalem, Meah Shearim. The other group, Gush Emunim, took the opposite approach: conforming to Zionist ideology, including its relaxation of certain *mitzvoth,* they have emphasized the superior benefit of one *mitzvah,* the sanctity of the land. Embracing settlement (*hitnahlut*) as their motto, they strive for the territorial expansion of the state to its "biblical" limits, limits that they themselves define.

It is important to remember that Christian and Jewish fundamentalists differ markedly from their coreligionists in interpreting nationalism. For most Christians and most Jews, it was the benefits of modernity, rather than perceptions of religious loyalty, that colored their reaction to nationalism. For the majority of Protestant American Christians, participation in the national ethos of the USA was a satisfying, if paradoxical, adjustment. For the majority of Jews, the foundation of the modern state of Israel signaled the end of nearly two thousand years as a fractured community in exile. In the words of one scholar, it was "as though Judaism for millennia had been a religion in search of a polity."[75]

The opposite was true for Muslims. Though Islamic expansion had been limited to the Afro-Eurasian *oikoumenē* or civilized world, it was a vast domain. Within its vast and disparate parts, Muslim elites had enjoyed political power and global preeminence for more than a thousand years, till the advent of the Technical Age. European commercialism challenged indigenous polities; its colonial agents created their own elite counterparts in the once-proud Muslim empires of West and South Asia. Nationalism arose as a derivate or mimetic reaction to colonial rule. It held out the promise of ending foreign domination, but at the same time it reneged on that promise because colonial values persisted even after the colonizers had left. For the entire Muslim world, twentieth century nationalism produced a cleavage of enormous magnitude, between Muslims and the dominant culture of Western Europe but also among Muslims, between those who openly accommodated to Western values and those who seemed to oppose them. Since both modernizers and their opponents tended to be urban elites, neither group expressed the fears or hopes of the majority. Throughout the twentieth century most Muslims, like most citizens of the third world, have remained rural and illiterate.

No matter how one ratchets Islam with nationalism, one cannot escape the implications of the mimetic theory of nationalism. According to the political theorist Richard Falk, global strife will be perpetuated by the dilemma of Afro-Asian countries: straightjacketed into an imposed system of governance, they cannot adapt it to their own precolonial values. In theory, when former colonies won their independence, they should have became nations, but in fact, they adopted the rubric of statehood without the substance of nationhood. They were state-nations hoping to become nation-states, but the gap between these two identities persists and it produces frustration as well as anger.[76]

The Muslim experience is immensely complicated by the fact that Islam, like Judaism, stakes out claims to be a holistic ideology, competent to address every activity of life and every sphere of human society. How well it does this, with what problems of internal consistency, is less important initially than the breadth and duration of the claim. Because Muslim elites encountered nationalism as the driving force of European expansionism, it was inevitable that it would evoke in them an empathetic response, to advocate their own nationalism against external aggression, to secure territorial freedom from outside interference. What was equally inevitable, however, was that not only Europeans but all others, including immediate neighbors, even immediate Muslim neighbors, would be excluded from the sacralized homeland. Nationalism became eulogized as patriotism in Muslim regions as in other parts of Africa and Asia. Little regard was paid to the double edge of that conflation: while patriotism evokes an appeal to ideals that are transterritorial and universal, closer to the notion of *umma* or corporate solidarity in precolonial Islam, patriotism, when conjoined with nationalism, suggests that the only ideal worthy of pursuit is territorial or, even more narrowly, racial. Both appeals lead their constituents to wave a banner of optimism that is at heart antireligious. Just as European nationalism rang the death knell for any hope of a Holy Christian Empire, so its echo response among Arabs and Asians precluded any ultimate success for a pan-Islamic movement.

Despite apologetic efforts made on behalf of the Arab nation, the stark reality is that nationalism did not arise in the East but in the West. It was part of the GWT that exploded into Muslim regions as into other parts of Asia, Africa, and Latin America. There is a voluminous literature on Arab nationalism, scarcely any on Muslim nationalism. Some have tried to argue that Arab nationalism does not conflict with Islam since the Arab nation is, after all, the heartland of the Muslim world. But that argument is belied by history as well as by geography. There has never been an Arab nation in the premodern period. Nor has Islam ever claimed any nation as its authoritative referent.[77] What it has claimed is one inclusive and determinative doctrine: *tawhid* (the sacrosanct unity of this world and the next, matter and spirit). To speak of the Muslim basis for Arab nationalism is as absurd as claiming Christian racism or Jewish materialism as the obvious outcome of innate religious dispositions. The universalist outreach of all three precludes their narrow stereotyping into a single ethos that privileges one race or one class. To pair Islam with Arab nationalism revalorizes the latter upward and the former downward. It is not only an essentialist and reductive exercise; it is wrong.

In part two we will examine the fundamentalist counterchallenges to several forms of nationalism. The outcome varies from Judaism to Christianity to Islam. But the crucial point of reference is ideological. Fundamentalism as a religious ideology is defined by its unremitting opposition to nationalism as the most tenacious ideology of the Technical Age. It is a battle of ideologies that will occupy us for the remainder of this work and also for the remainder of the twentieth century.

CHAPTER 4

Fundamentalism as a Religious Ideology in Multiple Contexts

We may define fundamentalism as the reaffirmation, in a radically changed environment, of traditional modes of understanding and behavior. In contrast to conservatism or traditionalism, which assumes that things can and should go on much as they have generations past, fundamentalism recognizes and tries to speak to a changed milieu, an altered atmosphere of expectations.

—R. STEPHEN HUMPHREYS

Two minor tasks remain. The first is to consider the objections raised to the broader study of fundamentalism. Some deny that fundamentalism can be cross-cultural and multicreedal. By restricting fundamentalism to beliefs and attributing those beliefs to EuroAmerican Protestant Christians, the objectors preempt a global consideration of the fundamentalist protest against modernism. In this chapter we will address their objections before discharging the final task of part one: to enumerate the characteristics of fundamentalism as a religious ideology that mobilizes not only Progressive Patriotic Protestants but also their Jewish and Muslim counterparts.

We begin by exposing the basis for all analytical investigation. Describe. Compare. Evaluate. Three steps. Sequential and cumulative, they should be present and discernible in any serious study of any field of human endeavor. Yet each bristles with tacit assumptions, unasked questions, logical dead ends.

To describe should be the simplest. Common sense has yielded the pervasive slogan: "Tell it like it is." But what to tell? To whom? For what motives? With what expectations? Contemporary philosophy, going back again to Nietzsche, posits that "we know no fact independent of interpretation; there is no vision of reality untainted by prejudice and perspective."[1] That means that there is no truth apart from the teller, who is at the same time the interpreter of truth. All history becomes, in Benedetto Croce's dictum, "contemporary history." Present-mindedness is inescapable, for as the biblicist Rudolf Bultmann observed: "there are no such things as presuppositionless readings of the past."[2]

Even in the sciences the same intimate reciprocity between subject and object, knower and known pertains; despite claims advanced by scientists, "there is [also], so far as human consciousness goes, no such entity as a universally objective physical reality."[3] What is to keep us from going back and forth through the swinging door of relativism? The persistent hope is also the major challenge: a rigorous selection of critical norms, a ceaseless self-examination of subsurface emotions and influences, and, above all, an openness to new evidence and variant views.

The obstacle course facing contemporary scholars is bewildering. To describe is to choose, and hence "the very first word of description contains a myriad of implicit methodological assumptions."[4] If this is a truism, it is doubly true when attempting to frame an interpretive model for understanding religious movements. Not only must one clarify the religious sphere in relation to other spheres of human experience, but one must also defend the choice of particular religious issues and agents, processes and prospects. The title of this book suggests what we intend to describe: opposition to the modern age and defense of the eternal unchanging God as a reflexive reaction among Islamic, Jewish, and Christian fundamentalists. But why is antimodernism so virulent in these *three* traditions? Does it not also arise among Buddhists, Sikhs, and Hindus? Or, alternatively, is it perhaps just a Christian phenomenon?

To describe is to make a category choice, either to create new categories or to breathe new life into what others have created. Since only Christian fundamentalists describe themselves as members of a group labeled, proudly and defiantly, "fundamentalist," the other two—Islamic and Jewish—are fundamentalisms invented by outside observers. The labels in each case allude to an orientation characteristic of some Muslims and some Jews that seems best characterized as "fundamentalist." But to describe Islamic and Jewish fundamentalists is to presume that they exist. Is the presumption justified? How do we know that they exist?

Before we can venture to compare them, we must make clear who "they" are. Labels do influence how we think about those labeled, and the label "fundamentalists" runs the risk of becoming just another stereotype. Used uncritically, it summons up a shorthand abstraction that may assist popular discourse but at the expense of damning the target group.

How can we demonstrate that fundamentalism is multifaceted, that among its adherents are particular groupings of pious Jews and committed Muslims as well as certain Progressive Patriotic Protestants? The answer is elusive. At one level, we do *not* know that either Jewish or Islamic fundamentalists exist. By the same token, we do not know that Christian fundamentalists exist. Those who might reply, "But of course they do!" could point to history and current usage. After all, fundamentalism began as a movement within Protestant Christianity at one point in the recent past,[5] and there are still certain groups in late-twentieth-century America who continue to claim that they are the faithful remnant, since they and they alone honor the fundamentals of Christian scripture, belief, and practice. Hence, one could argue, both the historical record and empirical observation prove that Christian fundamentalists exist. By the same criteria, other kinds of fundamentalists should be disallowed. Since no group within Judaism or Islam ever claimed to be fundamentalist, and since at present most Jews and Muslims, especially those labeled fundamentalists, reject the suitability of that nomenclature either for themselves or for their coreligionists, one must refrain from calling any group of Jews or Muslims fundamentalists.

The logic of this twofold argument is flawed. Its premises do not withstand close scrutiny. The first part—that Christian fundamentalists do exist—rests on the assumption that we have been identified as *the* fundamentals by one group is, in fact, their exclusive possession. Yet to the extent that all Christians stake their destiny on certain articles of faith, all qualify as fundamentalist. By this line of reasoning the claim that there are Christian fundamentalists becomes a tautology; all Christians are, or should be, fundamentalist.

The second part of the argument—that no non-Christians can be fundamentalist—is marred by reinforcing fallacies. One is the claim of exclusion by origin: if you didn't start it, you can't have it. The other is the nominalist retreat to performer privilege: if you don't want the name, I must take it back. Both fallacies need to be exposed. Their persistence denies fundamentalism any potential opportunity for broad scale, comparative assessment.

Those who advocate exclusion by origin, we will call "originists." They rest their argument on priority of place. Fundamentalism, in their view, is not transferrable beyond certain Protestant Christians of twentieth-century America. Why? Because no concept, belief, or practice is transferrable from its place of origin until the group to whom it is transferred accepts the place of origin, its formulations, and its experience as consonant with their own. Hence, one may speak of both Christianity and Marxism as movements that legitimately expanded and now exist in multiple contexts unrelated to their places of origin. In each case, several groups unconnected to either Palestine or England have acknowledged one person—be it Jesus of Nazareth or Karl Marx— as the pivotal figure whose scriptural testament has given direction and purpose to their lives. But, by the same argument, one may not speak of nationalism in the Middle East since most Arabs and many Iranians reject the European experience as an authentic antecedent mediating their own entrance into the twentieth century as nation-states. Christians are also caught in a dilemma. By this argument, they should not accept religion as a self-description of their outlook. The word "religion" is not found in the Old and New Testaments. A Latin word, its meaning reflects its place of origin, and the ingredient of faith, deemed crucial to post-Reformation Christianity, becomes confused by being subsumed under the alien category religion. One Protestant scholar has even gone so far as to suggest that the word "religion" should be eliminated from academic discourse. In its place we should substitute originary terms to reflect the component parts of religion. The most basic, irreducible parts are faith and tradition. Juxtaposed one with the other, they satisfy; lumped together as "religion," they offend.[6]

Yet the examples of nationalism and religion together reveal the absurdity of originist logic. Places are incidentally significant, not historically decisive in the development of socioreligious movements. Even though nationalism originated in Western Europe, the nation-state model has become a global transplant; it has pressed into its confines even groups that continue to be antagonistic to virtually everything else that Europe represents. Religion, for its part, has gained widespread acceptance as a blanket category encompassing all institutional expressions of human engagement with the sacred, the holy, the other. As Zwi Werblowsky noted in discussing Judaism as a religion, it is nonsensical to say that a term is restricted to those who first used it; Judaism *is* a religion, despite the fact that biblical Hebrew lacks a single word equivalent to "religion." After all, he reminds the originists, "the Hebrew language, like Hebrew and Jewish culture, has not only a biblical dictionary; it also has a history."[7] And the dictionary best services history when it is seen as instrumental rather than conclusive to establishing the meaning of a text or context.[8]

The nominalist argument parallels the originist argument. Shifting the invariant authority, it places primacy on a name. Whereas the originist, without regard to actual historical circumstances, isolates and prioritizes a geographical place, a founding figure, or an ethnographic referent, the nominalist latches onto a particular name, and then limits the legitimacy of that name to those who claim it as self-conscious exponents. In its starkest form, the nominalist argument restricts to performers the right to name themselves. If a group does not arrogate a name to itself, then no observer can use that name to describe its characteristic emphasis or normative profile. By that "logic," the only humanists are those who claim to be humanists; there are no teachers but those who teach in classrooms; clowns only are found in circuses. The argument could be ignored or ridiculed, except that it is so often and so guilelessly invoked. Many claim, for instance, that fundamentalism can *only* be used in its dictionary definition as "strict maintenance of traditional orthodox religious beliefs, for example, the inerrancy of scripture and literal acceptance of the creeds, as fundamentals of Protestant Christianity."[9]

To underscore the futility of adhering to any dictionary, Hebrew or English, in trying to write about religious movements, we have only to consider two other terms decisive for the religious history of twentieth-century America: secularization and civil religion.

By the nominalist canon, we would be led to conclude that there is no secularization in the world. After all, only a handful of armchair academics refer to such a process. Instead, one should depict developments in industrialized countries over the past two hundred years by focusing on what is visible and factual, namely, scientific discoveries and technological developments. More than that is inferential and suspect.

Such an argument is tantamount to empirical literalism. It misses the point by reading only letters, not words, for any perceptive observer of recent history has to note that science and technology have influenced the conceptual as well as the physical framework within which cosmologies are imagined, religious beliefs forged, and moral values exercised. A double process is at work. Private beliefs have become pluralized at the same time that public values have been relativized. Through both tendencies the modern world continues to reflect the impact of that elitist eighteenth-century German philosophical movement known as *Aufklärung* or the Enlightenment.

The twentieth century has moved beyond the view of the Enlightenment that its founders expounded. One may doubt that the Enlightenment of the few ever led to the secularization of the many. But that doubt leads to a debate over the scope of Enlightenment values. It should not cloud the separate issue of naming that random process which has occasioned the emerging modernist mindset. Secularization, more than any other term, captures the pervasive ambiguity that characterizes institutions as well as individuals who have become heirs to the Enlightenment. For that very reason secularization resists a narrow application. It remains central to the analysis of social change, especially among sociologists of religion, despite the fact that few moderns, no matter what their class, gender, or professional differences, would claim that they are practicing secularists.[10]

The case is similar with civil religion. It is a term of even more recent provenance in popular discourse than secularization. Indeed, civil religion is best viewed as a subset of secularization, for without the presuppositions of a nation-state powerful enough to elicit the loyalty of its citizens, a power vastly increased by the instrumentalities of modern-day technology and communications, civil religion would be jejune. Civil religion is little more than nationalist ideology recast in a "positive" light by being linked to religion. Civil religion upgrades nationalism while downgrading religion. Coined by Rousseau in the eighteenth century, civil religion was intended to connote the corporate identity that a republic self-consciously espouses. The sociologist Robert Bellah reintroduced it into late-twentieth-century American discourse on religion and society. It gained wide popularity in the sixties and early seventies. Bellah himself has voiced unhappiness with the phrase, yet he cannot replace it with a more suitable term. Recently, he has used the term even more broadly. Together with Phillip Hammond, he opted to stoke the debate about civil religion on a global scale: their coauthored book illustrates how civil religion exists in other parts of the globe (such as Mexico and Japan) where that term was never thought of, much less consciously advocated.[11]

On an individual level the nominalists' position is also confounded. Philosophers and social theorists often claim to map out a new position separating themselves from accepted schools of thought. Though they deny their link with the immediate past, they seldom succeed in making the clean break that they boldly announce. Karl Popper says, "I am not a positivist," yet in many respects he is.[12] Pierre Bourdieu says, "I am not a structuralist," yet he shares many of their emphases.[13]

Describe and compare. To describe fundamentalism in Christianity, Judaism, and Islam is to presume that it exists in all three. It is also to presume that what they hold in common as fundamentals is comparable. Though fundamentalism originated in Christianity and though certain groups of Protestant Christians use the term widely, there is ample precedent for expanding the category "fundamentalism" to other religions than Christianity. We can designate certain non-Christian groups as "fundamentalist" if the term draws attention to qualities among these groups that, when clustered together, make more sense of what they do, or claim to do, than other abstracting umbrella categories. No choice of technical terms is risk-free. Forfeiting self-reflection, we join the ranks of sloganeers unless our labels help to clarify the complex issues of social exchange.

Labeling is, therefore, the first act of description and the necessary prelude to comparison. It offers an *a priori* judgment about the success of that which has been chosen as the primary category of description. In the case of nationalism, religion, secularization, and civil religion, many would accept the continuous widespread reference to them as proof of their reality. Since they have succeeded in eliciting recognition from several quarters of the academy, media, government, and even churches, one might be excused for assuming that they describe something as real as it is varied. Yet they reflect a pattern that is common to each new term or neologism. It experiences initial acclaim or controversy before gaining public acceptance. It then acquires a paradigmatic force, sustaining its further usage even when those who introduced it or continue to use it may feel compelled to explain why that usage is not wholly adequate to the events, processes, phenomena, and people being described.

The formation of cultural paradigms is not unlike the formation of scientific paradigms. Their commonality is easier to accept when one realizes that they share a dependence on the "human factor" that belies scientific claims to absolute neutrality, value-free objectivity, or universal validity. Both types of paradigms augur a transformation of outlook in their respective audiences. The instinct to construct a new tradition informs all research, privileging some elements, ignoring others, and always supporting a version of truth that is never the whole truth. The boundaries of cohesion and dissemination for social scientists and humanists gravitating to a new cultural leitmotiv may be less clearly visible or traceable than it is for natural scientists charting a new law of the phenomenal world, yet the human element in paradigm formation is finally more significant than the distinction between investigators.

Fundamentalism is beginning to achieve paradigmatic stature as a global religious movement. Before we can demonstrate that it exists out there, beyond the confines of the original and continuing American context, we have to set forth hypotheses that must be tested and modified, verified or rejected in specific cases. *Only then is evaluation possible.* To decide whether or not fundamentalism discloses enough truth about the current religious condition of some human actors to warrant its continued usage is a judgment that follows, even as it depends on, accurate description and careful comparison.

It also depends, as did our analysis of ideology, on continuous vigilance in separating the denotation of words from their connotations. Many scholars would like to curtail the usage of fundamentalism because it "has become pejorative and implies an intolerant, self-righteous, and narrowly dogmatic religious literalism which, in its rigidity, is incompatible with 'progress' and 'rationalism'."[14] That approach, however, acknowledges only one level of historical usage, generalizing its force to all groups in all circumstances. Fundamentalism, like religion itself, has been and will continue to be variegated.

To examine the cluster of traits that define fundamentalism in *any* social context, we have to situate our analysis within the historical developments of chapter two and against the ideological challenge of chapter three. Only between the dialectic of history and ideology can we chart our skeletal profile of fundamentalism. Even that profile will remain provisional, its validity subject to the ongoing correlation of the traits it abstracts with the variety of detailed data from which they are abstracted. If successful, it will provide a guide to the immediate future of some religious groups. It will also warn of possible detours, though it cannot remap the road, much less indicate where or when it will end.

Fundamentalism is a multifocal phenomenon precisely because the modernist hegemony, though originating in some parts of the West, was not limited to Protestant Christianity. Through the Enlightenment it affected significant numbers of Jews, and due to the colonization of much of Africa and Asia in the nineteenth and early twentieth centuries, it touched the lives and destinies of many Muslims. The modernist hegemony did not end with World War II or with the attainment of political independence by so-called third world countries.[15]

Preexisting commercial and military dependencies were rarely forfeited by the former colonizers. Moreover, the mindset of modernist bias (quantity over quality, change over continuity, commercial efficiency over human sympathy) was often perpetuated by indigenous elites who took control in the first stage of national independence. The accelerating structural shift into a global economy put a premium on accommodation. At the same time it penalized isolation or lag-time response to new conditions.

To the extent that indigenous codes of behavior acted as a countervailing force to the homogenizing influence of commercial networks and communications accessibility, it is still valuable to think of Western and non-Western cultural spheres. One must recognize two features of this new phase: first, the modernist mindset was linked to the West by *both* sides, EuroAmericans who thought they were privileged by history or destined by God to control but also indigenous elites who admired or resented EuroAmerican power; and second, that part of the modernizing West that was excluded from power included not only Christians and Jews but also Muslims. Those who see the new hegemony in parochial terms, equating modern with Western with European, dismiss Islam as peripheral. Yet if we examine the reduced public role of all three monotheistic traditions, fundamentalism emerges as a potential development within each, its potential expanded by the peculiarly Western outlook that they hold in common, from the use of language to the formation of institutions to the projection of universal patterns of expectation (utopian) and disappointment (tragic).

Fundamentalism per se is neither a causal force nor a mere epiphenomenon of more basic, underlying forces, whether demographic, economic, or political. Rather, in our view, fundamentalism is a novel ideology congruent with the interests of specific groups responding to social tensions generated by the contemporary world. It is, moreover, a *religious* ideology since the beliefs of its adherents, their practices, their challenges, and aspirations, all are framed in discourse that authorizes action through scriptural, creedal, and moral referents.

But why must we speak of fundamentalism as an ideology first and a religious disposition second? During the late twentieth century, modes of scholarly discourse, like writing instruments, are changing. (Could one imagine authoring a book on a personal computer before 1980? Could one imagine being grateful for the absence of a computer virus before 1988?!) We must be faithful to the markings of the present phase of global history. In the Agrarianate Age, religion, despite its detractors, was the parent and superior of ideology. In the Technical Age (nineteenth and first half of the twentieth century), they were in latent conflict, operating in separate spheres: ideology referred to the public arena of politics and economics, religion to the private sphere of individual conscience and creedal profession. They seldom conflicted or overlapped, except in the minds of a few prescient scholars, such as Owen Chadwick and Eric Hobsbawm. But now in the High Tech Era (since 1950), ideology, despite its critics, supersedes and subsumes religion.

We are still adjusting to that shift of authoritative categories. It is central to understanding both the emergence of modernism and the fundamentalist reaction to its emergence. Most of the authorizing thinkers are European, whether one looks to the Germans from Kant and Nietzsche to Gadamer and Habermas, or to the French, most recently, Ricoeur, Bourdieu, Foucault, and Derrida. An occasional American, such as Dewey or Peirce, surfaces. The British have contributed Coleridge and Collingwood. But the names are initially less important than the sum total of what they collectively suggest as modernists. Meaning is to be separated from truth, function from metaphysics, human from god. What Nietzsche proposes as a theory of art, Kant requires as an axiom of morality. The end result is the same: ideology comes to supersede religion, just as theology is displaced by sociology.

We have said all this implicitly in the preceding three chapters. We now need to recapitulate if we are to cope with both the modernist threat to religion and the fundamentalist response to that threat. The shift in referential categories occurred during two centuries, the eighteenth and the nineteenth. Its proponents were from Europe, England, and America, and they were *all* privileged, by education if not by social and economic circumstance. One could go even further and specify that they were elite consumers of the new knowledge. Citizens of the university, they did not directly assist in the production of the new scientific discoveries; rather they reflected on the implications of these discoveries and their unprecedented power.[16]

Two quotations will help to illustrate the analytical force of the momentous shift from the Agrarianate Age to the Technical Age in Western thought. Both quotations also underscore the social limitation of Enlightenment exponents, despite their rhetorical nimbleness. Partisan to his subject, the leading historian of the philosophy of the Enlightenment declared, without a trace of hyperbole,

in the 18th century the intellectual center of gravity changes its position. The various fields of knowledge—natural sciences, history, law, politics, art—gradually withdrew from the domination of traditional metaphysics and theology. They no longer look to the concept of God for their justification and legitimation; the various sciences themselves now determine the concept on the basis of their specific form. The relations between the concept of God and the concepts of truth, morality, law are by no means abandoned. But their direction changes. *An exchange of index symbols takes place.* That which formerly had established other concepts now moves into the position of that to be established and that which hitherto had justified other concepts, now finds itself in the position of a concept that requires justification.[17]

The "exchange of index symbols" is emphasized because it summarizes the message of the entire passage. God becomes an index symbol, exchanged for truth, morality, law. It is a dramatic shift, yet Ernst Cassirer gives no hint about the size or composition of the group who accepted it as authoritative. He deems it to have been a momentous step for the influential *few*.

In the next century that step produced an epistemological about-face, again for the few. In the words of the literary critic Gerald Bruns,

since the beginning of the 19th century the interpretation of texts or statements has come to rely increasingly upon the separation of meaning and truth as an authorizing principle. "By Bentham," J. Stuart Mill once wrote, "men have been led to ask themselves, in regard to any ancient or received opinion, Is it true? And by Coleridge, what is the meaning of it?" ... This distinction, which ... became the first principle of historicism, was a death blow to the ontological seriousness—one might say the eminence—of the human sciences (not only literature and history but also philosophy and theology).[18]

Obviously, most people reading this statement choose to focus on its *force*. It reverses the traditional way of looking at the world. Yet it is equally important to take into account the *scope* of this statement. Who, if anyone, outside the academy welcomed this rigorous cleavage between meaning and truth, deemed to be authoritative by Coleridge as also by the budding cadre of historicists? Once adopted, it did lead to a widening spectrum of questions about religion, and even to a redefinition of religion in terms of the meaning that it held for its adherents rather than the truth that it claimed to reveal to all humankind. But the loss of influence was not universal; it was limited to those groups within or aligned to Enlightenment circles. Even within the academy, religion was not "dead."

Though theology may have lost its preeminence as an academic pursuit, religion did not cease to be less engaging for those historicists who tried to uncover the multiple mechanisms of human societies. Whether welcoming or fearing the criterion of value neutrality, sociologists and later, anthropologists became spiritual mutes. They systematically disengaged from any but the rationally defensible aspects of their subject. For them and for their successors, "religion is to be treated as a datum (the meaning of which is) to be explained." They removed themselves from "the religious man (who) sees religion as a human experience (the truth of) which needs to be understood in its own terms."[19]

In relating to fundamentalist discourse without accepting its premises or conclusions, we depend on ideology as a medial category. Ideology reflects the modernist mindset to which religion is the corrosive inertia of the past. While most political ideologues have been concerned with meaning rather than truth, a religious ideology conjoins truth with meaning. For this reason alone fundamentalism would be better understood as a religious ideology than as any other form of cognitive, moral, or social patterning.

But there are further reasons why it is useful to identify fundamentalism as a religious ideology. It conforms to a cluster of traits, what Wittgenstein might have called family resemblances. All of them separate fundamentalists both from their modernist opponents and also from their contemporary coreligionists. Five are especially important:

1. Fundamentalists are advocates of a pure minority viewpoint against a sullied majority or dominant group. They are the righteous remnant turned vanguard, and even when the remnant/vanguard seizes political power and seems to become a majority, as happened in Iran in 1979, they continue to perceive and project themselves as a minority.

2. Fundamentalists are oppositional. They do not merely disagree with their enemies, they confront them. While the evil other is an abstract sense of *anomie* or uprootedness, it is located in particular groups who perpetuate the prevailing "secular" ethos. Fundamentalists confront those secular people who exercise political or judicial power. Often they also confront "wayward" religious professionals.

3. Fundamentalists are secondary-level male elites. They claim to derive authority from a direct, unmediated appeal to scripture, yet because interpretive principles are often vague, they must be clarified by charismatic leaders who are invariably male. Notions of a just social order in Iran, or a halakhic polity in Israel, or a Christian civilization in America require continuous, repeated reinterpretation. In each instance what seems to an outsider to be arbitrary retrieval of only some elements from a common past is to fundamentalists the necessary restoration of an eternally valid divine mandate. And it is a mandate mediated through exclusively male interpreters.

4. Fundamentalists generate their own technical vocabulary. Reflecting the polysemy of language,[20] they use special terms that bind insiders to one another, just as they preempt interference from outsiders. *Halakha* for Jews, *sharīʿa* for Muslims, and "creation" for Christians represent three terms, each of which would be open to several interpretations but which fundamentalists invest with a particular meaning that exceptionalizes, even as it appears to validate, their ideological stance.

5. Fundamentalism has historical antecedents, but no ideological precursors. As Marc Bloch warned, one should never confuse ancestry

with explanation. Though the antecedents of fundamentalism are varied and distant—the Maccabean revolt for Jews, the Protestant Reformation for Christians, the Wahhabi revolt for Sunni Muslims, the martyrdom of Husayn for Shi'is—fundamentalism as a religious ideology is very recent. It did not emerge in Protestant America until the end of the last century. It has only become apparent within Judaism during the last fifty years, and since it represents a delayed reaction to the psychological hegemony of European colonial rule, it could only occur in majoritarian Muslim countries after they had become independent nation-states, that is, in most instances, after World War II.

All the above traits will be considered in detail in part two. The last is the sine qua non for our approach to fundamentalism. While other sectarian or separatist movements can be characterized by the initial four traits, about no other religious protest groups could it be said that they originated in direct response to that global pattern of change known as the GWT or modernization. Part two of our study will examine how these five traits cluster in the countertexts that provoked a fundamentalist revolt in several cultural settings: modern day quasi-Hasidim and *haredim* in Israel, Protestant Christians in America, Sunni Muslims in Malaysia, Egypt, and Pakistan as well as Shi'i Muslims in Iran and Southern Lebanon.

Part 2

COUNTERTEXTS

CHAPTER 5

The Living Word from the Eternal God

Thus Abraham said to this father Azar: "Do you accept idols as gods? I see you and your folk are in obvious error." Therefore we showed Abraham sovereignty over Heaven and Earth so he might feel reassured.

When night descended on him, he saw a star. He said: "Will this be my lord?" So when it set, he said: "I do not like setting things."

So then as he saw the moon rising, he said: "Will this be my lord?"; and when it set, he said: "If my Lord did not guide me, I would be a member of the lost folk."

So when he saw the sun rising (again), he said: "Will this be my lord? This is (even) greater." As it set, he said: "My people, I am innocent of what you associate (with God)! I have turned my face inquiringly to Him who originated Heaven and Earth. I am no associator."

—THE QUR'AN; 6:75–79

Out of its inner depths the Jewish people will yet sound the same call that was issued by the rock from which it was hewn (that is, Abraham). Out of its awareness of light and happiness, out of its profound compassion for every afflicted soul, for every confused creature, for the forms of national, social and moral life that proceed on paths full tangling thorns, because of the absence of a source of light to reveal to them that yearning for which the soul of all existence cries out in its pain, it will sound the call: Seek me, search after me, and live.

—ABRAHAM ISAAC KOOK

The God of Abraham praise
Who reigns enthroned above
Ancient of everlasting days
And God of love

—A HYMN

There is no fundamentalist movement apart from its constituent members. Who are these people? Is it Ayatollah Khomeini deriding former President Carter as the Satan of our day? Is it Jerry Falwell seeing enemies of Christ in every liberal legislator who supports legalized abortion and opposes prayer in public schools? Are they *haredim,* Jewish zealots protesting archaeological work undertaken near the ancient Temple site in Jerusalem by other Jews (who are equally zealous, committed Zionists intent on proving the territorial antiquity of Israel)? These images hardly mesh, yet they all come to mind when one asks: who are fundamentalists? They are either religious fanatics, extremists, obscurantists, dangerous men out of kilter with our age and its values, or they are paragons of virtue and defenders of the faith, self-declared renegades from a secular, moral, and pluralistic society.

Yet they may turn out to be something other than either of these two opposite images suggest. Fundamentalism as an aspect of religious history has a more complex series of antecedents than we can understand by looking at current events, whether in today's headlines or on evening news programs.

We can begin to understand the issues raised when we examine the interlocking of language, history, and ideology as the context for fundamentalism. Language presupposes the dyad within which fundamentalism is expressed as opposition to modernism, embodying latent as well as manifest dimensions, and striving for truth through power. A careful survey of Western and world history discloses the ascent of a second axial era, the Technical Age, in which Western origin does not assure Western dominance without numerous interim downturns and subsequent adjustments. Ideology focuses on the importance of interest groups marshaled to action in the public sphere on behalf of their own group and against others.

While we have demonstrated the need to analyze fundamentalism as a religious ideology, we have not examined the defining elements of that ideology from a fundamentalist perspective. Even though ideas alone do not determine patterns of action, the appeal of certain ideas requires us to reflect on their catalytic potential. The foundational idea for fundamentalists is monotheism, and monotheism requires attachment to the ultimate paradox, a divine being at once transcendent and unknowable yet omnipresent and all-knowing. The impetus for fundamentalism is shared by the three major monotheistic traditions of Western civilization: Judaism, Christianity, and Islam. From a purely doctrinal reading, every fundamentalist is a monotheist . . . and vice versa. As John R. W. Stott, the Anglican prelate, once intimated, "every individual Christian is a fundamentalist."[1] For to be a believer in any branch of monotheism, whether Jewish, Christian, or Muslim, whether one worships in a synagogue, a church, or a mosque, is to express a kind of prerational (magical, superstitious) thinking that would be labeled "fundamentalist" *from a modernist perspective.*

In part one we have noted that fundamentalism came into being, and continues to exist, only because of modernism. The French Revolution disenfranchised Catholicism as the state church of France, while Enlightenment philosophers and their successors repeatedly called into question the very idea of God. That double attack fueled the fundamentalist response: to protect and defend God from the multiple assaults of his enemies. All were moderns but not all were modernists. Because other monotheists had surrendered, either outright or by compromise, their priceless, premodernist legacy, fundamentalists were left as the last defenders of the fortress of faith. They were not defending simply themselves, or the church (synagogue, mosque) or scripture (Bible, Torah, Qur'an). They were defending GOD.

Conceived simply as an *idea,* the notion of God is arguably the most powerful abstraction that has ever been formulated. Its power derives from its abstraction, its nonrelation to the self-evident human experience of the material world. There are no proofs, no methods of verifying or denying, testing or refuting the existence of *God,* whether defined as Being, Presence, or Force. And in monotheism the notion of one God becomes an abstraction aggregated, that is, all the attributes and potentialities that have been linked to multiple "Others" are conjoined and imputed to this One. Transcendent, he cannot be called down, Immutable, he is beyond shifting human fashions. He is the Ultimate Unaccountable.

If one continues to apply modernist logic, looking at structure rather than theology, monotheism derives its extraordinary appeal from a two-stepped interlocking assumption that relates the most abstract to the most concrete. Participants in each monotheistic tradition are convinced that there is but One Other who combines in himself all that human beings are not but would like to be: immortal, all-wise, all-powerful (as well as a few things they could never imagine being: self-creating, invisible, patient). At the same time they are convinced that the Other is related to that which is most immediate, particular, and valuable for them. The wholly distant becomes the concretely immediate. For monotheists, it is less important how the two elements are brought together than to underscore the benefits of their concurrence. Making the abstract concrete and beneficial is also, of course, the pattern intrinsic to every ideology, and in that sense monotheism becomes not only the basis for all ideologies[2] but also itself the model ideology. Each monotheistic community always advocates the part against the whole, framing one group's self-interests as beneficial for all humankind. There are no testable universal givens, only mandated universalist norms.

If fundamentalism is a religious ideology, then it is only a limited case instance of that ideology common to all monotheism. To look at fundamentalism without understanding monotheism is like taking a picture of waves and imagining that you have captured the turbulence of the ocean. Fundamentalism projects itself as wave and light, fire and sword, but its source is monotheism. The source needs to be scanned before noting its downstream results. It has a threefold basis:

1. That there exists a unique, omniscient, omnipotent, beneficent yet zealous and jealous and, above all, personal Being. "Say: He, God,

is One; Eternal; not begotten nor begetting; there is none like Him" (Qur'an 112). "The Lord sits enthroned above the flood; the Lord sits enthroned as King for evermore. The Lord shall give strength to his people; the Lord shall give his people the blessing of peace" (PSALM 29:10–11).

2. That the same One created universes infinite in number and expanse, as also this universe, the heavens and earth, together with all life, not least human life, making it discernible (but only in part) through the finite intellect. "When I consider your heavens, the work of your fingers, the moon and the stars you have set in their courses, What is man that you should be mindful of him? The son of man that you should seek him out?" (Psalm 8:4–5). "God! There is no deity except Him, the Living, the Eternal! Slumber does not overtake Him, nor does sleep. What the Heavens and what Earth holds [belongs] to him. Who is there to intercede with Him except by His permission? He knows what lies before them and what's behind them, while they embrace nothing of His knowledge except whatever He may wish. His Seat extends far above Heaven and Earth; preserving them both does not overburden Him. He is the Sublime, the Almighty!" (QUR'AN 2:255–56).

3. That the same One is further capable of expressing, and chooses to express, his eternal will through particular persons (prophets such as Moses, Jesus, and Muhammad) in particular places (Mt. Sinai, Jerusalem, Mecca) at particular moments in history (Moses, ca. 1300 B.C.; Jesus, ca. A.D. 25; Muhammad, A.D. 612). "We have sent messengers before you, some of whom We have told you about, while We have not told you about others. No messenger may bring any sign unless it is with God's permission. Once God's command comes, (matters) will be decided correctly, and that is where the quibblers will lose out!" (Qur'an 24:78). "For our knowledge is imperfect and our prophecy is imperfect, but when the perfect comes, the imperfect will pass away" (1 CORINTHIANS 13:9).

These elements could not be sustained and developed, however, except for the prescriptive function that writing plays in the symbol production of each monotheistic tradition. ("We gave Moses the Book and followed him up with messengers later on. We gave Jesus the son of Mary evidence and assisted him with the Holy Spirit" [Qur'an 2:87].) The content of prophetic revelations becomes effective by being recorded in writing, not only recorded but canonically fixed, safeguarded, transmitted, and obeyed. Hence, the Torah, the Gospels, and the Qur'an are prescriptive documents; though they can be viewed as primarily literary specimens,[3] their major role is institutional to elicit solidarity within the "believing" community and to define boundaries against outsiders. The attitude to scripture is reverential not only because of what it says but because of what it does. For believers, their community identity is vouchsafed by the authenticity attributed to their original scripture. Their loyalty as individual believers is measured by their corporate assent to precepts set forth within the canon. The canon looms as the fixed measure and the standard of all revealed truth.

Yet that seeming rigidity of monotheism is also the key to its internal dynamic for change. Though the outer limits of canon are fixed, within the self-selected "revealed" texts of canon there are always ambiguous or ambivalent elements. They can either be ignored or, more likely, explained through the appeal to interpreters whose authority in judging the meaning and application of canon is accepted as superior to that of "ordinary" believers.

Scripture is enacted and reinforced through ritual, especially in the singing of music and the recitation of formulaic prayers or creeds. The leitmotivs of monotheism may be summarized in a pastiche of different creeds that reflects what monotheists hold in common:

I/we believe in one God, the Father Almighty, Maker of Heaven and Earth.

I/we believe in the agency of prophets as purveyors of the divine will and human exemplars for true believers.

I/we believe in a moment of reckoning at the end of time; and in a community that will be confirmed by the One who reckons.

I/we believe in the authority of scripture as the locus of what is most needed and eternally relevant to address the human condition in this world and the next.

The creed should sound familiar to most readers. It is a terse but systematic way of saying that all monotheists are not only fundamentalists but also creationists, i.e., they accept God as the creator of every speck of finite matter, from the grains of sand to the outermost moons of Uranus and beyond. They also acknowledge prophetic insight, discontinuous time, and scriptural supremacy. This influences the way they define themselves, the way they act as communities, and the way they relate to the rest of the world outside their communities.

The theological intent of monotheism is at once consistent and ambiguous. Jews, Christians, and Muslims believe in a universal God with exclusive designs. He acts in history but selectively, through a special set of agents randomly commissioned among groups (families, tribes, nations) that are seldom eager to be singled out, at least initially. Each divinely guided agent entrusts to his people a unique set of writings, a holy book, even though the canonical form of scripture is seldom fixed until after, sometimes long after, the prophet's death.

This pattern of enactment and belief characterizes all monotheists, whether Jewish, Christian, or Muslim. It sets forth a hopeful view of human existence. Life is imbued with meaning, a meaning commensurate with the message of the community's scripture. And so a system of reference, characterizing and reinforcing "the Judaic-Hellenistic canon," is set in motion. One can know God's will only through appeal to scripture. Through scripture the One God declares His purpose for the present. Through scripture He also provides directions for the future. But He does so indirectly, *not* directly, by calling the attention of the faithful reader-listener to what he has done in the past through prophets of old. What transpired on Mount Sinai ca. 1300 B.C., with the giving of the Torah to Moses, on the way to Calvary in A.D. 27, with the dying and returning of Jesus, as also at Mount Hira outside Mecca in A.D. 612, with the near choking of Muhammad by the Archangel Gabriel—all these events changed the way that some humans (Jews, Christians, and Muslims, respectively) thought about life in this world and went about the business of living. The One God had acted; his believers responded.

There are numerous ways of refining and defining this common monotheistic outlook. Some have called it scriptural, conservative, orthodox, nostalgic, even atavistic, but at the least it means that no one who is a believer in the God of Moses, Jesus, and Muhammad can disassociate herself or himself from an orientation to the past that infuses it with a unique authority. How can there be any future hope unrelated to that first hope? For it was in the past, not the present or the future, that there occurred the decisive revelatory event—what German theologians are fond of calling *lichtungsgeschichte,* the history of erupting light[4]—which dispelled the darkness of paganism, idolatry, and unbelief, setting the pattern of belief and action for those able to hear, to see, and to respond.

To the extent that monotheism is a shared perception of what life finally means, all believers in the God of Abraham are conservatives, wanting to preserve their memory of the past, just as all are fundamentalists, staking their faith on basic, unalterable assumptions about the universe, its nature, its inhabitants. Continuity, *not* change, is their motto. Tangible witness to what they believe may result in solitary meditation, or more likely, membership in religious institutions (church, synagogue, or mosque). It may induce creative silence, but more often, it impels periodic participation in ritual acts of remembrance, and weekend congregational services, whether they convene on Friday, Saturday, or Sunday.

But tangible witness to a living God also involves more. It fosters the desire to impose universalist norms on society as a whole. The notion that faith could and should be primarily a private matter emerged late in the annals of Christianity, as a consequence of the Protestant Reformation, with an assist from the French Revolution. For monotheists the notion of a universal God may have been abstracted from concrete, empirical reality, but the custodians of his Word forged and maintained institutions consecrated to his worship. Through believing men and women and their monuments, the divine dicta extended into all aspects of day-to-day life. How else could the Eternal One be omnipresent, the Omnipotent effective, the Living recognized?

By even the most secular reading of the religious past, Jews, Christians, and Muslims share an interlocking history, they comprise one group among the families of humankind. They agree on more than they disagree. They share articles of faith about God, prophethood, scripture, and the final judgment, even though to outsiders these same articles of faith may sound quaint, comical, or downright offensive. They accept the authority of the past. They support institutional religion and participate in ritual observance. They advocate the value of collective, public morality. They are people of conscience, vision, and hope. They are God's people.

The thrust of theology and scriptural narrative is to emphasize the potential nourishment that is to be derived from the original wellspring of monotheism. The dialogic hypothesis alleges that once Jews, Christians, and Muslims reexamine the roots of their common faith, then they will recognize that they jointly share equal, viable, and valuable membership in a common family. Reaffirming their true origins as a deeper bond of identity, they will end the protracted family quarrel which has caused so much bitterness, feuding, and actual bloodshed over centuries.

This argument—let us call it "ecumenical" for that is its intent—runs directly opposite to the fundamentalist claim. The ecumenist believes that one becomes more universalist by surrendering particularist claims; the fundamentalist believes that one sustains universalism only by asserting and reasserting the divinely sanctioned particularity that separates not only Christian from Jew from Muslim, but certain Christians from all others, certain Jews from other Jews, and the Muslim elect from unbelievers with Muslim names. Fundamentalism subscribes to an ideology of double election. Having been born a Christian, Jew, or Muslim one must reclaim that identity, while ecumenism believes that election exceeds community boundaries and can only be realized through the larger rather than the smaller community of believers.

The ecumenical urge has prompted recent efforts to revive cross-creedal dialogue and to locate it as the basis for spiritual affirmation beyond the constraints of any one monotheistic tradition. But do dialogue advocates resolve the universalist/particularist dilemma with compelling clarity? Do they have the possibility of marshaling a consensus among those for whom they speak, whether Christians, Muslims, or Jews? A brief review of two Christian spokesmen will illustrate both the difficulty of their position and its controvertibility into an interpretation of scripture favored by fundamentalists.

In *The Sons of Abraham*, James Kritzeck, the Roman Catholic Arabist, has provided a brief but brilliant essay on the tenor of monotheism.

Kritzeck tries to launch an irenic future from a close reading of the monotheistic past as set forth in its scriptural legacy. The locus of hope is Abraham, the patriarch of faith for Jews, Christians, and Muslims. In the Torah, he is the first of those who worship one God, not hesitating even to sacrifice his only legitimate son to the God who demands his blood (Genesis 22). In the New Testament, Abraham became, for the apostle Paul, the symbol of faith triumphant. Appearing prior to the Mosaic law, he transcended that law in the name of a higher law, the law of love validated in the last days by the blood of Christ poured out on a cross for errant humankind (Galatians 3). In the Qur'an, Abraham also looms large. He is the first true believer in one God. He is the rebel son who disowns not only his polytheist father, Azar, but also all the galactic idols of his family faith (the sun, the moon, the stars), embracing in their stead faith in the One beyond heavens and earth who yet created, sustains, and will ultimately judge both the heavens and the earth, the living and the dead (Qur'an 6:75–79).

Allegiance to Abraham is a common bond unique to monotheists. It seals them together in a sequential lineage of prophethood. They are pledged to a referent that supersedes race (Abraham was not Jewish), language (he did not speak Hebrew), and national hubris (his offspring are said to inhabit many nations). Should not Jews, Christians, and Muslims then enjoy a special discourse with one another? Should they not be able to work together for common goals as Abrahamic believers?

Kritzeck's vision is grounded in an expansive yet wary reading of scripture. As he notes in his conclusion, history has been unkind to the "sons of Abraham." The family has never coalesced, the metaphor has not been transformed into reality:

Moslems, Christians and Jews of any level of spiritual and intellectual attainment should be able to speak with one another more easily and with more fecundity than with others. Are they not all, in a special and sacred way, brothers? Is not Abraham the father of them all?

The Abrahamic symbol has been more fruitful in the minds of some monotheistic thinkers than in the shared experience of monotheistic communities. In spite of the common legacy of their religious faiths and the long and otherwise fruitful cultural interaction among them, there has never been a genuinely productive dialogue among the three.[5]

Kritzeck's despair is deflected by a prominent Protestant theologian. Writing in the aftermath of the 1979 Iranian Revolution, Harvey Cox finesses the historical primacy of Judaism and focuses instead on the thematic congruence of Christianity and Islam. He is certain that they are "much closer in history and doctrine than we might think." Why? Because Muhammad "believed he was living proof that the God who called and used previous prophets such as Abraham and Job, neither of whom was Jewish, could do the same thing again." In addition to the link through Abraham, they share similar rituals—profession of faith, fasting, alms, prayer, and pilgrimage. To strengthen their multiple bonds of belief and also make explicit their core example, Cox stresses the centrality of Jesus in Qur'anic revelation. Cox does not exclude Jews altogether: they could have a beneficial role as mediators, defusing rival truth-claims and "fostering conversation between Muslims and Christians." Yet the greatest hope, in his view, would derive from a mutual recognition of common origins among the two numerically largest communities of monotheistic belief, for did not Islam and Christianity begin with a shared vision of deliverance through hope in the ultimately triumphant justice of the one true God? Cox tries to make Islam palatable to Christian exponents of social justice, recasting Muhammad as defender of the poor, the ostracized, the adrift, the malcontent. Read in this light, the actual history of Islamic expansion and empirebuilding becomes "a kind of liberation theology gone astray."[6]

But this approach raises more problems than it solves. The exclusion or demotion of Jews undercuts the theological basis for dialogue, while the liberationist gloss falsifies it historically. Cox's recasting of dialogic variables is finally less hopeful than Kritzeck's, despite its pastiche of references to scripture, history, and contemporary politics.

The real problem with both approaches lies at a deeper level. By straining to find points in common between monotheists, they minimize the significance of conflicts that are at once theological and historical. What Jews, Christians, and Muslims hold in common is also what keeps them apart. All the points in favor of monotheistic collaboration and ecumenical harmony can too easily be reversed.

Abraham is the most tantalizing symbol of convergence because he seems to be the springboard for a chimera of hope beyond the present impasse. Other issues are often cited to indicate the chasm between Jews, Christians, and Muslims—the Christian claim of divine incarnation, offensive to Muslims and Jews alike, or the Jewish and Muslim emphasis on religious law (*halakha* and *shari'a*), for which there is no Christian counterpart. But Abraham and his offspring are the leitmotiv signaling the spectrum of insurmountable differences. Genesis 22 seems like a clear, unequivocal account of Abraham's commitment to God even at the expense of his own genealogical self-interest. Isaac is his only son. He will sacrifice him to God. He will forego the transmission of his name, his family, his worth to future generations. However, in supplementary Muslim scripture (*hadith*), the son about to be sacrificed often becomes Ishmael, *not* Isaac. The "alternate son" tradition is reinforced by cultic lore surrounding the Dome of the Rock in Jerusalem: for Muslim pilgrims to the Holy City, it was Ishmael rather than Isaac who was almost killed by their fiercely monotheistic father on that rock—which ranks second only to the Ka'aba in Mecca for its importance in Islamic ritual observance.[7] The tension implicit in the Jerusalem rock is confirmed by several Qur'anic passages (for example, 2:135, 16:120–24, 60:4) that signal Abraham as the point of pride for Muslims against both Jews and Christians.

Abraham, though a common symbol, is a different reality for Jews, Christians, and Muslims. There does not seem to exist a common ground of symbolic unity beyond the multiple interpretations, both literary and cultic, in stone and on paper, that monotheists project about the first patriarch.

The problem with Abraham also signifies the issues that fundamentalism raises as an outgrowth of monotheism in the modern context. It can be paraphrased as a subset of the universalism/particularism construct discussed in part one. All groups see what is particular to them as instrumental, and hence subordinate, to what is universal in their corporate identity. Yet they never disavow the need to particularize, that is, to delineate their faith assumptions in ways that do not allow all persons to be viewed as conscious, voluntary members of their community (except through conversion). Both the universalist and the particularist tendencies coexist in every monotheistic community. They complement but also compete with one another. The artifacts of scripture, liturgy, and history that emphasize continuous competition provide the ideological fuel for fundamentalists. Fundamentalists insist on choice but also action. "All should proclaim *our* version of the faith; why don't they? All should be uncompromising with evil; why aren't they?" No believer is exempt from the battle for truth. All are God's soldiers or His enemies. Every living creature owes his or her existence to the Creator, yet only some have a special, an elected, a "saving" role in His creation. It is the elect who are called as members of the communities that God has set apart by historical acts, prophetic delegates, and enduring scriptures. It is they who are empowered and required collectively to do great and mighty deeds.

It can be argued that fundamentalism is at one with the modernist tendency to interpret all distinctions as oppositional antipodes, irresolvable dichotomies. We have discussed Abraham. He is a symbol in scripture. He is, however, but one of numerous symbols. Scripture contains a collage of symbols. In reading scripture, we have to recognize that a pattern of symbols or ciphers exists, that they yield different results depending on the interpretive principles applied to discern their meaning. The endeavor to wrench meaning from symbols is called the science of interpretation or hermeneutics.

From the viewpoint of ideology, the differences sort out according to immediate, tangible group interests. All branches of monotheism are characterized by an appeal to God-prophet-book. That general system yields insight into specific groups only when we consider them separately and recognize their axial priorities or primary thought fields. Even if Steiner is correct that a characteristic worldview or culture pattern dominates Western elites,[8] it is a profile grooved with deep incisions, compartmentalizing each space from its neighbor. For Jews, it is the distinctiveness of a people, for Christians the uniqueness of a man, for Muslims the inerrancy of a book. All are abstractions, all disguise an aggregation that subsumes several concrete elements and formative precedents. It is twelve tribes who coalesce to become the people of Israel. It is the prophetic history of Israel that prepares for the man-God, and it is earlier prophetic testimonies that anticipate the final, complete Book given to Muhammad. Only when these denotative characteristics have been sorted out does it then become possible to interpret the malleability of symbols as devices for confirming and projecting specific group interests.

Monotheism appears to differ from all other religious outlooks because it encodes a sequential emphasis on one God, many prophets, a revealed book, and a community set apart and "saved." How these elements interrelate depends not on the pool of aggregate terms of overlapping referents but rather on the defining construct peculiar to each. For Judaism, it is God and his people; for Christianity, God and his son; for Islam God and his book. All monotheists are defenders of God, but are they defending the same God? For in each case, that which is most abstract is conjoined with that which is most particular. It is not one or the other, it is both together that define the prescriptive outlook for each. It is too simplistic to say, as Durkheim once did, that the deity is society transfigured and symbolically expressed. It is rather the interplay of the notion of God (real or imagined) with the variables of society that transforms the latter.

We have been careful in part one to distinguish latent from manifest, what is implicit from what is explicit. It must be stressed that there is always a difference between implicit, unconscious mediation of values, and explicit, conscious ranking of symbols and terms. The part of monotheism that is given in scriptures is only the manifest. Even the so-called higher criticism limits itself to words, and in that sense it can be said that all biblical criticism fosters fundamentalism because it pays attention to tracking the text, whether through lower or higher criticism. It is the Gadamerian sense of the text, the text as suspended from its authorship and speaking on its own, that needs constant reaffirmation.[9] Behind the words of scripture lie human interests. Whether scripture is inspired by God or not becomes less relevant for historians than how its words are interpreted by human beings. The crucial question to ask is: how did any ascriptive agent, whether God or blind fate, shape the constellation of interests that produced constructs of such pervasive power?

In every instance, social mores reflect the communication of truth through power, and the interfaced polarities that characterize each branch of monotheism also extend to the next level of what is prioritized for each. Scripture may be the highest explicit authority, but it is always cited to advance a principle that supersedes, even while acknowledging, scriptural authority. If Judaism is the construct of God and people, then what matters most is the delineation of group, ethnic, or national identity, and that comes through statutory laws. Scripture defines law, but the law takes on an autonomous expression as the sum total of what scripture is really all about. The *mitzvoth* have scriptural antecedents but enjoy their own juridical authority apart from different readings of the Torah. In the case of Christianity, the determinative construct is God and one man, and the purpose of scripture is to clarify the ways in which that man, Jesus of Nazareth, can be interpreted as the Messiah of Jewish eschatological-apocalyptic expectation. The preoccupation of Christianity is double: to explain one man as uniquely God, but also to express the universal God as a single Jew, an itinerant Palestinian rebel rabbi of the first century A.D. Following Jewish precedent, all scripture is deemed as authoritative, although in fact its usage is limited to those passages that anticipate or seem to confirm the distinctly Christian wrestling with the man-God issue. Law is reduced to an ancillary, dispensable role. For Muslims, by contrast, the construct is God and a book. Therefore the need is to trace all prior revelations as an anticipation of this revelation, all prophets as predecessors to this prophet. As in Judaism, law is also an outgrowth of preoccupation with the book. In some respects, the *shari'a* or Muslim law does resemble Jewish law (*halakha*) yet it also differs by positing the book as an open invitation to all humankind, not the confirmation of a limited number of tribes or a nation that represents an expansion of tribal identity. Although the Arabic Qur'an is functionally closed to non-Arabs, theologically it is open, membership in Islam being accessible to all who learn Arabic, or at the least memorize and recite certain passages in Arabic from the Book.

If we pursue the twin linguistic principles of aggregation and referentiality, it becomes clear how all three branches of monotheism converge in what they aggregate and at the same time differ in what they presume as authoritative referents. To distinguish monotheists in this manner, by specifying constructs and the personality traits or expected actions that emerge out of those constructs, is different than the relativist approach. That difference needs to be stressed, and it becomes clear as soon as one examines the relativist interpretation of monotheism.

For the relativist, if one cannot prove the existence or absence of God, one also cannot confirm the superiority of one theistic tradition over another. All prophets are equally right, all are equally wrong. All scriptures are true, and also false. All religious communities are sincere and, at the same time, hypocritical. Since none can be evaluated or ranked with reference to others, they are equivalent to any monotheistic, or atheistic, belief system. What matters is a community's self-definition. Once the boundaries are drawn, then each monotheistic tradition becomes as separate from other monotheists as from idolaters. Monotheists ipso facto have no more in common with one another than they do with those whom they oppose as idolaters, heretics, nonbelievers.

That is the relativist argument. It is explicitly the basis of the separation between church and state in the USA and also in other countries where a constitution authorizes the pluralistic expression of religious loyalty. It is also implicitly upheld in polities that advocate a state-supported religion yet do not tolerate any expression of religious beliefs or religiously motivated activity that does not support the group interests of the ruling elite. When religious dissent is treated as political treason, it is not monotheism but authoritarianism that is practiced.

Our view differs from relativism because we stress the interaction of monotheistic belief with group self-interest, and we evaluate that interaction as purposeful and effective. The resulting profile defines Jews, Christians, and Muslims in ways that differentiate them from one another but also lend strength to their individual claims to project a universalist impulse. One cannot ignore, as relativists tend to do, the catalytic force of religion, especially its role in nurturing social cohesion.

Despite the fact that each monotheistic tradition is molded by its adherents' attention to certain core elements, the process is unconscious for most. It does not directly concern either leaders or followers. Yet for fundamentalists, the process is externalized. It is made both conscious and compelling. While fundamentalism emerges only within limited segments of each monotheistic community, its members are intent on assessing the irreducible core elements of faith, belief, and tradition and defending them against *all* others.

Fundamentalists go beyond the rivalry that sets Jew against Christian against Muslim. To be corporate vehicles created, chosen, directed, and saved by the One, fundamentalists are intensely opposed to *all* "others" in their midst: Jews to other Jews, Christians to other Christians, Muslims to other Muslims. To understand the motivation for intracreedal rivalry, often exceeding in intensity the hostility directed to outsider others, we need to look at sectarianism.

Sectarian impulses, actions, and outcomes are endemic to monotheism. All too often the discussion of cross-creedal or interreligious strife obscures the reality of intrareligious, sectarian strife. Almost all popular commentary on religious groups is afflicted with an inflated use of aggregation bordering on what Owen Chadwick calls "stereotyping."[10] Jews, Christians, and Muslims are described as though it were self-evident what each represented. To the outsider that distinctive identity may be clear. Yet to the insider, the observant, committed follower of Moses, Jesus, or Muhammad, the creedal or liturgical marks of identity which would be universally accepted throughout his or her community are moot. Each is subject to reinterpretation, eliciting debate and even acrimony. The ability of individual believers to assert variant views and draw others into their circle is limitless. And conflict between believers inevitably results. Just as fanaticism has become the code word for describing fierce opposition between groups on the basis of religious belief, so sectarianism has come to have the same negative connotation when applied to strife among members of the same group on the basis of conflicting religious belief.

Sectarianism is, above all, a generational phenomenon. It derives from the impulse of each community to survive, to sustain, and therefore to institutionalize its belief system beyond the lifetime of the founding figure. In its initial stages, sectarianism derives precisely from the difficulty of institutionalizing the charisma of the prophet/leader/founder in successive generations after his death. The significance of his death is augmented by the death of those who first accepted his message, acknowledged his spiritual authority, and became his intimate followers. The cumulative loss of not only the leader but also his early followers weakens the initial bonds of group solidarity at the same time that it fosters the emergence of a distinctive communal identity.

At each stage in the history of Judaism, Christianity, and Islam sectarian strife derived from the construct identified as peculiar to each community. Among Jews the riveting context for defining consensus was corporate loyalty to the true Israel. But what was the true Israel? According to the Torah, it was a creed linked to a race: the covenant of faith forged by a dislocated, persecuted minority (the Diaspora) bound to one another through tribal associations traceable to the patriarch Jacob. Only secondarily was it territorial, spurred by warfare with neighbors over a disputed homeland, *Eretz Yisrael*, the land of Israel. Hence Jewish sectarianism derived from interpretation of the law. It focused on reflection about the nature of the *mitzvoth* because their collective primacy was presumed.

For Christians, the compelling consensus was individual loyalty to the extended body of Christ, the church of true believers who were to proclaim Jesus of Nazareth as the Risen Lord and apply his moral injunctions to their lives. True belief for Christians was kerygmatic as well as ethical. In both dimensions it rested on a scriptural foundation. But who was to interpret the double mandate? The process of canonization and creedal conformity could not have succeeded without the authorizing instrumentality of the Roman Empire (after A.D. 323). Truth was enforced through power; corporate hierarchy favored conformity rather than efforts at creative reinterpretation of scripture. The Reformation, insofar as it appealed directly to the individual believer, seemed to return him or her to center stage, yet the inescapable context for professing the faith remained a community of like-minded believers,[11] and so Christian sectarianism flourished in the aftermath of the Reformation.

For Muslims, by contrast, the first yardstick of loyalty has always been the community bound by a book and by custom (*sunna* of the Prophet). The centrality of the Book was above dispute. It defined individual and corporate identity. Prayer, like pilgrimage, was oriented to a rock in Mecca (the Ka'aba) and secondarily, to a rock in Jerusalem (the Dome of the Rock). All rules governing behavior were also defined in writing by a corpus of juridical decisions. Based on Qur'an and *hadith*, it was known as *shari'a*. Loyalty to its mandates was corporate. Most Muslims are better labeled Jama'i-Sunnis instead of simply Sunnis, since the prefix *jama'i*, familiar to all Muslims yet unknown to most others, connotes "community." Sunni Muslims are Muslims who share a sense of community across ethnic, regional, and cultural divisions. Similarly, those who dissent from the consensus code of Jama'i-Sunnis comprise a separate or Shi'i community. They are not a sect but an independent stratum of Muslim orthodoxy. Differences among Shi'i Muslims result in the formation of other divisions best labeled as sects. These are the Zaydis, Isma'ilis and Ja'faris. Often known after the last numbered Imam, or religious teacher, to whom each group accords ultimate authority, they are called Fivers, Seveners, and Twelvers, respectively.[12] Ithna 'ashari or Twelver Shi'ism will be our main concern in this study.

While sectarianism does not explain fundamentalism, its persistent recurrence in each of the monotheistic traditions provides the institutional setting without which fundamentalism could not have arisen in the twentieth century. The next three chapters examine the particular forms which fundamentalist sectaries have assumed in Judaism, Christianity, and Islam.

CHAPTER 6

Fundamentalists in Defense of the Jewish Collectivity

The Talmud says that the acts of the *zaddikim* are greater than the acts of creation of Heaven and earth. The meaning is that the act of creation involved the emergence of something out of Nothing, whereas the acts of the *zaddikim* involve the turning of something into Nothing. For in whatever they do, even if it be a physical thing like eating or drinking, they raise on high the holy sparks in that food and so in all that they do they convert something into Nothing.

—DOV BAER, THE MAGGID OF MESERITCH

The relationship of Judaism to fundamentalism is crucial for both Judaism and fundamentalism. For Judaism it provides the lens through which one can glimpse the struggle to assert the sharpest profile of Jewish identity in the modern world. For fundamentalism it offers the necessary third dimension of a religious protest against modernism conceived and sustained with reference to monotheistic loyalties. How do Jewish zealots relate to Muslim and Christian counterparts? The presumption is that Judaism, Islam, and Christianity can be correlated at the level of monotheistic belief, as we indicated in the previous chapter. Beyond that apparent convergence, one must draw attention to the fact that Judaism is more intensely related to practice, right practice, or orthopraxis, while Christianity stresses the notion of right belief or orthodoxy. If Jews are more prone to ask one another: "what do you do?" Christians are more more likely to demand: "what do you believe?" The contrast between the two outlooks makes it even more difficult to comprehend what the term "ultraorthodox" means in a Jewish context, as we will see below. Preliminarily, however, one can cite Islam as straddling the polar dispositions of Judaism and Christianity. While some observers are fond of pointing out that Islam, like Judaism, stresses orthopraxis, the concept of orthodoxy also looms large in the discourses of modernist as well as fundamentalist Muslims: for those engaged by Islamic symbols and rites, it is not only what you do but why you do it that matters.

Jewish zealots relate to both their Muslim and Christian counterparts. All three are inescapably shaped by their response to that global pattern of change that we, following Marshall Hodgson, identify as the Great Western Transmutation. To the extent that there is a distinctly Jewish reaction to modernity traceable through some segments of European Jewry during the past century, its complex elaboration within present-day Israel may be appropriately termed fundamentalist.

Every expression of fundamentalism, whether it be Jewish, Christian, or Muslim, whether it originates in the first or third world, has a double emphasis: the collective good above individual choice, and advocacy of one interpretation of the collective good against all others, especially all inside others. To the recurring question, Are there any absolutes in a changing world? fundamentalists respond with a triumphant "Yes!" Their "yes" always pits believers against believers. The level of bitterest conflict focuses on the authority, which is also the responsibility, for actualizing the collective good of the community.

The clearest initial contrast is between Muslim and Jewish fundamentalists, since in the case of Protestant Christianity, as we will see, a public ethos that requires collective assent did not emerge till the late Agrarianate Age, concomitant with the Reformation. Judaism and Islam contrast precisely because representatives for both have long asserted, and continue to assert, the priority of communitarian goals over individual rights. Among both Sunni and Shi'i Muslims, the battle is waged in the political arena. Fundamentalists require an Islamic state since the collective good of Muslims can only be realized through conformity to the *shari'a*, and only an Islamic state can fulfill the demands of a religious society by upholding the high standard of *shari'a* loyalty. Jewish fundamentalists, on the other hand, do not idealize the state. Unlike their Muslim counterparts, they are at best ambivalent, at worst hostile to the Zionist state. They challenge the government of Israel because of its pretensions: after centuries of Diaspora existence, it claims to be a polity representing Jewish aspirations for return to the Holy Land. The claim is as extraordinary as it is threatening to Jewish fundamentalists. While most attach importance to the notion of a Jewish state, such a state, in their view, can function only as a messianic reality. What is most required to prepare for and hasten the coming of the Messiah is strict adherence to Jewish laws, the cherished *mitzvoth*. If the state of Israel claims to be, even implicitly, the longed for Jewish Commonwealth, it preempts the messianic timetable. The *mitzvoth* would have to be suspended, their performance rendered nugatory. Such a perceptual dilemma cloys the imagination of Jewish fundamentalists. Their opposition to the implicit messianic function of the state of Israel makes it unlikely that Israelis will ever achieve consensus on the meaning of the Third Commonwealth as a *Jewish* state. While tacitly accepting the state's instrumental function, to maintain public order and to ward off external aggression, the most observant Jews publicly contend with others about the appropriate strategies for promoting that collectivity known as the people of Israel.

The oft told story of Judaism in the twentieth century pits the Jewish people against a host of inimical forces: European anti-Semitism leading up to but not exhausted by the Holocaust, the Palestinian resistance to the Zionist movement and since 1948, the further isolation of Israel from its hostile Arab neighbors. Those are the headline stories. They ignore the other story of Jewish resistance to assimilation and secularization. That resistance has issued in conflict. It has become an internal struggle. It does not pit Jews against the outside world but Jews against other Jews. It is a fight for the soul of Judaism. It is a fight to prove that Jews are not merely a special race with a piece of territory but a divine instrument with a universal mission.

The chasm is invisible to most because non-Israelis, even non-Israeli Jews, do not readily identify with this struggle as their struggle. It is an ideological struggle between those who defend the right of Israel to exist as a modern-day nation-state and those others who question the meaning of its existence. So much has been at stake in the former issue during the last forty years that the latter issue has seemed to pale in comparison. Those groups labeled extremist, or better, fundamentalists, focus exclusively on the question of Jewish identity and its consequences: Who is a Jew? What does it mean to be a Jew? What should a Jew do as a Jew? Others may raise the same questions but relate them to cultural, ethnic, or social concerns. For fundamentalists, the questions demand repeated asking on their own terms. They demand to be raised not for the existential well-being of the individual but for the long range ·good of the collectivity.

Were a political *modus vivendi* to be struck between Zion and its neighbors, public interest, stoked by fundamentalist passion, might move these questions of identity from offstage to center stage. Even in the absence of a diplomatic truce reducing external tensions, they may dominate the next phase of Israel's history as much as the right to exist as a state has dominated its first phase.

And those who can best be described as Jewish fundamentalists have already staked out their claim on one criterion. It is a single, encompassing canon of Jewish identity. To be a Jew means three things:

(1) living by the commandments of the Torah [the *mitzvoth*], but also
(2) obeying the directives of the sages who have been ordained to determine the *halakha*, and
(3) believing in the truth of everything that the Torah teaches according to the interpretation of scholars whose greatness in *halakha* also invests them with superiority in this area.[1]

Many would argue that it is possible to cast off the yoke of Jewish law and still be Jewish. After all, there is patriotic identity as part of a Jewish nation-state, modern Israel; outside Israel, there is cultural identity as part of a Jewish community wherever one happens to be in the Diaspora, no matter what the dominant culture. Yet for those who maintain that Jewishness is defined not by genetic code or familial memory but rather by observance of canonical commandments, all nonobservant Jews become apostates. One Jewish fundamentalist has gone so far as to declare there is "no difference between red apostasy and blue apostasy, between apostasy with a cross (converting to Christianity) and apostasy without a cross (becoming a secular Jew)."[2]

Almost all Jews living outside of Israel, and the majority within Israel, would be offended by such a narrow definition of Jewish identity. It is for this reason that groups advocating such views have been called "extremists" or "ultraorthodox" or, even occasionally before now, "fundamentalists."[3] The difficulty of evaluating them by hurling invectives or heaping up defamatory stereotypes becomes clear when one examines the linchpin of the system, that is, the personal force of the exemplars who embody the *mitzvoth* and withstand the challenges of the Enlightenment. At stake is the larger issue: who will ultimately succeed? Will it be those Jews who have survived the adversity of the contemporary world by adopting the Enlightenment mentality in general and the nation-state in particular, forging new institutions while also accommodating to new values? Or will it be those other claimants to Jewish authenticity who embrace the premodern concept of collectivity, who locate it in adherence to all the *mitzvoth* without compromise, even to the point of disallowing secular education and secular vocations, while also challenging other Jews either to follow that discipline or else forfeit their claim to participate in the millennia-old drama known as Judaism?

It is at base a battle of absolutes, universals couched as ideological appeals to particular interest groups. On the one hand is the modern crusade of openness, experimentation, and adaptation to the new or untried and opposition to closedness, perpetuation of norms, and compliance with the old and familiar. On the other hand is the definition of dark and light, bad and good, nonobservant Jew and observant Jew as ironclad equivalencies. Is it then a choice between myth and reality, or is it a choice between two ideologies each of which is partly myth-making, partly reality-defining? However that question is answered will depend on the influence of leaders who shape policies and inspire followers to specific ideological ends. All fundamentalists, whether they be Christian, Islamic, or Jewish, agree that the leadership of certain extraordinary individuals is decisive for the collective good. Since the values expressive of the collective good are abstract and universal, they must be actualized by specific human agents, almost always male, who represent the values for which the group as a whole is striving at any moment in its history. In Judaism, even more than in Islam or Christianity, one finds spiritual luminaries who defend a notion of collectivity. To preserve and also refine the *kehilla* (which is at once the political-legal structure of a local Jewish community and also the essence of that community) is the core value in traditional Judaism. Its staunchest preservers have become authoritative figures in all aspects of life for their followers. Some are rabbis of such personal piety and scholarly renown that groups of the devout nucleate around them. Others are not "mere" rabbis; they are *zaddikim* or *rebbes,* masters in that distinctly Jewish movement for spiritual renewal known as Hasidism.

It was Hasidism that provided the spiritual model for what has emerged as Jewish fundamentalism. Historically the Hasidim have been the exemplary group defending Jewish collective existence against foreign challenges. It was they who spearheaded the first Jewish resistance to Greek acculturation, culminating in the Maccabean revolt of 165 B.C. (or at least that is the claim of contemporary Hasidim in their reading of the Jewish past). It was also Hasidim who spurred outbursts against acculturation during the late Middle Ages, in twelfth-thirteenth century Germany, just as they have, from the eighteenth century on, sparked a widespread reaction to the Technical Age. In its latest manifestation, the Hasidic movement has had two phases: it first emerged among East European Jewry from the early eighteenth till about the mid-nineteenth century; then it began to attract followers amid the larger Ashkenazi community. It did not affect the Sephardic or so-called Oriental Jewish community.

What has distinguished Hasidism throughout the modern period, setting it apart from both its own prior history and also from all forms of non-Hasidism, is its doctrine of the *zaddik,* or righteous man.[4] Indeed, the history of the Hasidim since the eighteenth century can be encapsulated in the colorful biographical profiles of those pious sages known as *rebbes* or *zaddiks.* Not only did they respond to the gradual impoverishment of the Ashkenazi community beyond Germany, they also showed a way to cope with brutal pogroms, like those waged against the Jews of Ukraine in 1648. They offered as well an alternative to the failed Messianism of the Sabbatean movement, a movement that had erupted among the Sephardim in 1665–66 but the effects of which were felt long after among the Ashkenazim as well.

Mere compliance with the Torah and its interpreters did not meet the threat that Jews of Europe faced on the eve of the Technical Age. They were looking for solace and reinforcement at a personal level. They wanted mediaries who could both assure and uplift them. Hasidism produced such unusual men in the forms of *rebbes* or *zaddiks,* extraordinary "fools for God." They could be labeled mystics, miracle workers, or heretics, but they were above all devout and accessible mediaries, at once integral to their communities and yet valued above other pious Jews.

To grasp their influence on Jewish fundamentalism it is necessary to understand the *rebbes* as both theological innovators and social revolutionaries. Each *rebbe* became the embodiment of piety for his community. The *rebbe* was reckoned to be as different from other men as the Torah was different from other books. In a vertical cosmology that conceived of heaven and earth on a single axis, God communicated with humanity through a process of descent and ascent. All Jewish history became sorted out and remembered in two periods of equal measure: pre-Hasidic and Hasidic, a kind of Jewish gloss on the Jaspers division of world history into the pre-Axial, Axial, and Technical Ages. In the pre-Hasidic period, the Book was handed down to Jews on Mount Sinai in order to lift them up to heaven. Scholars endeavored to make the Book accessible to the whole community. But with the advent of the Hasidim, the *rebbe* took the place of both the Torah and the scholars: even though his authority implicitly rested on his knowledge of Torah and his ability to interpret it better than other rabbis, it was he who personified the Torah. He was the living Torah, and as such the *rebbe* was sent to show Jews the way back up to God.

In the quotation at the outset of this chapter, Dov Baer epitomizes the attitude of early Hasidic masters. He contrasts the simple acts of the *zaddiks* or *rebbes* with the creation of heaven and earth. In his view, the eating and drinking of the *rebbes* outshines even the creation of the universe! How can this be? Because through creation, according to Kabbalistic teaching, the Almighty made something out of nothing in a single holistic act, but the *rebbes,* by their unique sacramental power, continuously render something into nothing, even causing the food they eat to "raise on high holy sparks."[5]

The social function of the *rebbes* derived from their theological revaluation of spiritual authority. As demonstrated by Jacob Katz and more recently by Menachem Friedman, there developed in Eastern Europe during the nineteenth century "a kind of division of labor between the Hasidic *rebbe* and the traditional rabbi. While the latter mediated between the Jew and *halakha,* the former mediated between the pious individual (the *hasid*) and God,"[6] much as the Sufi *shaykh* in premodern times mediated between Sunni Muslims, the Prophet, and God. At the same time, the Hasidic community, known as *'eda,* came to be differentiated from the traditional community *(kehilla).* The former had no geographical boundaries but close voluntary ties, while the latter was restricted in both its geographical and legal functions. If the *rebbe* was not like other men, he was also not like other religious leaders. In effect, the *rebbe* did more than complement the role of the traditional rabbi; for a large segment of East European Jewry he supplanted the appeal of rabbinical authority.

It is not surprising, therefore, that the first opponents of the *rebbes* were the traditional rabbis, at once their neighbors and their rivals. The internal dispute between *rebbes* and rabbis remained intense till about the mid-nineteenth century. Often depicted as polemical duels between the Hasidim and *mitnaggdim* (the opponents), these contests were nonetheless internal to Judaism. Both contestants were seeking the same high ground, to preserve the people of Israel, whether through the *kehilla* or the *'eda,* by invoking the Torah as the mainstay of Jewish identity.

But by the mid-nineteenth century, the Enlightenment ethos, which had wreaked havoc on Western European Jewry in its initial outburst, began to impinge on the already weakened Jewish communities of Eastern Europe. The Hasidim responded by coalescing the *'edot* (pl. of *'eda),* formalizing their own ritual disciplines, and challenging their opponents. However, the *mitnaggdim,* or opponents, were no longer other traditional rabbis. The *mitnaggdim* had become the *maskilim,* those Jews who referred to themselves as "enlightened men" but who, in the view of the *rebbes,* had sold their soul to an alien ethos and, therefore, were no longer Jews but apostates. Claiming to be enlightened, they had actually enveloped themselves in darkness. For the *rebbes* and their followers, Enlightenment and Emancipation were interchangeable. They were twin terms for the same negative reality: the separation of Jews from their collective observance of the *mitzvoth,* or commandments of the Torah. The Emancipation, in their view, connoted not freedom but a new form of exile, a latter-day Babylon. Resisting all efforts to redefine Jewish identity in terms of Enlightenment and Emancipation values, the *rebbes* also opposed the Ashkenazi embodiment of secular Jewish hope, that nationalist movement which led to the formation of the new Zion, the Third Commonwealth,[7] the state of Israel.

The Hasidim were not the only Jews of the late nineteenth century who opposed Zionism as a secular ideology. A century earlier, when Hasidism was still flourishing in Eastern Europe, Jewish Orthodoxy had come into being as a reaction to the first stirrings of the Great Western Transmutation among West European Jewry. Like the notion of scriptural inerrancy among Christian fundamentalists or the *nizam-i mustafa* (the Muhammadan system) among Sunni Muslim fundamentalists, the idea of Orthodoxy itself reflected modern influences. The word "orthodoxy" has no Hebrew equivalent. Derived from Christian usage, it prevailed in the Jewish context to describe those who opposed the Enlightenment or *Haskala.*[8] The irony of Orthodoxy in its Jewish formulation has been aptly pinpointed by Gideon Aran:

Tradition itself was altered in the course of its confrontation with modernization and secularization. At about the end of the eighteenth century, the encounter gave birth to a new social phenomenon: Orthodoxy. While Orthodoxy represents itself as the sole legitimate heir of traditional Judaism, it is in fact only one stream among others—although it is arguably the closest to the original medieval rabbinic mold. Orthodoxy, in practice, is a defensive reaction against the other modern trends in Judaism which it views as contrary to tradition.[9]

The chief function of Orthodoxy is also defensive: to neutralize the acids of modernism that had begun to corrode the structures of Jewish religious and social life. Samson Raphael Hirsch, a Prussian rabbi, and Moses Sofer, better known as Hatam Sofer, a German rabbi who migrated to Slovakia (Bratislava), both inspired movements among non-Hasidic Jews which were later labeled as Orthodox. It was followers of Hatam Sofer who became, in the early 1870s, the first body of European Jews to win recognition as "an officially recognized Orthodox subgroup." When a decade later Samson Raphael Hirsch secured a similar concession from the Prussian government for his Frankfurt community, Orthodoxy was firmly launched as an expression of Jewish ritual and creedal observance.[10] The separatist impulse of the Orthodox, to keep themselves pure by withdrawing from the dominant group, was often frustrated. Particularly when it came to schooling for their children, the temptations were numerous to teach secular subjects alongside the traditional halakhic curriculum. Only that group which later became identified as the *haredim* stood firm by the pronouncement of Hazon Ish, that "foreign learning (i.e., secular knowledge) was not to be taught to *yeshiva* students."[11]

Many Orthodox, while eager to emigrate to Palestine, refused to participate in efforts to establish a Jewish commonwealth. How could Israel as a self-proclaimed Jewish state *not* represent the best interests of all Jews? Most non-Jews assume that it does. The Orthodox opposition to Zionism begs for further explication. It is at core a religious opposition, rejecting as incompatible with Talmudic observance any state that seeks to represent the aspirations of world Jewry. It is not merely fear that a Jewish state would not honor the *mitzvoth* as they had been honored in the prenational *kehilla* and *'edot;* rather, it was, as Jacob Katz has made clear, that "Jewish tradition did not foresee a middle stage between Exile and Redemption."[12] To the *haredim*, the idea of a Jewish state implies that history has stalled, that the God of Abraham, Isaac, and Jacob is no longer moving humanity inexorably toward a messianic closure. Some Orthodox rabbis have gone so far as to declare that "Zionism [is] a greater danger than the Enlightenment. The latter only led individual Jews astray, but the former undermined the very foundations of Jewish life."[13] Since symbols embody the values of traditional Judaism, the Zionist movement, by revalorizing age-old symbols, has preempted rather than simply rivaled Orthodoxy. It has dressed secularism in religious garb. Secularization, to the extent that it connotes more than the privatization of ritual observance, accelerates the transfer of religious values from their original context to a new context in which they serve nontheocratic purposes. It is in this latter sense that "Zionism [as a secular ideology] did effect a transposition and hence a transformation of significant meanings derived from traditional Judaism."[14]

Numerous Orthodox Jews, perceiving its threat to their spiritual heritage as evolved during the Diaspora, opposed Zionism. In Europe they formed organizations that challenged the advocacy of a Jewish state, at first passively and later actively. Just before the outbreak of World War I, successors to Samson Raphael Hirsch established the principal anti-Zionist organization, Agudat Israel. "This group declared its purpose to be the application, to all problems facing the Jews, of the perspective of traditionalism, i.e., the spirit of Torah. Thus it emerged as the Orthodox counterweight to the Zionist movement."[15] After the Holocaust, and in no small measure because of it, most of the Agudat Israel opted to migrate to Palestine or to settle in North America. Those in Palestine later became reluctant albeit permanent citizens of the state of Israel. To this day they continue to have separate schools (*yeshivot*) and refuse to acknowledge the public celebration of Independence Day. At the same time, however, most Agudat Israel members benefit from state-provided services. Only extreme Orthodox separatists, such as Neturei Karta, "actually refrain from any structural contact with the state's agencies." Most of them live a sequestered, if protected, existence in the heart of Jerusalem in the Meah Shearim quarter.[16]

Another group claiming the mantle of Orthodoxy came into existence at nearly the same time as Agudat Israel. Founded in Eastern Europe in 1902, they were subsequently known as Mizrahi, an abbreviation for Merkaz Ruhani (Spiritual Center). During the 1930s many of them, fleeing Nazi programs of internment and extermination, also migrated to Palestine. After the establishment of the state of Israel in 1948, they became members of that coalition now known as the National Religious Party (NRP). Theologically they dallied between Orthodoxy and Zionism. They espoused a kind of brokered messianism: not wanting to preempt the coming of the Messiah, they trusted that formation of the state of Israel might somehow assist in the process of messianic redemption. Yet they remained discomforted by the official laxity of the new state vis-à-vis compliance with the *mitzvoth*. They also looked askance at the secular overtones of the majority of the ruling elite. On both counts, they had to hope against hope that denial of traditional religious values might prove to be only a temporary aberration.

The tentativeness of the Mizrahi party members contrasted with the boldness of another European Jewish leader who migrated to Palestine in the early twentieth century. Rabbi Abraham Isaac Kook arrived from Lithuania about the same time that Mizrahi was coming into existence. He first took up residence in Jaffa. Eventually he became Chief Rabbi of Palestine. His thought is much more complex than his biography. To those who revered him he was a visionary. To those who couldn't understand him or refused to accept his authority, he was a muddled reactionary. By either reckoning, he went beyond the accommodationist posture of the Mizrahi Orthodox, even though he advocated their interests and enjoyed their public support while he was Chief Rabbi. Rav Kook, as he is affectionately known, placed extraordinary emphasis on *hitnahlut* or the resettling of the Land of Israel. It was, in his view, a sign of imminent redemption, at once global and evolutionary. All other facets of halakhic Judaism achieved their apotheosis in *hitnahlut*. No Jews could exempt themselves from working for that utopian goal. The secular Zionists, no matter how much they resisted recognition of the true value of their labors, were also integral to the divine plan: nation building was a religious task validated by Jewish history in order to reunite the Chosen People with the Holy Land. All other endeavors were preliminary, all other interpretations of Judaism trivial and wrong.

To try to understand Rabbi Abraham Isaac Kook is to come to terms with the multiple strands of premodern Jewish tradition that survived, albeit transformed, in the Technical Age. At a symbolic level, not only Rabbi Abraham Isaac Kook but also his son and successor, Rabbi Zvi Yehuda Kook, project the image of latter-day *Hasidim*. Gideon Aran has even suggested that the Kooks appealed to their followers (since 1974 known as Gush Emunim) with that charismatic tone of extraordinary awe which the *rebbes* alone had engendered in their followers.[17] One scholar has gone so far as to parallel the Kooks with Hasidic forebears:

Families (of Gush Emunim settlers) have specific readings: books published by the Merkaz HaRav Institute, commentaries of Rabbi Z. Y. Kook on the Biblical portion of the week. They show an increased religiosity, compared with the average religious Zionist outlook. They even have a dynasty: the Kook family with its two revered leaders, A. I. and Z. Y. Kook notwithstanding other rabbis from the same family. They express enthusiasm: love of the Land of Israel, certitude that to settle the Land hastens the coming of the Messiah. They have their quasi-ritual calendar including yearly commemorations of the death of both Rabbis Kook.

All these aspects have a striking similarity with Hassidic [*sic*] life. Born out of despair inflicted upon Jews from Eastern Europe, in the second half of the eighteenth century, by terrible sufferings . . . Hassidism [*sic*] offered the Jewish masses enthusiasm and a search for ecstasy as opposed to the Talmudic studies offered by the establishment for consolation. It flourished by creating groups united around their respective charismatic leaders, the "rebbes."

Born out of the Yom Kippur War, challenging the vacillating answers from both political and religious leaders, Gush Emunim developed their own type of Hassidism [*sic*]. They have their charismatic "rebbes," the Kook dynasty, and they express enthusiasm and search for ecstasy through the Land of Israel.[18]

One must be careful, however, in linking the Kooks to Hasidism. There is a crucial distinction between Hasidism as an historical antecedent to Jewish fundamentalism and Hasidism as a set of discrete spiritual lineages that provide the primary ideological identity for some modern-day Jews. The Kooks reflect the Hasidic legacy without being contemporary *rebbes*. While they may shadow the *rebbes* of Hasidic fame and while their followers may imbue them with a charismatic appeal reminiscent of the *rebbes*, neither the Kooks nor their successors can function as modern-day Hasidim. Why? Because their world and the world of the *rebbes* have been separated by the Technical Age. The Great Western Transmutation limits the autonomy of all religious movements. The Gush are no exception. They have been enveloped by a twentieth-century nation-state. Their leaders, like all Jewish zealots with Israeli passports, must function within the monitored reflexivity of the state of Israel. However much they may protest its profile, they cannot deny its impact nor alter its requirements as a nation-state. To the extent that Gush Emunim have any premodern historical antecedents, they are Hasidic, but to the extent that they are present-day citizens of the state of Israel, they are ideologically cleft from the great family dynasties. They remain quasi-Hasidic—nothing less, nothing more.

The fuller expression of Jewish fundamentalism only emerges when we consider its representation through both wings of Jewish Orthodoxy. They appear to be opposite: the non-Hasidic *haredim*, epitomized by Neturei Karta, and the quasi-Hasidic Gush Emunim. Moreover, the leaders of both groups are openly antagonistic to each other, yet what has come to be known as Jewish fundamentalism represents a transference of the bifurcation emerging within Jewish Orthodoxy. Unless we trace the numerous ways in which Neturei Karta and Gush Emunim, despite their differences, crisscross and often parallel in their relationship to Jewish identity,[19] we can understand neither the formation nor the future influence of Jewish fundamentalism.

Other scholars, notably Jacob Katz, Menachem Friedman, Gideon Aran, and Ehud Sprinzak, have recognized two wings of Jewish Orthodoxy or fundamentalism. They have also made claims about their contrasting qualities. Yet the political scientist Ian Lustick has asserted that Gush Emunim and Gush Emunim alone represent Jewish fundamentalism in present-day Israel. Moreover, Lustick traces Jewish fundamentalism as a worldview back to the Maccabean period.[20] Echoing the claims made by Katz et al., we restrict the timeline of Jewish fundamentalism to the Technical Age, just as we also extend its scope beyond the political realm. On both counts our analysis departs from Lustick's policy-oriented, behavior-driven inquiry into Gush Emunim.

Some would argue that we should expand our categorization of Jewish fundamentalism to include that name which insistently comes to the fore when discussing Jewish fundamentalism: Rabbi Meir Kahane. In our view, Kahane is a Jewish activist but not a fundamentalist. His is a personal, highly idiosyncratic interpretation of the Torah. He does not observe the radical traditionalism of Agudat Israel members. Nor does he engage the metaphysical challenge of the *Haskala*, as do the *haredim*. He fits the mold of neither Neturei Karta nor Gush Emunim. Openly antagonistic to its current leader, Moshe Levinger, he also rejects the Gush move to sacralize secular Jews. He inveighs against Hebrew-speaking *goyyim* as well as Arabic-speaking *goyyim*. While the Gush esteem fellow Jews, even if they be self-confessed secularists, Kahane interprets the process of divine redemption as demanding unequivocal assent. Following the Six Day War, he, together with many other religious activists, began to advocate an imminent messianism. As "talk about the redemption of the Jewish people in this generation became common in the 1970s,"[21] Kahane leaped ahead of the pack; he predicted a specific year for the advent of the Messiah. According to a pamphlet published in 1978, he calculated that the establishment of the state of Israel in 1948 had initiated a forty-year cycle of global transformation. The year 1988 would be the date culminating the challenge, the peril, and the redemption of Israel. Redemption did not come in 1988, at least not visibly, yet Kahane remains a messianic enthusiast.[22] Retrospectively, he sees his own making of *aliya* in 1971 as messianically motivated: all Diaspora Jews had to return to the Land of Israel for redemption to occur. Yet *aliya* itself does not guarantee individual redemption, for in Kahane's view, not all Israeli Jews will be saved; salvation is reserved for those who honor the one overriding *mitzvah*, war against the entire Palestinian people.

Shocking in its saber-rattling extremism, Kahane's approach superficially resembles Gush Emunim emphasis on resettling the Land, *hitnah-lut*, the land referred to being Judea and Samaria, that is, the West Bank of the Jordan River. Kahane also shares with Gush extremists a disdain for Arabs. He sees them as part of divine destiny only to the extent that they are opponents now and victims later. Any reference to human rights, whether by appeal to juridical norms or humane conscience, is irrelevant: those who understand the divine command will be honored; those who don't will be destroyed, whether they be Jews or Arabs.

Yet there is a decisive difference between Kahane and the Gush leadership. While both Rabbis Kook were theologians before they were transformed into ideologues, Kahane has been and remains an ideologue. As an ideologue, he has used all the instruments of modern-day media to promulgate his message and to gain support for his objectives. Early in his career he left the rabbinate to practice journalism. He has since disseminated his views through twelve books and numerous pamphlets. His deeds as well as his words keep him in the public spotlight. In the late sixties he organized the Jewish Defense League (JDL) in New York. He gained notoriety from JDL public demonstrations to protest perceived wrongs committed against Soviet Jews, New York Jews, all Jews. Since coming to Israel, Kahane has continued to commandeer press attention by violent acts against Arabs that he has either initiated or approved. He has formed his own right-wing political party, the Kach, and in 1984 he succeeded in winning election to the Israeli parliament, the Knesset. He had mounted what appeared to be a successful campaign for reelection in fall 1988, only to have his party debarred from the ballot at the last moment by the intervention of the Israeli Supreme Court.

Even had Kahane been returned to the Knesset, he would scarcely begin to have the impact on Israeli political culture that Gush Emunim enjoys. Marginalized, he exercises influence by irritating and goading. He irritates because his objectives coincide with the most extreme, underground elements in the Gush movement, those who would like to restore the Temple Mount to its Solomonic splendor by erasing the Muslim shrine known as the Dome of the Rock. He goads because he competes with Gush leaders for public attention and financial support, moving them still further to the right in their own political strategizing.[23] Either way, Rabbi Meir Kahane remains a counterfeit fundamentalist.

From a modernist viewpoint, the whole story of Jewish fundamentalism can be told as an Israel-specific variation of the closed mind/open mind dichotomy that the psychologist Milton Rokeach, following Fromm and Maslow but ultimately Freud, explained as the characteristic feature of several religious groups. Its thesis may be simply stated. "Open" and "closed" are category distinctions that apply both to individuals and to belief systems. The closed "provides a systematic cognitive framework for rationalizing egocentric self-righteousness and the moral condemnation of others," while the open broaches an exploratory framework that seeks out and confirms "tendencies toward growth, productiveness and self-actualization."[24] The motives for both are also opposite. For the closed, there is a dominant need to defend against threat, whether the threat is perceived as internal (anxiety resulting in ego dissolution) or external (anarchy leading to group as well as individual destruction). For the open, by contrast, there is a perpetual need to know, to expand the constellation of possibilities for human creativity and progress.

No individual, social group, or historical outlook is marked by one tendency to the exclusion of the other; rather there is a constant flux between these polar dispositions. In real-life experience there emerges a kind of dialectical relation between (1) the need to know and (2) the need to defend. The greater is (2), the less is (1). Emphasis on (1) leads to individual autonomy, while emphasis on (2) tends to produce reliance on an authoritative person.

The authoritative person, however, is all too often also an authoritarian personality. The closed mind locks into a closed system; all participants are enjoined to obey a human leader who embodies the symbols of authority that circumscribe their common world. Absolute belief is matched by unswerving loyalty, and it is this cyclical, reinforcing dogmatism that makes the closed system work. The exemplar leader inspires others to pursue the ideals of defense against a common enemy. The enemy is imbued symbolically with flaws that elicit only revulsion and hatred. The leader is marked by virtues that the entire community prizes. The leader and the enemy are a study in contrasts; the leader is the best of all people, while the enemy is never allowed to be perceived with that mixture of often ambiguous character traits that marks real people.

Rather than dismissing Jewish fundamentalists by stereotyping them, reciprocating the attitude that they too often adopt to their opponents, we can understand the nature of their protest more fully if we revert to history. We must retell the story of the Hasidim, and we must empathize with their ethos insofar as possible. The indispensable starting point is the *hasid/maskil* battles of nineteenth-century Eastern Europe. The previous enemy of the *rebbes* had been other rabbis who opposed their reinterpretation of religious authority, but by the mid-nineteenth century, the new enemy had become the enlightened Jew, for the enlightened Jew claimed to represent the ethical mandate of tradition even while pursuing the vocational opportunities of the emergent West. The change in enemy signifies a profound change in attitude. If all fundamentalism is a reaction against the corrosive effects of modernity, then the Jewish reaction exemplified by the Hasidim was an attempt to rescue the collectivity of Jews from certain death. The Enlightenment, in their view, represented an ideological cancer: at first it seemed to augur only a gradual change in external conditions among one segment of the *kehilla,* but it ended by infecting the whole *kehilla* and threatening to destroy its heart and soul, the Torah. It was, above all, the model of the enlightened man as modern citizen, emancipated from the binding traditions of the past, which struck at the heart of the Hasidic vision of Jewish collectivity:

External rather than internal in its impact, the Enlightenment withdrew the political basis of Jewry by extending to Jews the rights of citizens, and at the same time denying Judaism the authority over Jews it had formerly exercised. It encouraged the development of new type of person, the *maskil,* "illumined man," who mastered areas of human erudition formerly thought to be irrelevant to Jews. So the Enlightenment's processes of dissolution reinforced one another. The *kehilla* lost its legal standing, and some of its subjects opted out of it at the same time. . . . Had Jews merely converted to Christianity, it would hardly have affected traditional society; but many left that society and yet chose to remain Jews. They plunged [the Jewish community] into a crisis of identity which has yet to find resolution.[25]

The history of the Ashkenazim in Central and Western Europe did not, however, parallel the experience of the Hasidim in Eastern Europe during the eighteenth and nineteenth centuries. The Hasidim took the crisis of identity to be peculiarly their fate, as was also the mandate to pronounce the divine judgment on those Jews who had deserted the *kehilla*. For the Hasidim, twentieth-century atrocities committed against Jews were merely the outcome of conditions within the Jewish community. It was the loss of internal purity that had given rise to external disaster. Just as the *rebbes* were invested with powers that harked back to the moment of Creation, so each *mitzva* was seen as "an event of cosmic importance, an act bearing upon the dynamics of the universe."[26] So important were the *mitzvoth* that one could, in Emmanuel Sivan's words, "innovate in order to preserve [the] tradition [they embodied]." It was not enough to intuit the spirit of the *mitzvoth*, one had to pursue their compliance in the most excruciatingly small detail. The contemporary sage Hazon Ish compiled his famed commentary on the Orah Hayyim section of *Shulkhan Arukh*, (the sixteenth-century guide to halakhic behavior). The subject of investigation was *shi'urim* or canonical measurements. Among other items Hazon Ish calculated the difference in the size of olives used in the sixteenth and the twentieth centuries. Why bother with such a calculation? Because it was necessary to determine the quantity of unleavened bread *(matza)* to be used at the Passover *seder* meal: unless the amount of *matza* was "equivalent to an olive," which meant an olive of the size available in the sixteenth century, the most sacred of meals would be invalidated. Since the twentieth-century olives proved to be smaller, one had to use more than one olive in measuring the requisite size *matza* for *seder*.

Such seemingly minute distinctions went to the heart of the *haredi* worldview: one must scrupulously observe all the *mitzvoth*, or else run the risk of defiling that sacred trust, the Halakhic legacy bequeathed to the prophets and sages. Ritual slippage lessened the spiritual worth of the Jewish collectivity. Worse yet, it delayed the coming of the Messiah and the day of redemption. In short, salvation, not just for the individual but for the world, depended on the most fastidious compliance with all the requirements of the Law. It was an unending exercise in spiritual ascesis.[27]

Nor would it seem farfetched to the most conservative of East European Jewry to claim that the entire world was kept alive only due to the vigilance of educated Jewish males in observing the *mitzvoth*. Conversely, it was their neglect that invited upon the *kehilla* the expression of divine wrath, seen above all in the prolonging of the Babylonian Exile. For the *haredim*, that Exile did not end in 1948. Since the Messiah had not come, Exile continued. Why had he not come? Because other, "impure," unobservant Jews had through their neglect of the *mitzvoth*, delayed his coming.

Some Hasidim went further still. Divine retribution was the secret, as also the necessary, explanation for the horror of Nazi Germany. Who was Hitler, according to Hasidic interpreters, but "one of the evil geniuses used by God to chastise the Jews for not keeping the *mitzves?*" Or as one put it, graphically but grimly, doubt created Auschwitz.[28]

And since it was the Enlightenment that produced doubt, the Hasidic struggle continues. It did not slacken with the death camps of Auschwitz or the movement to create a modern Jewish state. Since the Enlightenment never ceases to stimulate new ideologies and to produce still further opportunities that lure Jews into the dominant culture, the modern-day Hasidim must respond to every encroachment on the *mitzvoth*. Even though those who chronicle their fortunes, such as the preeminent historian Simon Dubnow, are ready to concede that theirs has been "a losing struggle against new Hellenisms."[29]

When the most recent Hellenism, Zionism, became the dominant socialist ideology for twentieth-century Jewry, Hasidic masters, along with other religious loyalists, refused to conform. Some Hasidic leaders, like some non-Hasidic Orthodox rabbis, felt that it ought to be possible to absorb the Zionist platform within the Jewish tradition. Social reality, alas, clashed with traditional theology. The Enlightenment legacy divided some Jews from other Jews. It remained a bone of contention. In particular, the Eastern European Hasidim who migrated to Palestine refused to join those favoring a Jewish expression of the European Enlightenment, especially one that reidentified the Jewish people as a *nationalist* collectivity.

The independent legacy of Hasidism persisted in the Holy Land. Its defiant protest mood is epitomized by two Eastern European rabbis who came to Palestine when Zionism was still in its infancy. In the late nineteenth century, the rabbi of Brisk, Moses Diskin of Brest-Litovsk (1816–98), migrated to Meah Shearim in Jerusalem to escape the Enlightenment. At the turn of the century, as we mentioned above, Rabbi Abraham Isaac Kook migrated to Jaffa from Lithuania for the same reason. He later became the theological lodestar for Gush Emunim. Despite the fact that neither rabbi is formally linked with the Hasidim in conventional biographies, both demonstrate the influence of the Hasidic struggle against the Enlightenment. Fiercely committed to observing the *mitzvoth* as the irreducible test of Jewish identity, they also stress the need to defend the collectivity through allegiance to a spiritual mentor.

The Hasidic impress on the rabbi of Brisk is indirect and circumstantial. His lineage extended to Joseph Hayyim Sonenfeld, and then to Rabbi Amram Bloi, one of the most outspoken ideologues of Neturei Karta. Though the name Neturei Karta ("Guardians of the City") was not linked to the rabbi of Brisk or his followers till 1942, by the 1920s the ultra-Orthodox had distanced themselves from other members of Agudat Israel and from Zionist advocates. They abhorred dealing with *maskilim*, i.e., "enlightenment Jews." Since such Jews had ceased to observe the *mitzvoth*, they were no longer Jews; they were unbelievers. Just as the Hasidim had protested the Enlightenment, so Neturei Karta protested the state of Israel. Despite radically altered contexts, the two groups shared a continuity of purpose. Nowhere has that continuity been more graphically attested than in the actions of Rabbi Amram Bloi. In the 1950s he defended the picketing of a Jerusalem club that permitted dancing. Not only was the activity "immoral," and not only did the club have official sanction, but it was located opposite a house of study belonging to followers of the eighteenth century Hasidic master, Rabbi Nahman of Bratzlav. While it was the primary task of the Guardians to observe the *mitzvoth* within the confines of Meah Shearim, it was also their mission to defend other observant Jews, in this case the Hasidic followers of Rabbi Nahman, against secular defilement.[30]

Neturei Karta are but the most vocal component of that larger organization known as 'Eda Haredit (the "Pious Community").[31] All its members reckon themselves to be the truly pious (*haredim*). While Neturei Karta may be more extreme than others in their uncompromising opposition, first, to the Zionist movement and, second, to the state of Israel, all *haredim* view the core values of Judaism as incompatible with secularism of any stripe, including a socialist-nationalist ideology. Numerous are the means by which they have maintained the tension between existence in the contemporary world and adherence to the dynamic intent of *halakha*. Education has been the key to their continuous vitality. Menachem Friedman has demonstrated how the *kollel* or religious school functions as a unique institution protecting married *yeshiva* graduates. Traceable back to late nineteenth century Eastern Europe, the *kollel* was later institutionalized in Palestine by Rabbi Abraham Karlitz, better known as Hazon Ish. An elaborate network of commercial exchanges allows a subgroup of traditional Jewish male elites to be preserved from defilement in the secular world. Often it is their new brides who assist as breadwinners that they may pursue the Halakhic injunction: "Tarry in the house (of the Lord) all your days." While urban structures support most expressions of fundamentalist ideology, no other group exceeds the *haredim* in perpetuating a rigid dichotomization between modernity and tradition, material hedonism and spiritual purity in the very midst of the modern metropolis:

In the setting of the big city, the *haredi* ghetto provides a solid territorial base for the various subgroups in the community. It enables the *haredim* to maintain an independent culture which can borrow selectively elements from the surrounding culture, and to maintain a large measure of internal social control. The modern city thus affords the chance to sustain the *haredi* voluntary community in a dialectical balance of isolation from, and mingling with, the rest of the population.[32]

While this pattern has characterized the *haredim* in all the cities to which the remnant of Eastern European Jewry migrated after the Holocaust, it has been especially emblematic in Jerusalem, the heart of biblical and modern Israel. Neturei Karta identify Zionism with the maladies of a deracinated, permissive culture, yet they have followed the *haredi* practice of witnessing to purity in the midst of pollution; they continue to oppose the new Zion by residing in the holiest of cities, Jerusalem, in a section sequestered from nonobservant Jews.

Were their activities limited to Meah Shearim, Neturei Karta would be a sociocultural oddity but nothing more. However, the protest that they and other *haredim* make against other Israeli Jews as apostates from *Klal Yisrael* (the Jewish collectivity) has extended beyond Rabbi Bloi's picketing of a night club. It encompasses archaeological excavations in the Old City, as the most densely inhabited section of Jerusalem is called, and also commercial infringements on the observance of the Sabbath. Neturei Karta, despite their ghettolike residence, have become self-appointed moral guardians for the whole city of Jerusalem.

Gush Emunim, or "Bloc of the Faithful," represent a disparate reflex of Jewish fundamentalism. They have emerged in modern Israel more recently than Neturei Karta. They grew out of a secretive youth movement of the 1950s *(Gahelet)* which remained discreet even when it later merged with the Merkaz HaRav, the *yeshiva* founded by Rabbi Abraham Isaac Kook and developed by his son Rabbi Zvi Yehuda Kook.[33] Gush activists came into public view only with the opening of the West Bank after the Six Day War in 1967. They did not acquire a name until 1974. Accepting the legitimacy of the state in principle, they challenged its reluctance in practice to extend the borders of present-day Israel far enough to encompass all the biblically mandated territory of *Eretz Yisrael*. The ideological beacons for Gush Emunim, as we noted above, are the two Rabbis Kook. Rav Zvi Yehuda Kook was the only son of Rav Abraham Isaac Kook. Succeeding his father, Rav Zvi Yehuda Kook differed only slightly with his teachings: he justified Israel as a nation already redeemed rather than one on the path to redemption, as his father had continually stressed,[34] and he further specified three stages in which messianic redemption would occur. The first stage was "repentance of fear." It entailed return from the Diaspora to the Land. The second, "national reconstruction," heralded a symbiosis of the People and the Land. Only then could the third stage, a "repentance of love," begin. While it would ultimately usher in the messianic era, responsibility for accelerating this redemptive timetable rested with the repentant community. It was up to the Jewish people to attract the Messiah and produce the final redemption through their "increasing level of religious observance."[35]

While distinctions between the two Rabbi Kooks have occupied intellectuals, what has been more significant for the majority of religiously observant Israelis is that both Rabbi Kooks called Zion away from the drift of secularism and back to its spiritual moorings.

It is because of their emphatic religious stance, and their opposition to Enlightenment influence, that Gush Emunim combine with Neturei Karta to form the two wings of Jewish fundamentalism. Their common purpose is often obscured by their opposite views of the state: the one denies it any legitimacy, the other prods it to extend its legitimacy. Neither group can claim the allegiance of more than a small percentage of Israelis, yet together they stake out the spectrum of possibilities to which other religiously rooted Israeli groups must relate. None would go so far as Neturei Karta in denying any legitimacy to the state, few would go so far as Gush Emunim in compelling the state to expand its territorial claims, but all have to account for the constellation of issues that these two fundamentalist ideologies raise, for it is they who pose the stiffest challenge to the secular ideology that guided both the Zionist movement and the foundation of Israel.

Whether or not either group succeeds in its objectives, their importance will be finally measured on an ideological rather than a theological scale. The shift in valuation is crucial. It is only possible from a post-Enlightenment, modernist stance. The sociologist Gideon Aran has brilliantly illustrated how a particular group *(Gahelet)* and a peculiar set of historical circumstances (the aftermath of the Six Day War) converged with the radical elements of Rabbi Abraham Isaac Kook's theology. The group needed a leader, but the leader also needed a special set of followers. While granting Rabbi Kook great stature as a thinker, Aran judges the outcome of his intellectual enterprise to have been a dismal failure. Even his authority as Chief Rabbi of Palestine did not gain credibility for his unconventional ideas. Lustick notes that "Merkaz HaRav [the *yeshiva* he had founded] barely managed to survive into the 1960s as an ordinary seminary with no more than twenty students."[36] It was not till the *Gahelet* youth group became attached to the Merkaz HaRav *yeshiva* that:

Rav Kook's thought took on the aspect of a platform for political involvement and was harnessed to the aspirations of an active social force. In a parallel development, those aspirations [i.e., of the *Gahelet*] took on spiritual depth and enjoyed a new legitimation for what had until then been merely dreams and feelings. In the process, both assumed an essentially new and different significance. . . . Its distinctive and lasting expression is Gush Emunim.[37]

The peculiar wedding of theology and ideology through charismatic leaders is also true for Neturei Karta. Though their role is less dramatic and visible, Neturei Karta, like Gush Emunim, have been inspired by a defensive religious ideology: to reclaim the *Klal Yisrael* (the Jewish collectivity) in the changed context of post-Enlightenment twentieth-century geopolitics. Their leaders advocate religious goals under the umbrella of a secular state, yet they refuse to grant the state any intrinsic rights, either to define Jewish identity or to circumscribe the practice of

Jewish piety. They isolate the Meah Shearim section of Jerusalem from contamination by the impure Jews who surrounded them, but they also continue to attack those outside Meah Shearim who openly flaunt the *mitzvoth*. In the steadfastness of their endeavors, they draw admirers and even secular supporters.[38] However, from their own viewpoint, they remain a symbol of the Babylonian Exile: as Jews had suffered exile (*galut*) in the world, so they now suffer exile within Israel!

The ideological character of Neturei Karta, as also Gush Emunim, rests on a special appropriation of scripture. For Neturei Karta, the oral Torah represents the necessary complement to the written Torah. What was revealed to Moses on Mount Sinai continually needs to be updated in its applications. The Neturei Karta are not mere interpreters of the written Torah; they are also authentic voices of the living Torah. Gush Emunim have a similar reliance on oral Torah: for both Rabbis Kook and their successors, oral Torah is the necessary extension of written Torah. Without its resources charismatic leaders cannot relate to the pragmatic issues that most engage their followers. Consider the problem of making a precise territorial delineation of *Eretz Yisrael*. Since redemption will come only to devout Jews who reoccupy the Land of Israel, it is crucial to determine the boundaries of *Eretz Yisrael*. According to the written Torah, such boundaries remain imprecise, but in the Gush interpretation of oral Torah they expand well beyond the borders of the present-day state of Israel. Hence the Israeli invasion of Lebanon in 1982 was regarded by Gush leaders as a religious event since, in their view, all of southern Lebanon had been vouchsafed as a part of *Eretz Yisrael;* it had been divinely decreed to the tribe of Asher.[39]

While scriptural truth and charismatic authority blend together as naturally and compellingly for Jewish fundamentalists of the twentieth century as they did for the Hasidim of earlier centuries, neither Neturei Karta nor Gush Emunim are direct legatees of the *hasid/maskil* battle of the nineteenth century. Their joint experience has been mediated by the Great Western Transmutation. They are at once continuous and discontinuous with prior Jewish opposition to the Enlightenment ethos. Both movements claim historical antecedents, especially charismatic leaders, from the past, yet neither has an ideological precursor. Their forbears saw in Zionism a possible threat to messianic redemption, but since 1948 *all* Orthodox/fundamentalist groups in the Third Commonwealth have had to militate against an avowedly secular nation-state that embraced them despite their opposition to its existence. They might have recourse to other eras and deceased heroes, but they can only protest within a radically altered, a thoroughly modern polity. The righteous minority have become in-house critics against secular Zionism, whether they try to expand the scope of the *mitzvoth*, as do religious Zionists and now Gush Emunim, or they continue to challenge any definition of Judaism that trivializes the *mitzvoth*, as do Neturei Karta. It is a debate that will continue to reverberate beyond Israel, yet the sharpness of its focus there may well set the parameters of its engagement elsewhere. Who is a Jew is coming to mean, Who is an Israeli Jew within the imminent (or ultimate) messianic scheme of redemption in the Land of Israel?

Although, in the modernist view, both the Hasidic movement and its fundamentalist sequels may seem to be but further exemplifications of the closed-mind system, that judgment needs to be qualified. It is true that both Gush Emunim and Neturei Karta do rely on authoritarian personalities and a holistic code of religious commandments, to the exclusion of all other options for contemporary Judaism. Yet their opponents, the secular Zionists and their allies, are also exclusivist. They are prone to judge the Enlightenment as not merely a moment in Western history auguring the Technical Age and, more recently, the High Tech Era but also as a universal standard for judging all other human experience. Nationalism, that stepchild of the Enlightenment, becomes the criterion for Jews as for others to prove themselves citizens of the twentieth century. By such logic, the Zionist pioneers were justified to reconstitute a Jewish homeland, for whatever practical causes and under whatever ideological banner, because only as citizens of a common state could Jews mirror their European predecessors and also emulate their Western contemporaries. Israel had to be a nation-state like any other to survive.

Secular Zionists, in sidestepping the metaphysical question, cannot erase it. Is nationalism the ultimate goal, or is it conditional on other realities, instrumental to still higher goals? Must religion fit into the puzzle of national identity, or does it retain an independent and also transcendent reality? In examining Jewish fundamentalism, we have to be wary of the positivist axiom that *all* religion is merely the irrational mutterings of superstitious infants, unwilling or unable to accept scientific progress. As Gadamer and others have shown in criticizing the critique of ideology, the ghost of Comte still lingers behind the screen of putative objectivity. Those enlightened "we" who claim a dialectical victory over the superstitious "they" too often end by enthroning abstract symbols over concrete realities, the new over the old, the future over the past.

Reality is at once multileveled and complex. Nationalism has influenced but not superseded traditional Judaism. Many seemingly secular Israelis continue to search for religious meaning. The Enlightenment has neither preempted nor satisfied their quest.

Moreover, to the extent that modernism disguises itself as the only true tangent of modernity, it does pose a continuous threat to all monotheistic traditions. It is fundamentalists who have rallied to the defense of the God of Abraham, Isaac, and Jacob. Ruling out compromise on what is deemed fundamental, they make opposition in the name of religion inevitable and even virtuous. Once the fundamentals have been staked out and their value asserted, there is no other battle worth fighting, no other goal worth pursuing.

Despite their other differences, Neturei Karta and Gush Emunim concur in their opposition to secular Zionism. Both speak and act on behalf of their treasure. As observant Jews, they have but one treasure. It is the *mitzvoth* interpreted by worthy sages who embody what they teach. They are the Hasidim, inveighing against all the Hellenisms of the present age, even those introduced as expediencies, or lauded as goals, by a Jewish state.

It is important to stress the significance of naming Jewish fundamentalists before we describe their actions or evaluate their significance. The implicit emphasis of much scholarship has been to assume that the modern state of Israel has struck the delicate compromise between religion and politics; it has become a secular polity with a civil religion. Have not numerous religious groups demanded, and been given, a forum in the public domain? There is even a National Religious Party. But at the same time, Israel as a modern nation-state does not act on theocratic principles; nor have its leaders thus far advocated religious views as the primary basis for formulating policy objectives, whether domestic or foreign. One ideology has prevailed up till now in Israel, and it has been socialist-nationalist-secularist.

Yet the Six Day war produced a shift. It changed not only territorial boundaries, it also changed the moral frame of reference for Israel. The sudden, dramatic conquest of the West Bank of the Jordan River and also the reunification of Jerusalem under Israeli rule "precipitated a crisis of identity. . . . Israelis who identified themselves as patriots or nationalists, had no *moral* claim on the Holy Land."[40] Justifying the right to rule Judea and Samaria was an unexpected but inevitable consequence of military success. The politics of expansionism needed ideological buttressing beyond the appeal to national security.

The shift of perspective in Israel was gradual rather than immediate. Not till after 1973, and the seeming impasse of the last Israeli-Egyptian war, the Yom Kippur War, did religious Zionism acquire major political importance. It suddenly moved to the forefront of public attention with the New Zionism, represented above all by Gush Emunim. Followers of the Rabbis Kook challenged, and continue to challenge, the notion that the state can determine the future of Zion on its own terms. To a seemingly invincible secular ideology, they counterposed a superannuated religious ideology and, through their charisma, brought it back to life.[41]

The debate is so charged, the stakes so high that it is tempting to take sides, sorting out right from wrong, labeling one an open, the other a closed ideology. Is secular Zionism right because it accepts the ethos of the modern world? Is Jewish fundamentalism wrong because it rebels against that same ethos? Neither Zionism nor fundamentalism can claim universal validity. Each instead must depend on other elements to determine the outcome of its struggle. And to understand those elements one must suspend a preconceived ranking that pits us against them, good against bad, modernity against tradition, science against religion. Instead one must be aware of the stakes that motivate both sides.

In scanning the future of Israel, Jewish fundamentalists have underscored the central significance of a continuous spiritual identity. They oppose any effort to redefine, and so reduce, the scope of the *mitzvoth* within some larger nationalist outlook called "civil religion." Consider the judgment that "traditional Judaism expresses itself primarily through a system of law which the vast majority of Israeli Jews do not feel obligated to observe and a series of myths which many, if not most, do not find credible." [42] That would seem to justify the development of a civil religion as the only compromise ideology that would satisfy most Israelis. A civil religion could retain the aura of the past while voiding its substance through a modern-day secular Jewish state. Even after 1967, most Israelis seem to support the civil religion option. Statistics confirm what seems to be the continuing erosion of traditional Judaism:

The post-1967 period has seen less Sabbath observance and more bread on Passover. Tel Aviv cinemas have broken a long tradition of shutting down on Friday nights and have begun to open their gates to eager customers on the Sabbath. Few kosher restaurants exist outside the hotels which cater to tourists. Enrollment in religious schools . . . is on the decline and went down from 33 percent in 1959–60 to 25 percent in 1982–83. [43]

Yet an alternative reading of civil religion in Israel is equally plausible. The trends away from strict observance, far from eliminating religion, simply accentuate the tension between what is and what ought to be. The so-called masses of Israel are both religious and secular. "While the vast majority of them would reject adaptationist efforts to legitimate halakhic deviation, in practice many of them are adaptationists." [44] Such a statement lays bare the discrepancy between appearance and reality, between what we have termed elsewhere the manifest and the latent. It implies a process that sociologists describe as "inadvertent secularization": no matter what claims are made on behalf of tradition, modernity prevails.

But note how easily the same argument can be reversed. One could recast the above statement to read: "While in practice many Israelis are adaptationists, the vast majority of them would reject adaptationist efforts to legitimate halakhic deviation." The emphasis then shifts from what Israelis do or don't do and stresses the unswerving attachment that they feel to values that are premodern, nonsecular, Halakhic—that is to say, religious.

In the recent history of Israel, *both* statements are true. Before 1967, when the myth of the intrepid Sabra, the native son who was also a socialist pioneer, prevailed, the first reading was true; but since 1967, and even more since 1973, when religious values have reentered the mainstream of Israeli public discourse, it is arguably the second that prevails. Gush Emunim's New Zionism may not become the dominant ideology in Israel,[45] yet a momentous transition is occurring, one that is all the more puzzling because it was so little anticipated by secular analysts of Israeli society.

Jewish fundamentalism in Israel may be a passing phenomenon, but it may also be, as Ehud Sprinzak has argued, the tip of an iceberg. The iceberg, though still concealed, has the potential to loom larger and larger in the future of Israel.[46] To assess it properly a broad context is needed. While Israel may retain its distinctiveness as a Jewish homeland transformed into a modern nation-state by a people in Diaspora, Jewish fundamentalism is not unique. At least in its formative phase, it expresses the larger dilemma that all monotheistic traditions faced with the onset of the Technical Age. Judaism experienced the Enlightenment piecemeal. The initial disruption of Western European Jewry only partially afflicted the Jewish communities of Eastern Europe. Zionism arose in the "liberated" urban circles of Western European Jewry, but it also spread to Eastern Europe, so much that one could claim it only became a mass movement due to the large numbers of Eastern European secularizing Jews who flocked to its ranks. Yet Zionism did not find universal acceptance among Eastern European Jewry, and to the extent that it was accepted among the Orthodox and Hasidic Jews of Poland, Hungary, and Czechoslovakia, it was always in tension with the demands of tradition, symbolized above all by attachment to the *mitzvoth* and to sages and pietists who exemplified them. Victors tend to write history in their own image, and the success of Zionism in establishing the state of Israel and maintaining its viability against hostile "others" seemed to solve the problem of Jewish identity.

However, there was never an unconditional acceptance of the secular vision of what it is to be a Jew, and recent events merely resurfaced the religious counterimages that continued to animate émigrés to Israel, especially from the Hasidic communities of Eastern Europe, who were still living out the two-thousand-year-old drama of Diaspora Judaism. For them, as for new others, the preoccupation with collective survival as a nation-state, even one linked to ethnic Jewry, merely postponed the question of religious destiny; it did not provide an alternative worldview.[47]

Part of the problem is to find an idiom of discourse that does not preclude evaluating even that which might be unattractive or inimical to the outlook of the analyst. A necessary first step is to put civil religion into the same cage of ideology that "contains" fundamentalism. We must try to see civil religion as but one historical manifestation of a process that depends for its success on its ability to mobilize and also sustain interest groups on its behalf. Advocates of civil religion cling to secular Zionism as the shibboleth of Israeli identity. They are then forced to wedge the unexpected into a mosaic of definitions that uphold "civil religion" as the paradigm of what ought to be the basis for moral cohesion in a modern-day nation-state. The syncretizing or homogenizing view asserts that traditional Judaism must change; it must inflate the scope of its symbols to encompass activity and attitudes previously thought of as secular. Syncretists posit civil religion as the fail-safe net of national identity. Like Peter Berger's sacred canopy, civil religion becomes the overarching worldview which subsumes all other worldviews. Traditional Judaism must find its niche within civil religion, for only religion that is civil rather than sacred can serve the needs of the state, and those are the needs that finally count.

Another, more extreme, interpretation depicts the widening of ideological incompatibilities: "a hardening religious militancy and a movement to bring secular 'repentants' back to the fold on the one hand, and a growing secular hedonism on the other."[48] That is the bifurcating view. Its advocates posit an inevitable and continuous confrontation, even though they usually stop short of making ominous chiliastic predictions. They assume that a live-and-let-live ethos will prevail at the heart of Israeli society, no matter how explosive are the incommensurate views publicly aired. Israelis, in their view, will never allow ideological clashes to generate social cleavages that weaken the corporate solidarity or threaten the long-range vitality of Israel as a state.

But what sort of consensus stamps out divisiveness, and at what cost? If we examine what is latent and unspoken beyond what is manifest and boldly declared about Jewish fundamentalists, the religious option looks stronger than consensualists allow. And if we limit ourselves to Neturei Karta and Gush Emunim as the two most compelling exponents of Jewish fundamentalism in Israel, the persistence of religious symbols in the new Zion seems assured. Ironically, the purposes of Neturei Karta and Gush Emunim converge to the extent that their ideologies, though opposite to one another in form, stress an activist intentionality that remains adamantly, unremittingly religious.

At first, it is the differences between Neturei Karta and Gush Emunim that seem most striking. How can they be arrayed together as a religious front "united" against secularists when they appear as mirror, reverse images, one of the other? They, in fact, function as complementary branches of a single movement. They come close to exemplifying the two wings that Karl Mannheim and others since him have seen as characteristic of most ideologies. Ideologues are part chroniclers, part poets, and, in largest part, activists. Though their appeal is directed to history, it is couched in the tone of poetry, for like poets, ideologues rely on the ambiguity of language and symbols. To their opponents, that means they demonstrate a tendency to pathological polysemy,[49] but to advocates it means that they have found the essential formula for pouring old wine into new skins, or rather for ensuring that God's dicta—to worship only him and to keep only his laws—are preserved from new idolatries.

Beyond their opposite view of the state, the two wings of Jewish fundamentalism contrast starkly in their style of religiosity. Neturei Karta seem cast as the Jewish equivalent of Luddites, those inveterate enemies of all modern ways, including technology. In following the *mitzvoth* strictly, they do not watch TV, they segregate their womenfolk, they do not allow participation in secular education.[50] By the austere standard of Neturei Karta, Gush Emunim compliance with the *mitzvoth* is suspect. Though to some they may seem to be "scrupulously observant,"[51] they dress in contemporary, even fashionable attire, but more importantly, "their leisure-time activities are little different from those of secular youth: they watch television, go to mixed parties, and go to the cinema and theater."[52]

There are still deeper differences. Gush Emunim, in claiming to fulfill all the *mitzvoth*, are really raising one to exclusive supremacy, the *mitzva* of settling the land. Their adherence to this *mitzva* coincides with the secular interests of many nonobservant Israelis. Far from shunning such support, the Gush have cultivated it,[53] and unlike Neturei Karta, they do not press on other Israelis their own zeal for religious compliance with the standard *mitzvoth*.

The extent of the Gush willingness to compromise with secular society does render suspect their long-range identity as Jewish fundamentalists: how far can they compromise before losing their authenticity as observant Jews settling *Eretz Yisrael*? That question will be repeatedly asked. However it is finally answered, the Gush dalliance with secular Israelis has been publicly embarrassing on at least one occasion. The incident involved the archsecularist Ariel Sharon. It took place on 5 January 1980 when Sharon was then agriculture minister for the Begin government. He had been meeting with Gush Emunim in Elon Moreh, a contested settlement near Nablus. On the road back to Jerusalem his motorcade was stopped by Peace Now demonstrators. The army was brought in. A compromise was negotiated. Television recorded the scuffle, and Sharon's motorcade was allowed to proceed. "Forgotten in the excitement [however] was one fact: The minister's visit to the Gush settlement and the whole incident took place on the Sabbath, when under Jewish law driving is strictly banned."[54]

TV missed the *real* story: how could Sharon have visited Gush Emunim on the Sabbath? The fact that Gush members were willing to break even the Sabbath highlights the extent to which one *mitzva*, settling the land, takes precedence over others for their leaders.

Neturei Karta would not meet with government officials on any day for any reason. Their opposition to the state on religious grounds evokes grudging admiration. It has even attracted some unusual converts. If one judges by numbers, their influence is small, but if one reflects on the fact that tradition has always extolled the righteous few (who else were the prophets in their day?) and that individual penitence on behalf of the unrepentant collectivity is lauded by rabbinic masters, then the movement of Hozrim bi-tshuva, otherwise known as born-again Judaism, takes on powerful significance. One of the most dramatic conversions involved a secular Sabra TV personality who became an observant Hasidic Jew. Prior to his conversion, Uri Zohar promoted the Sabra myth: the best Israelis were the sons of Ashkenazi socialist immigrants who thrived on the kibbutz and, where necessary, on the battlefield. To abet Sabra solidarity, Uri Zohar provided humor, specializing in quips and anecdotes that delighted his Israeli viewers. But then he changed, not only his vocation but his person. "The Sabra hero was transformed into an Orthodox Jew: first the skullcap, then the side-curls, finally the beard and bearing of an Orthodox grandfatherly person. After he left public life and television, Uri Zohar completed this metamorphosis from sandal-shod native son to heavily garmented, bent *shtetl chasid.*"[55]

Though rare, the transformation of Sabras like Uri Zohar into *hasidim* evokes multiple contrasts. The homologies abound. Sabra/secular Zionist/modernist becomes counterposed to *chasid* (Hasid)/observant Jew/traditionalist. Is it a generational phenomenon or a pervasive mood reversal, or both? At the least it is ironic, and irony demands a literary encapsulation. Amnon Rubinstein provides the requisite mock humor by reverting the insight of Haim Hazaz, a famous post–World War II Israeli writer:

In the forties, Hazaz wrote that when a man cannot be a Jew any more, he becomes Zionist. By the eighties, a full circle has been completed. Many young Israelis feel that their traditional secular Zionism, with its emphasis on normalcy, has reached a dead end and that Hazaz's dictum is refuted and reversed by experience: when a man cannot be a Zionist any more (Zionist in the true Herzlian sense, which denies Jewishness while affirming Jews) he reverts to being a Jew.[56]

The ultimate irony, perhaps, is that there has to be such a choice, that Zionism should have seemed to be a disavowal of Judaism, with the result that the core value of what it is to be a Jew is linked to the anti-Zionist ghetto in the midst of the putative capital of the new Zion. The journey from Zion to Judah seems complete when,

occasionally, these Sabra-turned-chasidim join the most militant Orthodox groups of the Meah Shearim quarter in Jerusalem, from which they emerge to throw stones at cars travelling on the Sabbath. From the heartland of Israel they have traversed all the way to non-Zionist shelters of *galut* (diaspora) within Israel. Just as their fathers ran from Jewish isolation, seeking participation in current history and culture, so do these Sabra sons seek refuge from current history in a haven where Judaism, unaltered by the outside world, reigns eternal.[57]

But clearly the symbolic clash here is too great to be sustained by the majority of Israelis. One must constantly stress that those who go from Sabra to *hasid* are but a small minority of the second generation of European émigrés to Israel, even as the total population of *haredim* does not exceed 3 percent of all Israeli Jewry.[58]

Gush Emunim is still smaller, representing at most twenty thousand West Bank and Gaza Strip settlement activists.[59] Yet Gush Emunim represents another, opposite outlet of Jewish fundamentalist spirit. The Gush, too, proclaim attention to the *mitzvoth* as central to Jewish identity. Moreover, their pioneering spirit, harking back, as it does, to the *élan* of the initial settlers, especially the third *aliya*, 1919–23, compels tacit support from many secular Jews, open support from an influential few.

Moreover, as Ian Lustick has graphically demonstrated, in the aftermath of Camp David the Gush leadership developed an array of interdependent organizations that facilitated their political and cultural outreach, even as it allowed them to preempt and then infiltrate the National Religious Party.[60]

Does that mean that the Gush are not true fundamentalists and that only Neturei Karta are? Some might leap to such a conclusion, but it runs the risk of myopia, for both groups symbolize an explicit religious dimension that others also want to locate in modern Israeli society. Neturei Karta and Gush Emunim are like the inner and the outer, the limited and the extended, tangents of Jewish fundamentalism. Symbiotically, they cooperate to enforce but one authentic definition of Jewish collectivity: the People of Israel and the Land of Israel, conjoined and sanctified through the God of Israel.[61] Contrasting forms aside, Neturei Karta and Gush Emunim serve the same theocratic function.

Their complementarity becomes still clearer if we examine the interrelationship of language and history. Everyone associates Hebrew with Israel, but how does one interpret Hebrew as a canonical language of modern Israel? In the first decade after the creation of the Zionist state, the movement to change names was powerful. It caused many famous leaders to surrender their Diaspora lineages for Hebrew or, at least, Hebrew-sounding names. But that did not answer the larger question: what to do with the Diaspora as a part of the legacy of Jewish history? The Sabra and the Hasid offered opposite evaluations. To the Sabra, Israel was a welcome break from the Ashkenazi past; it was a completion of the true emancipation of Jews from the ghetto existence of premodern Europe. But to the Hasid, emancipation was but another term for Enlightenment *(Haskala)*. Both were mirages, subverting rather than enabling the collectivity. For all that had been intended in the *mitzvoth* was nurtured, winnowed, and preserved in those same European ghettos;

there could be no break with the past that was not at the same time a denial of Judaism. What resulted, after 1948, was

a collision between two different concepts of what "redemption" means. On the one side, stood secular Zionists from Left and Right . . . who denied the validity and relevance of Jewish history from the last revolt against the Romans (70 C.E.) to the Return of Zion (1948). On the other side, stood the traditional Jewish outlook which belittled the Jewish rebellion against the Romans and put its emphasis on the great works of scholarship created in *galut* (exile). The secular view went so far as to downgrade even the Talmud and the "oral Torah," the guide by which Jews lived and which embodied their own unique legal system. Constant efforts were made to exclude its study from the Yishuv schools' curricula.[62]

These are two mutually exclusive views of the Diaspora, and their opposition is nowhere more sharply apparent than in evaluating the work of the pioneer ideologue of Gush Emunim, Rabbi Abraham Isaac Kook. By one reading of his writings, he is an exponent of that view that could be called the "negation of the Diaspora." It has been alleged that he saw in the two-thousand-year Jewish exile "not only a period of dispersion and travail but an unfortunate social and spiritual experience characterized by closedness, divisiveness, spiritual weakness, and detachment from nature."[63] Yet Rabbi Kook also held an exalted view of what certain Jews, including the Hasidim, had accomplished in the Diaspora. His deft compromise of two antithetical attitudes toward the Jewish past is indicated in several of his writings. In "Fragments of Light: A View as to the Reasons for the Commandments," for instance, he offers an impassioned defense of the *mitzvoth* and their primacy in Jewish identity. And in his most famous essay, "The Road to Renewal," he defends the Hasidim. Hasidism, in his view, was the social movement that rescued spiritual inspiration from "the grotesqueness it had assumed in Sabbatianism [the seventeenth century messianic movement that subverted, by coopting, rabbinic Judaism]." Eventually Hasidism "led to the formation of a group that established a base for the return to *Eretz Yisrael* and a renewal of practical work for the rebuilding of our ancestral homeland."[64]

In other words, the Hasidim for Rabbi Kook were the true historical precursors of religious Zionists. Even though his son stressed the immediate timetable of Messianism and even though some recent Gush members seem indifferent to both Rabbi Kooks,[65] the Kook legacy will survive, especially since both father and son may be seen as cofounders of a movement that resembles yet does not replicate medieval Hasidism. The *rebbes* can even be invoked as role models for contemporary Gush activists, as they were in a recent article extolling the heroic but doomed efforts of a Gush engineer who tried to halt the 1982 evacuation of the Sinai.[66]

Links to the Kooks and vestigial Hasidism do not exhaust the relevance of history and language to Jewish fundamentalism. For Neturei Karta also, it was the Diaspora that produced true Judaism. The rabbinical movement persisted after the rebellion against Rome which led to the destruction of the Second Temple (70 c.e.). Its crowning achievement was to canonize one version of *mitzvoth;* the *Shulkhan Arukh* is itself a synopsis of a code of conduct that combined all earlier codes and "explored each law from its place in the Talmud through the latest sources."[67] Its author was a sixteenth-century Spanish mystic and scholar, Joseph Karo (1488–1575), who lived in Safed. He, together with Polish rabbis such as Moses Isserles, so simplified the *mitzvoth* that they were brought "within range of the common Jew. They have remained [ever since] the most potent force in orthodox Jewish life."[68] And what Karo did has been commented on and further refined by successors. While Solomon Ganzfried (1804–86) made a famous abridgment *(Qitstsur Shulkhan Arukh),* now translated into Western languages, for *haredi* Jews the most influential commentary was the *Mishna Berurah* by Rabbi Israel Meir Ha-Kohen Kagan (1838–1933). Since it dealt primarily with holiday observance and other ritual law, it was also referred to as *Shulkhan Arukh-Orah Hayyim.* Widely circulated among Eastern European Jewry, the title of the book supplanted the rabbi's patronymic, and he is better known as Hafetz Hayyim. In the next generation, another Eastern European rabbi, Abraham Yeshaya Karlitz (1878–1953), migrated to Bnei Braq, a suburb of Tel Aviv, where he became so esteemed by the *haredi* community for his commentary on Hafetz Hayyim's commentary of *Shulkhan Arukh* that he, too, is best known by the title of his book: Hazon Ish.[69]

Yet modern Israelis, even those who are schooled in the *yeshivot* (religious academies), have seldom become acquainted with either Hafetz Hayyim or Hazon Ish, much less the highly evolved intellectual tradition of the Diaspora that sustains the *haredi* worldview. The Sabras have been slow to recognize that "the Hebrew culture of the Bible is closer to the era of the kings and prophets who ruled ancient Judaea and Israel than to the late rabbinical traditions of the Pharisees. . . . [Because] the Hebrew culture that has been revived in Israel is in many ways pre-Jewish and pre-Christian, it is only in the last decade that the Sabras have begun to show interest in post-Hebraic Judaism [that is, the writings of the sages and pietists who inspire the Hasidim and now the *haredim*]."[70]

The cultural gap is also a linguistic and temporal gap. For Jewish fundamentalists there is no past tense. To ask the question, Who is a Jew? is to ask the question, Who was a Jew? Questions about identity over which Neturei Karta agonize continuously concern ancestors. They are revered ancestors buried in the Holy Land. Their bones are sanctified. They should be honored. Too often they are not. Consider that

Jewish burial seems to occupy a sightly higher position than Jewish marriage in the sociological Jew's scale of ritual priorities. Throughout the ages Jews have fervently hoped that at the end of their days their bodies would lie in consecrated ground—preferably in the company of their ancestors and, at any rate, in that of the faithful. [The Holy Land in general was deemed to be a burial ground of special sanctity. And] the choice of the four Holy Cities (Jerusalem, Hebron, Tiberias, and Safed) was dictated by the proximity of revered shrines. [Is it any wonder then that] the most heartrending expressions of protest to come from the pens of the Guardians of the City have been provoked by archaeological excavations and gardening operations—under the auspices of the Ministry of Religions for the benefit of tourism—around the graves of the teachers of the Mishnah and medieval luminaries [including Hasidic masters]?[71]

For Neturei Karta the grip of tradition on the present is symbolized by the mandatory veneration of the dead. Honoring holy graves is not a *mitzvah* that can be suspended or rationalized. It is the plumbline of spiritual continuity with the past. It must be retained at all costs.

Jewish fundamentalists will continue to resist efforts to assimilate them. Rejecting inclusion under an umbrella ideology that would merely extend the boundaries of religious Zionism without changing its context, they are not daunted by their own small numbers. Through their two wings, Neturei Karta in the heart of Jerusalem and Gush Emunim throughout the new frontier (Judea and Samaria), they challenge all secular Zionists with an alternative vision of Israel's past and also its future. They cannot be moved. Can they be overcome, and if so, for what? That question dwarfs all other questions about Israel. Even survival as a nation-state (now assured) only underscores the real question: is Israel to be a nation like other nations, or is there a special meaning to Jewish collectivity?

The emergence of Jewish fundamentalism is instructive for understanding the larger themes of fundamentalism in all three monotheistic traditions. The core identity, in this case the Jewish collectivity, has persisted despite the multileveled challenge of the Technical Age and now the High Tech Era. Secularization succeeded for the majority of Jews, as it had for others, but it did not remove the impulse to identify with myths, rituals, and persons who were deemed to represent an authoritative past. It was always a few who saw themselves as the faithful remnant upholding what others had abandoned or profaned. They did not confront modernism directly but always through those others in their midst who changed while trying to deny that change was harmful.

The faithful remnant, however, is itself ambivalent. It opposes those coreligionists who embrace the Enlightenment, and yet it also hopes to bring them back to those values abandoned, those rituals neglected. "Gush Emunim sees itself as charged to remain within the main body of Israel in order to transform the whole" and to reeducate those led astray by secular Zionism.[72] And Neturei Karta, despite its opposition to the state of Israel, remains as a holy witness to rabbinic Judaism within the heart of modern-day Jerusalem.

The faithful remnant also does not simply respond to timeless directives or to age-old scriptural truths. It requires their reexpression in living holy men, charismatic leaders of the present era, and it responds to particular events that embody the challenge of secularization to core values. Nowhere within contemporary Judaism has this sequence of fundamentalist logic been clearer than in the evolution of Gush Emunim. Settlement of the land became the prime *mitzvah*, superseding in importance all other *mitzvoth*, even observance of the Sabbath, and the Rabbis Kook emboldened others to promote the messianic era through adherence to this *mitzvah*. Political events of the three most recent Arab-Israeli wars—1967, 1973, and 1982—elicited a broader public support for the settlement ideology of the Rabbis Kook. More recent events have confirmed and extended their initiative. Gush Emunim opposed the Sinai withdrawal that was called for in the Camp David accord between Israel and Egypt; Sinai, in their view, was a part of *Eretz Yisrael*, divinely entrusted to the people of Israel. Its surrender would further postpone the advent of the messianic era. The aged Rabbi Zvi Yehuda Kook (he was then ninety-two years old) encouraged the Sinai settlers "to preserve the wholeness of the land, the holy inheritance of our fathers," just as he excoriated "a Jewish government which . . . violates the commandment of the Creator."[73] As if by divine decree, he died at the moment that the government of Israel was on the verge of fulfilling its treaty obligations, for despite the objections of religious settlers and activists, Israel did withdraw from Yamit and Sadot in the spring of 1982.

The double loss of both their beloved leader and also the sacred land should have been a setback for Gush Emunim, but instead it proved a spur to their further development. A new authoritative leader emerged in the person of Rabbi Eliezer Waldman, and a new cause in the Lebanese war, which began in the summer months of 1982, soon after the "defeat" of Sinai. For Rabbi Waldman, not only was southern Lebanon part of *Eretz Yisrael*, but those who fought there and died became heroes in advancing the redemption of Israel. After all, had not Rabbi Abraham Kook said, "When there is a war in the world, the power of the Messiah is aroused?"[74] The real enemies were those other Israelis who doubted the rightness of the war or refused to fight, for they failed to realize that Israel was "revealing the powers of redemption through the souls who act in the drama, those who are sacrificed and ascend."[75]

Gush Emunim may not survive the tempestuous cycles of Israeli politics. So crucial is the role of charismatic leaders that some doubt that any Gush personality will ever fill the vacuum created by Rabbi Zvi Yehuda Kook's death.[76] Even in the absence of another *rebbe*, Gush Emunim will continue to project its views and advocate its objectives through skillful use of media. Their own existence has been highlighted by Israeli press and TV, but even more importantly, they have developed a sectarian publication, the journal of the West Bank settlements called *Nekuda*. It has become a unique forum for voicing their internal debate over approaches to outsiders, those major segments of Israeli society that they need to influence if they are to succeed as the righteous vanguard.[77] While the Neturei Karta would seem to be handicapped by their aversion to the electronic media, they, too, have furthered their aims through a sectarian publication, the biweekly journal, *Mishmereth Homathenu*. It presents their view of events in Israel, just as it fosters debate about tactics within the circle of the Guardians.[78] And so, both wings of Jewish fundamentalism have made use of their own Hebrew language publications to marshal support for their concerns. Even in opposing modernism, they continue to acknowledge the value of modern print media. For them, as for other fundamentalists, media and ideology are inseparable. Jewish fundamentalists benefit from media coverage in a double sense: while secular media draw attention to their efforts and enhance their pariah status for outsiders, their own media present another view that reinforces and extends the loyalty of inside members. The modern world is rejected through its own instrumentalities. That is, after all, the ultimate hope as well as the day-to-day goal of fundamentalism.

CHAPTER 7

American-style Protestant Fundamentalists

It is almost impossible to overestimate the impact of historical consciousness upon religious thought in the West. It could be argued that Protestant and Catholic liberalism was virtually defined by its sympathetic
response to the historical understanding of culture. Liberals made their
peace with modernity in various ways, but in the end they all insisted
that God's self-revelation is mediated through the flow of history. . . .
[The opposite] insistence [,namely,] that the method and content of revelation were not a function merely of historical processes stood at the
core of what came to be known, especially in the United States, as fundamentalism.

—GRANT WACKER

The necessary context for American Protestant Christian fundamentalism was that axial event best depicted as the Great Western Transmutation. The United States was only a partial exception to the pattern of
technicalization that eventually transformed major parts of the globe.
Initially it was but one among the many traditional societies affected by
the overseas networking of European trading companies and the expansion of maritime travel. In time, however, the American continent became at once a showcase and a test case of the rapid change
characteristic of the modern era, due to the technical and commercial
acceleration of the GWT.

How was America transformed from a minor to a major actor in the
roll call of nations? There are many evaluative criteria, but the yardstick
of modern warfare offers the most graphic evidence. The United States
did not become a Great Power, a nation capable of waging war and
winning it beyond its own borders, till the beginning of the twentieth
century. Only Japan and China have been more recent entrants into the
Great Power game.[1]

But more than military prowess distinguished America's stature in the
twentieth century. Viewed from Europe, the United States became a
microcosm for charting the formation of the entire modern world. It
owed its origins to the Old World. Not only through its immigrant mi-

norities but also its ties to a European-based world economy, America was shaped by events in the Northern European theater. For the GWT was a global phenomenon and part of its expansionary force was directed to the American continent. There were other markets and pockets of resource: not only North American but also South American, South Asian, and East Asian coastal frontiers. All of them were located, some even discovered, and others redefined by European commercial expansion.

America was at once a part of the overall emergent pattern and also a region with distinctive variations. The Europeans who settled America came for a variety of motives. Yet it was the same mercantile entrepreneurs, operating with military superiority to natives and favorable economic and political support from home governments, who settled the several colonies. Sea power determined victory, and therefore the ultimate battle was between British and French navies. The rivalries that each had with Spanish, Portuguese, and Dutch forces were flickering skirmishes, diversions from the major struggle. America experienced the multiple colonization of expansionary Europe. The British and French colonized Indians; their successors continued the colonization of Indians and blacks. There were undeniable successes, notably the rooting of equality and tolerance as civic rights constitutionally enshrined, but there were also excesses and failures, none worse than slavery, institutionally uprooted by a civil war but economically and emotionally persistent into this century.

In short, colonial America, like every colonial society, was hierarchical, its class structure rife with inequality. Even after winning independence, Americans retained a mixture of class contrasts: the ruling elites publicly espoused egalitarianism, but they also tolerated, even encouraged a "legally imposed hierarchy" that protected and extended their own material and social interests. One need only read the literature on the debate about social Darwinism at the turn of the century to sense how alive was the need to justify social and economic elitism in the land of those who were free but still unequal.[2]

America was no exception to a global pattern of change. The foundation and development of the American republic was framed by the major force reshaping the world—the Great Western Transmutation. If there was a newness and a fresh hope in America, it was symbolized for many by the expansion westward. The frontier epitomized the American *élan*. As an image, the frontier has had lasting cultural and religious effects—the notion of regional autonomy, the assertion of individual initiative and protection, the promotion of group interest on a contractual rather than a covenantal basis.[3] Above all, the frontier evoked the hope that no boundaries are permanent, that all frontiers disappear only to be replaced by new and bigger frontiers. In January 1986, there occurred the worst disaster in the American space program: the explosion on takeoff of the shuttle *Challenger* killing all seven crew members aboard, and still many people rapturously confirmed the need to continue to explore space. As news commentators never tired of emphasizing, outer space is the last great frontier.

The Western frontier of America also offered a temporary escape valve for those trapped by the double-bind logic of institutional religion. On the one hand, all American churches, like every religious body, were shaped by what can only be phrased oxymoronically as a restrictive universalism. Every group claimed that it alone had the whole truth everyone needed, but at the same time, all would-be proselytizers were held in check by an explicit particularism. Each group had to accept the right of others to exist, and also to advance universalist claims of their own. Religious sectarians in theory could live anywhere, yet the frontier tolerated ecclesiastical experimentation more than the settled, rapidly traditionalizing regions of the Northeast and the South. Mormonism became the distinctive American frontier religion, California the birthplace of more religious sects than any state in the Union.

Even at the frontier, however, there were functional limits to religious freedom. It was freedom constitutionally mandated by an established government. Any religion could flourish except one that might threaten the physical security or contradict the social ethos of the Republic. A religion to kill white Americans or to promote socialist communes was effectively precluded—at least until the rise of the Nation of Islam in the 1930s and the Hippies in the 1960s. Absence of creedal uniformity provided a porous umbrella under which numerous ecclesiastical structures could and did exist side by side. Their only connection to one another, beyond physical proximity, was the common mandate to tolerate one another's difference. Gradually there came to be no religion *of* America except the general sense that America allowed *any* religion. The awkward paradox of this development was brought home in the fifties when President Eisenhower made the now famous pronouncement that "our government makes no sense unless it is founded in a deeply felt religious faith—and I don't care what it is."[4]

The impasse that brought America to the Eisenhower dictum was intimately linked to the church-state construct. No exhibit of cultural change through modernization is more glaringly American than the checkered pattern of church-state relationships. How do churches (and also synagogues and mosques) function in a modernizing pluralistic polity? It is not merely a matter of keeping religion out of politics. It is rather the complex task of charting how Protestant churches spearhead the search, common to all religious bodies, of securing their identity and purposes vis-à-vis an emergent American polity distrustful of organized religion.

What "modern" reason accomplished in science and economics was transferred into social values through the Scottish Enlightenment and its American disciples. The church-state construct became a political expedient of the founding fathers to separate state from church, and at the same time to remove church from state. By abstracting actual institutions and reifying processes in transition, they posed the two as somehow equal entities magnetically drawn to the same source of power. Only in the American context have church and state been ritually demarcated, on the assumption that they could and should function as complementary opposites. Hidden from public scrutiny is the unsettling recognition that there must exist an implicit, persistent tension between them since both claim to be reality-defining, allegiance-eliciting social organizations.

That peculiarly American development came at the hand of Protestant or post-Protestant Americans. The church-state construct remains as alien to Roman Catholics as it is puzzling to Jews and Muslims. For all of them the state-church separation retains the air of a "bogus" Protestant invention.

Although the American experience reflects only one tangent of the GWT, an examination of that tangent does help us to come to terms with its irresistible force elsewhere. Two questions seem crucial before focusing on the church-state issue. First, what was the role of the founding fathers in evolving the peculiarly American notion that the basis of true government (i.e., democracy) is the moral individual exercising common sense? And, second, even more basically, how was the individual thought to be superior to any other basic unit of social organization, for instance, the family, the church, or even hereditary elites?

The individual is morally rational. He or she exercises his or her freedom on behalf of society as a whole. Society should enhance rather than restrict or redirect one's freedom. The group exists for the individual, not the reverse.

Despite its naive optimism, the sanctity of individual autonomy echoes as a powerful clarion cry to American ears. It goes back to Jefferson as a founding father. It was he who stressed not only freedom of religion but also freedom from religion. While other founding fathers like Madison, Franklin, and Paine shared Jefferson's deep distrust of institutionalized religion, it was Jefferson who marshaled the forces of anticlericalism. He went further than others in asserting that the churches ought to be "servants of the state, even in their status as voluntary associations. The state was in effect the true guardian of the public welfare and the churches were [or ought to be] its allies."[5]

Jefferson, in effect, saw only the social usefulness or instrumentalism of the churches. Protected by the state, they were also subordinate to it. He did not see them as coequal defenders of the public good nor did he allow for the possibility that they could be alternate custodians of the public good whose autonomy permitted them to criticize other public institutions. The first role was irrelevant, the second irreverent to the state, and ecclesiastical dissent, ranging from annoyance to treason, was not to be tolerated. Free speech could be expressed through elected officials to Congress, social policies could be changed or confirmed by the courts, but the challenging of public priorities by anyone, including clergy, was seditious. It was not merely blasphemy; it was treason.

Jefferson did not see the dilemma that his views posed for the churches. If reason could be invoked to redefine faith as maintenance of the public good, the churches were reduced to serving as custodians of rationally perceived morality. They lost the uniqueness of their authority. They also forfeited their claims to legitimacy, for "virtually all the historic faiths of the West, Protestant and Catholic, Jewish and Islamic, understand themselves as communities of response, called into being not by logic but by a divine initiative. They are rich-textured religions of revelation that stand apart from as well as within the cultures where they are embedded."[6]

Nowhere has this dilemma of revealed religion been more clearly spelled out than in the writings of H. Richard Niebuhr. In *Christ and Culture,* Niebuhr postulated five stances of the Christ paradigm relative to culture: Christ against culture, Christ of culture, Christ above culture, Christ and culture in paradox, Christ as the transformer of culture. There are problems with Niebuhr's typology. For instance, in focusing on what was professed by individual Christian thinkers or leaders, he does not recognize the extent to which churches as social institutions take on a will of their own, often embodying the accommodationist impulse rather than opting for one of the conflictual stances. Yet Jefferson and his followers have fallen prey to the opposite tendency, ignoring the shortcomings of religious folk who merely mirror civic values and fail to question the inadequacy of *all* political structures. Indeed, "if the churches were to accept the Enlightenment rationalist thesis that religion is reducible to a common core morality discoverable by reason alone, they would have to acknowledge that most of their faith and life is irrelevant to society."[7]

It is ironic that Jeffersonian democracy, because it seems to favor the exercise of religious freedom, tolerates a pluralistic array of religious institutions. Precisely because it rejects the ultimacy of any creed, it fosters all creeds while arrogating to itself a privileged authority that implies, even if it does not claim, the sole custodianship of spiritual and moral values. Values are the core of culture; a state cannot operate without them; a church cannot function without challenging and reshaping them. The resulting tension is recurrent in all stages of history. The prophets challenged ancient Israel's myopic kings. Jesus mandated that what is Caesar's and God's be kept separate. Muhammad usurped power from his polytheistic elders. Yet under the impact of the GWT the transcendental dimension of church-state tension evaporates. Advocates of the Scottish Enlightenment, including the founding fathers of the USA, view it as immanent. No longer autonomous, the spiritual reflex depends on political goodwill.

Does the modern state in America usurp the function of the premodern church in Europe? Yes, for

the state finds itself creating the faith which it cannot locate outside itself, claiming that all its activities are ultimately informed by a commitment to "spiritual and moral values." These values include justice, order, and the rule of law, a concern for the common good, and a certain egalitarianism in "life, liberty, and the pursuit of happiness." They are more than political goals. They are said to be willed by God in the design of the universe. They are celebrated in patriotic speeches and documents major and minor, from the Declaration of Independence and the Gettysburg Address to run-of-the-mill election speeches. This is the content of the so-called "civil religion" (to use Rousseau's phrase, now popular again), also called by historians "republican religion," meaning "the religion of the republic."[8] It is of course a "natural theology," not a revealed one; but it is celebrated and ritualized in a way not unlike more traditional religions. . . . It (even) includes a formal acknowledgement of God, often in the favorite rational term, a "Supreme Being." . . . In short, the state creates a substitute highly forbidden state church. It practices its own kind of religiousness, while fending off the actual institutional embodiment of religion as it is found in living churches; and this is the fate to which it was foreordained by the original rationalist vision at the time of the Constitution.[9]

The parallelism of civil religion to traditional religion is itself a perilous redirection and reduction of the role that organized religious groups have played in the history of humankind. Civil religion is precisely not a religion. Common sense not faith is the universal chord whose ring it echoes, and conformity to its creed is local rather than global. Even Jefferson did not believe that all nations on the earth would subscribe to democracy.

To the extent that the new religion of the American republic is civil, it reflects its modernist origins. It is a child of what we have called the modernist hegemony. Its outlook is technical, quantity-prone, utilitarian, profit-maximizing outlook. There is a sense in which the only referent of ultimate values in the Technical Age is modernism. Modernism is the true religion of the High Tech Era. Modernism claims several churches, one of which is democracy, another, communism, and another, socialism.

The contradictions of Jeffersonian-style civil religion might not have become apparent in the early decades of the twentieth century had not the GWT also produced an outpouring of European immigrants from hard pressed, marginalized areas of the old West who sought a new life and brought with them their old values to the new West. It has often been stated that the immediate cause for the emergence of American-style fundamentalism was ideational: those who cared about the content of religious faith rejected the new rationalism embraced by liberal Protestants. But another powerful impetus for crystallizing a radically Protestant ideology was also at work. It was sociological. Dramatic demographic and economic changes occurred at the end of the nineteenth century. Till then constitutional equality had been an ideal to be proclaimed but not fully tested in the USA. It was on the eve of the twentieth century that the United States not only emerged as a Great Power, it also became a bona fide test case of "cultural pluralism."

So many immigrants of Mediterranean extraction came to the USA in the first two decades of the twentieth century that in 1924 Congress passed the Johnson Immigration Act. It drastically curtailed immigration from Eastern and Southern Europe while favoring immigration from the Protestant nations of Northern Europe.[10] Ironically in the same year (1924) Horace Kallen coined the term "cultural pluralism" to advocate the value of ethnic heterogeneity and Old World ties among a shifting American population. What was bliss to some became poison to others, and the pressure valve for venting both pleasure and protest was institutional religion. By the mid-twenties, it was becoming apparent that the increased ethnic amalgamation from different nations, the rapid expansion of the "middle class" within America, and the availability of instantaneous communications between all classes, whether by telegraph or telephone, by radio or newspaper, would elicit a public response from groups who felt deprived.

America the melting pot was always in danger of becoming America the boiling cauldron. The very plurality of groups and views caused some to be frustrated because they could not control the larger directions of their lives, above all in the public sphere. However much their creedal orientations and institutional autonomy were constitutionally safeguarded, it also seemed that the Supreme Court had become the ultimate referent, assuming the role of a divine surrogate, proclaiming what was admissible or inadmissible by the standard of civil law. The universalist impulse of the older established churches, both Protestant and Catholic, had never sought a correspondence or congruence between their system of beliefs and the particular style of government or ethos of society. But to some American Protestants the universalist claims of Christianity appeared as a biblical mandate that rubbed up against the constraints of the dominant American ethos, one that rightly came to be called "the Religion of the Republic." The Supreme Court became the ecclesiastical arm of the Religion of the Republic, public officials its high priests, patriotic Americans its laity, and the fundamentalists—its heretics. The rest of the history of American fundamentalism is a tracing out of that heresy.

It is a history that remains blurred. Much has been written about Progressive Patriotic Protestants, but with few exceptions, what has so far appeared in print reflects a close reading of dates, events, and, above all, people that tells only part of the story.

Fundamentalists themselves are partly to blame. Prolific producers of words, few became systematic historians, fewer still exploratory or integrative thinkers. Scholars on fundamentalism, coming out of the tradition of American church history, narrate the etiology of Protestant Christian fundamentalism as a variation, whether legitimate or deviant, of American evangelicalism. They expand the enemy beyond what fundamentalists themselves describe, but it remains "modernism" or a string of cognate -isms—liberalism, scientism, relativism, materialism.[11] What is omitted is the larger context that produced both fundamentalism and its opponents, the tidal changes in social and economic organization as well as intellectual and cultural fashions against which fundamentalists reacted but to which they themselves also became linked. The shift was global, though its origins were linked to the West. We have described it elsewhere as the Great Western Transmutation, the Technical Age and, since 1950, the High Tech Era.[12] It is to that resorting of temporal markings that Christian fundamentalism, like its monotheistic parallels in Judaism and Islam, must be related if we are to make sense of them.

The perceptual vantage point is not easily scaled. To investigate American Protestant Christian fundamentalism we need a methodological rule of thumb that separates out recorded data from unrecorded trends and unacknowledged forces. We must review explicit acts but also connect them to implicit motives and tacit influences. We are not faced with a simple, stark contrast of inner and outer, emic and etic perspectives. The insider's privileged account, when set against an outsider's hostile or "objective" account, does not yield a true understanding of the origins and development of American fundamentalism. Rather, the stories of each, outsider-observer as well as insider-fundamentalist, are so enmeshed one with the other that both run the danger of ignoring their common context. That context is not only the GWT in its initial form but also in its most recent phase, the High Tech Era. It is the furthest development of modernity in one of the youngest of the world powers.[13] It shapes Christian fundamentalists in ways similar to Jewish and Islamic fundamentalists, even though the outward forms of each are radically dissimilar. The motivating forces are cloaked beneath a thicket of scholarship that needs to be disentangled before comparisons or contrasts can be broached.

Most scholarship looks at Christian fundamentalism as a religious movement. Begun in the nineteenth century, it accelerated in the twentieth. Its seeds were planted in England, but it flourished in America. However nuanced, the temporal and spatial boundaries of Christian fundamentalism remain within the Anglo-American branches of late-nineteenth–early-twentieth-century Protestantism. Less clear is whether the fundamentalist movement should be treated as primarily a social or an intellectual happening. The social approach downplays the impact of doctrinal fires and looks instead at cross-creedal challenges. Fundamentalists were Protestants pitted against non-Protestants, first Jews in England, then Roman Catholics in America.[14] They fought external foes. By contrast, the intellectual approach takes seriously the doctrinal issues that fundamentalists themselves dwell on. It does matter whether or not certain Protestants accepted the Bible as inerrantly true, whether or not they adhered to a premillenial or postmillennial view of the end of time. Fundamentalists fought internal foes. Their leaders separated from mainline Protestant denominations, specifically Presbyterianism and the American Baptist Convention. They protested creeping rationalism within the church. They founded their own churches in order to maintain doctrinal purity and also to point out the defilement of those from whom they separated. "Expound and expose" was their clarion cry. According to one of its leading proponents, "historic fundamentalism is the literal exposition of all the affirmations and attitudes of the Bible and the militant exposure of all non-Biblical affirmations and attitudes."[15]

By either approach, the social-sectarian or the intellectual-separatist, the history of fundamentalism becomes an extended charting of doctrinal controversy and ecclesiastical conflict. It ends where it begins, in the recapitulation and appraisal of biographical profiles. Two examples, one from a fundamentalist scholar, the other from a scholar of fundamentalism, will suffice to show the difficulty in which they are commonly immersed, despite opposite predispositions. The fundamentalist scholar is George Dollar. The scholar of fundamentalism is Ernest Sandeen.

Dollar writes self-consciously as a faculty member of Bob Jones University. He tries to give the authentic profile, and also the working handbook, of American Protestant Christian fundamentalism. His study, entitled *A History of Fundamentalism in America*, is divided into three parts. In it he looks at the past one hundred years with alliterative key words. The period of 1875–1900 is Reaction and Restoration; 1900–1935, Revulsion and Revolt; while the latest period, 1935–1973 (when the book was published) becomes Reconstruction, Revival, and Retreat. The key to Dollar's book is its parade of people. His profile of American fundamentalism is peppered with biographical vignettes. Eliminate them and you have very little to say about the substance of the topic at hand. There are heroes and villains. The former, as might be expected, receive fuller treatment than the latter. But there are two kinds of villains: vague archenemies from the distant European past, and vivid others, their successors and supporters in contemporary America.

Dollar's enemies are the heroes of the European Enlightenment: Immanuel Kant, G. F. Hegel, F. C. Baur, Albrecht Ritschl, and G. F. Schleiermacher. "All five catapulted German philosophy and theology onto the American scene, philosophizing its theology, providing sharp tools to destroy the historic faith, and bringing into slavery the minds of the intelligentsia and the prospective leaders of the denominations."[16] Their villainous role is abetted by others, including Ernst Troeltsch, another German scholar (often regarded as the founder of the scientific study of religion) and, of course, Charles Darwin, whose *Origin of the Species,* published in 1859, launched the monkey trial, or what came to be known as the controversy over evolution.

If the attention given the European cast of villains is brief, their American successors fare little better. According to Dollar, the troika of American theological liberalism at the turn of the century consisted of William R. Harper, founder of the University of Chicago; William N. Clarke of Colgate Rochester Divinity School; and William A. Brown of Union Seminary in New York. Only Clarke's views are explored at length. The others are presented in synopsis form.

The case is different when we come to the fundamentalist exponents of the Word. First among them was A. J. Gordon, the Baptist biblicist from Boston who flourished till nearly the end of the nineteenth century, expiring in 1895. Literalist, fundamentalist, millenarian, he put forth his views not only from the pulpit but also in several books. His periodic paper, *The Watchword,* established a trend followed by other fundamentalist notables, from his contemporary James H. Brooke (*The Truth*) to John R. Rice (*The Sword of the Lord*): to embrace modern media, above all, to disseminate one's own views through a regular publication that circulates widely among loyal followers.

The rest of part one of Dollar's book documents other great figures in the first phase of American fundamentalism, though none approaches the stature of A. J. Gordon. Evangelists were active in this same period (1875–1900), and while Dollar does not claim their leading lights as fundamentalists, he is careful to note that the greatest of them, Dwight L. Moody (the congregationalist preacher who founded Moody Bible Institute), "was very close to A. J. Gordon and his group of Fundamentalists and upheld their meetings and convictions" while also not countenancing "Liberals in what they were teaching or doing to the Christian faith."[17]

In part two (Revulsion and Revolt, 1900–1935), the biographical lens becomes still sharper, in assessing blame as well as heaping on praise. During the early decades of this century liberalism produced its most appealing personalities in Harry Emerson Fosdick, Shailer Matthews, and Walter Rauschenbusch. Fosdick is given special and lengthy treatment. He heads the list of twentieth-century American churchmen who were partisan to the evils of Protestant liberalism. Others include Reinhold and H. Richard Niebuhr, Joseph Fletcher, James A. Pike, Norman Vincent Peale, and even Martin Luther King, Jr. They had their Continental counterparts, theologians such as Karl Barth, Paul Tillich, Rudolf Bultmann, and philosophers of the rank of Karl Jaspers, Martin Heidegger, and Nicholai Berdyaev. Together they have contributed to the decline of biblical Christianity, since "each one had played a significant role in the creation of ecumenical theology—one utterly devoid of Bible truth but Satan-inspired to blind millions to the saving grace of God."[18]

The heroes in the crusade for Bible truth, or the fundamentals of Christianity, were another American troika: J. Frank Norris, John Roach Straton and William Bell Riley. They were aided by a lonely defender of the faith north of the border, the Canadian Thomas T. Shields. Dollar goes into extensive detail on the merits and contributions of each man to the fundamentalist cause. But two summary statements set the tone for all the detail of this portion of his book. On the one hand, "fundamentalists need not look for their type again."[19] They stand in a class by themselves. Yet their separate and coordinated efforts did not produce a decisive victory for the cause they defended, and so one must acknowledge a shortcoming: "in the persons of Norris, Straton, Riley and Shields Fundamentalism produced its most inspiring, though erratic, giants."[20]

How great were these heroes of the halcyon years of American Protestant Christian fundamentalism? What made them seem "erratic" even to their admirers and defenders? All of them suffered "lesser" defeats, and perhaps the clearest way to measure their larger-than-life profiles is to acknowledge their mixed record. Norris was a Texan Baptist. A declamatory preacher who never learned the word "moderation," he fought all forms of infidelity, especially evolution, which he detected in the Southern Baptist Convention and also in his alma mater, Baylor University. In 1926 he became involved in a personal altercation with a local businessman. Words turned to physical violence; Norris shot and killed his opponent. For the remainder of his long life (he did not die till 1952 at the age of seventy five), he was haunted by this incident.

Straton experienced defeat of another kind. A Northern Baptist, he denounced sin in the modern-day replica of Gomorrah, New York City. Not only the ultraliberal Union Seminary but also the Protestant pulpits of New York City were deemed by him to be turnstyles for nascent liberalism. It was Straton who gave the reply to Harry Emerson Fosdick's 1922 sermon, which Fosdick rhetorically titled, "Shall the Fundamentalists Win?" In his rejoinder, sometimes called the second most important event of Christian fundamentalism, after the Scopes trial, Straton attacked both Romanism and Al Smith, the first Roman Catholic candidate for President (in 1928). But he suffered defeat when he challenged a leading Unitarian minister to public debate on the essential articles of faith. The debates were held at the end of 1923 and the beginning of 1924 in Carnegie Hall, with both those in attendance and those who listened on radio voting their preferences. Though Straton won the debate on the divinity of Christ, his opponent, Charles Francis Potter, carried the day on two crucial issues: most of those polled rejected both the infallibility of scripture and the virgin birth of Christ. The fourth debate focused on evolution. Its outcome was inconclusive. Ironically, the fifth and final debate, on the return of Christ, was never held![21]

Riley suffered defeat in a different guise. As a member of the Northern Baptist Convention, his most enduring contributions to the fundamentalist movement were organizational. He founded the Northwestern Schools (a seminary and liberal arts college for training fundamentalists), and he played a leading role in founding the World's Christian Fundamentals Association in 1919 as well as the Baptist Bible Union in 1923. No less than Straton he sought to debate leading modernist opponents. Clarence Darrow once agreed to debate him on evolution, but the touted confrontation never materialized. His biggest disappointment, however, was not to transform the Northern Baptist Convention, of which he remained a member till near the end of his life. On what he deemed to be key issues, many of his closest friends held back or demurred; they could not concur with his unalloyed adherence to the fundamentals.

Shields resembles Straton in his strident attack on Romanism. As a Canadian and the pastor of a Baptist parish in Toronto, he, like Straton in New York City, faced Roman Catholics on a daily basis in many dimensions of public life. He influenced Baptists in the United States, joining with Riley and others to found the Baptist Bible Union in 1923. Like Norris, he was attentive to the inroads of modernism into the university, fighting to excise the apostate appointments at McMaster University in Hamilton, Ontario. But he had to acknowledge defeat when the Ontario Baptist Convention sided with the McMaster administration after 1926. Also, like Riley, he suffered from the inability of friends to support his theological posture. Two who had worked with him for decades split to form their own seminaries, leaving the Toronto Baptist Seminary that Shields himself had opened in 1922. Curiously, by the end of his life he had allied himself with the anticommunist demagogue Carl McIntire. In 1948 Shields joined the International Council of Christian Churches, which paralleled McIntire's American Council of Christian Churches, itself a rival to the National Council of Churches.

What becomes evident in looking at the "lesser" defeats of the four giants of American fundamentalism is how much they hold in common. All became great in the first instance because they gained repute as tireless orators on behalf of biblical truths. They expanded their pulpiteering through the media, both electronic and literary, the radio as well as the pamphlet. One cannot read any account of any of their lives without being struck by the special emphasis on sectarian journals. For Norris, it was *The Fundamentalist*,[22] for Riley, it was *The Christian Fundamentals,* for Straton, *The Faith Fundamentalist,* later changed to *The American Fundamentalist.*[23] Shields called his journal *The Gospel Witness*.

The other form of zealous expression, besides pulpiteering and publishing, was organizing. Here Riley stands in a class by himself. Both Norris and Shields complemented most of his endeavors. Only Straton seems to have devoted a minimal amount of his energy and time to these endeavors, although he did help found the Baptist Bible Union and also the inconsequential Fundamentalist Leagues of New York. It is no accident that Jerry Falwell in his own biographical recitation of the heroes of fundamentalism gives greatest attention to Riley, Norris, and Shields, less to Straton: building a network of independent, locally responsible, grassroots, biblically based churches was crucial to the success of fundamentalism as a movement.[24]

The Baptist giants attracted company. They had other non-Baptist supporters among the mainline denominations, especially Presbyterians, like J. Gresham Machen of Princeton Seminary, Clarence Macartney of Pittsburgh, and William Jennings Bryan. Bryan, the three-time Democratic candidate for President of the United States who later served as Wilson's Secretary of State, is best remembered by fundamentalists for having attacked evolution and debated against Clarence Darrow in the 1925 Scopes trial. But chiefly these three operated through their own fundamentalist fellowships, siphoning off their followers from statewide Baptist conventions.

Retreat set the pattern for the next period of fundamentalism, depicted by Dollar as Reconstruction, Revival, and Retreat (1935–1973). The empires of the Baptist giants eroded, and a new enemy emerged from within. It was the new evangelicalism, claiming to be loyal to the Gospel but really imbibing liberal, modernist notions and encouraging association with infidels. If the dual challenge of fundamentalism is to expound and expose, it was the failure of Billy Graham to expose the apostasy of certain evangelical churches that led to the rift between him and the fundamentalists at his New York City crusade of 1957. Even though he had succeeded the legendary Riley as president of the Northwestern Schools in 1947 and had become a widely acclaimed preacher, Graham was excluded from fundamentalist pulpits after 1957, and the core of that spirit which had motivated Norris, Riley, and Shields was preserved through fellowships modeled after theirs. They all take their cue from the two pace-setting fellowships of the twenties, the World's Christian Fundamentals Association and the Baptist Bible Union. And like fundamentalism itself, they are as strong or as weak as the reputation of their charismatic leaders. It is for this reason that Jerry Falwell, in making his own assessment of the fundamentalist movement, exalts personalities over *any* issue which might be contested by persons of opposite views. Of the 1900–1930 era, he writes:

It is impossible to conceptualize the confrontation fully without a detailed analysis of the personalities involved. The controversy of Modernism and Fundamentalism was much more than a confrontation of ideologies. In many respects it was a confrontation of charismatic personalities, climaxed by the Scopes trial in 1925. The trial became much more the confrontation of Darrow vs. Bryan rather than of evolution vs. supernaturalism. Often the ideas became subsumed within the personalities of the people who represented those ideas.[25]

It would be tempting to continue the roll call of Dollar, depicting the latest heroes who have participated in the fundamentalist battle against modernism in the late seventies and eighties. That exercise would lead us into still another evaluation of the relationship between American Protestant fundamentalists and conservative political movements. We would conclude, as have most serious observers, that the marriage of religion and politics is an anomaly with limits as well as benefits to both partners; some fundamentalists at some points in their history may feel impelled to engage, in order to reform, the body politic, but others have defined their life's work in spiritual terms that either tacitly ignore political issues or actively oppose political involvement.[26]

What has too seldom been done is to test the parameters of fundamentalism as an intellectual enterprise. The cultural historian Ernest Sandeen has made a fruitful start in this direction. In *The Origins of Fundamentalism: British and American Millenarianism, 1875–1914*, Sandeen maintains that at the heart of American-style evangelicalism is precisely a battle of ideas, and the key term around which all other ideas cluster is millenarianism. "Fundamentalism" looms as an ambiguous term. It was not coined till 1920, and then by a journalist. It can refer to a socioecclesiastical movement spurred by separatist Protestants, but, in Sandeen's view, it is rather the latest phase in a theological controversy going back to nineteenth-century England and involving most branches of evangelical Christianity. Though precipitated by the so-called higher criticism (that tries to explain the human origins and hence the textual discrepancy of scripture by rational techniques, including archaeological and linguistic evidence), it was not circumscribed by exegetical issues, nor was it etched by any list of fundamentals, whether that list was phrased synecdotally as five or expanded to seven, nine, or twelve.[27]

The heart and soul of fundamentalism, according to Sandeen, was the millenarian spirit. "For it is millenarianism which gave life and shape to the Fundamentalist movement." Indeed, "fundamentalism ought to be understood partly if not largely as one aspect of the history of millenarianism."[28] By that standard, of course, fundamentalism is not simply or mainly a product of American social and religious history. Rather, as the subtitle of Sandeen's book suggests, there is an historical interface and continuous causal relationship between British and American millenarianism.

Yet, like Dollar, Sandeen attaches great importance to personalities in the formative period of fundamentalism. For him that period is *not*

1900–1935, as Dollar and Falwell maintain. Rather, it is the roughly forty years from the launching of the annual Niagara conferences in 1875 till the outbreak of World War I in 1914. In searching for the origins of fundamentalism, Sandeen attaches more importance to the nineteenth than the twentieth century. The prima donnas of fundamentalism, as Dollar had depicted them, are either absent or scaled down in his study. Norris belongs to a later period; he is not even mentioned. Shields and Straton come up only in passing. Riley is the sole prima donna who merits significant treatment, mainly because he was a millenarian advocate who also organized, first the Northwestern Schools and then, in the twenties, the World's Christian Fundamentals Association and, together with Straton and Shields, the Baptist Bible Union. But for Sandeen, the crucial biographical component to fundamentalism belongs to the pre-War period. It is a composite profile spelling defeat for millenarianism rather than the victory that by 1893 it seemed on the verge of attaining within two major denominations, the Baptist and the Presbyterian. It has a lengthy cast. Over thirty millenarian leaders had promoted the crusade against modernism during the latter part of the nineteenth century. The giant among them, A. J. Gordon, died in 1895, and another major leader, J. H. Brooke, died in 1897. By 1911, all but five of the twenty leading American millenarians from the first generation had died. In Sandeen's view, it was this loss of leadership, rather than any other social or intellectual factor, that dealt an irrevocable blow to the millenarian movement. Those who survived and the younger men who were coming up, such as R. A. Torrey and A. C. Dixon, could not wear the mantle of their pioneering predecessors. A crisis occurred in millenarianism. It fought new battles, but without its pioneers the millenarian movement itself was transformed into a movement now called fundamentalism.

Was it then the same phenomenon by a different name? Is American Protestant Christian fundamentalism but British-American millenarianism recycled and relabeled? Sandeen argues that the change was, in fact, little more than nominal:

As a result of the 1919 World's Conference on Christian Fundamentals (which led to the foundation of the World's Christian Fundamentals Association in 1922), the millenarian movement had changed its name. The millenarians had become Fundamentalists. Whether they were the only ones with exclusive rights to the title remains to be seen, but there is no doubt that the movement which we have traced from its revival in the early nineteenth century had dropped one badge and picked up another *without altering its basic character or drive.*[29]

Are those same millenarian-fundamentalists evangelical? Sandeen may have underestimated the radical separatism of those who came to be called fundamentalists. In embracing the term fundamentalist to describe their doctrinal views, some evangelicals were hoping to set themselves apart from other evangelicals who may have claimed to uphold the fundamentals but, in their judgment, did not. The evangelical theologian Kenneth Kantzer accuses Sandeen of "confusing fundamentalism and conservative evangelicalism."[30] In fact, what Sandeen tries to do is to collapse the former into the latter. The term "fundamentalist" has only a partial debt to semantic precedents. The annual Niagara conferences did outline the "fundamental" articles of faith. The pamphlets commissioned by the Stewart brothers and published between 1910–1915 were *The Fundamentals,* and the Presbyterian Church did affirm "five fundamentals" in 1910 and again in 1916 and 1923. In short, a kernel of faith was held up as the litmus test of true belief for numerous conservative Protestant Christian groups at the end of the nineteenth and beginning of the twentieth century.

Yet it is essential to distinguish concern with certain fundamentals from the self-consciously fundamentalist movement that emerged in the twenties. Riley was the crucial figure. His name can be linked with Dixon and Torrey, both of whom died before the end of the decade (in 1925 and 1928 respectively), or with Shields, Straton, and others who continued the crusade against modernism beyond the twenties. All these defenders of God and Christ welcomed their definition as fundamentalists. Yet they took on the battle against modernism in terms that were not congruent with other conservative Christians or with the tone of the Fundamentals, as outlined in the famous pamphlets of 1910–1915. The Fundamentals had stressed defense of the Bible, especially the notion of biblical inerrancy, against the inroads of higher criticism. But their defense—namely, reliance on the doctrine of verbal inspiration—had not moved beyond positions of late-nineteenth-century millenarians. In particular, the Fundamentals had paid little attention to the conflict between science and religion, only three of thirty articles dealing directly with the issue of evolution.[31]

By contrast, the fundamentalists of the twenties who chose to be known by that name and not by any other, were separating themselves from their own millenarian past as well as from other conservative Christian contemporaries. They maintained allegiance to the "fundamentals" without, however, defining too closely what was meant by fundamentals. Any pretense to forge a new doctrinal posture within the major denominations was abandoned when the leading Presbyterian intellectual, J. Gresham Machen, left Princeton to found the rival Westminster Seminary in 1929 (even though the actual schism in the Presbyterian Church did not take place till 1936). If the enemy at the turn of the century had been "Romanism, ritualism, rationalism" out there, it now became "liberal modernism" in here, i.e., among the very denominations that were supposed to be defenders of the faith.

Despite Sandeen's pioneering endeavor, fundamentalism cannot be inextricably linked to millenarian origins and directions. More than a

mere social movement, fundamentalism is the direct consequence of neither doctrinal symbiosis nor sectarian disputation. It is, above all, a religious protest against modernism, embodying more strengths than
millenarianism and combating more enemies than higher criticism.

The battle against evolution marks the most graphic fissure between
millenarianism-evangelicalism and fundamentalism. Looking only at the
Fundamentals, or at doctrinal defenses within Northern Baptist and
Presbyterian circles, one would be hard pressed to predict, even in 1920,
that evolution would become a major doctrinal battle line for fundamentalism. The reason why it did is not hard to find: the evolution issue
surfaced in the aftermath of a protracted social battle, the battle to
outlaw drinking alcohol. By 1920, it seemed that that battle had been
fought and won, for in the preceding year the Eighteenth Amendment
to the Constitution had become law in the United States. Prohibition not
only barred the legal consumption of alcohol; it seemed also to curtail
the laissez-faire mentality of nonevangelical Americans. Millenarians
and their conservative allies could dare to hope that they were winning
the battle against Romanism—by which was meant not just the authority
of the pope but the right of increasingly large numbers of non-English
speaking immigrants, both Catholic and Jewish, to pursue an "immoral"
lifestyle.

It was only after the "victory" of Prohibition faded that emerging
fundamentalists sought another issue on which to focus public attention
and confirm their own purity. That issue became evolution, culminating
and collapsing in the Scopes trial of 1925. Unless one looks at the broad
social as well as the narrow ecclesiastical controversies of the twenties, it
is impossible to address the insistent question: "How could such an outmoded viewpoint, lingering on like a spiritual appendix, suddenly begin
to function with renewed vitality [at this point in American history]?"[32]

The problem partly lies in the presumption of the question. Not
everyone saw the fundamentalist posture as "outmoded." For a great
many Americans, the fundamentalist defense of biblical verities func-
tioned as a clarion cry to Truth, not "a spiritual appendix." The intellectual historian Henry F. May lays bare the soft side of deism:

By very early in the new century one kind or another of biblical religion was
everywhere triumphant and it was the deists (i.e., those who believed in a single
beneficent God running the universe according to perfectly natural laws) who
were reduced to little sectarian groups, bravely resisting extinction . . . Deism
and its liberal successors, always proclaimed as the religion of the republic's
future, never became the religion of more than a small elite group.[33]

The triumphant majority who advocated biblical religion were neither
strict millenarians nor evangelicals obsessed with millenarian concerns.
Sandeen's attempt to posit a conceptual continuity between the millenarian movement and the fundamentalist groups of the twenties fails be-

cause the issue of evolution eclipsed the advocacy of millenarianism. Some protagonists against evolution were millenarians, but since millenarians "did not believe that legislative action could produce pure morals," few of them joined in sponsoring the thirty-seven antievolution bills that were introduced into twenty state legislatures between 1921 and 1929! Moreover, the most famous of the twenties standard bearers for biblical creation, William Jennings Bryan, "was not a millenarian and never made an adequate theological defense of those doctrines that they did accept."[34]

By the late twenties the fundamentalist movement had outstripped its millenarian associations, and the belief in America as the land of divine destiny compelled many a biblical literalist to work for the realization of an earthly utopia. Intemperance had been but one barrier to that dream. Evangelical revivalists who fought for Prohibition now took a public stance on the biblical teaching of creation. Evolution symbolized the threat of science at every level. It came to be seen as a greater threat to utopian, absolutist idealism than alcohol consumption had been.

The choice of evolution as an opponent altered the tone as well as the direction of the fundamentalist movement. Through examining the interaction between evolutionists and fundamentalists, we move close to the vortex of the modernist mindset. We come face to face with "the exchange of index symbols"[35] that evoked the fundamentalist response.

EVOLUTION AND THE CONTROVERSY OVER CREATION

Evolution became an issue for the fundamentalists because they alone among Protestant Christians sensed the shattering challenge that modern science posed to the foundations of Christian belief. According to Owen Chadwick, very few Europeans in the mid-nineteenth century were disturbed by the effect of evolution, even though it seemed "to throw into doubt all external evidence for a sense of design and purpose in the world." Some rationalized that evolution "looked to make the world more purposeful by bringing more phenomena under the reign of (natural) law."[36] By the end of the nineteenth century, many Protestants, clergy as well as laity, had gradually accommodated to the idea of evolution.[37]

The success of evolution crowned the growing agnosticism that had surfaced since the Enlightenment and been voiced by Hume, Kant, and others.[38] Was Hume right that while science could not disprove a single miracle, it rendered all miracles irrelevant? The iron grip of determinism seemed "proven" by Darwin's theory of natural selection, namely, that human as well as animal life was subject to a sequence of measurable interactions between species and environment. Consider, for instance, a present-day geneticist's summary of the significance of Darwin's legacy:

Evolutionary theory represents the apotheosis of a bourgeois worldview. . . . It was for Charles Darwin [building on the zoological speculations of de Lamarck and his own father, Erasmus Darwin] to frame the mechanisms for evolutionary change in terms of natural selection . . . [His] observation set the stage for the *final* conflict of science with religion. . . . For . . . Darwinian theory was a direct challenge to the residual hold of Christianity as the dominant ideology of Western society and was seen as such by friend and foe alike.

In retreat since Newton, orthodox Christianity had fallen back into the belief in a God who was first cause of the natural world and still remained the day-to-day controller of life—and especially of human destiny. Darwinism wrested God's final hold on human affairs from His now powerless hands and relegated the deity to, at the best, some dim primordial principle whose will no longer determined human action.

The consequence was to change *finally* the form of the legitimating ideology of bourgeois society. No longer able to rely upon the myth of a deity who had made all things bright and beautiful and assigned each to his or her estate, . . . the *dominant class* dethroned God and replaced him with science. The social order was still to be seen as fixed by forces outside humanity, but now these forces were natural rather than deistic. If anything, this new legitimator of the social order was more formidable than the one it replaced. It has, of course, been with *us* ever since.[39]

What is astonishing about this statement is not only its source but its timing: the geneticist R. C. Lewontin wrote this essay in 1984, as if to confirm the Orwellian prophecy. Lewontin would have us believe: first, that science and religion are set on a course of inescapable conflict; second, that Darwin ushered in the final battle between religion and science; and, third, that in terms of the dominant class, science has won the contest, displacing the biblical deity with random genetic permutations and their social equivalents!

Much of the problem derives from the scientific search for absolutes, which involves not just discoveries that point to new laws of nature but hypotheses and conjectures, none of which are failsafe,[40] but the thrust of which is to prove the self-sufficiency and self-disclosure of the natural world. Even in a cursory reading of Lewontin, one would be hard pressed to say that his is *not* a religious claim. It is not, after all, based on the scientific method, scientific reasoning, or scientific evidence. It is instead a collection of faith assertions made by a scientist who still claims to be speaking as a scientist even though he has shifted subjects. In the shift, however, he forfeits his credentials as "expert."

If the boundaries between science and religion are too easily blurred, who is at fault? The frequent target of vilification is those who claim to be presenting traditional or fundamentalist Christian views. Yet it was the Harvard paleontologist Stephen Jay Gould, himself a dialectical positivist, who once allowed

we scientists are no different from anyone else. We are passionate human beings, enmeshed in a web of personal and social circumstances. Our field does recognize canons of procedure designed to give nature the long shot of asserting itself in the face of such biases, but unless scientists understand their hopes and engage in a vigorous self-scrutiny, they will not be able to sort unacknowledged preference from nature's weak and imperfect message.[41]

Most scientists do not share Gould's attempt at self-examination, though arguably even he does not go far enough. They implicitly reject Gadamer's call for excising the prejudice against prejudice.[42] They speak with the authority of science even when they have gone beyond the boundary of their own discipline or science as a whole.

Fundamentalism is not the sole nor even the most appropriate response to scientific hubris. The response that fundamentalists have made to the problem of evolution entails its own excesses. Often fundamentalists seem to abuse both the Bible and science in their retort to the challenge of evolutionary theories.[43] Yet no one can dispute that they have keyed in on a crucial issue: does God exist as creator of heaven and earth, and if so, how does that faith affirmation of his cosmic magisterium mesh with either concrete data from the natural world or the opaque happenstance of human affairs?

Many modernists have confronted the question of theodicy, that is, the vindication of God's justice in the face of inexplicable suffering. Theodicy has preoccupied sociologists of religion, from Max Weber to Peter Berger.[44] But fundamentalists have focused on the prior question: does God exist, and how can he be said to exist if he does not function as the Creator cited in the Genesis account and confirmed elsewhere in scripture?

The debate between science and religion encompasses more than the issue of evolution versus creationism. It stretches back beyond Charles Darwin to the beginning of the Enlightenment. It is coextensive with the Axial Age, if we agree with George Steiner, that Western civilization is at base dyadic, formed through the admixture of Hellenic and Judaic epistemes. To the extent that Lewontin represents a popular reflex in modernist thought, he is promulgating a "pop or vulgar sociobiology."[45] He pushes the debate between religion and science to a choice of incommensurates. Evolution as a scientific theory is counterposed to creationism as a biblical "myth." Darwin enters center stage, either as hero or as villain.

Yet the parameters of the debate are not clearly defined. In the latter part of the nineteenth century, multiple issues, agendas, and constituencies converged through oblique happenstance. Segments of the historical puzzle can only be pieced together from disparate sources. Locating the right balance is the most essential, and the most difficult, task of all. It is not a matter of misplaced emphasis, i.e., some scientists fighting some men of the cloth, and then claiming that the outcome of their struggle augurs the *final* victory of science over religion, for even that one-sided judgment rests on a selective updating of the complexities that emerged in *fin de siècle* Europe. As the end of the twentieth-century approaches, and the centennial of Darwin's death has already been observed (1982), there remains the task of sorting out underlying issues in a manner that permits the multipartisan assessment of their relevance for humankind.

Historians of science share with fundamentalists the predisposition to take biography seriously. At the heart of all biographical assessments of Darwin is one's attitude toward the man and his legacy. The very domination of his theories has made the evaluation of their worth more difficult. Some praise or vilify him with scarcely a ripple of recognition that the record is ambiguous. Most defend Darwin's understanding of evolution.

There are five levels at which it is possible to look at his work: first, Darwin's self-estimate, especially his implicit Comtian bias and strong dislike of injecting teleological arguments into scientific theory; second, the view that fellow scientists in his own field had of his work; third, the judgment of scientists in other fields; fourth, the assertions and distortions of quasi-scientists who were enamored of progress, change, and power as embodied in science; and fifth, the general public. Before assessing each of these levels, one ought to note that the one which has least concerned scientists themselves has been the public at large. Most theorists of science depicted scientific researchers as supermen, pioneering the future that all humankind were destined to live. Few thought of themselves as successors to Auguste Comte, having to establish a new religion of Man that would displace the old religion of God. That kind of vigorous proselytization for science as not only a cognitive tool but an ersatz religion did not emerge full blown until the sociobiology crusade of the mid-seventies. Spearheaded by E. O. Wilson, its proponents fully expected that *if* humankind could only trample traditional religion under foot, one could transform passion for religion into passion for the "real" absolute, namely, science.[46]

Given the attitude of scientific publicists toward the general public, it is hardly surprising that the contempt has been returned, often veiled in ignorance, misunderstanding—or reaffirmation of religious fervor. The legacy of Darwin needs to be reviewed. To understand its shadows as well as its strong lights, one must look at the biography of Darwin and intercalate the man with an assessment of his major work, *The Origin of the Species*.

Darwin was an eminent Victorian scientist. Even in his day science had begun to evince the rough edges of specialization. He was drawn to the earth and life sciences: geology, botany, biology. He disliked both mathematics and physics, distrusting their techniques and discounting their results. His own theoretical speculations relied on induction. His approach, as he explained, was to "to establish a point as a probability by induction and to apply it as hypotheses to the parts and see whether it will solve them."[47] It was philosophers of science, not research scientists themselves, who established the criteria of success or failure. By the standards of his own day, Darwin had mixed success as a theorist: two of his hypotheses were proven wrong; two were deemed correct. One of the latter was evolution.

Evolution was accepted and acclaimed, but as an original hypothesis, not a documented discovery. If one traces out the distinctions between method and hypothesis that Darwin's contemporary and countryman, John Stuart Mill, outlined, Darwin's theory of evolution lacks confirmatory proof. It remains a hypothesis, and therefore one's response to his argument depended not on recognizing and understanding some infallible scientific principle but on gauging the attractiveness of his speculation. Darwin had criticized a fellow scientist, Herbert Spencer, declaring that his generalizations "do not aid . . . in predicting what will happen in any particular case."[48] If, however, the measure of a scientific hypothesis is its testability—to be verified or falsified, either to predict and be vindicated or to miss and be discarded—then *The Origin of the Species* is also unscientific.

Darwin is often bracketed with another hero of British science, Isaac Newton. In its simplicity, elegance, and influence, Darwin's theory of evolution is paralleled with Newton's theory of gravitation. Yet Newton, too, had not bolstered his argument with a universally valid proof. His theory had succeeded because it had been accepted, becoming part of the scientific canon. To paraphrase Thomas Kuhn, evolution became a new paradigm, challenging, modifying, and displacing previous paradigms. Or did it?

At first, Darwin's theory was not acknowledged by philosophers of science precisely because it did not fit the Newtonian paradigm. When later philosophers of science did come to accept Darwin's theory of evolution, they did so grudgingly, none with more critical disdain than Charles S. Peirce. Peirce condemned Darwin with hollow praise:

His [Darwin's] hypothesis, while without dispute one of the most ingenious and pretty ever devised, and while argued with a wealth of knowledge, a strength of logic, a charm of rhetoric, and above all with a certain magnetic genuineness that was almost irresistible, did not appear, at first, at all near to being proved; and to a sober mind its case looks less hopeful now than it did twenty years ago.[49]

This remark was made in 1893. If one tracks the subsequent course of Darwinism within the scientific community, its prospect for long-term success looked bleak at the turn of the century. "Physicists to a man had proved that the earth was not nearly as old as Darwin's theory required. Geneticists . . . were claiming that mutations were discrete, not gradual; thus, Darwin had been wrong in thinking that evolution was gradual. The excesses of evolutionists like Ernst Haeckel and the disputes concerning orthogenesis and neo-Lamarckianism had earned for evolution a decidedly bad reputation."[50]

But this record of the downturn in scientific esteem for Darwinism is only one part of the story. It must be meshed with accounts of the reception of Darwinism at other levels of Victorian society. "By the 1880s [i.e., during Darwin's own lifetime] a well-entrenched school of Darwinism had become a dominant feature of the scientific establishment," despite the fact that "natural selection itself continued to be a highly controversial topic."[51] The prestige of Darwinism, ironically, was confirmed by the amount of attention that was drawn to its controversial—and unproven—hypothesis. Those who were attracted to the ensuing debate as pro-Darwinians were successful in marshaling support for their views. Darwin himself did not enter the polemics directly. He depended instead on the oratorical skill of British partisans like T. H. Huxley; he was also aided by the inability of scientific opponents to muster a suitable counter theory to natural selection.[52] Even in being challenged, he was able to sustain interest in his views. When in the 1930s a remarriage of physics and genetics enabled Darwinism to come back, his reputation was secure as the pioneer and pacesetter of evolution.

The formation of Darwinism depended as much on the writings of its late twentieth-century proponents as on Darwin's own experiments. Proponents of Darwinism were able to marshal support without, however, demonstrating the scientific validity of its premises. The foremost historian of the Darwinian legacy could write in 1973 that

[From the 1930s on] the unit of evolution became the gene, and evolutionary change was to be measured in terms of changes in gene frequencies. Even so, the situation with respect to verification did not improve much. Given modern evolutionary theory, knowledge of mutation rates, rates of differential reproduction, and so forth, the best that a modern evolutionist could do was to provide a distribution function of possible outcomes.[53]

That minimalist perception of what had been accomplished through Darwin's theory and its sequels stands in stark contrast to Lewontin's maximalist claims that the final battle between religion and science, having been posed by Darwin, was then fought and won on behalf of science. A more modest conclusion seems warranted. Evolution prevailed not on its intrinsic merits but because Darwin benefited from the general prestige conferred on science as an independent inquiry that heralded progress but lacked firm criteria for correlating truth with success.

Once evolution has been understood as dubious science seeking acceptance as a universal ideology, it becomes possible to make sense of the entanglement of Darwin with religious issues. The natural selection of the species precluded any divine agent or ulterior purpose in the genesis of human life. A battle of "orthodoxies" was inevitable, not only because of Darwin's truculent disposition but also because of the expectations of his scientific colleagues.

No two readings of the evidence coincide. The differences between the social historian Neal Gillespie and the philosopher of science David Hull are particularly instructive. In his book *Charles Darwin and the Problem of Creation*,[54] Gillespie argues that there are two contrasting epistemes (following Foucault) or paradigms (following Kuhn). That is to say, there are two incommensurate worldviews or ideologies. They do not characterize all people all of the time, but they provide a sense of the gradient shift that was going on within the scientific community and, by extension, the significance of that change for the rest of Western society. For Gillespie, the contrasting worldviews or ideologies are best labeled creationist and positivist. The former affirms traditional religion and its influence within the scientific world, the latter the victory of the scientific view over both its metaphysical and theological rivals. This staged view of human history derives directly from Comte. It is itself an expression of evolutionary exclusivism, that is to say, it asserts that all human history can be divided into three stages, the first of which is mythical (theological), the second of which is metaphysical (philosophical), and the final of which is positivist (scientific).[55] Even while claiming objectivity, Gillespie clearly favors positivism. Nor does he hesitate to claim Darwin as a pacesetter in the decisive wave of positivism that catapulted evolutionary theory to the forefront of scientific claims for progress, enlightenment, and a materialist utopia:

With the full emergence of the positivist episteme during the nineteenth century, science as a whole for the first time only developed a completely natural world system, one that was neither logically not theoretically obligated to theology in any way. The striking thing about science in the later nineteenth century . . . was the willingness of so many scientists, even pious ones, to dispense with the "God hypothesis" as a part of the presuppositions of scientific work. . . . Owing to increasingly refined practice and to the increasing volume of successful science, practitioners began to feel that a theological domain in nature which neither yielded to nor permitted scientific investigation was an actual obstacle to the full development of scientific knowledge. . . . Many Victorian scientists were uneasy or skeptical about the role of religion *within science*, and as the century wore on their numbers grew. This was the focal point of the conflict, and it turned on the question of knowledge. The episteme shift under consideration did not require the repudiation of religion as such. It only required its rejection as a means of knowing the world.[56]

There is nothing scientific about this statement. It postulates the task of mustering believers for a new religion, science, which is now set forth as superior "because of its increased refinement and success." The bellwether group, however, is the scientific community itself, *not* all strata of society. The Comtian premise of an elite vanguard preparing all humankind for ultimate progress is later spelled out:

Just as science shifted from a theological ground to a positive one, so religion—at least among many scientists and laymen influenced by science—shifted from religion as knowledge to religion as faith. The attempts to defend science from the charge of irreligion . . . required real, if subtle, redefinitions of religion and especially of Christianity. . . . The Bible as history went the way of the Bible as science and gave way to the Bible as myth. Myth was thought of not as error but as symbolic theological truth. Ethics replaced ritual purity and behavioral conformity as the center of concern. Christianity became hard to distinguish from a vague belief in some sort of spiritual dimension in life. . . . [In short, scientists had a role] in weaning a large portion of the public away from Biblical literalism and changing the nature of that public's understanding of Christianity.[57]

Gillespie never specifies the stages by which the public at large was transformed to a metabiblical, nonliteralist interpretation of Christianity. And his profile, of course, omits reference to the crystallization of Protestant evangelicalism, and eventually fundamentalism, that was going on at the same time. Not everybody, it seems, was ready to be weaned.

In the late nineteenth century, two incommensurate epistemes emerged. This was "not simply a clash between science and religion, but between two antagonistic scientific epistemes: one with a deep theological commitment, the other with none."[58] Each claimed to have the key to truth and ultimate victory. For scientists, the clash looked to be weighted in favor of the new warrior. While "the old science invoked divine will as an explanation of the unknown, the new postulated yet-to-be-discovered laws. The one inhibited growth because such mysteries were unlikely ever to be clarified; the other held open the hope that they would be."[59]

In effect, Gillespie has prejudged his evidence. He draws up irreconcilable camps of opposing scientists. On the one side are new, positive, exploratory, growth-minded scientists, on the other are old, limited, inhibitory, tradition-bound mythologists claiming to be scientists. His goal is to confirm evolutionary positivism, and he claims help from Darwin's corpus in making his case. Gillespie threads together those passages from Darwin's correspondence and autobiography that allow Darwin to remain a theist, while also stressing his opposition to any level of divine intervention in the evolutionary process. On religious grounds Darwin advocated uniformity or natural selection rather than special creation or catastrophism. Those who challenged his thesis are simply stuck "in Comte's theological stage of science."[60]

Gillespie's reading of Darwin is controverted by Darwin's own life history. There is clearly a shift in emphasis from the early Darwin to the late Darwin,[61] and from Darwinists to social Darwinists. The latter apply evolution as a "proven" scientific theory to the analysis of social change and historical development, an extrapolation of Darwin's thought that is, if anything, still more controversial than his scientific speculations. It is too easy to impose a consistent pattern on all phases of Darwin's life and legacy, too easy to read back into the British botanist one's own view of what he should have said. Gillespie falls prey to this tendency. His interpretation of Darwin reflects as much his own predispositions as the thrust of Darwin's writings.

Some scholars go so far as to claim that it was the Darwinists who are responsible for the distortion of Darwin's legacy. The Darwinist misunderstood their eponym, unable to maintain that balance and openness to criticism and change which had characterized the author of *The Origin of the Species*.[62]

However, the preeminent philosopher of science David Hull makes clear that the problem goes back to Darwin himself. In Hull's view, Darwin fueled the evolution controversy needlessly by failing to see the extent to which he had shifted from his early affirmation of the Newtonian paradigm to an extreme, isolationist position. As a young student, he had affirmed that the work of the scientist and the work of the theologian were clearly demarcated. A scientist had merely

to fill in the details of Newton's great structure, perhaps expanding upon it, but always within the Newtonian framework.... Not only were scientists making great contributions to the noble edifice of science and to mankind by applications of science in medicine and industry, but their discoveries also lent support to religion through natural theology. As they discovered more clearly how nature worked, they showed how great the creator's wisdom had been [i.e., they confirmed the argument from design]. In his youth Darwin had hoped to join in this great parade of scientists and men of God marching arm in arm to produce a better world.[63]

Instead, with the publication of "The Origin of the Species," Darwin stopped the utopian parade of scientists and theologians dead in its tracks. Hull observes that not just life and earth scientists contemporary with Darwin but also philosophers of science greeted *The Origin* "as just one mass of conjecture. Darwin had proved nothing! From a philosophical point of view, evolutionary theory was sorely deficient. Even today, both Darwin's original efforts and more recent reformulations are repeatedly found to be philosophically objectionable. Evolutionary theory seems capable of offending almost everyone."[64]

David Hull is not a creationist. He is a respected authority on the history and philosophy of science. Yet Hull does not share Gillespie's positivist bias nor is he writing about the popular reception of evolutionary theory. Instead, he is looking at the core group of scientists, "a few key biologists and geologists" and philosophers of science, those whose views Darwin himself was most concerned with. He raises questions that go to the heart of Darwin's methodology and to the masked or disguised logic that he invokes. Not surprisingly, he finds that Darwin, in deflecting the criticisms of others, appeals only in part to the actual scientific method (statistical verification of empirically testable hypotheses). In larger part, he relies on the "common sense" appeal of his own rejection of theistic motives for doing science, even though he is arguing against contemporaries who are as qualified as he to engage in scientific research.

It is possible to review late-nineteenth-century science without speaking of two mutually exclusive paradigms or two logically incommensurate epistemes, one representing good science because it outlaws God, the other bad science because it still refers to the divine authorship of creation! According to Bowler, whose study of evolution is among the most recent and also the most balanced,

> more militant writers of the post-Darwinian era tended to assume that there must be automatic hostility between science and religion. Thus the Lyell-Darwin axis was hailed as the key to scientific objectivity, while the catastrophists' interest in religious issues was thought to have hindered the development of science. What occurred was not so much a conflict between science and religion but a series of attempts to solve religious problems universally admitted to be relevant to science. More recent studies have pointed out the *scientific* achievements of the catastrophists. Their religious concerns did not prevent them from being good geologists. On both sides of the debate there was an integral relationship between scientific and religious positions, each generating something of permanent value.[65]

The cooperative relation shifted to an antagonistic one partly due to the rhetoric of Darwin in his correspondence but more because of the stance of his British, American, and German defenders. It was they who claimed on behalf of Darwin the breakthrough at last to a new view of science as a self-sufficient worldview, the Promethean religion of a new age.

It is necessary to distinguish the three roles of Darwin: as transmitter, transformer, and symbol of scientific positivism. He transmitted the British naturalist tradition. It was that tradition that prompted both him and his advocates to look at "religious problems universally admitted to be relevant to science." Outside Britain there was a fierce debate between the American naturalists, Louis Agassiz and Asa Gray, with the former opposing and the latter offering only qualified support for "the Darwinian scheme of random variation and selection." In France neither Darwinism nor evolutionary speculation ever took off. In Germany Darwin's theories were welcomed less for their scientific value than for their political currency. The Germans promoted Darwinism as "a symbol opposed to traditional religion and a promise of progress in human affairs."[66] Only in Britain did Darwinians succeed in taking over the scientific establishment and changing public opinion. They did not create a "wide understanding of his theory but [rather] a growing willingness on all sides to admit that the world somehow is governed by law rather than divine caprice."[67]

In other words, the Darwinians, like the Newtonians before them, engineered an ideological revolution to support their contentions. In that sense, Darwin not only transmitted but also transformed scientific positivism. While Darwin, together with his cohorts and his advocates, did succeed in getting other scientists and philosophers of science to focus on theories of evolution, few concurred with Darwin about what evolution meant. Some of his most respected collaborators within the scientific establishment relied on some version of the argument from design. Charles Lyell is the best known. Though he abandoned what came to be known as "Mosaic geology," he adhered to what Gillespie calls "nomothetic creationism," i.e., belief that there was a divine purpose and pattern underlying the creation of all species.[68] Others shared related views of creation by design, including Asa Gray, William Carpenter, and the man who with Darwin was credited with discovering the law of natural selection, Alfred Russell.

In overcoming scientific opposition and arguing that only evolution by random selection explained the origin of the species, Darwinians were aided in part by the growing prestige of science as a professional pursuit in Victorian England but also in part by the heightened role of journalism in marshaling public opinion. Retrospectively, positivism vs. creationism was seen as a tidy debate between two clearly different and irreconcilable sides. The actual messiness of what occurred is aptly illustrated by the famous 1860 debate between Bishop Wilberforce and T. H. Huxley. The popular image is of Wilberforce as an ignorant man of the cloth, popularly known as "Soapy Sam," and Huxley as a no-nonsense man of science, "Darwin's bulldog." Huxley humiliated Wilberforce and helped turn the tide of public opinion towards evolution. At least that was how Huxley *later* interpreted the matter. But the actual debate must have been different, since Wilberforce was holding forth "not as a bishop but as a scientist, vice-president of the British Academy, with good ornithological work to his credit."[69] Huxley, his opponent, wanted a strict division in sphere of labor. While Darwin had been a broad naturalist, earning income from other sources, Huxley hoped to establish himself and others as "full-time, fully paid, specialized scientists." He also disagreed with the Anglican church's creedal stance as summarized in The Thirty-Nine Articles. "Wilberforce therefore personified both Huxley's hates, being an amateur scientist as well as a bishop."[70] It was that level of personal animosity rather than the dispassionate weighing of opposite views that prompted Huxley's recollection of the famous debate.

This debate would have been extraordinary, however, even if it had taken place exactly as Huxley recalled it. It shuns calm exchange of views for passionate confrontation of beliefs. By the tone rather than the substance of the issues, it posed a choice, with triumph or defeat the only possible outcomes. The most telling aspect of the debate was its visual quality. It focused on the dramatic effect of images to convey the substance of the densely complex issues. The bishop is remembered for having challenged Darwin's (and Huxley's) view that humans descended from the apes. Cartoons, essays, and editorials recalled it as "the monkey question," and ever since that has been the most visually vivid and frequent recollection of the Darwinian stance on evolution.

Darwin's exchange with scientific colleagues had been imbued with a truculence not unlike Huxley's. Once the debate had been joined, it tended to perpetuate itself in terms of those who defended natural selection exclusive of any other principle, material or metaphysical, and those who rebelled against Darwin's insistence that they had to make a choice.[71] Thomas Kuhn has asserted that scientific revolutions depend less on the triumph of truth over falsehood than the success of one group in arguing its viewpoint against all proponents of alternate viewpoints.[72] Such an analysis also applies to Darwin's theories and the controversies evolving from them. Darwin did not convince all scientists that he was right; what he advanced was an hypothesis, not a proof. As philosophers of science have noted, he repeatedly applied the principle of induction by eliminating (without disproving) alternative hypotheses.[73] Twice he was confronted with data that falsified his hypotheses, yet in such circumstances, Darwin would not adduce new facts in support of his own viewpoint or advocate another tangent of logical wizardry; instead "he turned to the venerable tactic of *reductio ad absurdum*."[74]

The antipathy between religion and science that Darwin accelerated has not abated since his time. If Darwin had been dealing merely with scientific issues in *The Origin* (as he had in his earlier studies), it would be possible to concentrate on the critique of Darwinism as bad science, and one could proceed to establish alternative hypotheses. But in both *The Origin* and subsequent debate, Darwin pushed his theory into the religious domain, challenging not only the God hypothesis but also its moral and cultural extension. The creationists may have been wrong to pose their model of a biblical genealogy against the evolutionary model of paleontology, but they were right to sense that the exclusion of God from science also had implications for the moral order. It was the moral, or rather amoral, consequence of evolution that elicited the ire of American fundamentalists, from Riley to Straton to Bryan.

Fundamentalists continue to react to evolution less as science than as symbol. At this level Darwin succeeded in a fashion that few other thinkers do in any period of human history. Freud attests to that "accomplishment" when he links his own claims to Copernicus and Darwin.[75] Despite its momentary eclipse at the turn of the century, evolution persisted as a key word, a cipher, a symbol, or, more often, as a stereotype. It was less important for what it meant than what it evoked. For some it stood for the accomplishments of science, confirming that what had been achieved in the Technical Age separated it from all preceding epochs and also exalted its accomplishments above theirs. Social Darwinists were the first to appropriate it in a larger sense.[76] Sociobiologists have proved to be their contemporary successors, claiming on behalf of evolution their own superiority as geneticists.[77] Their goal is clear: to exclude God from every branch of science and to seek protection for their pursuits under the Enlightenment principle of separate spheres—public and private, universal and particular, hard and soft. In their view, science, like law and politics, relates to the first, while religion, together with art and literature, relates to the second.

For those steeped in the Christian tradition, there was a necessary choice: either accept the claims of science and adjust the teachings of faith or else challenge science as bad faith. The former approach was adopted explicitly or implicitly by many of the major Protestant denominations prior to World War I. The latter has been the response of those labeled fundamentalists since the twenties.

From 1860s England to 1920s America, from the Wilberforce-Huxley debate to the Scopes trial, the monkey business has persisted. The debate is no longer restricted solely to fundamentalists. Creationism has become a cottage industry in its own right, claiming to set forth an alternate view of science which does not presuppose or depend on biblical or theistic referents. It is seldom noted that most of the leading fundamentalist preachers of the twenties deserted Bryan in his hour of need.[78] But the issue of evolution did not disappear with Bryan's humiliation. The laws making the teaching of evolution illegal in Tennessee, Mississippi, and Arkansas remained in effect *for more than forty years* after the Scopes trial. Only in 1968 were they declared unconstitutional by the Supreme Court. The issues that sparked the laws did not die out in those and other "Bible-Belt" states. Hence it was in Arkansas, a mere fourteen years later, in January 1982, that a district court had to rule on whether or not to give equal time to the teaching of creation science. The Supreme Court and the district court cases are related. Their contexts differ only in that creationists now present their case as "scientists," not as defenders of the faith:

The creation model [of the origins of life, according to the prolific creationist, Henry Morris] does not need to be formulated in "religious" terminology. . . . It states simply that the major categories of nature were formed by special creative and cataclysmic, purposive processes in the past which are no longer in operation today and which therefore are not accessible to empirical observation.[79]

In other words, since the point at which creation began can not be replicated, it cannot be tested. It is subject to neither confirmation nor falsification by scientific methods. Both the creationist and the evolutionary view of origins are, therefore, "unscientific."

The real issue for creationists remains the moral damage of evolution resulting from its exclusion of the God hypothesis. Bryan thought that "all the ills from which America suffers can be traced to the teaching of evolution."[80] Morris was even more explicit: "Evolution is the root of atheism, of communism, nazism, behaviorism, racism, economic imperialism, militarism, libertinism, anarchism, and all manner of anti-Christian systems of belief and practice."[81] Present-day creationists, like fundamentalists since the Scopes trial, argue that the religious, and specifically biblical, testimony about the origins of life is unassailable. "Creationists are not really arguing about the validity of the theory of evolution but the existence of God."[82] Morris said as much when he remarked:

The Biblical doctrine of origins of course is foundational to all other doctrines, and if this could be refuted, or even diluted, then eventually the other doctrines of Biblical theology would be undermined and destroyed.[83]

William Jennings Bryan put it still more starkly when he said, "It would be better to destroy every other book ever written, and save just the first three verses of Genesis."[84]

The shortcomings of creation science are easy to score, whether as science or as religion. Numerous authors have pointed out that the scientists who defend creation science are not themselves contributing to the frontier research in geology or biology.[85] They are advocating theology relabeled as science to show the limits of what claims to be objective science. Their difficulty is greater than that of Darwin's opponents. They cannot postulate a principle that has the seeming clarity and elegance of Darwin's theory of natural selection. Even Morris finds himself quoting Darwin to defeat Darwin.[86] But in addition, they have to fight against the self-sufficiency of science as a multifaceted profession and esteemed extension of modern civilization. T. H. Huxley won the battle in both senses. Not only did he impress the caricature of Bishop Wilberforce as Soapy Sam on future generations but more importantly, science as a profession became adamantly separated from the God hypothesis. The extent of that separation becomes evident when scientists such as Carl Sagan claim in the name of science that they have solved the God problem. It is no less evident in the ridicule heaped on scientists who still try to invoke "God of the gaps," as did Robert Jastrow in 1978.[87]

The real battle began and will continue in the courts. The Supreme Court functions as a reality defining agency. Its diffuse authority becomes clear when one looks at the juridical input into the creation vs. evolution controversy. Unlike the 1860 debate, the 1924 debate between Bryan and Darrow took place in a court of law, and in 1968, the 1924 laws prohibiting the teaching of evolution were declared unconstitutional by another court, the Supreme Court. In 1982 when the Supreme

Court ruling was upheld, it was a federal district court judge (in Arkansas) who decided against the creationists.

The religious influence of the American judicial system is enormous yet few are the reflective inquiries into its ideological limits. When authority is vested in "impartial" custodians of the law to decide between science and religion, it is seldom possible for such custodians to examine their own implicit preconceptions about the nature of science. Consider Judge Overton's statement that

the emphasis on origins as an aspect of the theory of evolution is peculiar to creationist literature. Although the subject of origins of life is within the province of biology, the scientific community does *not* consider origins of life a part of evolutionary theory.[88]

That statement becomes nonsensical when a geneticist such as Lewontin can claim that science during the past century has replaced God as "the new legitimator of the social order." Evolutionary theory as such may not be a threat to religious belief, but when extrapolated as a comprehensive ideology, as it has been from Darwin to Lewontin, from Huxley to Sagan, it does make claims about origins and it does infuse those claims with religious significance.

One must stress the benefit of creation science along with its shortcomings. It calls attention to the hubris of Darwinians, especially the neo-Darwinians or sociobiologists. The latter do not adduce data in support of socially charged theories and yet claim them as part of the process of scientific investigation. The supporters of sociobiology frequently resort to a version of Darwin's *reductio ad absurdum* arguments to dodge their critics.[89]

"A full understanding of human beings," including origins and destiny, is what evolutionary theory tries to provide.[90] Even contemporary exponents of evolution must admit that the arguments for its validity rely as much on ideology as facts.[91] The pretense to scientific objectivity needs to be unmasked, the claim to universal validity scaled down.

Just how difficult this task is for evolutionary scientists becomes clear in reviewing the densely argued book of Philip Kitcher. *Abusing Science: The Case Against Creationism* is the most thoroughgoing attempt by any philosopher of science to discredit creationism as science and also to loosen the popular appeal it elicits in tandem with American Protestant Christian fundamentalism. Kitcher sees himself as defending not only evolution but the entire edifice of modern science. For him the two are inextricably linked:

Evolutionary biology is intertwined with other sciences, ranging from nuclear physics and astronomy to molecular biology and geology. If evolutionary biology is to be dismissed, then the fundamental principles of other sciences will have to be excised.[92]

The linchpin of Kitcher's case, however, is his defense of what constitutes true science. To prove that evolution is science, he argues against logical positivists, such as Karl Popper, who have asserted that evolution is not science but rather a theory. Why is it a mere theory? Because it is not subject to testing and hence to modification or falsification. Kitcher challenges Popper's reliability:

The falsification criterion adopted from Popper—which I shall call the *naive falsificationist* criterion—is hopelessly flawed. It runs aground on a fundamental fact about the relation between theory and prediction: On their own, individual scientific laws, or the small groups of laws that are often identified as theories, do not have observational consequences [i.e., they cannot be experimentally tested]! . . . [Instead,] hypotheses are tested in bundles. . . . We can only test relatively large bundles of claims.[93]

Yet Kitcher never lays out the basis for testing "large bundles of claims." Nor does he examine the claims of sociobiology. As the Darwinian apologist Michael Ruse makes clear, sociobiology raises a dramatic test case about the soundness of evolution as a discipline addressing the array of human problems. Positivism persists as an undercurrent of much evolutionary thought. It holds up science as the cumulative progression from a lower to a higher order of thought, holding out a utopian vision for the liberation of humankind from the bondage of tradition.[94]

It is only in the final chapter of his book that Kitcher tries to demonstrate how the claims of evolutionary theory are at base *theological*. How then do they reconcile with classical Judeo-Christian belief? He purposes two tactics: first, to confirm Freud's reflection that "humanity had suffered three blows to its self-esteem: through the Copernican revolution (earth no longer the center), the Darwinian revolution (man no longer the center) and his own (man no longer rational)," and second, to postulate the possibility of a special relationship between God and man that need not be exclusive. In effect, Kitcher advocates a curious form of pop theology. It warrants summary recapitulation here:

If we are simply one among innumerable species who have occupied and will occupy our planet, then we are not compelled to conclude that we are not the focus of a special care. . . . To conceive of God as a Father we need not suppose that we are His *only* children. It is enough to suppose that He cares for each in ways that are appropriate to its abilities and needs. . . . .

Evolutionary theory emphasizes our kinship with nonhuman animals and denies that we were created separately. But it does not interfere with the central Judaeo-Christian message that we are objects of special concern to the Creator. It simply denies us an exclusive right to that title.[95]

That minimalist perception of a covenanted relation hardly leaves room for invocation or adoration, much less intercession or submission.

It allows a creator deprived of ninety-nine names and attributes, denuded except as a generalizable postulate. It offers the God of the deists revivified. It commends a surrender to scientific superiority *not* as a more efficient instrument for exploration but as a comprehensive ideology. It summons us to transfer belief from church to laboratory, from pew to courthouse, from creation to evolution.

Yet few church leaders see the larger issue at stake in the creation-evolution controversy. Moderate critics of creationism, writing from within mainline denominations, Catholic as well as Protestant, often echo Francis Bacon's allusion to the two books of God. They are

the book of God's Word in Scripture, which concerns the ultimate nature and destiny of humanity, and the book of God's Works in Nature, which contains the created order.[96]

It is implied that science and faith will conflict irreconcilably only if we insist upon confusing and conflating the two "books" of God. Yet the evolution debate has repeatedly demonstrated that scientific queries do touch on religious sensibilities, that professional scientists have had serious disagreements about the extent to which their enterprise forecloses or confirms the God hypothesis. The instance of Robert Jastrow makes clear that even agnostic scientists are inclined to locate "God of the gaps." Other scientists, however, are not willing to have even this residue of theism creep into their speculations.

The notion of two books, like the reliance on dyadic theory to which we alluded in chapter one, presupposes a world of light and dark, white and black. The High Tech Era, like its parent, the Technical Age, is suffused with gray.

Creationism is not the sole issue over which fundamentalists continue to clamor for recognition and change in the public sphere. Abortion, gay rights, pornography all elicit declamations from the Moral Majority and other conservative groups often linked to the fundamentalist movement. Evolution has often been downgraded as a major concern preoccupying fundamentalists. Just as fundamentalist preachers deserted Bryan in his hour of need in the Scopes trial, much of the contemporary literature by or about fundamentalists tends to view evolution as an aggregate or cluster concern subordinated to other shibboleths of protest against modernism or its agents, "secular humanists."

The deemphasis on evolution, whether by fundamentalists or those who study and try to understand them, needs to be redressed. The 1920s fundamentalists were right to focus on the issue of evolution. What their present-day successors need to review is first, the extent to which creation science has become an educational and polemical issue apart from religion[97] and second, the irrelevance of scientific facts to the underlying social issue, namely, the authority most Americans accord "reality-defining agencies" that tend to support what Lewontin has called "the dominant class." The intellectual historian George Marsden has written eloquently about the contrary images that American Protestant Christian fundamentalists have of American society: Is it Israel or Babylon? Do they share the Promised Land or wait out exilic deprivation?[98] The answer to these questions would go a long way toward sorting out the relation of fundamentalist tenets to the implicit structure of American society, for it is at that subsurface level that a tension persists between the claims of scriptural election and the counterclaims of pervasive pluralism.

Nor is this tension peculiar to American Protestant fundamentalists. It is a felt tension, albeit with different symbols and different outcomes, for Jewish as well as Islamic fundamentalists. Both are more openly confrontational of the societies in which they find themselves than is the Moral Majority or any other fundamentalist public advocacy group in the United States. Jewish fundamentalists, whether Gush Emunim or Neturei Karta, and Sunni Islamic fundamentalists, like the Takfir wal-Hijra group in Egypt, recognize the persistence of an exilic situation. They confront the defiled larger community in which they are located. By contrast, American Protestant Christian fundamentalists so closely identify with some of the ideals of the American republic that they try to transform rather than reject society at large. The Moral Majority, despite its excesses, has aimed at recovering the high ground for America as a whole, not at destroying its constituent parts.

Fundamentalists would do well to reconsider whether the claim of creationism to be a science is any longer worth fighting. Alternatively, they could, and should, look at sociobiology for the direct confrontation that it poses to theistic belief. Public debate is the warp and woof of the American social fabric. Affirming that there are "real" scientists who have challenged the too expansive scope of evolutionary theory, fundamentalists could make common cause with them in the search for alternatives to evolution.

Uppermost in all facets of the debate is the riddle of language. As the physicist Edward Harrison points out, the word evolution has had to bear too much freight in the history of the life sciences. The positivism of Comte, accepted and augmented by Darwin, Huxley, and a host of others, has made it impossible to separate "evolution" from progress. Evolution, in Harrison's view, should be restricted to sciences such as astronomy and astrophysics, where it can relate to "a mechanistic treatment in the physical universe." Natural historians and scientists, especially sociobiologists, groping for catchall terms to encapsulate a variety of phenomena, should abandon reliance on "evolution." Instead they could describe processes of change as natural or, better, random selection.[99]

Having opened a Pandora's box, can humans put the genie back in the bottle? Probably not. Evolution is now such a badge of pride in scientific thought that it is almost impossible to imagine Harrison's proposal getting the serious hearing it merits. At the least, all concerned parties can pay closer attention to the preconceptions that cloud the interface of science and religion.

One must begin by recognizing that creationism vs. positivism is not the neat clash of epistemes that Gillespie and others project. There are fuzzy edges on both sides. Creationists fail to realize the extent that they have not invoked true scientific principles because they are not trying to identify new, testable hypotheses but rather to cast doubt on those hypotheses that already exist. Yet at the same time positivists falter in not recognizing the ideological and nonuniversal character of their claims on behalf of science. Facts and values are enmeshed in all human activity, including science, and the desideratum is not to eliminate prejudice but only to clue the lay reader and listener, as also the scientific practioner, to its existence.

In my view, the debate on creation will remain peripheral to the leading philosophical minds of the High Tech Era. The crucial metaphysical frays of the twentieth century have been and will continue be staged *within* science, not *between* science and religion. Even as a public spectacle, the debate on creation is less an objective inquiry into knowable facts from value-free perspectives than it is a testing of constituencies who advocate two variant worldviews. The outcome cannot be decided nor closure achieved as long as the competing symbols continue to attract constituencies in each generation. The best alternative may be to decide that the issue is no longer worth debating, as the French apparently did long ago.

In the meantime antievolution is the shibboleth that most accurately defines fundamentalist opposition to the modernist hegemony and its relativizing force. Other propositions, such as millenarianism or dispensationalism, do not confront scientistic hubris as boldly as does creationism. Progressive Patriotic Protestants may have made their most enduring contribution to global fundamentalism by staking out one end of the cognitive spectrum called science and labeling it "the Genesis account of creation." While they may be doing bad science, it is senseless to claim that they are not doing science, especially when so much that engages the human imagination and modern institutions rests on the deepening of mystery, and the doubting of a fix on ultimate certainty, through the exercise of the scientific method.

CHAPTER 8

Fundamentalists in Pursuit of an Islamic State

On *Jihad* or Holy War in Islam

The basis for the existence of colonialism in Muslim countries is those government officials (who claim to be Muslims but are not). . . . We are required to focus on our Islamic duties, first to apply the Law of God (the *shari'a*) and the Word of God. And there can be no doubt that the first battleground of *jihad* is the removing of those shackles of unbelief that constrain us and substituting for them an Islamic order.

—'ABD AS-SALAM FARAJ

Imagine some group that says to the Muslims who are delivering the call of Islam to a nation: "You have no right to say what you are saying. We do not allow it." In these circumstances it is not permissible for us to fight with that nation, with those people who are blameless and unaware. But is it permissible for us to fight against that corrupt regime which props itself up with a putrid ideology that it uses like a chain around the necks of people to imprison them in a blind alley isolated from the call of truth; a regime which acts as a barrier against that call? Is it permissible for us to fight that regime so as to remove that obstacle? Or, in real terms, is it permissible for us to fight against that prison of repression or is it not? In view of Islam this *is* permissible, for this itself would be a form of uprising against *zulm*, against injustice and oppression. It may be that the *mazlum*, the wronged, the oppressed, are not aware of the nature of the injustice and have not requested our help, but in fact there is no need for them to request it.

—AYATOLLAH MORTEZA MUTAHHARI

This chapter is divided into four sections: first, a general assessment of Islamic fundamentalism in the aftermath of the Iranian Revolution; second, a confrontation of the gap between the rhetoric of Islamic activists and the reality of Muslim polities; third, a country-specific survey of Islamic fundamentalism in three Sunni polities: Indonesia, Pakistan, and Egypt; and finally, fourth, an inquiry into the unique circumstances of hieratic Shi'ism in Iran and its accommodation to the Technical Age. We will conclude with reflections on the long-term viability of Islamic groups that cluster and cohere as fundamentalist cadres.

There is an urgent need to decode the rampant sloganeering that clouds Islamic fundamentalism. Since Imam Khomeini's ascent to power in Iran in early 1979, Islamic fundamentalism has been targeted by the American news media as the *bête noire* of American interests in the Middle East. It has manifest and ugly implications. It implies the usurpation of political authority by militant religious ideologues. It implies a process of destabilizing the "true" leaders of the Muslim world, leaders who are deemed to be "true" because they are moderate, which is to say, West-oriented. It implies replacing "true" leaders with atavistic clones of Saladin or Genghis Khan. Above all, it implies implementing policies that ignore the "major" ideological struggle of the twentieth century, the struggle between capitalism and communism, and instead attaching importance to premodern religious values by absolutizing scriptural norms.

Islamic fundamentalism is a historical accident that some tend to invoke as an inevitable process. Islamic fundamentalism precedes Khomeini, yet it is the unexpectedness and now the durability of the Iranian Revolution that have caused Western observers to look for Islamic fundamentalism everywhere. Any actor who has an Arab or Muslim name is deemed to be a potential fundamentalist, and any movement of opposition to the government in power has to be scoured for fundamentalist motivations. Two questions pervade media coverage of Islam: will the Islamic revolution in Iran be repeated elsewhere and what will the impact of the Khomeini regime be on other Muslim polities? The great danger of the press, to which Alvin Gouldner called attention (see chapter four), is its obsession with crises. A concomitant danger is the need to compress diverse complexities into ready slogans that seem to explain crises. Islamic fundamentalism, recited as a polysemous slogan, evokes the threat of religious zeal generally and Islamic loyalty in particular.

For many sensitive and respected scholars of the Muslim world, Islamic fundamentalism has become an unacceptable rubric, too damaged by journalistic distortion or popular reflex to be useful. We take the opposite stance. We argue that Islamic fundamentalism can still be reclaimed as an analytical category, but only if it is properly delimited. It requires twin limits, the one structural, the other temporal. The first pertains to polity: Can ruling elites be labeled "fundamentalist" without violating the intrinsic quality of fundamentalism as protest? Could there ever be a circumstance when those in power would reflect a fundamentalist ideology? The second limit pertains to history: What are the implications of framing fundamentalism as a conflict with modernism? When in the Technical Age does there appear a time line marking the emergence of fundamentalist cadres? Is it the French Revolution? Is it World War I or II? Is it later? Both sets of questions entail limits to the use of fundamentalism in an Islamic context. Their exploration will occupy us in this chapter.

As the historian Marilyn Waldman shrewdly observed, we have yet to "develop a framework commensurate with the magnitude of contemporary Islam."[1] While we must try to resist ethnocentrism and stereotyping, we must also avoid falling into hopelessly obscure scholarly distinctions. Islamic fundamentalism, like fundamentalism itself, represents a major challenge to academic discourse. So varied is the landscape of the Muslim world that the most appropriate first move in approaching Islamic fundamentalism is to set out disclaimers. Islamic fundamentalism requires attention to what it is not before one can make sense of what it is. In previous chapters, we have stressed that fundamentalist cadres are invariably oppositional. Fundamentalists oppose the prevailing ethos—whether they define it as secular or modernist or Western—but they also oppose those in political power who perpetuate the prevailing ethos. Muslim rulers are the natural enemies of Islamic fundamentalists, and yet since the debacle of 1967 in the third Arab-Israeli war, most heads of state have moved to recognize the appeal of Islamic symbols. Not fundamentalists, they have nonetheless tried to disguise their own adherence to the prevailing ethos by themselves engaging in Islamic rhetoric. Are most Muslim heads of state therefore subject to the charge of hypocrisy? Are they preaching what they dare not and cannot practice? Perhaps, but no less so than other non-Muslim politicians who resort to religious symbolism in their public discourse.

Custodians of the nation-state, the political elite are its beneficiaries. They seek to maintain the status quo through their control of the instruments of symbol production: the government bureaucracy, the print and visual media, the schools, and often also the mosques. In the seventies and the eighties, because Islam has superseded every other ideological support as a basis of appeal for sustaining the legitimacy of the state, Muslim politicians have not only resorted to Islamicly coded messages, they have also occasionally outstripped the fundamentalists in their advocacy of an Islamic utopia.[2] But precisely because they are ruling elites, they cannot be regarded as fundamentalists. By virtue of being at the center of power rather than on the margins, they exclude themselves from that vital quality of fundamentalists: to oppose the prevailing ethos rather than to embody it; to advocate change rather than to maintain the status quo.

The oft invoked distinction between radical and conservative fundamentalists blurs the actual character of Islamic fundamentalism.[3] Arab kings do not serve as conservative exponents of fundamentalist ideology. Monarchism as an institution is incompatible with fundamentalism as an ideology. Neither the Alaoui Malikites of Morocco nor the Saudi Hanbalites (sometimes called Wahhabis) of Arabia qualify as fundamentalist ideologues. Both regimes are firmly entrenched monarchies. Their claims to legitimacy as Muslim royal families are long-standing, the Alaouites going back to the seventeenth century, the Saudis to the early nineteenth. While both rely on religious ideologies, in each case they are religious ideologies in the service of nationalist goals. The Alaouite monarchy is constitutional and accountable, at least in theory, to an elected parliament. It persists as the symbolic cornerstone of national independence from a much detested and vigorously resisted French colonial rule. The Alaouite king functions as "Commander of the Faithful" for all Moroccans, appealing to the spiritual patrimony of Maghribi history while also trying to modernize a country that remains predominantly rural, tribal, and preliterate. The Saudi monarch also has a religious title. He is "Protector of the Holy Places." The holy places he is committed to protect are transnational centers of Islamic ritual loyalty, the Hijazi cities of Mecca and Medina, yet he protects them as the head of a modern-day nation-state. He has an unenviable task: to ensure the hegemony of one tribe, the Al Sa'ud, over an area larger than the US east of the Mississippi River. Not all Saudis are Sunnis or Wahhabis. A disaffected Shi'i populace inhabits the strategically significant eastern province of the kingdom.[4] On the other hand, both demography and economics assist the Saudi monarch: the total population of native Saudis is less than five million, despite published statistics to the contrary;[5] the vast income generated by petroleum production and export continues to provide, even with the reduced power of OPEC since the mideighties, the basis for large-scale modernizing strategies. Yet for King Fahd of Saudi Arabia, as for King Hassan II of Morocco, the role of religious ideas is limited: clerical functionaries (the 'ulama) may legitimize the existence of the state as a Muslim polity, but they do not determine the dominant tone nor do they set the planning agenda of that state. To speak of either a Saudi monarch or a Maghribi monarch as "fundamentalist" is to make nonsense of both monarchy and fundamentalism.[6]

Muslim polities of the left do not qualify as expressions of fundamentalism. Libya, for example, is not a case of fundamentalist fervor triumphant over secular opposition. Mu'ammar Qadhdhafi has evolved his own version of Islam. The Third International Theory is a sui generis creation of his lively imagination. Though claiming to wrest the mantle of Arab socialism from his early hero, Gamal 'Abd al-Nasir (Nasser), Qadhdhafi owes more to Chairman Mao than to either President Nasser or the Prophet Muhammad. Set forth in *The Green Book*, "which in style and name recalls Mao's *Red Book*,"[7] the Third International Theory is a bold attempt to dispense with Islamic functionaries, the 'ulama, and to establish Qadhdhafi as "a new *imam* competent to shape an Islamic code for modern men."[8] Yet Qadhdhafi's views remain peripheral to the Arab Muslim world, just as Libya itself parrots but does not embody the cultural norms of that world. By any canon of Islamic orthodoxy, Qadhdhafi has to be adjudged an apostate. He "has subordinated the *shari'a* to his own ideology and has interpreted it with a view to rationalizing policies that owe nothing to Islam."[9]

Neither Arab monarchs nor African socialists qualify as Islamic fundamentalists because they coopt Islam rather than marshaling support for a revolutionary Islamic order. Only movements in direct contact with the dominant world order, itself reflecting ascendant European capitalism, could and did spark the beginning of what emerged as Islamic fundamentalism. The putative father of Islamic fundamentalism was the late nineteenth century Persian activist, Jamal ad-din al-Afghani,[10] but it is two movements in the twentieth century that have set the tone for Sunni-style Islamic fundamentalism: al-Ikhwan al-Muslimun in Egypt and Jama 'at-i Islami in Pakistan. One cannot exaggerate the significance of their place of origin. Both Egypt and that portion of North India which later became Pakistan were shaped by European colonial rule. It was rule imposed for the sake of commercial gain. Whatever the attendant political or diplomatic considerations, the major impetus for colonization was the hope of commercial gain, growing out of the market needs of the Technical Age. Al-Ikhwan al-Muslimun and Jama'at-i Islami arose as socioreligious movements opposed to colonial rule. Their founders were Muslim laymen who perceived Western values as the polar opposite to their own sense of cultural authenticity. They disregarded the authority of religious functionaries (the 'ulama) because the latter, in their view, had accommodated to the West. Fundamentalists challenged not only colonial administrators but also those among their own compatriots, fellow Muslims who seemed to embrace and project colonial, which is to say, European-Western-Christian values.

For Sunni Muslims, the Ikhwan and the Jama'at remain the historical precursors to present-day Islamic fundamentalists, even though they were not often depicted as fundamentalists until the 1970s. It was the dramatic price increases spurred by OPEC in 1973 that inadvertently caused the public manifestation of Islamic loyalty now known as fundamentalism. The increased income of certain OPEC and OPEC-dependent Muslim countries made possible new opportunities for economic expansion never before imagined,[11] but at the same time it brought home to marginalized Muslim elites, whose numbers also increased in the seventies and eighties, the gap between the industrialized West and the so-called third world. Despite the OPEC profits of the past fifteen years, all OPEC countries remain part of the third world. The dilemma of development is perhaps best epitomized by a member of the Saudi ruling elite who once lamented to an American audience: "We Saudis are rich but you Americans are wealthy. I'd rather be wealthy," by which he meant, as he went on to explain, that while one criterion of national prosperity may be the number of schools, hospitals, roads, banks, and industries, the *true* criterion of national prosperity is the ability of a country to design, construct, and maintain modern facilities, including their technological underpinnings, without foreign assistance. By that criterion, Saudi Arabia, like every other OPEC country, including Iran, remains underdeveloped and, therefore, dependent on others for what it needs to exist and to compete as a modern nation.

In effect, the OPEC price revolution produced a regional revolution of expectations rather than an upward revaluation of the global socio-political power of the leading OPEC producers. The disparity between "worlds," especially between the first world for whom oil was being produced, and that portion of the third world which served as producers, remained visible. For those Muslim elites who looked beyond bulging bank accounts, Mercedes Benzes and swimming pools, it brought home the persistent burden of the Great Western Transmutation. A compensatory reaction has been to stress the importance of Islamic symbols and to reassert the need for Islamic values. Begun in the seventies, the drive to massive government-sponsored Islamization found numerous outlets, whether expressed through new political entities such as the Conference of Islamic Nations or through national sponsorship of Islamic banks and Islamic insurance companies. But all these devices attenuated without removing the underlying problem: the sense of exclusion from the major issues and the ongoing dramas of the Technical Age felt by Muslim elites and nonelites alike.

The greatest field of play was and will continue to be science. No frontier epitomizes the marginality of Islam to scientific discovery more than space exploration. The major competitors in outer space are also the two archrivals of first and second world ideologies, the United States and the Soviet Union. The exclusion of Islamic participants has not gone unnoticed. In the summer of 1983, newspapers from Cairo to Jakarta ran a front-page story that excited the imagination of many Muslim readers. It concerned Neil Armstrong, the first astronaut to land on the moon. While walking on the lunar surface, Armstrong had heard an eerie noise. He had no idea where it was coming from or what caused it. It remained in his mind, although it escaped his official debriefing, after he returned to earth. Some years later, while on a US sponsored tour of nonaligned countries, Armstrong was walking through Cairo when he heard the same wailing noise echoing in the streets. He stopped a passerby and asked what it was. On being told that it was the Islamic call to prayer, coming from the muezzin of a nearby mosque, he immediately converted to Islam. But, alas, when he returned to the US and to his native Cincinnati, he was told that if he made a public profession of his newfound faith, he would be fired from his government job. The story may seem silly, but it has a very serious point. Neil Armstrong the American astronaut becomes, like America itself, an ambiguous symbol for Muslim audiences. On the one hand, he attests to the splendid discoveries of the Technical Age that were ordained by Allah for the benefit of all humankind; even non-Muslims were used to confirm the truth of the Qur'anic revelation, to wit, that He (Allah) is the Lord of the universe (*rabb al-'alamin*). But at the same time, America has not accepted the special role it could have and should have played in the Islamic dispensation. The first astronaut on the moon, discovering belatedly the Muslim validation of his mission, has to hide his own Islamic identity. Practicing *taqiya* (the concealment of one's faith for self-preservation), he keeps his conversion to Islam a secret. Otherwise he would lose his job since public acknowledgment of his newfound faith would scandalize the secularized Jewish/Christian elites who control America.

The ability to mythologize lunar explanation and bring it within an Islamic worldview also extends to oil. Only certain Muslim nations and only a limited number of Muslim elites within these same countries have benefited from the OPEC price revolution. Yet the Saudis have claimed the gift of black gold, or oil, as a double blessing vouchsafed by Allah on their behalf. It confirmed their singular leadership in the Muslim world, just as it seemed to propel the Muslim world as a whole to the fore in the arena of Great Power politics.

Others who did not share immediately in the newfound prosperity of the Kingdom of Saudi Arabia or its neighbors also attached special religious significance to petroleum discovery, production, and export. Consider the case of Malaysia, a Southeast Asian state with a bare Muslim majority. "[In the seventies] the oil boom was taken in Malaysia as a sign of Islam's validity since worldly success was always a sign of Allah's grace. . . . Furthermore, oil was discovered in offshore Malaysia, fulfilling the folk wisdom about the divine distribution of good things in this world. EuroAmerica received science and technology; the Jews intelligence, acumen, and solidarity; the Chinese diligence and business sense, but the Malays received Islam and now oil, reserved for the Muslim peoples of the world." [12]

The mythologization of oil in an Islamic context is crucial to some elements of Islamic fundamentalism. Those who received its benefits were nought but instruments of Allah's will, even when to outsiders there often seemed to be an invisible line separating testimony to divinely bestowed worldly success from crass, self-serving consumerism. The same Allah who had given the Qur'an as a first symbol for the success of Islam had now given black gold to Muslims as an instrument for their material redress in the present century. That century began in 1979.

It was the beginning of the fifteenth Islamic century. Ironically, its beginning was signaled by a revolt against the Saudi monarchy that took place in the heartland of Arabia in November 1979. The leader of the movement was a disaffected National Guardsman who had become a theological autodidact. In the province adjacent to the holy sites of Mecca and Medina, Juhayman ibn Sayf al-'Utayba preached against the corruption of Saudi society and advocated the toppling of the monarchy. Young theological students, disillusioned and disoriented by the rapid changes taking place in the kingdom during the late seventies, were attracted to his movement. Not only did he preach that loyalty to the *shari'a* entailed criticism of the Saudi regime, he also believed that the expected *mahdi,* a messianic figure for Sunni as well as Shi'i Muslims, would arrive to usher in the new century. He surprised even his followers by proclaiming his own brother-in-law as the *mahdi* and then summoning them to join him in marching on the Great Mosque of Mecca. Once they gained control of its sacred precincts, Juhayman was convinced that Allah would intervene, assisting his small band to overcome the counterattack of unbelievers, i.e., troops loyal to the Saudi regime.

It was a bold if suicidal move. Juhayman's makeshift militia, which may have numbered several hundred, did surprise thin Saudi security forces. They did occupy and control the liturgical center of the Islamic world for exactly two weeks. But the embarrassed authorities, after first obtaining a *fatwa,* or legal decree, from the state financed *'ulama,* moved to crush the revolt. The false *mahdi* and numerous others were killed in the ensuing engagement, but Juhayman was captured alive. He, together with sixty-two others deemed to be the ringleaders, were quickly tried and publicly hanged. The Saudi authorities blamed the whole incident on outside interference, and international oil companies, temporarily scared to the point of hiring risk analysts to assure them that the outburst was abnormal, calmed down by the early eighties. Their executives, like the Saudi ruling elite, took consolation in the revolt's immediate suppression. No one attempted to address the challenge that Juhayman had briefly raised: has the House of Sa'ud gone too far in its implicit accommodation to modernist values?

The fundamentalist challenge in Arabia has had echoes elsewhere. From Mecca to Tehran to Kuala Lumpur, 1979 signalled more than the beginning of a new Islamic century. It also signaled the possibility of a restoration of Islamic values to the center stage of world events. Secular elites could no longer claim Islam as exclusively *their* cultural patrimony. The mantle of Islamic loyalty was also now seized by marginalized, out-of-power groups. Sometimes termed the petite bourgeoisie, these are the estranged urban dwellers who continue to have attachment to rural roots and premodern values. They may be poor and disenfranchised, but more often, they have experienced a breakdown of traditional expectations: obtaining the rudiments of secular education, either unknown or denied to their parents, they also seek better employment. And the number of such petits bourgeois has dramatically increased in the latter half of the twentieth century, for in numerous Muslim countries, the postindependence years have witnessed accelerated birth rates. Coupled with falling infant mortality rates, higher birth rates have caused enormous population booms and severe pressure on limited resources in the most populous Muslim countries: Egypt, Pakistan, Indonesia and, of course, Iran.

The cycle of Islamic fundamentalism has become so much more vicious in the eighties than in the seventies because the Muslim ruling elites who raised hopes in the seventies could not sustain or fulfill them in the eighties. It is the vision of the dispossessed that drives a certain class of male elites. Most are not only urban but upwardly mobile: whether educated in modern universities of the Islamic world or EuroAmerica, they have become scientifically professionalized. One may characterize them as fervently Qur'anic, patriarchal, ascetic, and anti-Western, but they are, above all, unemployed or underemployed. Whether frustrated engineers, disaffected doctors, or underpaid bureaucrats in meaningless public jobs, potential Islamic fundamentalists are *petits bourgeois* in search of a purpose from the meaningful past to preempt the uncertain future.

By geography and history, Malaysia is peripheral to the Arab heartland of Islam, yet the Malaysian perspective helps to illumine other areas of the Muslim world. There members of the *dakwah* movement advocate strict adherence to Islamic values. They believe in a puritanical, abstemious style of life that sets them apart from other Muslims. In their view, Islamic ideology can best be practiced through emigration (*hijra*) from the larger world which corrupts, distorts, numbs, and blinds. Because it is a movement at once nativist and retreatist, it is

a reservoir of turbulence and could move on to the next phase of nationalist Islam, or on to militant Islam challenging other religious and state structures, or even on to the highest form of fundamentalist, revolutionary Islam.

The prognosis is grim because the conditions for forestalling fundamentalism are impossible to meet. Until the third world has accommodated itself to the challenge of Western modernity, and until Islam no longer has a feeling of inferiority, and until Muslims have strong and prideful identities, we can confidently expect manifestations of fundamental Islam, with varying degrees of vigor, disruption and political success.[13]

It is such shortfalls, between the first world and the third world, between the West and Islam, between dignity and displacement, that produce Islamic fundamentalists who also are often the terrorists of airport notoriety. They want to achieve power in this world. Confident that Allah will direct their deeds and increase the number of "truly" loyal Muslims, they are willing to perish in cars, buses, or trucks, on tarmacs or battlefields because they are bound by their ideals. They are certain not only of their own celestial reward but also of the ultimate terrestrial triumph of their viewpoint.

The historian Ira Lapidus has noted that "Islamic movements have to be understood as the expression of a utopian dream that shatters all categories of analysis."[14] He is correct, but at the same time it is necessary in every instance to distinguish between the rhetorical expression of utopian hope voiced by fundamentalists and the parameters of possibility in the real life experience of Muslim societies. The rhetoric is both inflammatory and inflationary. Like this chapter's epigraph from Ayatollah Mutahhari, it urges physical assault on the enemies of Islam, and it presumes that a guided few can speak on behalf of the interests of all Muslims, even when it is necessary to confront others who also claim to understand and to act on behalf of Islamic ideals. Another ayatollah has offered the most sweeping vision of a triumphalist Islamic future. Ayatollah Muhammad Mahdi al-Shirazi looks forward "to the government of the thousand million" Muslims. He conceives this commonwealth to be in structure a traditional Shi'i state with modern amenities. The state will evolve through a long process of educational reform that will reach the Muslim masses, organizing them into small, active cells of dedicated workers. In this manner, through evolution not revolution, a new and lasting Islamic commonwealth will be built, even if its completion requires fifty years.[15]

Contrasting with this vision is the negative assessment of Muslim polities that characterizes much contemporary Western historiography. Although paying only lip service to the Oriental despotism of the noted sinologist Karl Wittfogel ("all Asian governments are doomed because their rulers are unbridled tyrants"), Marxists adhere to a version of the Asiatic Mode of Production. Middle Eastern countries, and by extension the entire Muslim world, cannot succeed because their societies have not been transformed from traditional feudalism into fluid commercialism. One of the more eloquent formulations of this argument declares that

Western history is dynamic; Middle Eastern societies are stagnant before colonial penetration. Western societies were based on some form of class stratification which is regarded as a condition of industrial development; Islamic societies are based on a mosaic of social groups. In the West, the critical transformation from feudal/religious culture to industrial/secular culture required the services of an autonomous, commercial middle class; in the Islamic Middle East, such a class was missing. [Hence] Middle East societies have not been galvanized by successful bourgeois revolutions.[16]

The implication of this analysis is that the change which did take place in Muslim societies was a version of the recycling of elites characteristic of Oriental despotism. Actors, faces, names change in a series of *coups d'état*, but the underlying socioeconomic discrepancies within each society, as also the disparity between Muslim society as a whole and the West as a whole, remain. Indeed, they are magnified with the passage of time. Yet, like the accent on nationalism that characterizes Gellner's projection of an insurmountable divide between East and West, the above analysis exalts theory above description, substituting dichotomous juxtapositions for complex ambiguities. All the stereotypes that promote the West as progressive, rational, scientific, secular have their obverse in the East, which is deemed to be traditional, superstitious, feudal, religious.

In looking at the actual Muslim world and assessing the likely future of Islamic fundamentalism, we have to move beyond both the utopia of Ayatollah Shirazi and the dystopia of Marxist fiction. Between rhetoric and reality lies the gradient of historical change best labeled the Great Western Transmutation. The Muslim response to that change predates and informs Islamic fundamentalism. For Muslim elites the change has produced negative results. It has registered an index of loss that is at once political and cultural. There are at least two reasons why the reversals that accompanied the GWT affected Muslims more harshly than Jews and Christians. First, Islam alone among the great monotheistic traditions enjoyed a public preeminence before the beginning of the modern era. Even if we gauge power by the ability to wage war on an international scale, the Ottoman Empire remained a force to be reckoned with until the end of the nineteenth century.[17] By any other index, especially symbolic power at multiple levels within a society, it persisted longer than the Roman Catholic papacy and on a wider scale than rabbinic academies or Hasidic networks. Second, the majority of Muslims, despite long periods of colonial conquest and rule, never acknowledged the cultural superiority of post-Christian Western powers. Denied every other vehicle of protest, it was Islam that they could and did assert as their nativist heritage. The French in North Africa, for instance, refused to allow Muslims citizenship unless they became Christian. Almost none opted to become French at the cost of forsaking Islam. The reverse was also true: to be a colonial was to enjoy a higher style of life abroad than at home but never to become Muslim. In both instances, the boundary of civilizational identity was religious.

European colonialism paved the way for the Muslim appropriation of nationalism, but the process was far from uniform. If all labels are too tidy ciphers of controversial complexities, the coding of a Muslim response to nationalism becomes defiantly diverse; it threatens to make nonsense of popular labels. Indonesia and Bangladesh, for instance, became secular republics, even though the majority of their citizens are practicing Muslims. Syria and Iraq embraced the same secular ideology, yet became rival socialist dictatorships. Algeria and Libya, though self-defined as radical Islamic polities, have religious classes disaffected from the government in power. Jordan and Morocco survive as benign Muslim monarchies which enjoy the support of their religious leaders, even though one king (Hussein) is less publicly devout than the other (Hassan II). Egypt and Sudan are constitutionally committed to pluralism, yet the Christian minorities in both states elicit suspicion in their Muslim compatriots. Saudi Arabia has garnered the distinction of being a puritan theocracy, Sunni-style, yet it faces the problem of disaffected Shiʻis in its Eastern province.

In every instance, however, nationalism became part of the Western challenge to the credibility and integrity of Islam as a holistic ideology.[18] The expansionist *élan* of an emerging ideology challenged the ideology of a traditional civilization. Rival ideologies, they are irreconcilable opposites, doomed to battle one another.

The crucial stumbling block for crusading modernizers is that Islam, like Judaism, does stake out claims to be a holistic ideology, competent to address every activity of life and every sphere of human society. How well it does this, with what problems of internal consistency, is less important initially than the breadth and duration of the claim. Because Muslim elites encountered nationalism as the driving force of European expansionism, it was inevitable that it would evoke in them an empathetic response to advocate their own nationalism against external aggression and to secure territorial freedom from outside interference. What was equally inevitable, however, was that not only Europeans but all others, including immediate neighbors, even immediate Muslim neighbors, would be excluded from the sacralized homeland. Nationalism became eulogized as patriotism, in Muslim regions as in other parts of Africa and Asia. Little regard was paid to the double edge of that conflation: patriotism evokes an appeal to ideals that are transterritorial and universal, closer to the notion of *umma* (i.e., corporate solidarity) in precolonial Islam, but by being conjoined with nationalism, it suggests that the only ideal worthy of pursuit is territorial or, even more narrowly, racial. Both appeals lead their constituents to wave a banner of optimism that is at heart antireligious. Just as European nationalism rang the death knell for any hope of a Holy Christian Empire, so its echo response among Arabs and Asians precluded any ultimate success for a pan-Islamic movement.

Islamic fundamentalists, recognizing the non-Muslim origins of modern-day nationalism, have refused the opiate of any nationalism as the cure for failed Islamic idealism. They have taken an unequivocal stance against Arab, Persian, Turkish, Pakistani, Malay, and Indonesian nationalisms. At a latent level what the fundamentalists have grasped is the holistic challenge of nationalism to the holistic claims of Islam. It is not, however, a battle of equals. Nationalism projects the gradient change of the GWT, including the immense power invested in the contemporary state. It exercises a monolithic authority, enforcing what one writer has called the state as an "obedience context," so that compliance with the party in power is tantamount to exercise of religious loyalty, or bluntly stated, political dissent is equated with religious heresy. Its authority extends to all the apparatus, including education and the media, at its disposal. For each state presides over, maintains, and is identified with, one kind of culture, one style of communication, which prevails within its borders and is dependent for its perpetuation on a centralized educational system supervised by and often actually run by the state in question, which monopolizes legitimate culture almost as much as it does legitimate violence, or perhaps more so.[19]

This assessment applies not only to communist or totalitarian states. It applies equally well to Islamic polities in most of Asia and Africa. The modern state commands an awesome array of instrumentalities for exercising and maintaining power. It projects what it pronounces as truth through what it can muster as preemption or coercion of other views. The monolithic state delimits the degree of change that any oppositional group can promote.

Phenomenal claims, eliciting fears of unprecedented catastrophe, are often made by proponents of Islamic fundamentalism. Rhetorical truth does not easily translate into social reality, however, and before one can grant credence to any fundamentalist stance, one must first distinguish between the temporary success of particular protests, the most dramatic being the assassination of political leaders, and the long-range durability of the state as the only context within which change can take place. Fundamentalists may overthrow a government, but they can not abolish the state. Even the possibility of changing the state through revolution depends on a rare concurrence of specific group interests with exceptional historical circumstances.

Islamic fundamentalism arose as a response to the failure of Muslim nationalisms. Had the transition from dependence to independence worked as its advocates thought it should, there would have been no Islamic fundamentalism, or at most it would have been a modest movement with about as much political influence as Carl McIntire and his American Council of Christian Churches. Instead, independence proved a severe disappointment to most Muslims.

The fundamentalist view derives its strength in part from the clarity of its antinomies. It opposes all statutes and policies that do not accord with the *shari'a* as a timeless code of conduct. Modern-day Sunni Muslim polities, whatever their ideological posture, cannot operate as juridical heirs of premodern Islam. They must accommodate to the civil law of the colonizers and the exigencies of a global economy. Even leaders who might be privately devout must publicly espouse policies and pursue actions that belie their commitment to an Islamic state.

Colonialism, a direct outgrowth of the GWT, was the vehicle for Western domination in Muslim lands. Its long-term consequences have yet to be exhausted. Its durative influence is scarcely beginning to be understood. For fundamentalists more keenly than for their coreligionists, colonialism has never ended; after independence it merely assumed new guises, Western ideology but with native, i.e., Muslim, masks.

The experience of Iran has been determined as much as the experience of its Sunni neighbors by the interaction between indigenous elites and those foreign colonizers who served as commercial and political agents of the GWT. The major difference has been the unique discursive power of Shi'i Islam. It long antedates either the Pahlavi state or Imam Khomeini. Twelver Shi'ism in Iran symbolizes at once the hope and the frustration of Muslims in the face of a century of Western colonial expansionism and, since World War II, continuous political dominance. Unlike their neighbors, Iranians never faced the problem of defining nationhood, only in winning freedom.[20] From the sixteenth century to the twentieth, their leaders accepted the identity of Iran as an ethnic-cultural-religious grouping. Shi'i nationalism was the religion of the majority of those who gained power or exercised influence in Iran, whether as secular leaders or as clerics. Though much has been made of the opposition between clergy and state in Iran, it is essential to remember their underlying continuity as embodiments of *iraniyat,* an untranslatable code word for what it is to be distinctly Iranian. A foundational element of *iraniyat* is territorial independence: constantly threatened by hostile neighbors, and later, by colonial powers, Iran has never been fully subjugated by any non-Iranian polity.

And so Iran pursues its own course. Far from signaling the future path of opportunity for Sunni fundamentalists, the Islamic Republic of Iran demonstrates how well Iranian isolation as a Shi'i polity prepared it for the ordeal of an embattled theocracy. Since the 1979 revolution, the ideologues of the Islamic Republic have offered a categorical redefinition of Islam as the basis for a modern nation-state. They have devised a Western-style constitution that excludes non-Islamic modes of behavior. They continue to promote an Islamic revolution abroad while on their western border fighting a territorial war with modern weapons, both activities being made possible only through reliance on a source of income that is generated by non-Islamic, capitalist needs: the export of petroleum.

To grasp the uniqueness of Shi'i Iran, we must first examine more closely the experience of nationalism among select countries from the Sunni Muslim fold. With the exception of the Turks, nearly all polities that could be labeled Sunni Muslim experienced the profound ambivalence of nineteenth–twentieth-century nationalism. Initially, nationalism was a resistance movement. It entailed defensive actions against foreign encroachment, but then with the winning of independence, it had to become recuperative. Its leaders were confronted with the awesome task of forging a polity that could survive as a modern nation-state, both against Western manipulations (no longer just European but also American and Soviet) and also against other postcolonial emerging powers, many of them neighboring Muslim states.

For Arab and Asian Sunnis committed to Islamic ideals, it is only since the winning of independence from colonial rule that opposition to the modernist hegemony has been possible. Yet the legacy of external domination has preempted the option to frame a prenational Islamic polity. Nationalism, first embraced as a temporizing device to oppose foreign domination, has lingered. After independence it has been reinstitutionalized as *the* form of Muslim polity. The nation-state has become as normative a structure for Muslim as for non-Muslim countries. It embodies little of Islamic ideals for social justice. It projects either tribal stratification or military authoritarianism, or both.

And Islamic fundamentalism is destined to remain an elitist male protest movement because most Muslims in most countries have not had the luxury to be concerned with the shift in central authority that political independence signaled. Beyond the coercive power of the ruling elite to engage them either militarily or commercially, most Muslims have had to seek the basic staples of survival, to wit, food, water, clothing, shelter, and only rarely have they had the "luxury" to pursue secondary concerns like better employment for themselves, higher education for their children, religious conformity for their country, or status revision for their gender.

The last concern relates particularly to women since patriarchal structures prevail throughout the Islamic world. Although women do not appear as fundamentalist leaders, their role in Muslim societies remains crucial to understanding the strength of the fundamentalist appeal. No topic has occasioned more prejudgment, protest, and reinterpretation than the idealized status of the Muslim woman. One must first consider the third world context of most Muslim families. Only then can discussion relate to the actual conditions of Muslim women and the weight of their domestic duties. Only when gender is socially embedded in the day-to-day experience of its subjects can it become viable as an analytical rubric. Consider Islamic dress codes. The image of a sea of black veils suggests forced female retirement from the public sphere and seclusion within the home. Yet it has now been amply demonstrated that the veil, and other clothing ensuring a woman's modesty, can be used as a strategy for social advancement.[21] By the norm of human rights, a more apt index of women's improved status would be changes in implementing the *shari'a*, changes that assure women the equality with men that was scripturally mandated for them in the Qur'an.[22] No society, however, conforms to foundational texts.

In practical terms, therefore, the most significant issue for Muslim women is their position within marriage, since marriage is the expected lifelong experience of most Muslim women. While polygamy has attracted much attention, it is less odd from a Western perspective than *mut'a*, or temporary marriage. A seventh century custom never denounced in the Qur'an, it allows a man to cohabit with a girl or woman for a limited period of time in exchange for an agreed upon sum of money. There is no marriage contract and hence no divorce. Forbidden by Sunnis, *mut'a* marriage is still practiced by Shi'i Muslims. Although repressed under the Pahlavis, it has been reinstated with renewed justifications in the Islamic Republic of Iran. The arguments for or against *mut'a* marriage are less significant finally than what it symbolizes as an institution: marriage, *all* forms of marriage, exist to further the goals of the Muslim *umma;* private rights or individual wishes are dismissed as a fiction of Western cultural hubris. We make a mistake when we try to isolate gender issues, like marriage or women's rights in marriage, from the defining elements of an Islamic social order. The recurrent emphasis is on the corporate good (*maslaha*); it, rather than individual freedom, remains the highest priority.[23]

Since World War II, defining the corporate good has preoccupied those Muslim male elites who have had the "luxury" to be concerned with status issues in the public sphere. Direct, often bloody encounters with European colonial powers ended foreign military occupation and outside political control. But independence did not produce freedom. Nationalism after independence became a new oppressor, spawning European-related heresies, whether socialism under Nasser in Egypt (1952–69) and Sukarno in Indonesia (1950–67), or military authoritarianism, thinly veiled as constitutionalism, under Ayyub Khan in Pakistan (1958–69). Each case requires further review if we are to understand the basis, as also the limits, of the fundamentalist response to the contemporary crisis of Islamic identity.

None of these examples is taken from the Arab heartland usually identified as the core region of Islam. The choice is deliberate. It is not anti-Arab but pro-Islamic, for the strength of Islam as a world religion has been its ability to exercise internal decolonization. No one group can arrogate to itself the exclusive right to speak on behalf of Islam. In the premodern era, that decentering of Islam was a virtue. Now it becomes a liability, since each modern nation-state creates its own orthodoxy, revalidating Islamic symbols, coopting the *'ulama,* and setting the tenor for public observance of Islamic loyalty. The oleaginous fluidity of competing Muslim identities makes it difficult to determine what are universal Islamic norms, apart from the appeal of particular ideological claims.

In trying to channel the religious impulse into national objectives, ruling elites often engage in masked battles with religious functionaries. Though the end result is the same, to ensure the hegemony of the state over all competing loyalties, the battles take a different form in each Muslim polity. We will explore the encounters that have occurred in three predominantly Sunni nations. They are among the most significant Muslim countries on a global gradient. Indonesia is demographically the largest Muslim country in the world with over 120 million Muslims among its 160 million citizens. Their participation in the *umma* is undisputed, but the nature of their loyalty to Islam is a subject of continuing debate. Pakistan is the pivotal state signaling the nature of Islamic identity for its own 90 million citizens and, tangentially, for another 185 million Muslims in both India and Bangladesh. Though it has existed as an independent polity for a mere forty years, its role vis-à-vis other Muslim nations is crucial. Egypt is the swing state intersecting the Mediterranean Sea and the Indian Ocean; it is the crossroads of Eastern Africa, the Arabian peninsula, and the Fertile Crescent. It *is* the Middle East, straddling Europe and Asia at many levels. It totals 40 million Muslims among its 45 million inhabitants.[24]

INDONESIA

The political theorist John Armstrong has argued that "it is the symbolic rather than the material aspects of common fate that are decisive for identity."[25] If he is right, then Islamic ideology in Indonesia reflects the multiplicity of cultural factors that predate Islam and shape its development in Southeast Asia. The same process of interaction between an external, cosmopolitan cultural force and an indigenous, regional symbol system characterizes Islam everywhere. What draws attention to the Indonesian case is that Islam succeeded numerically there, but not without being simultaneously redefined. All historical notations frame the argument of Islamic identity in one of two directions, toward a notion of normative Islam lying beyond Indonesia, or toward Indonesia as a self-defining norm in which Islam is domesticated without being detached from its West Asian foci. The ultimate question concerns cultural markings: which changed more, Islam or Indonesia, through their mutual interaction? To answer that question we have to test the truth of that age-old axiom: history is geography over time.

Indonesia is an island culture, and unlike Egypt or Iran, both of which are contiguous land masses, Indonesia did not become politically united until the period of Dutch colonial rule in the nineteenth and twentieth centuries.[26] Although Islam played a major role in the development of Indonesian nationalism, when independence from Dutch rule was achieved in 1945, the constitution was framed in terms of what future President Sukarno declared to be the five principles of national life: belief in God, humanitarianism, national unity, democracy, and social justice. In their vagueness, as also in their Sanskrit labeling (*pancasila*), the principles appeal to all religious communities without privileging Islam. Muslim nationalists were understandably unhappy with this compromise. They tried repeatedly to bring Indonesian constitutional law and public policy closer to the ideal of an Islamic state, in particular urging that Muslims be required to adhere to the *shari'a*.

They lost out, despite the Masjumi constitutional movement and the Dar ul-Islam antinationalist rebellion, both of which extolled Islamic symbols but enjoyed only a limited popular success.

Under Sukarno and also his successor, Suharto (1965–), it has been secular nationalism, with a predisposition to religious pluralism, that has dominated in Indonesia. Both Sukarno and Suharto are viewed as model secular humanitarians. Muslim leaders cannot match their flexibility in public life. In a sense, they and Islam have been the victims of regional politics, for at the national level it is Javanese syncretism that has prevailed, repressing the Muslim statist ambitions of Sumatrans and particularly Achchinese. The most prominent politician favoring Islamic reform since independence has been the Masjumi advocate, Mohammed Natsir. Yet his very identity with legalist Islam handicaps his success in Javanese politics.[27]

The slogan "Pancasila" has so dominated Indonesian political discourse that even the advocates of an Islamic state have had to wage debate with reference to its five principles. "While almost everybody in Indonesia now agrees with Pancasila," writes a Dutch scholar in 1983, "the Muslim activists feel that the government wants to 'secularize' the five principles; on the other hand, the government feels that the Muslims want to 'Islamize' them."[28] Nor is the debate limited only to a choice between monotheistic creeds, rituals, and prescriptive laws. For through its Ministry of Religion, the government of Indonesia promotes "a kind of pluralism that permits adherence to one of several salvationist doctrines, either monistic or monotheistic in character." In other words, the cornucopia of religious options is made as broad and elastic as possible in order to foster national unity, or what Indonesians are fond of calling "unity in diversity."[29]

In such a cultural potpourri, to speak of Islamic fundamentalism is a blatant catachresis. Indonesians have never had a collective national past with a singular religious orientation that locates its authority beyond the archipelago. There are numerous indigenous myths, values, and symbol systems. Collectively they neither comprise a golden era nor evoke a sense of nostalgia that can be labeled Islamic. The enforcement of the *shari'a* on Muslim Indonesians would be a novelty not a recurrence. There are too few whose self-interests could be defined and served through an Islamic state. Indonesia becomes important, therefore, not as a distant hotbed of future fundamentalist eruptions but rather as a test case signaling the limits to which generalizations about Islamic fundamentalism can apply.

Mohammed Natsir may be as committed to the ideal of an Islamic state as Imam Khomeini, yet the constitutive elements of Indonesian nationhood preclude the possibility of a substantial challenge to secular ideology on the basis of Islamic loyalty. The difference between Iran and Indonesia is not doctrinal; both project "true" versions of Islam, but in one case religious custodianship is vested in a clerical class that enjoys popular support, in the other religious values are dispersed, denying any Islamic group the capacity to project its self-interests as the interests of the whole.

PAKISTAN

Unlike Indonesia, Pakistan is not an island or an archipelago but part of the Asian subcontinent. It is linked by history to India, by faith to Central and West Asia. The three hundred years of sustained Mughal rule provided Muslim elites in North India with a sense of their continuity to Central Asian forebears, but it was British colonialism that shaped the profile of present-day Pakistan: Lord Mountbatten presided over the partition of a vast region along communal lines, religiously defined. It was a fatal error, resulting in the physical death of millions but also destroying the dreams of other millions. Not all Muslims were drawn to the ideal of an Islamic state. In 1947, and afterwards, many Indian Muslims chose not to migrate to Pakistan. They stayed behind, ensuring that the secular state of India had a Muslim minority that continues to number over 12 percent of its populace.

Many who favored a separate Muslim polity did not want to be joined together in the same Islamic state. The subsequent rift between East and West Pakistan resulted in the formation of Bangladesh in 1971, again with much bloodshed. Two incompatible parts came unbound from the mold into which they had been cast in 1947. The result was three separate nation-states that held in common only a constitution as the frame of governance: one dominated by Hindus and Sikhs was constitutionally secular (India), another with a Muslim plurality had an avowedly Islamic constitution (Pakistan), while the third (Bangladesh), though dominated by Muslims, was constitutionally secular.

Even some of those who migrated to Pakistan did not accept it as a bona fide expression of Muslim political aspirations. Among them was Mawlana Abul-'Ala Mawdudi. Trained as a journalist rather than an 'alim or religious professional, he had a powerful second conversion to Islam in his twenties and became a prolific pamphleteer, spokesman, and activist on behalf of Islamic causes. To some he is the preeminent Muslim reformer of South Asia, to others he is fundamentalist with cultural blinders, to still others he is a preacher gone astray, hopelessly compromised in his ideals by the realities of postindependence Pakistani politics.

It is important to distinguish between what he said and what he did. In 1941 he founded the Jama'at-i Islami, an organization dedicated to Islamic reform within India. He was opposed to the Pakistan movement, arguing that the Muslims of India were effectively irreligious and that the creation of a separate state would not help them any more than it helped the irreligious Muslims of Iran and Turkey. But when Pakistan was created in 1947, he migrated to Lahore. The Jama'at-i Islami became his sole public voice, and through it he repeatedly challenged the government's claims to be Islamic, risking imprisonment and even the death penalty (in 1953). After being freed, he came to terms with the military government of General Ayyub Khan, and from 1962 till his death in 1979, with intermittent suspensions, he continued to work through the Jama'at-i Islami.

Mawdudi's life, despite the imprisonment, harassment, and death threats he endured, is much less eventful than his writings. His success with the 'ulama is due to the fact that they could not "produce any figure who would match his intelligence, talents and international standing."[30] From his initial publication of a book on *jihad* till his subsequent essays on virtually every domain of contemporary Muslim life, Mawdudi applied the hermeneutical principles of the supremacy of the Qur'an and the possibility of deriving a single, correct interpretation of its meaning for the present age.[31] It is as if he took upon himself the enormous task of "proving Islam's ability to supercede modern secular ideologies."[32] He is most renowned for his argument that no Islamic state can be set up unless there has *first* been an Islamic revolution. By that criterion, only Iran would qualify as an Islamic state; all Sunni polities would be condemnable as un-Islamic, their rulers *kuffar*, or unbelievers.

In Mawdudi's view not only was Pakistan far removed from being a religious state, but the situation of the righteous vanguard in the Ayyub reign was similar to that of religious parties in Indonesia under Sukarno. "Ayyub during his regime did what Sukarno had done in Indonesia," he told a reporter in 1970. "All religious elements were crushed and the administration went into the hands of the leftists. Press, news agencies, radio and television in fact all the organs of mass media were used by the leftist forces [while] Jama'at-i Islami had very little opportunity to work."[33]

Mawdudi's words echo the concern that other fundamentalist ideologues have had with media control. But at least one of his former followers felt that Mawdudi did not go far enough. According to Dr. Israr Ahmad, Mawdudi after his release from prison retreated from his "fundamentalist position and instead sought allegiances, first with the religious groups and then with avowedly secular political parties." Mawdudi, in the view of Dr. Israr, found himself tacitly cooperating with the same government he had criticized: he had only deluded himself into thinking that he was restoring democracy to Pakistan.[34] As a result of the contrast between ideals and realities, words and actions, Dr. Israr, also a Punjabi, also a layman (though a medical doctor not a journalist), resigned from the Jama'at in 1957. Then in 1974 he formed his own organization, Tanzim-e Islam. Dr. Israr's project was in many ways a clone of Mawdudi's, with two differences. First, he was unremitting in his effort to exclude women from the public work force and to "honor" them for their domestic roles. (Mawdudi had written about the seclusion of women but in the 1964 elections had supported, half-heartedly, a woman candidate for president against Ayyub Khan!).[35] Second, he understood that a religious movement required modern media. Dr. Israr skillfully used both television and overseas travel to project the image of a worldwide organization: reading beyond Pakistan, he reinforced his local, regional, and also national standing as the bellwether of Islamic ideals. Until the Zia al-Haqq government realized that their tacit support of this overzealous Punjabi activist could redound against them, he used media professionals, whether journalists, radio commentators, or TV program planners, to his own ends. In 1982, there was public brouhaha about the Israrization of Pakistan. His growing influence was feared, especially among professional women.

The worst did not come to pass; his movement may even be in permanent eclipse. Yet the meteoric rise of Dr. Israr Ahmad from comparative anonymity to worldwide acclaim demonstrates dramatically the power of the contemporary communications revolution. In its content and its instrumentality the organizations of Israr Ahmad and Jerry Falwell bear comparison. The televangelistic program of the foremost American Protestant fundamentalist has its parallel in the Markazi Anjuman Khuddam al-Qur'an of Dr. Israr Ahmad. The Pakistani example reflects a global pattern, all the more intriguing because its geographical remoteness from Europe and America obscures its development on a Western pattern with reliance on Western instrumentalities.

However, the limits of Dr. Israr's movement are also instructive. Instant, extensive communications means that "others" must respond to what we make of their experience. Dr. Israr could galvanize an instant reaction, but he could not control its ultimate consequence. When the Zia al-Haqq regime found that its purposes no longer coincided with his, he was denied the platform on which he had built his earlier success. The nation-state, in Pakistan as in Indonesia, shaped the decisive obedience-context. Once Benazir Bhutto came to power in the fall of 1988, Israr suffered a further setback: female domesticity as the sole model of Islamic womanhood seemed anachronistic.

EGYPT

Egypt, like Indonesia and Pakistan, has been stamped by the colonial experience—an experience that goes beyond the national borders of Egypt. Chapter titles of books signal the evaluation of Egypt that permeates not only the popular but also the scholarly imagination. The major American Islamicist of the twentieth century, Marshall Hodgson, entitles a chapter of his *magnum opus, The Venture of Islam,* "Egypt and the East Arab Lands: Revival of Heritage."[36] The implication is that

Egypt represented *all* the East Arab lands (as distinct from the West Arab lands of Morocco, Algeria, Tunisia, and Libya). The political scientist Fouad Ajami more recently alluded to the same sense of Egypt's centrality when he titled a chapter of his book on the Arab predicament, "Egypt as State, as Arab Mirror." Because Egypt is located at the crucial juncture of the *oikumenē*, or civilized world, it has spearheaded both the expansion of European commercialism and indigenous reaction to external manipulation. The bitter reaction of its intellectuals to British occupation was echoed in the newly founded presses of Cairo and Alexandria. In calling for the expulsion of foreigners, Egyptians tried to challenge European world hegemony by counterposing to it the strength of a revitalized civilization at once Arab and Islamic, with Egypt at its core. "Egypt, the epitome of Arab distress" might have been the caption for popular commentary on Cairo's plight as a colonial city. Yet many of the Egyptian elite accommodated to the shift in political management, while the large majority of their compatriots were hardly affected. They remained peasants *(fellahin)*, and for them survival was— and is—the overriding concern.

For others, the urban activists who galvanized the drive against colonial rule, the road to freedom was long and hard. Muhammad 'Abduh is remembered as the pioneering theorist of Islamic modernism. He inspired the Egyptian nationalist Sa'd Zaghlul, founder of the opposition Wafd Party. But Zaghlul died soon after Egypt gained independence from Britain in 1922, and for the next thirty years, Cairo and its tributaries, that is to say, all of Egypt, were ruled by a self-indulgent king who ignored both the needs and the will of his populace. It was only with the army coup of 1952 that eventually brought Gamal 'Abd al-Nasir (Nasser) to power (though he didn't assume full control till 1954) that Egypt could at last try to rid itself of the vestiges of British colonial control. Instead, however, Nasser established a centralizing bureaucratic state that changed the rhetoric but very little of the substance of the Farouk era. Despite the contemporary clamor, Egypt did not experience a revolution under Nasser.

Nasser was not antipathetic to Islam, for, like other officers who cooperated in the coup of 1952, his "first views had been shaped by religious training."[37] Religion, in his view, played an instrumental role, to strengthen the bonds between Egypt and other Muslim nations but above all, to draw attention to Egypt as the hub of the Muslim world. He did not accept the notion of an Islamic state. For him, as for Ayyub Khan in Pakistan or Sukarno in Indonesia, the albatross signaling public commitment to Islam was the *shari'a*: if its tenets were applied, the honor of Islam was defended, if relaxed, or worse, denied, Islam was defamed. While never officially denying the *shari'a*, Nasser did reshuffle it into his secular aims.

One writer has summarized the gap between the appearance of the *shari'a* and the reality of its function under Nasser as follows:

The revolutionary regime consolidated the legal system. First, the mixed courts, despised symbols of British colonialism, were abolished in 1954. Two years later the *Shari'a* and minority religious courts were absorbed into a single state secular system. From then on there was to be one single court system with one code of laws applied uniformly to all regardless of religion or nationality. With regard to matters of personal status such as marriage and divorce, a person's religion was still to be taken into consideration. The single legal code did, of course, incorporate elements of *Shari'a* but it was more European in character and, above all, it was a *secular law having no sacred basis.* The *Shari'a* itself no longer had the force of law; it was purely a matter of voluntary and personal application. Indeed, it was applicable in this fashion only insofar as it did not conflict with the established secular law in Egypt.[38]

Nasser's image so overshadowed the fifties and sixties that even communist critics label 1952–67 "the era of Nasserism."[39] His dominant philosophy has been described as socialist, since in his frequent displays of public oratory Nasser claimed to represent not only Islam but also the oppressed masses of Egypt. His model political leader was Marshal Tito of Yugoslavia.[40]

Yet contemporaries were quick to point out that Nasser was searching for an ideology; he was not launching a revolution. "By dressing up European ideas or myths in Arab clothes," Nasser was simply appealing to Arab middle classes who wanted to maintain the status quo. He was retarding instead of advancing the cause of economic justice and social redress without which there could be no true Arab unity.[41] The rapid and catastrophic defeat Egypt suffered in the 1967 war with Israel only confirmed in the eyes of his critics what they had said all along about Nasser: his temporizing policies could not withstand the test of time.

Anwar Sadat inherited the mantle of Nasser in 1970. He adapted the authoritarian structure of the Egyptian state to his own ends, but like Nasser, he failed to deal with the massive, underlying social inequities perpetuated by what one writer has called the "hydraulic politics of the Nile."[42] Under Sadat, despite the fictive victory over Israel in the 1973 war, the gap between the desire for an Islamic system, deeply felt by many, and the reality of a secular government became even more apparent, especially after the Camp David Accords of 1978.

Was it then evitable that Sadat would be killed by a cadre of Islamic fundamentalists, as he was in 1981? Or should the question rather be: did Khalid Islambouli and his collaborators hope to eliminate Sadat the image rather than Sadat the man? The answer is: the image. They attacked the image of a despot controlling a non-Islamic state system. They wanted to kill the Pharaoh. Sadat merely symbolized the Pharaoh whom fundamentalists but also others had come to revile.

Yet fixation with Pharaonic images—either praising or vilifying, immortalizing or killing the Pharaohs of each era—overlooks the major problem that confronts Egyptian-Arab society. The *shari'a* has persisted as a symbol of Islamic loyalty, and all politicians have recognized that "Islam remained the widest and most effective basis for consensus despite all efforts to promote nationalism, patriotism, secularism, and socialism."[43] All attempts at constitutional legitimation in Egypt have reflected the pervasive loyalty to Islam. In 1964 and again in 1971, Islam was designated as the state religion of Egypt. The people's council (*majlis ash-sh'ab*), appointed by the government, has continued to receive proposals for heightening the state's public commitment to the *shari'a*. Opposition political parties vie with one another as well as with the government in claiming the mantle of Islamic legitimacy.

It is in contemporary Egypt that two distinct interpretations of *shari'a* are thrown into sharpest relief. Egypt prides itself on its intellectual leadership of the Arab-Muslim world, and issues raised there have an either/or clarity, not confused by cultural syncretism as in Indonesia or by national identity as in Pakistan. Whichever perspective is adopted also determines the outcome of the debate on secularism. If one chooses to look at the encompassing power of the nation-state and its impingement on all realms of public life, then incontestable secularism had held sway in Egypt under Nasser and Sadat, and will hold sway under Mubarak and any future Pharaoh. The head of state was, and remains, less important than the system that grants power to his secular instrumentalities.

However, one could also take another view: the continuous, public link to Islam as a state religion means that the essence of secularism is denied. There cannot be a private sphere where religious principles prevail and a public domain where rational, secular concepts apply. Secularism is not authenticated by the mere dominance of the autocratic state over the religious beliefs, practices, and ecclesiastical structures of its citizens.[44]

Egypt is a crucial test case for secularization theory. If one argues that state control over religion has succeeded, then Egypt is secular, but if one argues that the underlying values remain religious and preclude separation of life into public and private domains, then secularization is but a public veneer, with no deep roots or transformative potential in society as a whole.

The argument is easier to resolve when one begins to look at either view of the *shari'a*-state conflict as an ideological stance. The socioeconomic disparities in contemporary Egypt mean that the debate only occupies the "Westernized" urban elites, principally in Cairo (though one prominent blind preacher, Shaykh Kishk, comes from Alexandria). Those who have been identified as fundamentalist invariably come from upwardly mobile middle-class backgrounds: revolutionaries are not the poor, downtrodden, and dispossessed but those who have sufficient education to perceive another reality than the one they daily confront. In the Egyptian context, the most notable protest group is the Muslim Brethren (al-Ikhwan al-muslimun). From their founding in 1936 by a school teacher, Hassan al-Banna, they challenged the government of King Farouk. Initially, they favored the officers' coup of 1952 that brought Nasser to power, but Nasser, after being threatened by them in 1954, moved to prohibit their activities, to jail or to kill their prominent leaders. Among them was the most prominent spokesman of the Ikhwan after Banna, Sayyid Qutb. Sentenced to death for sedition, he was publicly executed in 1966.

Sadat, on coming to power in 1970, attempted to preempt the Ikhwan. Initially he removed the public proscription against their activity. Ikhwan spokesmen once again became visible advocates of Islamic values but at a reduced level. Recognizing the durability of the state, they have since attempted to influence the national tenor of Egypt by joining the government rather than opposing it. When they ran for parliamentary elections in 1983, Ikhwan candidates only captured 8 seats in the National Assembly, but in the last elections they raised that total to 37, winning perhaps 10 percent of the popular vote.[45]

During the last fifteen years, the radical critique of Egyptian politics has moved to the right of the Ikhwan. Its proponents have argued that the entire government is tinged with apostasy (kufr) and that the only hope for implementation of an Islamic polity is through resort to violence. By 1977, they coalesced into a group calling itself Jama'at al-Muslimin (The Society of Muslims), though more popularly they came to be known as al-Takfir wal-Hijra, which means "declaring apostate and migrating," because they viewed Egyptian society as a whole to be corrupt and hence migrated elsewhere.[46] They posed a peripheral threat to the Sadat regime, but they would have been ignored had not internal leadership disputes prompted them to kidnap and then execute a former minister of awqaf (religious endowments). A quickly convened military trial in mid-1977 led to the conviction and execution of their principal leaders.

Jama'at al-Muslimin were succeeded by a group still more radical in tone. Jihad, as its name suggests, believed in Holy War against the regime in power as the only tactic for building an Islamic state. Whereas the Society of Muslims sought to migrate and consolidate their forces, Jihad's leadership aimed to kill Pharaoh, and they succeeded: having infiltrated key units of the Egyptian army, they gunned down Sadat at an army review stand in October 1981. Like their predecessors from the Society of Muslims, the Jihad leaders, including their principal ideologue, 'Abd as-Salam Faraj, were subsequently tried and executed.

Did the fundamentalist cadres in postindependence Egypt succeed? From the Ikhwan to the Jihad group, they have produced martyrs for the cause of Islamic purity. They have brought national and even international recognition to their grievances, but any evaluation of their actual or potential success must look at the resources for accomodation to the modernist hegemony within their *casus belli*, the *shari'a*.

The rhetorical capstone of fundamentalist opposition to the government in power is neglect of the *shari'a*. By replacing it with Western codes, even while claiming to maintain it, the ruling elites, according to fundamentalist critics, implicitly separate religious from secular authority. In so doing, they violate Muslim history and destroy the essence of Muslim society. The Ikhwan, claiming loyalty to Islamic ideals, oppose modernism in its nationalist guise. Yet they are no nostalgic atavists. They recognize that the ideal Muslim state was only briefly realized at one point in the seventh century A.D. They also recognize the power of the nation-state as a West-originated concept adopted by non-Muslim as well as Muslim polities. They are concerned to reclaim the Muslim difference, and to do it through an emphasis on fundamentals. Nothing is more fundamental than the *shari'a*, but it has to be rescued from the obfuscation with which medieval jurists overlaid it. A major task, therefore, is exegetical, to relate the *shari'a* to its own scriptural basis, the Holy Qur'an. The Qur'an becomes at once the glory and the nemesis of *shari'a* advocates. The Qur'an consists of a series of intermittent revelations given to the Prophet Muhammad over a twenty-two-year period from 610 to 632. In their lyrical force they are unequalled, yet amid the 6,666 verses of the Qur'an, only five hundred, some would say as few as two hundred, deal directly with legal issues.[47]

Such a thin base does not foster or sustain a comprehensive juridical system. One traditional way of expanding Islamic scriptural evidence for law making has been resort to *hadith,* or Prophetic traditions. While the Qur'an consists of divine revelations, traditions are nonrevelatory dicta ascribed to the Prophet Muhammad. They enjoyed a common system of ascription, traceable through generations of those who had known those who had known still others who had known the Prophet. Yet they differed widely in their content, especially between jurists of the Sunni and Shi'i branches of the *umma*. When Muslim judges made decisions on the basis of both Qur'an and traditions, they exercised a principle known in Muslim jurisprudence as *ijtihad,* and these decisions in turn became part of what was acknowledged as *shari'a* in the premodern period.

For the Ikhwan, the expansion of legal authority that *ijtihad* permitted was not justified. If traditions were seriously reexamined, as both fundamentalists and modernists have proposed, most of them would have to be abandoned. Jurisprudence therefore stands in need of extensive review. Such an intellectual process requires much time and effort. In the face of corrupt governments and threats to even the distant potential of restoring Islamic order, the Ikhwan opted instead for the direct inspiration of the Qur'an. It is no accident that Sayyid Qutb's main intellectual endeavor was a new Qur'an commentary, *In the Shadow of the Qur'an*. It extended to thirty volumes.[48]

In reworking Islamic fundamentals, the Ikhwan changed the notion of *shari'a*. It was no longer the cumbersome *shari'a* of old (subject to interpretation only by the *'ulama*) that the Ikhwan and other fundamentalists wanted to appropriate. Rather, they asserted the need for a streamlined *shari'a*. It was, in Mitchell's words, a *shari'a* that was general, flexible, developing, and universal in scope, prescribing principles of action that led to progress and happiness in all times and places. It was also a *shari'a* that was accessible to popular understanding.

As with Mawdudi, the Ikhwan were less immediately concerned with an Islamic state than with an Islamic order. Unless the latter preceded the former, there could never be a genuine application of the *shari'a* to the lives of Muslims.[49] The facets of this order are clearly spelled out by a contemporary Jordanian jurist. They are divinely decreed, not humanly constructed. They stand at the heart of Islamic civilization, binding Muslims to one another and regulating their conduct under God. They promote the five preservations essential to human life:

(1) self-preservation, enjoining what is proper to eat and drink, while prohibiting indulgence in prolonged fasting;
(2) preservation of the mind, or mental health, encouraging literacy and education while prohibiting alcohol, hashish, or drugs;
(3) preserving the species, requiring marriage while also limiting the number of wives to four, and making even that option remote by mandating conjugal parity;
(4) preserving wealth and property, by honoring labor and investment of money while also prohibiting unfair interest or usury or excessive accumulation of wealth; and
(5) preserving belief since belief in God as One, in Muhammad as His final prophet, and the Qur'an as His perfect revelation are enjoined on Muslims, while superstition and idolatry in all forms, including the elevation of country above God [nationalism], are prohibited.[50]

By its simplicity and comprehensiveness as an ideal, the *shari'a* precludes division of life into public and private domains. The crucial objection to Western cultural imperialism is the insistence of its proponents that all authority be sorted out into two realms, with the public domain projecting corporate, political ideals, and the private allowing individual moral suasions. That bifurcation of human social exchange is, for the fundamentalists, a malevolent legacy of the West. Appropriate to conditions of EuroAmerican history, it remains antithetical to the legacy of Islam. True Muslims cannot tolerate the separation of church and state because Islam is both. The Arabic words *din* (religion) and *dawla* (state) are conjoined within the meaning of Islam. In Banna's words, "politics is part of religion. Caesar and what belongs to Caesar is for God Almighty alone. . . . Islam commanded a unity of life; to impose upon

Islam the Christian separation of loyalties [into church and state] is to deny it its essential meaning and very existence."[51]

In other words, Islam is not merely a religion. It is a religion and more. It encompasses both the spiritual and the political, the private and the public domains. Attention to one sphere presumes engagement in the other. To do less is to trivialize and confound Islam. To talk about a church-state division in Islam is to talk about dividing Islam.

Yet, for the Ikhwan and for other fundamentalists, emphasis on the unity of Islam does not imply the creation of a theocracy. As Sunni Muslims, they attach minimal importance to a religious class in Islam; the 'ulama are ordinary Muslims who happen to be religious functionaries. It is for this reason that the context of Shi'i Iran is incomprehensible, and also secretly unacceptable, even to radical Sunni Muslims. As one writer has said, Islamic fundamentalism represents the revitalizing synthesis of Muslim laymen not clergy.[52]

Nationalism becomes the most despised front edge of secularism because it demands the state act as an obedience-context. In its stead, there should be emphasis on the general welfare of all Muslims (maslaha) exercised on behalf of the believers against the prevailing ignorance (jahliya) of time. Nationalism is doubly wrong: first, because it is an idea imported into Muslim countries from nineteenth century European state system; second, because it asserts that ultimate loyalty of the individual is to "my nation, right or wrong." Nationalism resurrects the kind of tribalism or jahliya that Muhammad opposed and which early Muslims, temporarily, overcame. In its stead, there should be a patriotism that seeks the benefit of all states of society and of Muslims everywhere, i.e., patriotism should replace the qawmiya (or ethnocentrism) of one group with the wataniya (or solidarity) of all groups as equal participants in the Islamic umma. Sayyid Qutb stressed the distinction by making the fundamentals into a string of homologies that paralleled yet transformed nationalism. In true Islam, according to Qutb, "nationalism is belief, homeland is Dar al-Islam, the ruler is God, and the constitution is the Qur'an."[53]

The ideas that Ikhwan leaders and also Mawdudi have expressed appeal to many middle-class Muslims, those urban males who have the time, education, and inclination to concern themselves with religious ideology. While Mawdudi was implicitly an elitist,[54] Dr. Israr talks openly about the enligthened vanguard. In both cases the emphasis is on action: deed over idea, program (minhaj) over reflection (fikra).[55]

What distinguishes fundamentalists from traditional Muslims is the force with which they take certain ideas and apply them as a challenge in particular instances, confronting—at risk to themselves but also to those being confronted—the evils in the society of their day.

The issues of understanding and applying the shari'a in any contemporary context become dramatically focused on the subject of jihad. Allegedly it means "commitment to wage war," and sometimes it is depicted as the sixth pillar in Islam, but it has a spectrum of meanings, including struggle against one's own innermost selfish tendencies. It is no accident that Mawdudi's first, and in some sense most controversial, writing was on *jihad*.[56] Nor is it happenstance that the recent expression of Islamic fundamentalist theory by 'Abd as-Salam Faraj was entitled *The Missing Imperative*. The imperative that had been missing from Egyptian public policy, due to the secularist corruption of its rulers, was *jihad*. Only its restoration, in Faraj's view, could bring about the possibility of an Islamic order, an Islamic state, and a future upsurge in the condition of Muslims worldwide.[57]

Fixation on Islamic order will not of itself transform Muslim societies or produce that revolution in Sunni Muslim countries that will be the counterpart or echo response to its occurrence in Iran. Attempts to redefine *jihad* by nationalizing it, as did an Azhar *'alim* (religious scholar) in justifying the 1973 war against Israel,[58] or as did Qadhdhafi when he wished to ward off a rumored American attack on Libya in early 1986, may have the effect of diluting its force. And it may also be that the nation-state system will find ways of surviving even terrorist attacks on its leaders.[59]

For those predisposed to condemn fundamentalists or dismiss their threat, it is easy to demonstrate, as does the Arabist Rudolph Peters, that

only their style and way of presentation . . . distinguishes fundamentalist from classical texts on *jihad,* since both views on the relationship with unbelievers are essentially identical. The fundamentalists have wrapped up these old ideas in a modern packing, by using phrases like 'permanent revolution,' etc., that are all borrowed from modern political usage. This style shows striking resemblances with that of the tracts of the various Jesus-movements in western Europe and the U.S.A., that by using similar catch-phrases with a politically progressive connotation, try to disguise their conservative message.[60]

Elsewhere the same author argues that ideology plays only a secondary role in the course of history, which is primarily determined by economic and social factors. Following the French Marxist Maxime Rodinson, Peters takes a materialist rather than essentialist approach to Islam. On this approach, any ideology, including *jihad*, is doomed to failure because Muslims have not experienced the social and economic transformations that produced the GWT. The standard of comparison is not explicitly stated. It is suppressed. The modern West becomes the *locus classicus* of success in the GWT. The author forgets that the West is not a standard for world history, since even in the West symbolic identity is neither identical nor congruent with economic and social indices. Challenges to their symbolic identity often motivate groups to produce dramatic change. As Fouad Ajami, who wavers between semiotic and materialist explanations of history, once argued, "A society's professed symbols cannot war with its realities for very long."[61]

And so a deeper question emerges: whose symbols war with whose realities? A single society has different classes. In the premodern period, there was often more horizontal identification between elites of different regions in the Islamic world than vertical identification between members of the same society.[62] Is it reasonable to assume that fundamentalism, more than nationalism, will appeal to the masses in Muslim countries?

Some have argued that it will. They see a cleavage between the ruling elite and the fundamentalists. What works against the ruling elite and in favor of the fundamentalists is the low level of socioeconomic-educational attainment in most countries. Ernest Gellner had hypothesized as the necessary concomitant of nationalism three qualities: literacy, homogeneity, and anonymity. They do not exist as a rule of life in most Muslim countries: the advances of OPEC over the past fifteen years have only exacerbated the cleavage between the few rich and the mostly poor. While the effective appeal of nationalism is to a limited, sophisticated, urban elite of the Muslim world, the power of the modern state allows these same elites to exercise coercive authority over a much wider segment of the population. And fundamentalists, despite the religious idiom of their discourse, seldom appeal to the greater number of their semiliterate, urbanite countrymen, whether they be unskilled workers or the so-called lumpenproletariat.[63]

The late Iranian scholar Hamid Enayat has tried to summarize the threat of Islamic fundamentalism in an analysis that meshes doctrinal and class conflict:

The doctrinal irreconcilability between Islam and nationalism, the simplicity of Islamic tenets for the masses, versus the relative sophistication of the nationalist ideals, . . . the rough correspondence between the nationalist-religionist rift, and the 'patrician-plebeian' dichotomy in the social structure . . . [all have] had one definite result: in any real trial of strength between the nationalists and the religionists, . . . the latter enjoy a potential tactical advantage in terms of popular support, which can be turned into actual superiority through shrewd leadership and manipulation of the masses.[64]

The argument stands or tumbles on its initial premise that Islam and nationalism are irreconcilable in every instance and that, therefore, the masses will always side with religious leaders (religionists) against political rulers (nationalists). Yet it is only from an Iranian perspective that such a statement acquires validity, since in Iran more than any other Muslim polity nationalism has been construed as a secular undertaking divorced from the religious ideals of the clerical class. The incommensurability of Shi'i nationalism, sponsored by the Shahs, and national

Shi'ism, advocated by the clergy, is peculiar to Iran. What distinguishes the Iranian context is not opposition to nationalism but the solidarity of the clerical class as the group opposing it.

The example of Iran demonstrates how difficult it is to speak of Islamic fundamentalism as a single, seamless category. While Iranians do not have the problem of national identity that afflicts many Arabs, Pakistanis, and Indonesians, the internal cohesion of Twelver Shi'i Iran as a minority branch of the Muslim world isolates Iran from its neighbors, both near and remote. Southern Lebanon represents a complex theater of limited opportunity,[65] and elsewhere in the Arab-Asian world, Iran cannot export its revolution except by force. Its staunchest Arab allies, Syria and Libya, are both autocratic regimes that derive none of their legitimacy from Islam, despite Qadhdhafi's much heralded claims. Even if the Islamic republic's forces were to win the Iran-Iraq war, topple Saddam Hussein, and extend military control over part of the Persian Gulf, their success would depend more on the exercise of power or its threat than on the ideological tenor of Khomeini's view of Islam.

Consider Khomeini's most popular book, *Islamic Government*. Written in Persian, it was translated into Arabic by a well-known Cairene leftist intellectual, Hasan Hanafi. Yet its sales in the capital city of Egypt were slow, their volume small.[66] Most Sunni Muslims, even those distraught with the modern nation-state, cannot identify with an Iranian construction of the Islamic utopia. The reasons are not hard to find. Even a casual reading of the English version of *Islamic Government* indicates Khomeini's reliance on the authority of uniquely Shi'i scriptural or quasi-scriptural sources.

However, the limits of Iran's appeal in the Muslim world do not negate the effects of its most recent political saga on the history of the twentieth century. Along with the Bolshevik Revolution, the 1979 revolution will rank as a significant milestone in the reevaluation of the Enlightenment legacy. The Bolsheviks excluded God; Khomeini enthroned Him. Neither reversal is "rational" but both are durative, and the religious dimension of what has happened in Iran is better encapsulated in the term "fundamentalism" than in any other -*ism*. For even in its brief history the Islamic Republic of Iran reveals not only the tension but also the convergence between religious fundamentalism and contemporary scientific-secular society. The key to both is technicalism.

It is no accident that the only two expressions of religious fundamentalism to have succeeded in the public domain are the Moral Majority and the Iranian Revolution. Both depend on sectarian cleavages within Islam and Christianity that benefit from emerging technicalism. Each leadership cadre has resisted the relativizing, secularizing force of technicalism because of their own commitment to "absolutist idealism."[67] They harness the instrumentalities of the modern world to ends that modernists reject as "antiquarian" and "superstitious."[68] Yet for the historically neglected, the socially marginalized, and the spiritually dislocated, the ends work; they justify all means, even the most modern.

Some scholars have underscored the historic coincidence of Iranian Shi'ism and the Protestant Reformation.[69] Both movements show how deep-seated antagonism between religion and a dominant ethos does not preclude their elective affinity. The Protestant Reformation opposed privileged structures, both ecclesiastical and political. It also rejected the notion of an enchanted world, stressing instead the mediation of an elect in this world. In so doing, it prepared for the capitalist and technological revolutions of the eighteenth century. For their part, the Shi'i hieratic classes (i.e., the "clergy") challenged the virtual Sunni monopoly of political power. In supporting a distinctly Shi'i polity, they stressed attention to the present age while also upholding the authority of their own leaders as links to the pure Islamic past.

In both cases a universalist impulse was at work. The Protestant Reformation produced a series of polities that expressed de facto pluralism and in time gave rise to constitutional pluralism. The theistic moorings of Protestantism may have been distorted, but they were not uprooted by the relativism of its progeny. The challenge of the Great Western Transmutation caused Protestant fundamentalists to affirm a timeless gospel: rejecting secular humanism, they could be both Progressive and Patriotic because they were, finally, Protestants.

The same is true of the Safavid empire. Beginning in the sixteenth century, the Safavids transformed Iran into a Shi'i state. The Safavid rulers forged a monarchical polity that for a time was capable of encouraging Shi'i loyalty while repressing the Shi'i clergy who had helped confirm their legitimacy. Yet the clergy never abandoned their will to protest.[70] The period of their denial was a time of gestation for reappearance in greater force. They could not be killed off, they could only be bought off, and if unwilling to surrender either to sword or to purse, they became a continuous, if rearguard, threat to all attempts at recasting the image of Iran as a nation-state accelerating progress and embracing secular-style pluralism. By supporting the 1906 constitution, the clergy showed their willingness to compromise with instrumentalities of Western power, but in the 1981 constitution they showed that the intent of their compromise was to reaffirm a religious state and also the patriarchal values on which it is predicated. The state was borderless: Iran became the center of an expansive polity whose limits were defined only by the limits of Islamic loyalty.

Neither American Protestants nor Iranian Shi'ites, however, were prepared for the assaults on their time-honored ideals that came in the present century. Further battles with modernism, whether masked as cultural progress (America) or national development (Iran), compelled an ideological reassessment of the past. Moments of glory could not be nostalgically invoked nor their effervescence recaptured. One had to restate fundamentals. That restatement of fundamentals was itself a radical, even a modern move. It signaled departure from past certainties and acceptance of present ambiguities. It was, for Iranians as for Americans, a coming to terms with the Great Western Transmutation.

When the Protestant Fundamentals were published (1910–1915), their impact was not immediate, yet over time they came to symbolize the religious defiance of relativism; they became for many the bedrock manifesto of militant American Protestantism. Few would deny that the long-term symbolic effect they have enjoyed has been enormous.[71] In 1985, seventy-five years later, *Fundamentals of Islamic Thought* appeared.[72] They represent a Shi'i manifesto against secularism. Their author was among the most respected Iranian clerics, a man whom Khomeini once described as "the fruit of my life" and "a part of my flesh."[73] Although the Ayatollah Morteza Mutahhari was killed in 1979 near the outset of the Iranian Revolution, his Fundamentals may well have an influence that outlives the Islamic Republic of Iran. They represent the same challenge to modern, secular, scientistic discourse that the earlier Protestant Fundamentals signaled. If anything, the Ayatollah's suasions are more holistic. They have a dual foundation. Building on the premises of Islam as a complete way of life, their author takes sides in the science vs. religion battles of the last fifty years. Mutahhari advocates Islam in philosophical terms that acknowledge while also refuting scientific challenges to a divine transcendent. Foremost among such challenges is the challenge of evolution.

Mutahhari denies evolution yet also affirms it. He denies the notion of evolution as articulated by Judeo-Christian apologists and deistic scientists. While the Qur'an, like the Bible, says that "God is the Author and Creator of life, . . . it does not refer to the first day and contrast it to later days."[74] Rather, according to the Qur'an, as Mutahhari interprets it, "the systematic transformations of life within the human embryo" constitute creation, and they *are* evolutionary. "[Just as] an animal or a human being continuously undergoes creation in traversing the stages of evolution [so] the whole universe is continuously undergoing creation." For Mutahhari the "marvelous logic" of the Qur'an is to affirm creation without attaching it to a particular moment or implying a retreat to negative theology. He goes so far as to acknowledge different scientific models of evolution, distinguishing the gradualistic model of Lamarck and Darwin from its successor, the punctuational model formulated by Ernst Mayr.[75] At the same time, Mutahhari remains ambivalent about the Genesis account of creation, preferring to bracket it from scientific investigation or philosophical discussion as a different language, the language of poetry, which serves a rhetorical rather than a logical function.[76]

However one finally evaluates Mutahhari's writings, what is initially most striking is the distance between his thought world and that of

Sunni theorists. So opposite is Iranian Twelver Shi'i fundamentalism from Arab or Pakistani or Malay Sunni fundamentalism that it is straining credibility to call them both "Islamic fundamentalism." The problem is at heart linguistic: how to avoid overaggregation while still making sense of human experience? Tyson, Peacock, and Patterson have sounded a salutary warning that "distinctive differences [can be] hidden in a lumping category such as fundamentalist."[77] If for expediency we speak of a category called "Islamic fundamentalism," it seems preferable to adopt a variant of Mannheim's two-wings principle in elaborating differences among Islamic fundamentalists as we did earlier in examining Jewish fundamentalism. Every ideology spawns a spectrum of responses to its basic premises. Politically or socially they can be described as going from right to left, from conservative to liberal, or vice versa, but they vary according to concrete, historical circumstances that were not anticipated by the founders of any ideology and can only be understood retrospectively.[78]

The two divisions or wings of Islamic fundamentalism that we examined are best categorized as "antinationalist," in the case of Sunni activists, and "modified nationalist," in the case of Twelver Shi'ites. The distinction between them becomes starkly evident when we review the use of the term "Islamic ideology" in contemporary Iran. Ideology was first exposited in a positive vein by the popular opponent of monarchism, 'Ali Shari'ati. Using a direct transliteration from the French-Roman into Perso-Arabic script, Shari'ati depicted ideology as "a magic word." In his view, it became "a religion consciously chosen by the people" and hence preferable to the customary religion of one's parents. Religion as ideology is no longer mere belief. It is instead "belief which is chosen, relative to existing inconsistencies, for the purpose of translating an individual's class, or a group's beloved ideals, into reality."[79] Embracing ideology, Ayatollah Mutahhari followed Shari'ati's lead, despite the other differences between the two men. Mutahhari's essay "Man and Faith" appears as a central chapter in *Fundamentals of Islamic Thought*. In it he tries to move beyond the science/faith dichotomy, as he also did in his treatment of evolution, he embraces ideology, or at least a certain strand of ideology. He quotes a host of Western intellectual giants, from Descartes and Kant to William James, Bertrand Russell, and even Erich Fromm, in order to posit two kinds of ideology. The one, corporate and particular, only mobilizes limited group interests. The other, universal and human, aims at "the salvation of the whole human species." Islam conforms to this second type of ideology. Its instrumentality is a comprehensive juridical code, the *shari'a*, its ultimate aim "the victory of humanity over animality, science over ignorance, justice over injustice, equality over discrimination, virtue over iniquity, piety over dissipation, *tawhid* over *shirk*."[80]

While there are inconsistencies in Mutahhari's appropriation of ideology, they are initially less significant than his use of a category that to Sunni theorists falls altogether outside the realm of acceptable Islamic vocabulary: ideology. Ideology has no Qur'anic, juridical, or lexical history in the Muslim world prior to the High Tech Era. A product of the worldview that Islamic fundamentalists are combating, it is nonetheless pressed into service by them to establish the force of their own counterargument. That strategy is understood, even if only at an implicit level, by Twelver Shi'i Iranian theorists. The valorization of ideology makes their writings at once more nuanced and less atemporal than the corpus of their Sunni counterparts.

The disjuncture between Sunni and Twelver Shi'i exponents of Islamic fundamentalism also illustrates the adaptability of fundamentalism as a global phenomenon. Fundamentalists respond to the concrete, circumstantial interaction of their ethos with the Great Western Transmutation. Above all, they oppose particular members of their own identity group (Jews, Christians, or Muslims) who have been infected by the disease of modernism and compromised by its value system. While the potential for fundamentalist ideology is framed by the discrepancy between an indigenous, universalist ethos and the external, rationalizing stance of the GWT, the actual impetus to reject modernism and to form fundamentalist cadres is triggered by specific incidents and living embodiments of the felt discrepancy. Hence the gradient of response always varies, in some cases on a broad spectrum determined in part by the brand of monotheism embraced.

For Islam, the core element is the Book mediated by the community. Among Sunni fundamentalists, the Book (whether conceived as the Qur'an or the *shari'a* expanded to have an authority equivalent to the Qur'an) is closed, hence it needs new and better implementers. The Sunni response to modernism is defensive, to reclaim the Book from the historical retardation that it has experienced at the hands of its traditional custodians, the *'ulama*. Compromised by the force of the GWT, the *'ulama* have invoked the time-honored principle of *ijtihad* (reinterpretation), but in reality they have forfeited their right to implement the *shari'a*. They have sided with the nationalists who enjoyed political power and social prestige. They have forsaken the *tawhid*, or unity of Islam, for the *shirk*, or polytheism, of the modernist hegemony.

But the case is different with Twelver Shi'i Islam. While the moral contaminator is once again Western civilization, it is the *'ulama* who are the custodians rather than the compromisers of tradition. It is they who carry the banner of Allah against all secular incursions. For Twelver Shi'i jurists, the Book is not closed but open. Its ongoing interpreter is the Twelfth Imam. Though hidden since the eighth century, he directly inspires faithful heirs of the 'Alid legacy. The Book remains accessible to a long line of living interpreters. Each relies on the oral transmission of *'irfan,* or anagogic wisdom. Khomeini is one such interpreter. His doctrine of *vilayet-i faqih* posits responsibility *(vilayet)* for the entire Muslim community in the hands of the foremost jurisconsult, the *faqih.* Debate about the role of the *faqih* goes back to the eleventh century. Khomeini is merely drawing out the latest tangent from a hallowed concept. He does not advocate an innovation, as some of his critics would have us believe.[81]

It is the historical embeddedness of Twelver Shi'ism as an expression of *iraniyat* that gives the Islamic revolution in Iran its characteristic force. The ruling clerics can claim that they are the moral custodians of what is most distinctly Iranian *(iraniyat).* It is they who have resisted the allure of the modern world. Against the chimerical relativism of satanic Westerners, they offer the utopian idealism of the Book as mediated by the Hidden Imam's only authoritative spokesmen, the clergy. Though some like Mutahhari may invoke the language of Islamic ideology, they do so only to reinforce the incommensurability of age-old opposites, God and Satan, light and darkness, Iran and others, the familiar dichotomies of the premodern era.

And so there are two groups who lead the Islamic revolution against secularism. Both groups are fundamentalist. Both agree upon the need to act on behalf of group interests. They are ideologues, not theologians or philosophers. But they are religious ideologues, because it is above all religious principles or fundamentals that they feel are threatened. Both are opposed to the same corrosive elements of modernity, above all, in the diminution of the Islamic character of the public sphere. Where they differ is in the mediating groups whom they support as the authoritative agents to reassert fundamentals, to reformulate purity as public order, to strive even to the point of *jihad* where necessary.

The comparison with Judaism in Israel illumines the Muslim difference. The *haredim* are more graphic in detailing what issues of Halakhic observance have been threatened by the dominant secular tone of the Israeli state. Unlike Muslims who have to react to leaders who claim to be enforcing the *shari'a* while neglecting or overriding it, Jewish fundamentalists are faced with a state context where observance is publicly challenged in the name of the higher principle of Zionism. It is much clearer what is neglected and who neglects, but the warfare is once again in the public arena. Hence what is challenged is the governmental sanction for the public neglect of specific observances: dietary laws must be kept, the sabbath quiet enforced, ancestral graves revered. Underlying all these demands is the larger question about whether any Jewish state, even one that had the Torah for its constitution, might be flawed because it preempted the Messiah. Messianic expectancy seldom erupts into public view, however, (unless one accepts Meir Kahane as a Jewish fundamentalist), so much more immediate and pervasive is the other tension relating to specific commandments and their neglect.

It is possible to reach some summary conclusions about Islamic fundamentalism and Muslim polities. There is no single reaction characteristic of all Muslims. The parameters of possibility are framed by two poles: first, mediation of the Book within tradition and, second, the level and degree of colonization. In every instance, the importance of political statutes for Muslim identity and the hegemony of modern state apparatuses have meant that the battle between modernism and fundamentalism in Islam is joined in the public order, above all in the capital city. It usually pits some elites against other elites, but it seldom involves nonelites at the highest level of decisionmaking. The public welfare (maslaha) is not expanded to mean welfare of the masses; rather it is the welfare of those who ally themselves with, or at least choose not to oppose, the interests of fundamentalist leaders.

Islamic loyalties are diverse—Sunni and Shi'i, Arab and Asian, first world and third world.[82] It is instructive to contrast the status of Islamic loyalties in Indonesia, Pakistan, and Egypt. In the case of Indonesia, Islam is debarred as the state religion. *Pancasila* as a secular umbrella encompasses Islam and appeals over the head of religionists to nationalists. The appeal is very effective in a country that has never known national cohesion till the colonial and postcolonial periods. In the case of Pakistan, the effort to enshrine Islam as a state religion was delayed. The secular socialist Zulfiqar Ali Bhutto arranged for its inclusion in the 1973 constitution, along with the provision for an advisory council on Islamic ideology. Bhutto's successor, Zia al-Haqq, arranged to have Bhutto hanged, but still implemented the council that Bhutto had launched. Even after Zia al-Haqq's unexpected death in an air crash in August 1988, the religious parties remained under the supervisory control of the government and continued to complain that Pakistan had yet to become a fully Islamic state. Only in the case of Egypt has there been an effective agitation to have the *shari'a* implemented in the public sphere. Here too, however, the responses have been piecemeal, each new effort marred by controversy. Though Islam was declared the state religion of Egypt in 1971, the *shari'a* did not become the main source of legislation till the plebiscite of March 1980. Since then its practical implementation has been subjected to procedural delays.[83]

The likelihood that fundamentalists will succeed anywhere in the Muslim world beyond Iran is minimal, if by "succeed" we mean to be able to introduce an Islamic order that opposes Western cultural norms and curtails non-Muslim political interests. The great temptation is to aggregate the entire Muslim world. Journalists, like government policy makers and academics, must resist that temptation. Instead one must look to the local factors fueling a fundamentalist ideology. The starting point is invariably an implicit index of power that is linked to Islamic prestige in the precolonial era. Marginalized male elites experience socioeconomic disparities as cultural loss, and they are drawn to participate in fundamentalist cadres in order to militate against nationalist structures that they deplore as un-Islamic because they are, above all, ineffective.

Yet the staying power of the modern nation-state is such that even when its instrumentalities are coopted by fundamentalists in the name of Islam, as happened in Iran, the codes of modernity are honored. The Islamic Republic of Iran is defined by a constitution, just as it is empowered by an oil-exporting economy. Sunni Muslims, should they succeed in restoring an Islamic order, would also conform to the nation-state model. Even short of total success, many, like the current leadership of al-Ikhwan al-Muslimun in Egypt, opt to work within the system, seeking elected seats in student unions, trade associations, and, of course, the national parliament. Like their American Protestant counterparts, Sunni Islamic fundamentalists want to take over the system rather than overthrow it. Fundamentalists can only succeed by adapting to that which they oppose. The outcome is no different for Muslims than for Jews and Christians.

Conclusion

The historian Fernand Braudel, whose writings were cited mainly in chapter three but whose influence pervades our study, once remarked: "There is no problem which does not become increasingly complex when actively investigated, growing in scope and depth, endlessly opening up new vistas of work to be done."[1] Comparative research on fundamentalism, already complex, will open up still further vistas as more become convinced of its importance and engaged by its opportunities. When those engaged are EuroAmerican scholars, they will be impelled to look beyond their own cultural legacy. In examining the multiple religious responses to modernism, one cannot remain confined to a single tradition, not even the supposedly foundational tradition of Progressive Patriotic Protestantism. Only an intercreedal, cross-cultural investigation reveals the true nature of fundamentalism, that all expressions of fundamentalist fervor are shaped by the redefining and restructuring of religion that takes place in the modern world, and it is modernism, emerging as the dominant ideological strand of modernity, that has decisively shaped the latest chapter, the High Tech Era, of global history.

Nowhere is the triumph of modernist ideology more firmly enshrined than in the nation-state. The social theorist Anthony Giddens examines the process of nation-state formation about as well as anyone. Without amplifying his distinction between core, periphery, and semiperiphery structures, we can concur with his general thesis that what characterizes the High Tech Era, above all, is "the diffusion of the means of waging industrialized war."[2] The effectiveness of this diffusion has made the nation-state system the inescapable political norm for all humankind. Fundamentalists, whether in the first or third world, have to elicit followers and mobilize movements within a reflexively monitored, hierarchically structured polity that neutralizes all moral absolutes under the rubric of its own unassailable sovereignty. Nationalist ideology preempts other invocations of transcendence; fundamentalists must perform on a stage that they did not construct and which they cannot destroy.

The instrumental strength of the modernist hegemony shields without erasing its cognitive limits. Apart from the intrinsic bias against religion, one must note other limits. Based on technicalism, it has a single monolithic view of reason. It is adept at enumeration; inventories proliferate in the High Tech Era. Yet it is weak in analysis, substituting origins for beginnings and often neglecting causal relationships of a basic nature.[3]

Nor are modernists prone to take account of limits. Given the pervasiveness of cognitive and emotive codes within the Western tradition, one might have expected a tradition of skepticism, if not self-criticism, to emerge among more philosophically-minded scientists. Yet novelty itself has been so enshrined in the modernist canon of sciences and technology that only the literary disciplines or human sciences of Western culture are criticized as premodern, traditional, irrational.

The modernist hegemony, by its very emphasis on change, has disguised the extent to which it itself embodies continuity and opposes change. George Steiner is only half-right when he observes that "the novelty of content and of empirical consequence in the natural sciences and technology have obscured the determinist constancy of tradition, but in philosophic discourse and the arts, where novelty of content is at best a problematic notion, the impulse to repetition, to organization via backward reference, is sovereign." For however much they obscure, the natural sciences cannot ignore "the determinist constancy of tradition"; like philosophy, they, too, are often governed by "the impulse to repetition, the organization via backward reference."[4]

An innovative mathematical theorist illustrates the problem of how the intrinsic appeal to referentiality becomes cloaked beneath the patina of scientific discourse. In the introduction to *Metamagical Themas*, Douglas Hofstadter explains why he is drawn to the study of mathematics. He is trying to discover the relationship between the mind, creativity, and music. Mathematics, in his view, "more than any other discipline, studies the fundamental, pervasive patterns of the universe, . . . [and] the deepest and most mysterious of all patterns is music, a product of the mind that the mind has not come to fathoming *yet*." Hofstadter sets for himself the task of unlocking *now* the mystery of musical creativity:

> In some sense, [he allows], all my research is aimed at finding patterns that will help us to understand the mysteries of musical and visual beauty, . . . [and] even though I find the prospect [of reducing music to mathematical formulae] repugnant, I am greatly attracted by the effort to do as much as possible in that direction . . . [especially since] in computers [we have] the ultimate tool for exploring the essence of creativity and beauty.[5]

Hofstadter, in effect, is divinizing his research program. On the one hand, he eschews the endeavor to render musical creativity formulaic, but at the same time, he dedicates himself to that endeavor because he now has an efficient tool, in fact, "the *ultimate* tool for exploring the essence of creativity and beauty" (my emphasis). To a modernist, the contradictoriness of this proposition is not problematic. He perceives himself to be the courageous explorer of a new frontier of problem solving. Yet his audacity presupposes that his readers continue to associate ultimacy with *Truth*. And to any reader who has the faintest memory about theological claims that the source of creativity and beauty is *divine*, it is Hofstadter who seems blasphemous, his quest not unlike that of Pascal: "to make God a mathematician whose secrets they could discover, and so come perilously near to identifying one's human power as a mathematician with *ultimate Truth*."[6]

It is only against the background of the modernist apostasy, launched long before Hofstadter and embraced by others than him, that we can consider ideologies alternative to the ethos dominating privileged male culture in Asia and the Middle East as well as in EuroAmerica. Among those ideologues who advocate a scriptural idiom and claim the public sphere as sacred space are the secondary male elites labeled "fundamentalist." The sociologist John Wilson located the crucial relationship when he declared that "the strident reassertion of a presumed tradition in a condensed, purified, or even reductionist form" is itself "a response to modernity, [for] fundamentalisms . . . are no less than modernisms determined by the modern culture that they so stridently reject."[7]

The indispensable starting point is to locate fundamentalism in contemporary discourse. Though it has religious labels, fundamentalism functions as an ideology. Fundamentalist leaders are self-proclaimed churchmen or observant Jews or faithful Muslims, but they are in reality ideologues because they must operate within the modernist hegemony while challenging not only its original premises but also its pervasive authority. They intuit as much as they verbalize the discrepancy between their worldview and the dominant worldview. They act boldly on behalf of their values.

In this study we have attempted to specify which subgroups within Christianity, Judaism, and Islam are fundamentalist, namely, one branch of Protestant Christians in America, scattered groups of quasi-Hasidic and *haredi* Jews in Israel, and certain cadres of Muslims—Sunnis in Egypt, Pakistan and Malaysia, Shi'ites in Iran and southern Lebanon. We have also addressed the nature of the issues that fundamentalists seize upon, stressing that despite their religious labels, each is identified with a particular ideology of opposition to the Technical Age, or more recently, the High Tech Era. The common object of their revulsion is the modernist hegemony. For Muslims, it is a third world ideology of protest; its defining characteristics relate as much to the third world socioeconomic condition of the majority of Muslims as it does to universal Islamic creedal appeals, for either Shi'ites or Sunnis. For Protestant Christians, on the other hand, fundamentalism is a first world, overtly capitalist ideology of reform. Progressive Patriotic Protestants are but narrowly separated from their politically conservative but often agnostic fellow citizens, those whom Henry May has labeled Progressive Protestant Patriots. Only for quasi-Hasidic and *haredi* Jews is it an ideology seeking to transpose premodern religious values into a modern nation-state. Neither first world nor third world but between worlds, Jewish fundamentalism comes close to being an ideology of recuperation.

The labeling "fundamentalist" helps us to see what these groups have in common. Too many of the arguments used to refute fundamentalists, or even to deny that they are fundamentalists, rely on etymological sleights of hand that miss the major point: something did happen on the way to the twenty-first century. The seismic divide separating the High Tech from antecedent eras needs to be recognized by advocates of modernization as well as by their opponents.

The deepest level of power derives from economics, and it would be foolhardy to discuss the GWT or its result, both in the first and the third worlds, without recognizing the commercial edge of technicalization. Yet the most immediate level of authenticity depends on religion, for no projection of power can escape the cultural constraints of religious observance, as even Japanese high-tech executives have come to acknowledge. Most studies fail to examine one or the other. Understanding fundamentalism requires attention to both economics and religion, especially their interaction at several levels—global, national, and local.

Fundamentalism is a concerted movement of disparate, mutually antipathetic groups. American Protestant fundamentalists provide the first explicit test case of the modernist/fundamentalist struggle. The movement, like the word fundamentalism, initially emerged among rural and urban Presbyterians and Baptists in the early decades of the twentieth century. Its checkered history only partially conforms to the criteria for fundamentalism we set out in chapter four. While they were openly confrontational to representatives of liberal Christian doctrine, Progressive Patriotic Protestants did not oppose the American political system. They tried to work within it to change its direction. Their viewpoint always remained that of the unsullied minority. They remained a minority even when they joined with others to press for legislation that banned alcohol and later tried to introduce creation science into the curriculum of public schools. Secondary male elites provided their leadership, extolling women as mothers and custodians of family values but never recognizing an individual woman as authoritative teacher. Their technical language, communicated through their own literary media and eventually through television, demarcated Protestant American fundamentalists from other Christians, though evangelicals rivaled them for the mantle of gospel purity and also staked out claims to their symbolic space.

Jewish fundamentalism did not surface till after the establishment of a Zionist state in the late 1940s. Fundamentalism within Judaism nonetheless has roots that predate all others. The social origins of Jewish fundamentalists are traceable to the ghettoization of European Jewry (the Ashkenazim) in the eighteenth and nineteenth centuries. Alienated by culture from the mainstream of the European Enlightenment, many provincial Jews, especially in Poland and Hungary, did not benefit from the commercial successes of renascent Europe. There were exceptions to the rule. They were the individual Jews who succeeded by becoming part of the dominant culture not as Jews but as modernists, and to the extent that they modernized or Westernized, they were regarded by other Jews, especially those from East European ghettos, as renegades to the ancestral legacy. Unfaithful to the embodiment of Jewish values, namely, the Torah, "enlightened" Jews appeared to their quasi-Hasidic and *haredi* counterparts as non-Jews. The tension between these opposite and incommensurable views of tradition, though never resolved, did not explode into the public domain till the formation of Israel in 1948. Hence Jewish fundamentalism seems more recent than Protestant American fundamentalism, despite the fact that its origins are, in fact, older.

The case is different with Islam. We can only begin to understand the varied sources for Islamic fundamentalism when we accept the extreme complexity of Islam itself. The question has often been posed, Are Muslims too varied an aggregate to be discussed under a single rubric such as "the world of Islam"? Yet the same question could be posed of Jews and Christians. To talk of scripture, e.g., Qur'an,Torah, Bible, is one thing, but to speak of communities that relate to that scripture, with any honest recognition of ethnic, linguistic, geographical diversity—and the stubborn "idols" each entails—is to admit the persistence of de facto pluralism, whatever the monotheistic creed or unifying mandate of scripture. Yet if we conceptualize Jews and Christians as worldwide communities, we must also admit that Muslims belong to a single, coherent *umma*. The *kehilla*, the church, the *umma*—each does exist. Each has points of cross-cultural identification and transnational loyalty. One must assert them while at the same time *not* claiming them as authoritative markings in any particular instance without also acknowledging the persistent force of local counterclaims.

It is especially important to note Islamic fundamentalists as a group apart from other Muslims. First cited by the British orientalist H. A. R. Gibb in the 1940s,[8] fundamentalism did not become a widely recognized Islamic phenomenon until the success of the clerically led Iranian Revolution in 1978–79. Prior to 1979, Egyptian and Pakistani oppositional groups were more often called extremist or militant than fundamentalist. They only became fundamentalist after the Iranian Revolution, by association with and comparison to Iran. Bluntly stated, without the Iranian Revolution, Islamic fundamentalism does not exist as an inclusive designation for antimodernist Muslim activists. In its stead, you have dissident radicals, a descriptive epithet that some scholars still prefer but one which has pejorative political connotations.

The cauldron of religious ideology in which Islamic, as also Jewish and Christian, fundamentalism has been brewing needs to be carefully examined. Its practitioners offer a unique cure for the ills of the High Tech Era: they rely on modern instrumentalities while rejecting the goals of modernism.

There is a grave danger, and a logical error, in exceptionalizing what occurred in early twentieth century America. The latent forces that prompted fundamentalism to erupt in the USA were also at work elsewhere in the world under the impact of the GWT but at a much more gradual rate, with a masking of both the scope of challenge and the depth of change that was occurring. Despite its scientific veneer and the military prowess of its beneficiaries, the GWT has proved to be an untidy, helter-skelter process of change. The level of mass participation may have increased, but ours remains a world whose major institutions and public policies are controlled by a small elite of "enlightened" men. Radio, like journalism, and later like TV, provided a venue through which it seemed possible to protest what was occurring. Yet the politics of twentieth century nationalism remained intransigent to religious aspirations. With few exceptions, political office became a platform for advocating modernist values, its mechanisms controlled by ideologues denying the autonomy of religious actors and institutions, notwithstanding the appeal of some politicians to religious sensibilities.

While most observers tend to discuss fundamentalism as a reaction against the modern world, we prefer to emphasize not only the fundamentalist reaction but also the threat against which fundamentalists are reacting. We call this "antimodernism" because it is the dominance of strategies and values labeled "modernist" that characterize the Technical Age and especially the High Tech Era. There are reactions against modernism other than fundamentalism. There are motives for fundamentalist groups other than antimodernism. But the core contest is between two incommensurate ways of viewing the world, one which locates values in timeless scriptures, inviolate laws, and unchanging mores, the other which sees in the expansion of scientific knowledge a technological transformation of society that pluralizes options both for learning and for living.

The seriousness of the modernist challenge to religious values, symbols, and worldviews is concealed by the shield of material ease that privileges major segments of EuroAmerican society. It is difficult to challenge that which seems basic to everyday life, from digital clocks to compact disc players to hard disk personal computers. The technological achievements of the High Tech Era do not, however, produce a single set of ideological projections. The challenges we have reviewed in chapters six, seven, and eight relate to specific modernisms: the nation-state as obedience-context for Jews and Muslims, the ubiquity of civil religion in America, the claims of sociobiology for scientific investigators of every continent. The cumulative effect of these chapters is to suggest that although the forms of fundamentalist protest may be questionable and even offensive to nonfundamentalists, there is ample evidence to support the fundamentalists' contention that religious symbols and claims have been devalued in the public discourse of many societies. The nation-state has defined and then occupied the space of symbolic purity.

In this conclusion it is necessary to stress that few modernists recognize the conflict with fundamentalism as anything but a rearguard mop-up operation. The *real* issue in their view is to delineate the nature of a postmodern (or postliberal or postneoorthodox) world. Once emergent, that world, it is presumed, will put to rest questions about scriptural authenticity and institutional autonomy advocated by fundamentalists on behalf of "true religion."

While speculations that promote a nontheistic worldview inclusive of the present epoch in global history are the grist of Marxist philosophy, the most resounding death knell to God-talk comes from a contemporary non-Marxist German philosopher. The philosopher is Hans Blumenberg. His major work, *The Legitimacy of the Modern Age,* has been hailed as "a great sweeping history of the course of European thought." It is, in fact, the most extensive effort yet mounted to disassociate modern science from *any* religious antecedents. By implication, the modern age would also be severed from all preceding epochs of world history. The title itself poses a rhetorical question: is the modern age legitimate? Can it claim authoritative points of identity that assure its independence? Is it self-referential rather than linked to legacies of the past or prospects for the future? The answer to all these questions, for Blumenberg, is a resounding "yes." He targets religious categories as the *bête noire*—to be isolated, defined, attacked, and demolished. Their persistence, despite Enlightenment critiques and competitive ideologies, is most evident in the attempts of other philosophers to explain the modern age as a *continuation* of premodern notions in new verbal guise. Even Nietzsche is suspect since he once commented that "how science could become what it now is can only be made intelligible from the development of religion."[9] Instead of legitimizing modern discourse with reference to its prior religious impulses, Blumenberg wants to sever the Gordian knot and proclaim the *de novo* character of both human self-assertion and theoretical curiosity in the modern age.

Blumenberg finds the secularization thesis itself to be a lumbering antediluvian relic of theologizing philosophers and social scientists. In his view, "the secularization thesis is an indirectly theological exploitation of the historiographical difficulties that have arisen with regard to the philosophical attempt at [formulating] a beginning of the modern age."[10] Implicit in the notion of secularization, he argues, is the previous valuation of the sacred, the transcendent, the other as a primary point of reference. Even when sacrality loses its functional force through the interjection of another outlook that is profane, immanent, and self-enclosed, he claims that it retains its historical primacy. Secularization, precisely because it must displace sacrality, is invariably understood to be the negation of prior sacred values. It is this inescapable reflexivity—of language but also of consciousness—that prevents secularization from expressing the privilege of the current epoch of world history. Therefore, in Blumenberg's view, the best approach to the secularization thesis in the modern age is to discard it as an anachronism. In its stead, he suggests, we ought to embrace and proclaim worldliness as the characteristic feature of our time. Worldliness is a self-referential category. Worldliness does not have to be claimed as the result of secularizations. Like the modern age, it stands on its own.

Blumenberg's arguments may or may not capture the imagination of EuroAmerican intellectuals. They do, however, offer a plumb line by which we can measure the efforts to assess fundamentalism within the academy. Most of the debates thus far mounted have been polemical quibbles or rhetorical asides. Consider the attempt to differentiate fundamentalists from evangelicals in the EuroAmerican context of Protestant Christianity. From scholarly monographs like Sandeen's *Roots of Millenarianism* to a collection of popular essays like Wells and Woodbridge's *The Evangelicals*, much attention has been drawn to the distinction between evangelicals and fundamentalists. While evangelical modernists like James Barr have tried to distance themselves from Protestant fundamentalists, fundamentalist preachers like Jerry Falwell have come forward to depict themselves as the *true* evangelicals, inviting others to join them.[11] The jousting over sectarian identity, however, misses the larger point: in neither camp is there a sustained *intellectual* counterchallenge to the issues posed by the Technical Age, issues that could be best summarized as scientific positivism. It is these issues that threaten the metaphysical basis of human thought and the search for ethical guidelines in human conduct. The threat is recognized by fundamentalists yet the response mounted to it, for instance in the creationist controversy, seems overly defensive and rhetorically freighted.

Another debate has been waged within Judaism: to try to establish what are the defining characteristics of the Jewish collectivity and to maintain them against all secular assaults. The divergent responses from Neturei Karta and Gush Emunim have puzzled those who want to exalt nationalist identity, specifically loyalty to the state of Israel, as the highest allegiance of the Jewish collectivity. It is a battle that at first seems remote from Blumenberg's appeal for a confirmation of the independent, nonreligious authenticity of the modern age. Yet the process of

Israel's formation as a nation-state in the High Tech Era lends partial support to Blumenberg's thesis. The majority of Israel's political leaders have come from segments of European society caught up with Enlightenment fever. They migrated to Palestine and worked to create a new polity that promoted technical skills, ensured the autonomy of its citizens, and strove for progress. If one could strip Israeli society of its minority dissidents, i.e., the National Religious Party and the contemporary zealots who belong to Neturei Karta and Gush Emunim, the Zionist state might come closer than any other modern state to fulfilling Blumenberg's model of a legitimate nonreligious polity. Even the Talmudic ritual antecedents that color Israel's civil religion might fade in a couple of generations. But that secularist utopia will not appear in Israel precisely because a religiously vocal minority does intrude into the public sphere. Politicized as religious ideologues, they insist on the historical continuity between the pre- and post-Enlightenment Jewish collectivity. They cannot be silenced or ignored, and so their aspirations for an uncompromisingly Jewish identity in the modern nation-state guarantee at the least a creative tension between them and their less observant Jewish compatriots. More frequently, as in the official response to the recent Palestinian demonstrations, that tension between religious and secular Jews erupts into physical confrontations within Israel that preempt compromise, preclude peace, and ensure protracted stalemates in Israel's external relations.

So radical is Blumenberg's reappropriation of modernity that the force of his arguments trivializes the search for some label other than "fundamentalist" to describe the numerous religiously motivated protests in the Islamic world. "Revivalism," "radicalism," "extremism," "activism," "militancy"—each has been touted by certain observers as a less culturally charged, more descriptively neutral substitute for the term "fundamentalism" in examining the religious protest common to Israel and its Muslim neighbors. Some go so far as to suggest that English vocabulary must be abandoned altogether and that one must resort to the French equivalent for fundamentalism, *intégrisme*. Still another move is to reclaim George Steiner's model of bifurcated linguistic-cultural spheres: upholding the specificity of any group's language and history as incommunicable, we must accept "the failure of Western secularized languages and Western historical parallels to provide *perfect* analogies for realities within the Muslim [or non-Western] world."[12]

By their nature, no analogies can be perfect. But the problem with monadist, atomistic logic, as we pointed out in chapter four, is the blindness of its advocates to the universality of certain themes and problems. While Muslims are not to be lumped together with Christians and Jews, they do have common concerns that are often best drawn out in a comparative frame of reference. Comparison must not be jettisoned. It is tough work that can yield results once technical terms are justified and analytical categories established. Aggregation and referentiality are inescapable, but prejudice can be minimized, positivism blunted.

The measure of how well our analysis of fundamentalism succeeds depends on the adequacy of the five criteria outlined at the end of chapter four. Are fundamentalists best described as (1) minority advocates of scriptural idealism who are (2) oppositional to the dominant ethos? Do their leaders and followers tend to be (3) secondary-level male elites who are bound to one another by (4) a religious ideology that relies on insider, technical language? Despite their own claims to distant and near antecedents, are fundamentalists (5) only to be found in the Technical Age as tenacious opponents of modernist ideologies that challenge their scriptural ideals and spiritual loyalties?

Each case needs to be reviewed with reference to these questions and the criteria they set forth. While Progressive Patriotic Protestants are not vocally opposed to the nation-state system of the United States of America, they conform in other respects to the normative outlook and behavioral pattern that characterize Israeli Jewish and Egyptian-Pakistani Islamic fundamentalists. All reject the dominant ethos of the society in which they live. All are marginalized male elites, coopting women by claiming to protect them as custodians of domestic space. All use a technical vocabulary that reinforces minority group identity, even as they try to reclaim the public sphere as a space of symbolic purity, whether it be for the observance of *mitzvoth* in Israel or enforcement of *shari'a* precepts in Islamic countries or furtherance of the ideals of Christian civilization in America. And none can be understood outside the parameters of religious ideology. The pattern of their emergence as self-conscious groups depends on the variant force of the GWT, as it first surfaced in Protestant America at the turn of the century, in Israel after the achievement of statehood (1948), and in Muslim nations most fully since the 1970s.

The overlap of fundamentalists in their defining characteristics allows comparison, but it does not overcome the profound distinctions between them. The major distinction is historical. It is, therefore, also socioeconomic. Fundamentalists have not equally appropriated the Technical Age. The clearest divide is between Christian and Muslim fundamentalists. Their competitive creedal assertions are exacerbated by divergent historical experiences. The Technical Age, as also the High Tech Era, has produced a cultural gradient that reinforces the other differences between first and third world societies.[13] Those who have been excluded from the front rank of technicalizing societies suffer structural inequities within their own societies of a different order than first world societies. To compare Christian and Muslim fundamentalists without acknowledging the disparate horizons of opportunity that their respective societies allow is fruitless. The obvious handicaps that most Muslims experience as third world citizens need to be reiterated: political limitations, reflected by the prevalence of military dictatorships or clan rulership permitting limited popular participation; economic inequities, situating a few landed or mercantile rich above masses of urban poor with minimal possibilities for the emergence of a middle class; educational restrictions, reflected in the existence of few universities and almost no high-tech training institutions, compelling the children of elites to study abroad; and gender asymmetry, using tradition as an excuse to exclude women from the public sphere even though it is the prevalence of unemployed men vying with one another for the few available jobs that reinforces the need to curtail women's professional horizons.

Much could be said to expand this portrait of gloom and doom. Enough has been said to underscore the impact of socioeconomic factors on Islamic fundamentalism. It creates two intersecting trends: first, all the above conditions of disparity apply in Muslim countries where fundamentalism has been most evident (Egypt, Iran, and Malaysia), with the stature of these countries being measured less vis-à-vis their immediate third world neighbors than distant first world excolonizers; and second, the groups that have mobilized as fundamentalists are not the most wretched but those who have had some contact with the West, who understand the horizons of possibility denied them by the inequities of the world system. Their ideology weds political-economic despair with a claim to cultural authenticity that derives from religious values. In Egypt, for instance, the failure of a Western-style educational system helped fuel the Islamic fundamentalist protest to the Sadat and now Mubarak regimes. Layleaders of both al-Takfir wal-Hijra and Jihad were incipient but thwarted technocrats: trained in the hard sciences, they still faced unemployment or, equally frustrating, underemployment at poverty-level wages.[14]

The situation in each third world Muslim country will get worse, not better, for the remainder of this century and well into the next. Objective realities will not allow an economic miracle to rescue oil-poor Egypt or oil-rich Iran, much less rubber-dependent Malaysia. Even the Islamic revolution in Iran has not reduced the massive economic disparities of an aridisolatic society, a society in which patterns of aridity and irrigation still determine vocational opportunities and class structures.[15]

Inequitable distribution of resources may fuel popular discontent and heighten the appeal of fundamentalist Islam in the short run, yet it does not brighten the prospects for an ultimate fundamentalist success, either in Iran or elsewhere. State obedience will always win out, even after a revolution. Fouad Ajami's shrewd assessment of Egypt after Sadat's assassination remains true. Echoing David Apter's analysis, Ajami depicts the examination of terrorism as itself a "growth industry" flourishing under the jurisdiction of the modern nation-state:

What begins as a challenge to the state ends up confirming its rationality, its monopoly on steering a reasonable course in a world that either is mad or is capable of becoming so at any moment. The state is said to be (by its custodians, by its many, many spokesmen) the only dike against great upheaval and disorder. This is a game that all states play; this also happens to be a game at which the Egyptian state is particularly skilled.[16]

The prospect for Jewish and Christian fundamentalists is similarly limited by the nature of the modern-day nation-state system, increasingly conservative during the High Tech Era. Technology acquisition and scientific advances depend on the availability of large sums of capital. Only nation-states, and in EuroAmerica large corporations, can provide that level of expenditure, and their custodians will always ensure that they also control the ends to which their investments are directed. As long as the marriage of statehood to modern instrumentalities remains viable, displacement by foes, whether representing fundamentalist aspirations or other marginalized interest groups, will not succeed. Self-interest will compel dominant groups to coopt or suppress all foes.

What fundamentalists have done or tried to do, on the one hand, and what their several activities represent to the rest of humankind, on the other, are two separate issues. We have spent most of our study addressing the first. We also need to examine the second. The crucial question may be framed as follows: how do we understand the valence of religious values as autonomous from the modernist construction of the material world? Is the Algerian-born French Islamicist Muhammad Arkoun correct when he asserts about the Muslim world that "the so-called religious revivalism is a powerful secular movement disguised by religious discourse, rites, and collective behaviors"?[17] The same query could be made of Christian and Jewish fundamentalist movements. But the word that needs to be stressed is "disguised," for the dominance of technology is such that if by secularization Arkoun means "the domination of nature to increase the powers of man," then there is no escape from the secular, even though proponents as well as opponents of revivalism-fundamentalism may not recognize the secular residue of their thoughts and actions.

Yet secularization, as we have seen earlier, is a term admitting of several definitions. Arkoun himself provides two other definitions for secularization that could apply in an Islamic setting: first, a decaying of the former capacity for receiving divine inspiration and guidance and second, a cultural and political program of emancipation from theological thinking and ecclesiastical dominance.[18] Neither of these definitions, however, applies to Islamic fundamentalists. They feel certain that divine guidance, if not inspiration, is still available and that they alone are guided to do God's will. They also are convinced that emancipation from either the *shari'a* or *shari'a*-mindedness is impossible for Muslims; an Islamic society and state can emerge only with the full implementation of the divine law. The sole definition of secularization that fits, therefore, is the one that links secularization directly to its technological preamble: the domination of nature to increase the powers of the human. And so we come full circle back to our original premise. Islamic fundamentalists, whether consciously or more often unconsciously, must be secular insofar as the instrumentalities they rely on to project their views are technical in origin, prized for their proficiency rather than their purity.

Yet fundamentalists continue to be distinguished from other moderns by their persistent identity as a minority religious subculture. Modernization theorists until recently had been convinced that the scientific positivist notion of linear progress or evolution would prevail: when the new and better comes, the old and less efficient will die away. Thomas Kuhn's book *The Structure of Scientific Revolutions* acquired fame in part because Kuhn tried to demonstrate how communities of scientific researchers helped advance new theories by their aggregation in support of one theory or paradigm over another. The new scientific truth does not triumph "by convincing its opponents and making them see the light, but rather because its opponents eventually die, and a new generation grows up that is unfamiliar with it." [19]

Human societies, however, do not work as macrocosmic extensions of scientific research groups. In contemporary EuroAmerica there is no consensus about what comprises the common good and how one ought to proceed in order to assure its perpetuation for future generations. The benefit of pluralism is also its liability: there are several competing subcultures whose adherents all believe that they can wrest the mantle of the future from others if only their views can be projected through the most efficient medium to the widest possible audience. By the scientific reasoning of modernization theorists, fundamentalism should have been expelled once liberalism became sufficiently integrated into the scriptural studies and theological outlook of mainline Protestant churches. In fact, however, the threat that the Enlightenment posed to religion in its liberal-modernist guise became accentuated. Instead of reducing, it heightened the fundamentalist appeal, especially to secondary elites.

The protagonists were different, yet the process of fundamentalist coalescence in quasi-Hasidic and *haredi* Judaism and Sunni (but not Shi'i) Islam was similar to its first emergence in Protestant American Christianity. The modern state relentlessly improved its capacity to function as the court of ultimate reference, the context of inclusive, enforceable obedience. For Judaism, the premodern period had allowed the development of many responses to the Enlightenment in Europe. It was only when refugees from the Enlightenment clashed with emissaries of the Enlightenment in Palestine that the religious issues at the core of their struggle became hardened and the state had to serve as the enforcer of its own quasi-religious ideology. For Sunni Muslims, it was the period of colonialism that masked the full extent to which the *shari'a*-minded were isolated from their coreligionists who deemed some accommodation to the dominant European powers as inevitable. Gaining nominal independence, Muslim elites continued to rely on EuroAmerican instruments of social exchange (newspapers, radios, and, in time, TV) as well as on institutions of military-political control (professional armed forces, constitutions, and national holidays). Reliance on them ensured that the modern nation-state would remain the forum of ultimate power.

The period of the great military patronage states (Ottoman, Safavi-Qajar, and Mughal) lasted in the Muslim world from the sixteenth till the end of the nineteenth century. During that period, there was always an ambiguous relationship between religious dissent and political treason. With the advent of the nation-state, the two merged. To profess a variant interpretation of Islam was treason, and vice versa: if one wanted to make a statement against the government in power, religion became the most visible and evocative vehicle of protest. Although there was enormous variation in the way that modern Muslim nation-states handled the explosive issue of religious conformity, nearly all reduced rather than increased the scope for creedal dissent, linking it to political disloyalty. Sunni fundamentalists reacted by claiming that both the rulers in power and the official religious classes were corrupt. The Shi'i opposition to the shah claimed that he had not preserved the right of the clergy to speak on behalf of the faith, and so had forfeited his own right to rule. In both instances, opposition to the state increased when it drew on religious resources, but by the same token, religious specialists could only succeed by controlling and directing the modern nation-state apparatus to their own ends. In Iran, the Shi'i *'ulama,* after coming to power in 1979, had to be both fundamentalist and modernist. It was, and remains, a challenge redolent with contradictions. They are contradictions that will continue to test the staying power of the young Islamic Republic of Iran.

In the long run, fundamentalists will not be able to control the tone of discourse or activity in the public sphere of any major nation-state. By the end of this century (reckoning on a Christian calendrical model), the post-Khomeini era of Iranian history will have demonstrated the near impossibility of juggling theocratic and technocratic goals in a premillennial Shi'i polity. In Israel, the likelihood of a continued ascent for Gush Emunim depends on their willingness to compromise with the pervasive statist ideology of the major political parties; Neturei Karta will remain spoilers, not principal actors. And the Moral Majority, or their future equivalent in the United States, have perhaps the least chance to succeed in dominating pluralist America. In the past, their predecessors met with occasional success, as in the fundamentalist-inspired prohibition movement, but the gains proved temporary. Fundamentalists themselves felt uneasy with continuous involvement in the political realm, and the pendulum swung back toward the majority will of an American electorate rededicated to pluralism after they had rejected the excesses of puritan denial.

If failure in the political realm is inevitable, how can fundamentalists succeed? They must recognize the intellectual impulse behind their present symbol production. In the High Tech Era, they must mount a counterchallenge to modernism that makes sense of the spiritual mandate they claim as eternal. They must confront issues of first and third world economic disparities without postponing them to millennial solutions. Above all, fundamentalists need to redefine issues that have been too narrowly the province of scientific specialists.

One critical approach not yet attempted by fundamentalists is to review and refute scholarship by scientists that invokes God-talk. Much of the scientific writing that engages theology reflects the narrow notion of reason that Comte had enthroned. It confuses creedal assertions about the spiritual world with empirical investigation of the material world. No scientific discovery, whether molecular or interplanetary, can nullify the God principle. Yet so powerful has been the prestige of scientific accomplishments that when practicing scientists like Lewontin and Hofstadter put on their "theological cap," they are more warmly and widely acclaimed among literate elites than so-called religious professionals.

The field for challenge, engagement, and eventual refutation also extends to the social sciences. A cornerstone of social scientific methodology is the axiom of equal access. It declares that no field of inquiry enjoys a privileged position. All are fair game, all are open to human investigation, observation, classification, and understanding. Religions, like languages and societies, cannot be ranked. In the words of one observer, all enjoy the same status vis-à-vis an *absent or present God.*[20]

Fundamentalists ought to feel impelled to challenge the ahistoricism of social scientists on their own turf. What is the further implication of methodological agnosticism? Is there a deeper relationship between meaning and truth? How, for instance, can one speak of Islam unless its primary actors and defining rituals are also analyzed? And how does one explain monotheistic religion without reference to some notion of the divine, by whatever name the Other is called?

The alternative to constructive engagement and criticism is to dismiss *all* social science as a closed field, out-of-bounds to the true faithful since social scientists are loathe to question their basic preconceptions, many of which revert to the perpetual seesaw of dyadic antinomies examined in chapter one. A challenge to social scientific method has already been raised by feminist scholarship. Instead of remaining detached from the academy, feminists have entered the mainstream of scholarly discourse and redefined basic categories.[21] A comparable revisionism could also be mounted at a different level by fundamentalists.

Fundamentalists of some stripe will survive for a long time to come. Even if they do not change tactics, they will probably appeal to a variety of marginalized male elites. On the other hand, scientists of all stripes will continue to be the most powerful brokers of modern culture. Even though they may lament that their respective fields are in an epistemological quandary, they remain hermeneutical foragers engaged in a common quest once summarized by the philosopher Richard Rorty as

the attempt to free mankind from Nietzsche's longest lie, 'the notion that outside the haphazard and perilous experiments we perform there lies something (God, Science, Knowledge, Rationality, or Truth) which will, if only we perform the correct rituals, step in to save us.'[22]

For Rorty, as for most scientists, there is nothing out there *pragmatically.* One can believe what one will, but belief has no acknowledged place in scientific method. There remains an unbridgeable chasm between the head and the heart, despite the fact that both science and belief are projections of the human spirit. Reprieve from the modernist hegemony will not be easily won. The battle joined by modernists and fundamentalists has to engage others if there is to be a postmodernist future that offers unity instead of division, hope rather than despair, God beyond human echoes.

Among those others who peer in at the battle from the sidelines are investigators of religion in the academy. They must precipitate a post-Enlightenment evaluation of the study of religion. It cannot be a recycling of the modernist-postmodernist exercise in critical theory that is now occurring in literary circles. It has to take account of what Gadamer has termed "the prejudice against prejudice," a prejudice that up till now has precluded the ability not only to perceive ideology as an inescapable analytical category but also to accept religious ideology as a generic caption for reviewing social movements that either claim or exhibit a scriptural motivation. Social scientists together with humanists have to stake out disciplinary positions that project an authentic discourse, ones that make sense of data without prejudging or displacing the role of human participants. The contribution of social science will be valuable to the extent that its proponents go beyond dimorphic reasoning. The elegance of model building or taxomorphic symmetry can only approximate the messy reality of human existence. Theorems do not need to hark back to mathematics or other natural sciences to gain intellectual plausibility and widespread acceptance. As cultural historians together with historians of religion have demonstrated, the investigation of data in numerous settings adduces points of tension between the ideal and the real, the center and peripheries, elites and nonelites that in themselves go a long way beyond "mere" description and allow for levels of interpretation, if not explanation, of the groups investigated.

Fundamentalism, to be understood, requires the microstudy of communities on a scale at once comparative and global. That task, barely begun, ought to engage social scientists as well as humanists. Both must pursue a degree of methodological self-examination, with reference to their academic disciplines as well as their personal backgrounds, that takes account of the limits of Enlightenment presuppositions concerning the origins of the Technical Age.

No analysis of fundamentalism will succeed unless it also comes to terms with the influence of the media. It must heed the near total exclusion of religious priorities from the public sphere. While ample attention has been drawn to the fundamentalists' use of the print and visual media in furthering their own ideological objectives, this approach too often tends to create a simple and satisfying half-truth: fundamentalists become religious fanatics who are also the ultimate terrorists. They are seen as caricatures of Milton Rokeach's closed-mind individuals. Opposed to the modern world, they also debase human nature and disregard reality itself. They embody what a pair of itinerant journalists have labeled *Holy Terror*.[23] Such an approach, however, misses the larger point. Due to the modernist hegemony, religious authority is not only controlled in the public sphere, it is largely excised from the day-to-day symbol production of the major media. Despite the fact that fundamentalists appear to terrorize through their zealous defense of fundamentals, they at least ensure that reference to religious ideals will not be excluded from all opinion-molding discourse.

An example will illustrate the dilemma of fundamentalists, and also provide a point of closure to our study. Televangelists endeavor to pack the media programming of heartland America, yet they seldom reach those professionally engaged upper-middle-class Americans for whom the evening news on one of the major networks or on Public Broadcasting Stations (PBS) is their chief contact with the "outside world." Some professionals only have time for National Public Radio (NPR), whether listening to the late afternoon program or to news summaries that begin at 7:00 A.M. Many must have been startled at the programming for National Public Radio on Tuesday morning 6 October 1987. On the public issues spot at 7:25 A.M., a Harvard astrophysicist was introduced to discuss the debate about teaching creation science in the public schools. Though he denied that creation science should be cycled into the required curriculum, he went on to discuss the crisscrossed relation of science to religion in the Technical Age. During the seventeenth and eighteenth centuries, he noted, God-talk was frequent among scientists. Most researchers were unabashed about injecting the God hypothesis into the discussion of their experiments as scientists. Even until the mid-nineteenth century, he suggested, it was commonplace to find some scientists engaged in their work as scientists from a deeply held set of religious convictions. He went on to stress the integrity of the scientific method. One could not, for instance, follow the vision of the theologian-computer whiz who, as the hero of John Updike's recent novel *Roger's Version*, tries to "prove" the existence of God through programming acrobatics. Yet at the same time, many scientists known to this Harvard astrophysicist still share the vision of Isaac Newton expressed in the conclusion of his major work, *Principia*, namely, that it is impossible to think of the majesty of our universe without attributing its beginnings to some divine force. He himself was intimately engaged in efforts to uncover the process by which the universe was created, and yet, he concluded, he and other scientists could only succeed in answering the question, *how?* —they could never broach the question, *why?*

Restraint bordering on confirmation of the God hypothesis characterized this Harvard astrophysicist's discourse on science and religion. What needs to be stressed is the pretext for its airing. It was scientific creationism, growing out of the generations-old fundamentalist concern with the divine origin of life as biblically inscribed, that provided the pretext for this five-minute spot on prime-time National Public Radio. Even if fundamentalist ideology does no more than elicit discussion of religious issues in the mainstream of public discourse in late twentieth century America, it will have served a useful end. Of course, it will try to do more, not only in America but also in Israel and in the Arab-Muslim world. It will agitate for the imposition of a religious lifestyle in all sectors of society. Though its adherents are unlikely to prevail, their brief moments of public notoriety will cause others to rethink the quandaries posed by the Technical Age, and in the High Tech Era we may yet dare to hope for the emergence of a universalist vision that admits the authenticity of the motives of fundamentalists without surrendering to their apocalyptic conclusions.

In the meantime we must guard against the innate human urge to mesh our own end as finite, physical beings with the end of all recognizable time. Pervasive concern with the end of "ordinary" time preoccupies both modernists and fundamentalists. Intrinsic to the Judeo-Hellenic circumference is the search for a moment beyond time. It is the search for absolutes untainted by transient time. However much one expands (or, like Rorty and Blumenberg, denies) the "greekjew" synthesis at the heart of Western culture, the quest for catharsis it launches seldom finds resolution. It is a quest that races to the future yet lingers, fearful of its own presentness. Only the deepest level of self-reflection, yielding equal draughts of ambivalence and certitude, can permit us to look at the destiny of humankind beyond the cognitive as well as biological limits that constrain our own most powerful endeavors to exert control. The final word, as Ayatollah Mutahhari once noted, must belong to the poet or seer rather than to the philosopher or scientist. It is the poet Wallace Stevens who perhaps best evokes the conundrum, which is also the hope, we share as moderns: to discover that "we believe without belief, beyond belief."[24]

Notes

PREFACE

1. Jonathan Z. Smith, *Imagining Religion* (Chicago: University of Chicago Press, 1982), 35.

INTRODUCTION

1. See Marshall Berman, *All That Is Solid Melts Into Air: The Experience of Modernity* (New York: Simon and Schuster, 1982), 345. An extraordinary endeavor to make sense of the contradictions in the theme of modernity/modernism, Berman's book isolates as one of its subthemes the disparity between the great writers and thinkers of the nineteenth century, those who first tried to reconcile the tension between modernization and modernism, and those more contemporary thinkers of our own era, especially since World War II, for whom the absence of spiritual imagination has obliterated the distinction between modernization and modernism, impoverishing us all.

   We collapse modernization and modernity into a single category. It is not because we disagree with Berman's major thesis, nor with its brilliant subsequent elaboration by Perry Anderson (see "Modernity and Revolution," in *Marxism and Interpretations of Culture*, ed. Cary Nelson and Lawrence Grossberg [Urbana and Chicago: University of Illinois Press, 1988], 317–38). Rather, it is in order to frame the contradictory nature of fundamentalism, specifically to look at the broad historical forces that shaped both modernity (or the Great Western Transmutation) and its multiple responses, including fundamentalism. See chapter three below for an elaboration of this approach.
2. Ibid., 345–46.
3. Ibid., 131–32.
4. See Stephen Bruce, "The Moral Majority: The Politics of Fundamentalism in Secular Society," in *Studies in Religious Fundamentalism*, ed. Lionel Caplan (Albany: State University of New York Press, 1987), 184.
5. The distinction between Sunni and Shi'i "fundamentalism," especially the clerical influence in the latter, will concern us throughout our study but particularly in chapter eight.
6. See Robert Wuthnow, "Indices of Religious Resurgence in the United States," in *Religious Resurgence: Contemporary Cases in Islam, Christianity and Judaism*, ed. Richard T. Antoun and Mary E. Hegland (Syracuse, NY: Syracuse University Press, 1987), 32.
7. James Barr, *Fundamentalism* (Philadelphia: Westminster Press, 1978), 7.
8. Ibid., 182 (my emphasis).
9. Two articles by William E. Shepherd that discuss Islamic fundamentalism and the comparison of Christian with Islamic fundamentalism suffer from the same endemic weakness: the author asserts rather than demonstrates what qualities fundamentalists

share with one another. By serializing traits, in a kind of slipshod neo-Weberianism, he locates antimodernism as but one of several characteristics of fundamentalists. No wonder that in both articles, after extensive referencing to every available source, he can only conclude either (1) that we should not use the term fundamentalism ("Islam and Ideology: Towards a Typology," *International Journal of Middle Eastern Studies* 19 [1987]: 321) or (2) that we can use it but only in quotation marks ("Fundamentalism: Christian and Islamic," *Religion* 17 [October 1987]: 367). For a detailed critique of Shepherd's approach, see *Religion*, January 1990.

10. Note, in particular, Dennis MacEoin, "Bahai Fundamentalism and the Academic Study of the Bahai Movement," *Religion* 16 (January 1986): 57–84, and Angela Dietrich, "The *Khalsa* Resurrected: Sikh Fundamentalism in the Punjab," in Caplan, *Studies*, 122–37.

11. See Berman, *All That Is Solid*, 309–10.

12. A critical bibliography on Protestant Christian fundamentalism has been compiled by Ernest R. Sandeen, *The Roots of Fundamentalism: British and American Millenarianism, 1800–1930* (Chicago: University of Chicago Press, 1970), 285-89. The opening line summarizes, even as it deplores, the state of scholarship on fundamentalism prior to 1970: "the fate of Fundamentalism in historiography has been worse than its lot in history" (p. 285). Sandeen launched a new tradition of scholarship that has attracted some able American proponents, among them George M. Marsden and Grant Wacker, but relative to other fields of American Christianity or comparative religious history, the study of fundamentalism retains a lowly, near pariah status.

13. Robert Bellah, Introduction to *Religion and America: Spirituality in a Secular Age*, ed. Mary Douglas and Steven M. Tipton (Boston: Beacon Press, 1983), ix. In a similar vein, but with a more detailed distinction between the religiosity of social and natural scientists, see Robert Wuthnow, "Science and the Sacred" in *The Sacred in a Secular Age*, ed. Phillip E. Hammond (Berkeley and Los Angeles: University of California Press, 1985), 190–91.

14. It is possible to extend the hard/soft contrast to the point of absurdity, as Richard A. Shweder does in the following passage: "When I talk to social scientists they tell me that what they do is soft science and that the real hard scientists are the physical scientists. When I talk to physical scientists who are meteorologists or geologists they tell me that what they do is soft science and that the real hard scientists are the physicists. And so it goes. The experimental physicists, feeling a bit soft, point me to the real hard scientists, the theoretical physicists. The theoretical physicists point me to the mathematicians, where the linear algebraists, feeling a bit a soft, point me to the hard cutting edge, the typologists, who tell me it's all very mystical and intuitive (i.e., soft)." "Storytelling among the Anthropologists" (*New York Times Book Review*, 21 September 1986, 39). It is fittingly ironic that a member of the social science division is trying to undercut the value of the hard/soft construct. For most university administrators, who were never consulted in his random sampling, the hard/soft segmentation of their faculty is neither as fuzzy nor as meaningless as Shweder implies, and it is, of course, the social scientists who are deemed to be the "softest" of the academic scientists.

15. Jan de Vries, *The Study of Religion: A Historical Approach*, trans. K. W. Bolle (New York: Harcourt, Brace & World, 1967), 45.

16. See especially Paul. R. Mendes-Flor, "Rosenzweig and Kant: Two Views of Ritual and Religion," in *Mystics, Philosophers, and Politicians: Essays in Jewish Intellectual History in Honor of Alexander Altmann*, ed. J. Reinharz and C. Swetschinski (with K. P. Bland) (Durham, NC: Duke University Press, 1982), 315–41.

17. To an older generation, Muhammad 'Abduh was the forerunner of a movement toward Muslim rationalism or modernism that seemed destined to attract more and more followers. See H. A. R. Gibb, *Modern Trends in Islam* (Chicago: University of Chicago Press, 1946) and later, E. I. J. Rosenthal, *Islam in The Modern Nation State* (Cambridge: Cambridge University Press, 1965), but more recent works on Islam in

Egypt scarcely mention him. Among the most notable are Fouad Ajami, *The Arab Predicament: Arab Political Thought and Practice Since 1967* (Cambridge: Cambridge University Press, 1981) and Emmanuel Sivan, *Radical Islam: Medieval Theology and Modern Politics* (New Haven: Yale University Press, 1958). On Sayyid Ahmad Khan, consult Christian Troll, *Sayyid Ahmad Khan: A Reinterpretation of Muslim Theology* (New Delhi: Vikas, 1978), and Bruce B. Lawrence, "Mystical and Rational Elements in the Early Religious Writings of Sir Sayyid Ahmad Khan" in *The Rose and the Rock: Mystical and Rational Elements in the Intellectual History of South Asian Islam*, ed. B. Lawrence (Durham, North Carolina: Duke University South Asia Program, 1979), 61–103.

18. See Wilfred Cantwell Smith, *The Meaning and End of Religion* (New York: MacMillan 1962), 230, where the author also allows that Kant was among the first to distinguish between the Christian religion and Christian faith.

19. Note the similarity in approach between the Antoun volume on religious resurgence (see above, note 6) and the Caplan volume on religious fundamentalism (see above, note 4). Both shade their interpretations toward the authenticity of nonreligious factors, motives, and outcomes as they apply to current episodes of tension and conflict. Particular authors are more or less sensitive to the issue of religious autonomy, that is, to the portrayal of religion as something more than a mere epiphenomenon of underlying social, political, or economic malaise. But both volumes suffer from the difficulty of trying to make a coherent point in an edited work combining several literary hands and often incompatible methodologies.

20. Bryan Wilson, *Religion in a Sociological Perspective* (New York: Oxford University Press, 1982), 13.

21. George Devereux, *From Anxiety to Method in the Behavioral Sciences* (The Hague: Mouton, 1967), viii.

22. Frederick Streng, *Understanding Religious Life* (Belmont, CA: Wadsworth, 1985), 226–27.

23. Marvin Harris, *Cultural Materialism: The Struggle for a Science of Culture* (New York: Random House, 1976), 32–45, especially p. 45.

24. Clifford Geertz, *Local Knowledge* (New York: Basic Books, 1983), 54–70.

25. Ibid., 69.

26. Paul Rabinow, "Humanism as Nihilism: The Bracketing of Truth and Seriousness in American Cultural Anthroplogy," in Norma Haan et al., *Social Science as Moral Enquiry* (New York: Columbia University Press, 1985), 67.

27. William McLoughlin, *Revivals, Awakenings, and Reforms: An Essay on Religion and Social Change in America, 1607–1977* (Chicago: University of Chicago Press, 1978), 9–17, especially p. 10.

28. Ibid., 12. At least two sociologists see the discovery of electricity as a more decisive signpost of modernism than evolutionary theory. Why? Because it compelled the retreat of religion from the realm of magic! While Stark and Bainbridge's hypothesis is arresting "(Secularization, Revival and Cult Formation," *Annual Review of the Social Sciences of Religion* 4 (1980) 1: 89–90), the measure of influence, as gleaned from subsequent religious history, rests with evolution.

29. Paul R. Brass, "Ethnic Communities in the Modern State," in *Identity and Division in Cults and Sects in South Asia*, ed. Peter Gaefke and David A. Utz (Philadelphia: Department of South Asia Regional Studies, University of Pennsylvania, 1984), 13.

30. Francis Robinson, "Islam and Muslim Separatism," in *Political Identity in South Asia*, ed. David Taylor and Malcolm Yapp (London: Curzon, 1979).

31. Brass, "Ethnic Communities," 18.

32. Ibid., 19.

33. We use modern-modernist in a slightly different sense than Marshall Berman. Like the aquatic imagery that abounds in his probing book, Berman glides between modern and modern*ist* as two polar images of location in the High Tech Era. Looking back at the divide of the Technical Age from what preceded it, we stress the religious dimension of that move toward cultural authenticity that seeks to claim both modern-

ity and its premodern impetus. Moderns have a collective past that informs their individual presents; modernists see only a single thread tracing their particular instincts, needs, and desires.

CHAPTER ONE: THE MAKING OF A CONSTRUCT

Epigraph 1: Genesis 11:1-9, RSV.
Epigraph 2: Abu Rayhan al-Biruni, eleventh-century Muslim polymath, cited from Alberuni's *India,* trans. Edward C. Sachau (London, 1910), 60.
Epigraph 3: James Boon, *Other Tribes, Other Scribes: Symbolic Anthropology in the Comparative Study of Cultures, Histories, Religions, and Texts* (New York: Cambridge University Press, 1982), 235.

1. Hal Lindsey, *The Late Great Planet Earth* (New York: Bantam, 1981). First published by a church press (Zondervan) in 1970, this book went through over sixty printings, totaling sales above fifteen million copies. It has a single theme, which is also a prediction: the imminent, cataclysmic destruction of the earth, due to the fulfillment of biblical prophecy, especially the return of "the Jew" to the Promised Land (see chapter four).

2. A. J. Toynbee, *An Historian's Approach to Religion* (New York: Oxford University, 1956), especially pp. 10–17 and pp. 136–40. His idealist approach is flawed by a too limited and arbitrary cleavage of ideologies from religions, but his attempt at a global survey of historical-religious worldviews is both provocative and insightful.

3. George Steiner, *After Babel: Aspects of Language and Translation* (New York: Oxford University Press, 1975), 158.

4. Ibid., 161. The parenthetical addition is mine, to capture the sense of a long passage in a brief citation.

5. Jonathan Schell, *The Fate of the Earth* (New York: Alfred A. Knopf, 1982). The perspectival hubris implicit in Schell's book was hinted at by Langdon Gilkey when he observed that "Schell seems not quite aware of the paradoxes he is generating . . . !" (*University of Chicago Magazine,* Fall 1983, 7).

6. Steiner, *After Babel,* 158 (my emphasis).

7. John U. Nef, *The Conquest of the Material World* (Chicago: University of Chicago Press, 1958), 216.

8. Even the ineluctable relativism of analytical thought has to be explained by analogy to mathematics. The British sociologist Rodney Needham illustrated the dilemma in the tenth—and crucial—chapter of his wide-ranging study, *Belief, Languages, and Experience* (Chicago: University of Chicago Press, 1972) when he stressed that "there will always subsist, as inescapable factors, an uncertainty and a variability in the categories by which any language whatever secures an order . . . in the organization of collective thought and action . . . [for] ultimately we cannot ever achieve an objective certainty in conceptual analysis. To paraphrase Einstein, as quoted by Waismann, on the laws of *mathematics:* so far as our categories refer to reality, they are not certain; and so far as they are certain, they do not refer to reality" (p. 223). What Needham never justifies is the analogy to mathematics as proof that there must be not merely a tension but also a chasm between certainty and reality, precluding linguistic universals or their religious equivalents, e.g., belief in a transcendent reality.

   The double-edged result of resorting to mathematics as the queen of sciences has also been pointed out by Horkheimer and Adorno: "by identifying nature with whatever can be comprehended mathematically, and by equating the latter with truth, the Enlightenment absolutized a methodological technique which eliminated the exercise of critical thought as such." See Max Horkheimer and Theodor W. Adorno, *Dialectic of Enlightenment,* trans. John Cumming (New York: Seabury Press, 1972), 27.

9. Robert Alter, *The Art of Biblical Poetry* (New York: Basic Books, 1985), 168–69.

10. To unpack the culturally conditioned linguistic substratum of Freud's therapeutic method would be a tedious exercise with dubious yield. The best effort to contextualize his antinomies remains Philip Rieff, *Freud: The Mind of the Moralist* (New York: Doubleday, 1961).

11. See Michel Foucault, *The Order of Things: An Archaeology of the Human Sciences* (New York: Vintage Books, 1973), especially chapters nine ("Man and His Doubles") and ten ("The Human Sciences"). Allan Megill, *Prophets of Extremity: Nietzsche, Heidegger, Foucault, Derrida* (Berkeley and Los Angeles: University of California Press, 1985) has rigorously dissected the structuralist tenor of Foucault's *böse Blick* or "malign glance" in his chapter on Foucault, 183–256.

12. James A. Boon, *Other Tribes* (Cambridge: Cambridge University Press, 1982), 53.

13. Ibid., 235.

14. In addition to Megill, *Prophets of Extremity*, see P. Major-Poetzl, *Michel Foucault's Archaeology of Western Culture* (Chapel Hill: University of North Carolina Press, 1983) for a sustained critique of Foucault's notion of episteme, especially pp. 199–200.

15. Roman Jakobsen, with M. Halle, *Fundamentals of Language* (The Hague: Mouton, 1966).

16. Two well-known examples of unexamined, or at least unexplained, reliance on *system* are Carl J. Fredrich's definition of ideologies, which begins, "Ideologies are action-related *systems* of ideas", (*Man and His Government* [New York: McGraw Hill, 1967], 89) and Clifford Geertz's definition of religion as a cultural system, which begins, "Religion is a *system* of symbols" (*The Interpretation of Cultures* [New York: Basic Books, 1973], 90), my emphasis.

17. Steiner, *After Babel*, 158 (my emphasis).

18. Edmund Leach, *Levi-Strauss* (Glasgow: Fontana/Collins, 1974), 35.

19. Owen Chadwick, *The Secularization of the European Mind in the Nineteenth Century* (Cambridge: Cambridge University Press, 1975), 44 (my emphasis).

20. Thomas S. Kuhn, *The Structure of Scientific Revolutions* (Chicago: University of Chicago Press, 1962).

21. Foucault, *Order of Things*, 343.

22. Talcott Parsons, *The Social System* (New York: The Free Press, 1951), as quoted in Barbara Hargrove, *The Sociology of Religion: Classical and Contemporary Approaches* (Arlington Heights, IL: AHM Publishing Corporation, 1979), 55. See, however, Talcott Parsons, "Evolutionary Universals in Society," *American Sociology Review* 29 (1964): 339–57. This article has been widely discussed and criticized by other sociologists, notably Robert Nisbet and Alvin Gouldner. The latter sees a drift toward Marxism in Parsons and other functional theorists. For a lucid *précis* of the leading figures and issues, see *Religious Change and Cultural Domination*, ed. David Lorenzen, (El Colegio de Mexico: Mexico City, 1981), 3–9.

23. Richard A. Shweder and Edmund J. Bourne, "Does the Concept of the Person Vary Cross-culturally?" in *Cultural Conceptions of Mental Health and Therapy*, ed. Anthony J. Marsella and Geoffrey M. White, (Dordrecht, Netherlands: D. Reidel Publishing Company, 1975), 98 (my emphasis).

24. Smith, *Imagining Religion*, especially pp. 6–8. The reference linking biological methodology to history is lodged in a note on p. 137, while the actual text goes on to explain that advances in biology have come through reliance on a morphological basis of comparison that excludes history (pp. 24–25). The model scholar for Smith seems to be the Pan-Babylonian historian, Alfred Jeremias, who tried to historicize morphology from within (pp. 26–27). Smith himself opts for a bridge position: the integration of a complex notion of pattern and system (cosmology) with an equally complex notion of history (p. 29).

25. See ibid., 3, for Smith's classification of the walnut and other nuts. It was Wittgenstein who preferred artichoke imagery, ridiculing the pursuit of higher-order generalities as a search for the "real" artichoke by peeling off its leaves (Shweder and Bourne, "Concept of the Person," 100).

26. Edmund Leach, *Levi-Strauss*, 113.

27. Ibid., 43.

28. Ibid., 16.

29. John B. Thompson, *Studies in the Theory of Ideology* (Berkeley and Los Angeles: University of California Press, 1984), 188–267.

30. Steiner, *After Babel*, 74, 106.

31. Ibid., 462 (my emphasis).

32. Megill, *Prophets of Extremity*, 311, quoting from J. Derrida's essay, "Violence and Metaphysics."

33. Steiner, *After Babel*, 463.

34. Frank Manuel, *Changing of the Gods* (Hanover NH: University Press of New England, 1983), 143, 165.

35. S. N. Eisenstadt, *Tradition, Change and Modernity* (New York: John Wiley and Sons, 1973), 27.

36. Peter L. Berger, *The Heretical Imperative* (Garden City, New York: Doubleday/Anchor, 1979), 27 (my emphasis).

CHAPTER TWO: REINTERPRETING THE RISE OF THE WEST

Epigraph: Barrington Moore, Jr., *Reflections on the Causes of Human Misery* (Boston: Beacon Press, 1972), 11–12.

1. Marshall G. S. Hodgson, *The Venture of Islam: Conscience and History in a World Civilization* (Chicago: University of Chicago Press, 1979), 3:204.

2. See the series of perceptive articles cast as a review symposium of Said's *Orientalism* (New York: Pantheon, 1978) and featured in the *Journal of Asian Studies* 39 (May 1980): 481–517.

3. Of the numerous critical studies on Weber and Protestantism, two stand out: Herbert Luethy, "Once Again: Calvinism and Capitalism" and Carl Antoni, "Religious Outlooks and Classes," both appearing in *Max Weber* ed. Dennis H. Wrong (Englewood Cliffs, NJ: Prentice-Hall, 1970), 123-40. The best, and also the briefest, encapsulation of what Weber intended is to be found in Julien Freund, *The Sociology of Max Weber*, trans. Mary Ilford (New York: Pantheon, 1968), 303–8.

4. John U. Nef (*Conquest*, 238) criticizes Weber for interpreting the Reformation too narrowly in terms of asceticism.

5. Fernand Braudel, *Civilization and Capitalism*, vol. 2, Translated by Sian Reynolds (New York: Harper & Row, 1982), 2:566–81. Braudel stresses that Weber is too obsessed with locating the origins of capitalism in the work ethic of a Protestant-Puritan minority. Braudel casts doubt on Weber's thesis by examining the alternative thesis of his contemporary Werner Sombart who, in Braudel's words, "exaggerate[d] Weber's thought, the better to destroy his case" (p. 568).

6. Atwood D. Gaines, "Cultural Definitions, Behavior and the Person," in Marsella and White (eds.), *Cultural Conceptions*, 179 (my emphasis).

7. Ibid., 180.

8. Ibid., 182–84.

9. Wolfgang Schluchter, *The Rise of Western Rationalism* (Berkeley and Los Angeles: University of California Press, 1981), 174.

10. Marc Bloch, *The Historian's Craft*, trans. Peter Putnam (New York: Vintage, 1953), 32.

11. Braudel, *Civilization and Capitalism*, 458, (my emphasis). His argument sounds like a recycled version of the monadist thesis, despite the beguiling abstraction of his imagery.

12. See John U. Nef, *Western Civilization since the Renaissance* (New York: Cambridge University Press, 1963), 273–76; and also, *The Conquest of the Material World*, 122n.

13. Moore, *Causes of Human Misery*, 12.

14. Nef, *Conquest*, 272. Unlike Braudel, who downplays technology as a major factor in the emergence of the modern world, Nef accents its critical role, as does Hodgson. Even Braudel seems to qualify his position in vol. 3 *Civilization and Capitalism*, when he attempts to look at all sectors in the world economy (pp. 69f.) as well as in individual countries, like Britain and France (pp. 557f.).

15. Hodgson, *The Venture of Islam*, 2:180, 183. What Hodgson does not make clear is how these investment patterns relate to overseas commerce and long distance trade. It is Braudel (*Civilization and Capitalism*, 2:248, 400f.), who makes the necessary connections, though Hodgson's formulations still pertain.

16. Each of these ages has been the subject of a Mentor paperback. Intriguing in themselves, they collectively make the implicit claim that the major philosophical issues arising out of the Western world can be, and indeed have been, etched in these slim volumes. The whole sequence, going back to the medieval period, is Anne Fremantle, ed., *Medieval Philosophers: The Age of Belief* (New York: Mentor, 1954); Stuart Hampshire, ed., *17th Century Philosophers: The Age Of Reason* (New York: Mentor, 1956); Isaiah Berlin, ed., *18th Century Philosophers: The Age of Enlightenment* (New York: Mentor, 1956); Henry D. Aiken, ed., *19th Century Philosophers: The Age of Ideology* (New York: Mentor, 1956); and Morton White, ed., *20th Century Philosophers: The Age of Analysis* (New York: Mentor, 1955). The only nonedited volume is the original and provocative monograph of Eric Hobsbawm, *The Age of Revolution*, 1789–1848 (New York: Mentor, 1962).

17. Hodgson, *The Venture of Islam*, 3:189.

18. McNeill, *The Pursuit of Power: Technology, Armed Forces and Society* (Chicago: University of Chicago Press, 1982), 151.

19. Ibid., 161.

20. Jack S. Levy, *War in the Modern Great Power System* (Lexington: University of Kentucky Press, 1983), 47.

21. Hodgson, *The Venture of Islam*, 3:200.

22. The crucial article on the development and use of "third world" nomenclature is Carl E. Pletsch, "The Three Worlds or the Division of Social Scientific Labor, circa 1950–1975," *Comparative Studies in Society and History* 23 (October 1981): 565–90.

23. A Yiddish term, *golem* is roughly equivalent to the Frankinsteinian robot: a machine out of control, with enormous, unchallengeable power.

24. Hodgson, 3:189 (my emphasis).

25. Edward Shils, *Tradition* (Chicago: University of Chicago, 1981), 325.

26. Nef, *Conquest*, 278.

27. McNeill, *Rise of the West*, 558.

28. See Braudel, *Civilization and Capitalism*, vol. 2, and G. Barraclough, *The Times Atlas of World History* (Maplewood, NJ: Hammond, 1982), Section 6: "The Age of European Dominance."

29. McNeill, *The Great Frontier: Freedom and Hierarchy in Modern Times* (Princeton: Princeton University Press, 1983), 57–58.

30. McNeill, *Pursuit of Power*, 152.

31. Two historical monographs that provide detail and close reasoning on the high human cost of nativist resistance to colonial rule are Michael Adas, *Prophets of Rebellion: Millenarian Protest Movements Against European Colonial Rule* (Chapel Hill, NC: University of North Carolina Press, 1979) and Louis Brenner, *West African Sufi: The Spiritual Heritage of Cerno Bokar Saalif Taal* (Berkeley and Los Angeles: University of California Press, 1985).

32. Barraclough, *An Introduction to Contemporary History* (Hammondsworth, Great Britain: Penguin, 1967), especially pp. 9–23.

33. David Hume, *Enquiry Concerning Human Understanding,* quoted and criticized in Richard Olson, *Science Deified and Science Defied: The Historical Significance of Science in Western Culture* (Berkeley and Los Angeles: University of California Press, 1982), 13.

34. See Henry F. May, *Ideas, Faiths, and Feelings: Essays on American Intellectual and Religious History, 1952–1982* (New York: Oxford University Press, 1983), 171–72. The introduction of modernist norms into religious discourse has long been noted, but the most extreme analysis is also among the most recent, namely, James Turner, *Without God, Without Creed: The Origins of Unbelief in America* (Baltimore: Johns Hopkins University Press, 1985). Turner downplays the usual theorization that traces the source of unbelief in Europe and America to scientific discovery or social upheaval. In his view, "religion caused unbelief. In trying to adapt their religious beliefs to socioeconomic change, to new moral challenges, to novel problems of knowledge, to the tightening standards of science, the defenders of God slowly strangled Him" (p. xiii). Most fundamentalists would agree. What Turner does not emphasize sufficiently is the

extent to which those who he scores as the clerical agents of unbelief are themselves a limited socioeconomic group; their views did not permeate British society nor prevail in America. Turner's data is limited to late nineteenth century America. Two works that deal with the subsequent period and put his observations into broader perspective are Robert S. Michaelsen, *The American Search for Soul* (Baton Rouge: Louisiana State University Press, 1975) and William R. Hutchinson, *The Modernist Impulse in American Protestantism* (Cambridge: Harvard University Press, 1976).

35. Shils, *Tradition*, 94.
36. Nef, *Conquest*, 317. Nef acknowledges the continuing relevance of A. N. Whitehead, *Science and the Modern World* (1925; reprint, New York: Macmillan, 1967).
37. Nef, *Conquest*, 318.

CHAPTER THREE: IDEOLOGY BETWEEN RELIGION, PHILOSOPHY, AND SCIENCE

Epigraph: Paul Ricoeur, *Lectures on Ideology and Utopia*, ed. George H. Taylor (New York: Columbia University Press, 1986), 258 (my emphasis).

1. The separation of "religion" from "ideology" is adumbrated in the several entries under each term in the *International Encyclopedia of the Social Sciences*, edited by David L. Sills (New York: Macmillan, 1968). Its most eloquent formulation is set forth by Geertz, *Interpretation of Cultures*, chapters four and eight.
2. See Thompson, *Theory of Ideology*, 4.
3. The most recent effort comes from Ricoeur, *Ideology and Utopia*. Other efforts include Thompson, *Theory of Ideology*, and Lewis S. Feuer, *Ideology and the Ideologists* (New York: Harper & Row, 1975). The basic problem is overloading the definition, often by reasoning backward from the consequences of ideology to its initial features. Consequences should never be equated with originary traits, as Ruth Willner has made clear in assessing the sociological debate on charisma; see Willner's *The Spellbinders: Charismatic Political Leadership* (New Haven and London: Yale University Press, 1984), 10–12.
4. Braudel, *Civilization and Capitalism*, 2: 458.
5. Shils, *Tradition*, 139. One philosopher of the social sciences has gone so far as to say that "the social sciences are continuous with literature." See Richard Rorty, *Consequences of Pragmatism (Essays: 1972–1980)* (Minneapolis: University of Minnesota Press, 1982), 203. Erik Schwimmer also debates about whether anthropology is to be considered among the social sciences or the humanities, but he concludes that in the last resort "anthropology is an ideological science." See Schwimmer, "Semiotics and Culture," in *A Perfusion of Signs*, ed. Thomas A. Sebok (Bloomington: University of Indiana, 1977), 163, 171.
6. Karl-Otto Apel, *Understanding and Explanation: A Transcendental-Pragmatic Perspective*, trans. Georgia Warnke, (Cambridge: MIT Press, 1984), vii. Jorge Larrain looks at the same issue but his argument is less focused than Apel's. See Larrain, *The Concept of Ideology* (Athens: University of Georgia Press, 1979), 173–76.
7. S. C. Brown, ed., *Philosophical Disputes in the Social Sciences* (Atlantic Highlands, NJ: Humanities, 1977), viii.
8. Steiner, *After Babel*, 34.
9. David A. Martin, *The Religious and the Secular* (London: Routledge and Kegan Paul, 1969), 9, cited in Michael Hill, *A Sociology of Religion* (London: Heinemann, 1973), 229. Owen Chadwick moves beyond dictionary definitions, proposing that historical evidence confirms that a process equivalent to secularization did, in fact, occur in the minds of certain nineteenth century European intellectuals. See Chadwick, *Secularization of the European Mind*, 2.
10. Eric Sharpe, *Understanding Religion* (New York: St. Martin's Press, 1983), 108–24 provides a list of secularist challenges as well as religious reactions.
11. Hobsbawm, *Age of Revolution*, especially 261–63.
12. Chadwick, *Secularization of the European Mind*, 192.

13. Alvin Gouldner, *The Dialectic of Ideology and Technology* (New York: Seabury Press, 1976), 18.

14. Paul Ricoeur, *Hermeneutics and the Human Sciences*. Edited and translated by John B. Thompson (Cambridge: Cambridge University Press, 1981), 76.

15. Jürgen Habermas makes this argument concerning both science and technology in *Toward a Rational Society*, trans. Jeremy J. Shapiro (Boston: Beacon Press, 1970), 81–122.

16. Habermas's formulations on the relation of speech to rationality are summarily presented in his article "Interpretive Social Science vs. Hermeneuticism," in Haan, *Social Science*, 251–69.

17. While devoting little attention to Popper, Habermas simultaneously elaborated and criticized Weber's thought; see Thompson, *Theory of Ideology*, 279–99.

18. Ibid., 300–301.

19. A. N. Whitehead (*Science*, 156) long ago pointed out the need for a constructive discourse between science and philosophy, but he also noted the lack of motivation among scientists to engage in such reflection on their work. Gouldner has attempted to meet the need in his own idiosyncratic manner. Paul Ricoeur would seem to be another contemporary philosopher to consider, especially since the recent publication of his sequel to Mannheim's classic titled *Lectures on Ideology and Utopia*, ed. George H. Taylor (New York: Columbia University Press, 1986). Yet he persists in a pervasive negativism about ideology that reflects only one tangent of its history, as becomes clear in his essay, "Science and Ideology," in *Hermeneutics and the Human Sciences*, ed. John B. Thompson.

20. Georgia Warnke in her introduction to Apel, *Understanding and Explanation*, xiii–xv.

21. Ibid., xvi.

22. Ibid., xix.

23. Thomas McCarthy in his introduction to Hans-Georg Gadamer, *Reason and the Age of Science* (Cambridge: MIT Press, 1983), vii; xxiii–xxvii.

24. Ibid., 100.

25. Ibid., (my emphasis).

26. Ibid., 102.

27. Ibid., 103–5.

28. Ibid., 106–7.

29. Gouldner, *Dialectic*, xiv.

30. See ibid., 25.

31. Ibid., xv–xvi.

32. Ibid., 3–4.

33. Ibid., 6.

34. The harsh rebuke of sociologists (and, by implication, anthropologists) for their social indifference needs to be partially qualified. Paul Rabinow has explained how at least Franz Boas was engaged by the issues he raised, even though his successors, including Clifford Geertz, have not been. (See Rabinow's "Humanism as Nihilism," in Haan et al., *Social Science*, 52–75).

35. N. Smart, *Beyond Ideology* (London: Collins, 1981), 208.

36. Gouldner, *Dialectic*, 86. Smart (ibid.) also stresses the commonalities shared by religion and ideology.

37. Gouldner, *Dialectic*, 87 (my emphasis).

38. Ibid., 42.

39. Ibid., 103.

40. Ibid., 107, 111.

41. Ibid., 160.

42. Ibid., 285.

43. Gadamer, *Reason*, 163.

44. The relationship between poetry and science is complex. Owen Chadwick (*Secularization of the European Mind*, 189–90) separates them as incommensurates: all science, in

his view, is prosaic, while "religion and poetry are bedfellows." Yet poetry is a form of artistic expression, and even if poetry is perceived as the highest art form, which it often is, there remains the critique of Derrida and others that "art is as much under the sway of the Greek logos as philosophy is," and hence it cannot escape the critique that is leveled against the entire Western episteme, both logical (scientific) and lyrical (poetic). See the involved discussion, "Deconstructing Kant," in Allan Megill, *Prophets of Extremity*, 332–37.

45. Gouldner admits the accuracy of some criticisms directed at his early study, *The Coming Crisis of Western Sociology;* see *Dialectic,* p. 284n. Of a different order is the critique of Gouldner in Thompson, *Theory of Ideology,* 83–90. While Thompson offers useful commentary on certain aspects of *Dialectic,* he never acknowledges the force of Gouldner's historical perspective. He is content to discount Gouldner as a minor ideology theorist, at least in comparison with those whom he deems to be the Continental giants: Ricoeur, Bourdieu, and Habermas (but *not* Gadamer).

46. Hobsbawm, *Age of Revolution,* especially 294–98.

47. The most scathing critique, extending to Habermas, is broached in chapter twelve, "From Ideologues to Technologues," 250–74.

48. Among American philosophers, Richard Rorty has strongly objected to the nominalist character of German philosophy, without, however, offering an alternative approach as deliberate and detailed as Gouldner's; see, for instance, his essay on "Method and Morality" in Haan et al., *Social Science,* 155–76.

49. Paul E. Sigmund, *The Ideologies of the Developing Nations* (New York: Praeger, 1969), quoted in Karl D. Bracher, *The Age of Ideologies,* trans. Ewald Osers (New York: St. Martin's Press, 1982), 4, n. 1.

50. Clifford Geertz, *Interpretation of Cultures,* 220.

51. Bracher, *Age of Ideologies,* 4.

52. Ibid.

53. *International Encyclopedia of the Social Sciences,* s.v. "Ideology (concept and function)."

54. Larain, *The Concept of Ideology* (Athens: University of Georgia Press, 1979), 155–56.

55. Gouldner, *Dialectic,* 281.

56. Ibid., 26.

57. Ibid., 280.

58. See ibid., p. 285 for an explanation of the contradictory relation between the whole and the part.

59. Geertz, *Interpretation of Cultures,* 230–31.

60. I am indebted to Fredric Jameson's majesterial summation of the principal issues in "Theories of Ideology," a photocopied class lecture prepared for his graduate seminar on Marx and Freud, Duke University, Spring 1986, pp. 11–13.

61. Ibid., 11.

62. Hobsbawm, *Age of Revolution,* 258–76.

63. Charles Adams, "The Ideology of Mawlana Mawdudi" in *South Asian Politics and Religion,* ed. Donald E. Smith (Princeton: Princeton University Press, 1966), 371–97. Adams makes a detailed and compelling argument that Mawdudi, despite his voluminous protestations to the contrary, is a cryptomodernist; he is deeply influenced, indeed transformed, by the very ideologies that he is seeking to oppose. Numerous other scholars have expounded on Islam as a religious ideology, many following the lead of Richard P. Mitchell who analyzed the Muslim Brothers as ideologues in his seminal monograph, *The Society of the Muslim Brothers* (New York: Oxford University Press, 1969). Few, however, discuss the distinction between Islam and ideology. A recent review article by W. E. Shepherd ("Islam and Ideology: Towards a Typology," *International Journal of Middle Eastern Studies* 19 [1987]: 307–36) mistakenly presumes that the major issues have been addressed, and one has now only to chart variant approaches. The truth is more complex. At heart Islam and ideology, like Christianity and ideology or Judaism and ideology, pose a paradox. Their linkage cloaks the variety within each tradition and reduces the force of nonideological elements. The anomalous position of Iranian Muslim thinkers, especially Shari'ati and Mutahhari,

has been assessed by Hamid Dabashi in his essay, "Islamic Ideology: Perils and Promises of a Neologism," in *Post-Revolutionary Iran*, ed. H. Amirahmadi and M. Parvin (New York: Westview Press, 1987). The Southeast Asian context has been preliminarily examined by Sharon Siddique in an article suggestively titled "Conceptualizing Contemporary Islam: Religion or Ideology?" in *Annual Review of the Social Sciences and Religion* 5 (1981): 203–23.

64. Michael Walzer, *The Revolution of the Saints* (Cambridge: Harvard University Press, 1965), 27–30.

65. Ernest Gellner, *Nations and Nationalism* (Ithaca, NY: Cornell University Press, 1983), 138.

66. Crawford Young, *The Politics of Cultural Pluralism* (Madison: University of Wisconsin Press, 1976), 66. One of those rare comparativists with a repertoire of theoretical as well as narrative skills, Young stresses how the modern state became a normative, self-enforcing concept, especially in newly independent third world countries.

67. Kenneth Cragg, *The House of Islam* (Belmont, CA: Wadsworth, 1969), 96.

68. Gellner, *Nations and Nationalism*, 142.

69. Anthony D. S. Smith, *Nationalism in the Twentieth Century* (New York: New York University Press, 1979), 42.

70. Ibid.

71. Jean Bethke Elshtain, "On Patriotism," Chancellor's Lecture, University of Massachusetts at Amherst, 18 October 1984, 7. Elshtain presents two stunning examples of patriots who were at the same time antinationalists: Martin Luther King, Jr. and Dietrich Bonhoeffer, pp. 18–20.

72. Henry May, *Ideas*, 171–72.

73. Jerry Falwell's outlook echoes Hal Lindsey, *The Late Great Planet Earth*, even though the source he quotes on Israel as the locus of chiliastic redemption is Jack Van Impe, *Israel's Final Holocaust* (Nashville: Thomas Nelson, 1979). See Falwell's *Listen, America!* (New York: Doubleday/Bantam, 1980), 93–103.

74. For an exceptionally lucid treatment of the fundamentalist-evangelical support of the constitutional amendment auguring Prohibition, see A. James Reichley, *Religion in American Public Life* (Washington, DC: The Brookings Institution, 1985), 216–19.

75. Norman L. Zucker, "Secularization Conflicts in Israel," in *Religion and Political Modernization*, ed. Donald E. Smith (New Haven, CT: Yale University Press, 1974), 95.

76. Richard Falk, *The Endangered Planet* (New York: Vintage/Random House, 1971), 222–27.

77. See especially Muhammad Ghazzali's deprecation of nationalism. He is a major expositor of the Sunni fundamentalist perception of Islamic statehood. His views are discussed at length in Hamid Enayat, *Modern Islamic Political Thought* (London: Macmillan Press, 1982), 87–93.

CHAPTER FOUR: FUNDAMENTALISM AS A RELIGIOUS IDEOLOGY IN MULTIPLE CONTEXTS

Epigraph: R. Stephen Humphreys, "Islam and Political Values in Saudi Arabia, Egypt and Syria," *Middle East Journal* 33 (Winter 1979): 3.

1. Karsten Harries, review of *Nietzsche: Life as Literature*, by Alexander Nehamas, *The New York Times Book Review* (19 January 1986), 14. Harries imputes to Nietzsche the philosophical outlook of perspectivism, i.e., "the notion that all truths can only be understood from the perspective of the person depicting them." This is a variant of subjectivism or relativism, and as such is counterposed to scientism, i.e., the view that there are objective, observable realities out there waiting to be discovered, and once made known, the power of these natural forces can be harnessed to social ends. The social sciences have a *human* subject, however, and as we indicated in chapter three above, that median position complicates the imagined clash between scientific theorems and perspectival truths, rendering it neither as inevitable nor as fearful as is often imagined.

2. Steiner, *After Babel*, 134.

3. Ibid., 88.

4. This is the import of Peter Berger's prolix second appendix titled "Sociological and Theological Perspectives" in *The Sacred Canopy* (New York: Doubleday/Anchor, 1969). Berger makes a bold attempt to show that the two disciplines are not irreconcilable, however disparate their methodologies, aims, and outcomes. While it is easy to criticize Berger's circular reasoning (see, e.g., Hill, *Sociology of Religion*, 40), his vision of a mutually fruitful exchange between religion and sociology has yet to be advanced by others.

5. At which point American Protestant fundamentalism began is not clear. See chapter seven for a detailed discussion of variant views.

6. W. C. Smith, *The Meaning and End of Religion* (New York: Macmillan, 1962), introduction.

7. R. J. Zwi Werblowsky, *Beyond Tradition and Modernity: Changing Religions in a Changing World* (London: The Athlone, 1976), 55n.

8. Northrup Frye has explicated, both in illustrative diagram and narrative prose, how every word always has two meanings: its dictionary or conventional meaning and its context-specific uniqueness. See Frye's *The Great Code: The Bible and Literature* (New York: Harcourt Brace Jovanovich, 1982), 57.

9. *The Concise Oxford Dictionary of Current English*, 7th ed., s.v. "fundamentalism."

10. Among recent entries in the secularization debate among sociologists is Phillip E. Hammond, ed., *The Sacred in a Secular Age: Toward Revision in the Scientific Study of Religion* (Berkeley and Los Angeles: University of California Press, 1985). Its several essays maintain the viability of the sacred/secular antinomy, unlike Douglas and Tipton's edited volume, *Religion and America*. The clearest, single-authored book addressing the topic is Henry F. May's *Ideas, Faiths and Feelings* since May manages to combine chronological precision with ironic detachment in interpreting the most recent chapters of American religious history.

11. Bellah has expressed disenchantment with his own terminological triumph; see Bellah, Robert, with Phillip E. Hammond, eds., *Varieties of Civil Religion* (San Francisco: Harper & Row, 1980), 9.

12. Larain, *Ideology*, 192: "Popper refuses to be called a positivist . . . [yet] he is still concerned with only one particular mode of knowledge and experience."

13. Thompson, *Theory of Ideology*, 64–66, where Bourdieu's emphasis on form or style over content or substance is underscored and criticized.

14. Umar F. Abdallah, *The Islamic Struggle in Syria* (Berkeley, CA: Mizan Press, 1983), 23.

15. A rare effort to explain the persistent diffusion of modernism in sociological terms is to be offered by Roland Robertson, "The Sacred and the World System," in Hammond, *The Sacred*, 347–58.

16. The continuum from Whitehead to Habermas and Foucault becomes indecipherable on any other criterion: they are/were privileged elites of both Western society and the modern university.

17. Ernst Cassirer, *The Philosophy of the Enlightenment* (Princeton, NJ: Princeton University Press, 1951), 159 (my emphasis).

18. Bruns's reply to H. G. Gadamer's article "The Eminent Text and Its Truth" is set forth in *The Horizon of Literature*, ed. Paul Hernadi (Lincoln and London: University of Nebraska Press, 1982), 217.

19. Keith Dixon, *The Sociology of Belief: Fallacy and Foundation* (London: Routledge and Kegan Paul, 1980), 105.

20. Steiner, *After Babel*, 34.

CHAPTER FIVE: THE LIVING WORD FROM THE ETERNAL GOD

Epigraph 1: The Qur'an: The First American Version, trans. T. B. Irving (Brattleboro, VT: Amana Books), 6:75–79.

Epigraph 2: The Essays of Abraham Isaac Kook, trans. Ben Zion Bokser (New York: Paulist Press, 1978), 285.

Epigraph 3: "The God of Abraham Praise," in *The Hymnal of 1982 (According to the Use of the Protestant Episcopal Church)* (New York: Church Hymnal Corporation, 1982), no. 401.

1. John R. W. Stott, *Fundamentalism and Evangelism* (Grand Rapids: Eerdmans, 1959), 6.

2. Feuer sets forth the most extreme version of this hypothesis in asserting that "every ideology in some fashion repeats the Mosaic myth" (*Ideology*, 1). Not all the evidence of his seminal essay confirms this hypothesis, but he tries to strengthen its plausibility by reverting its premise in a too brief concluding exposition of "prophets as ideologists" (pp. 197–202). The distinction that he needs to clarify is between prophets as referents for ideology (which they frequently are) and antecedents for particular ideologues (which they almost never are).

3. The locus classicus for the display of the Bible as a literary text is Northrup Frye, *Great Code*. Efforts by John Wansbrough to approach the Qur'an from a similar perspective have been less successful. See Wansbrough's *Quranic Studies: Sources and Methods of Scriptural Interpretation* (Oxford and New York: Oxford University Press, 1977) and *The Sectarian Milieu: Content and Composition of Islamic Salvation History* (Oxford and New York: Oxford University Press, 1978).

4. The danger of dissolving all theological discourse into a parody of antinomies has been signaled by H. Richard Niebuhr. Especially in *The Resurrection and Historical Reason* (New York: Charles Scribner's Sons, 1957), Niebuhr calls attention to the falsity of dividing "historical consciousness into the disjunctive either/or of internal, dynamic *Geschichte* or external, inert *Historie*" (p. 64).

5. James Kritzeck, *Sons of Abraham: Jews, Christians and Moslems* (Baltimore: Helicon, 1965), 74.

6. Harvey Cox, "Understanding Islam: No More Holy Wars," *Atlantic Monthly*, January 1981, 77.

7. *Shorter Encyclopedia of Islam*, s.v. "Isma'il."

8. See chapter one above.

9. The radicality of Gadamer's position is attenuated once it is recognized that his consuming passion is to construct an antipositivist hermeneutic that is respectful of texts but not subservient to them.

10. Chadwick, *Secularization of the European Mind*, 44.

11. The limits of Reformation-inspired individualism have been sharply etched by William A. Clebsch in *Christianity in European History* (New York: Oxford University Press, 1979), chapter five. The approach followed here has been mindful of Bryan R. Wilson's several writings, in particular, his study of the Exclusive Brethren in the volume, *Patterns of Sectarianism: Organization and Ideology in Social and Religious Movements*, ed. Bryan R. Wilson (London: Heinemann, 1967). We disagree with his equation of fundamentalism and orthodoxy (p. 35) while applauding his broadened application of ideology to the study of sectarian movements.

12. Tracing these distinctions in a manner that does not privilege one group of Shi'is over another is itself a herculean task. The twelver or Ithna 'ashari branch has been comprehensively summarized by a Baha'i scholar, Moojan Momen; see *An Introduction to Shi'i Islam: The History and Doctrines of Twelver Shi'ism* (New Haven and London: Yale University Press, 1985).

CHAPTER SIX: FUNDAMENTALISTS IN DEFENSE OF THE JEWISH COLLECTIVITY

Epigraph: Dov Baer, the Maggid of Meseritch, quoted in Louis Jacobs, *Hasidic Thought* (New York: Behrman House, 1976), 75.

1. Eliezer Schweid, *Israel at the Crossroads*, trans. A. M. Winters (Philadelphia: Jewish Publication Society of America, 1973), 21.

2. Emile Marmorstein, *Heaven at Bay: The Jewish Kulturkampf in the Holy Land* (London: Oxford University Press, 1969), 195. The quote itself indicates the disparity of viewpoint in the sources. Zucker tells the same story of Brother Daniel, a Jewish convert to Catholicism, but does not include the provocative remark here cited from the

Neturei Karta newspaper account of the event. See Norman L. Zucker, *The Coming Crisis in Israel: Private Faith and Public Policy* (Cambridge: MIT Press, 1973), 179–80.

3. Charles S. Liebman, in his article "Extremism as a Religious Norm" (*Journal for the Scientific Study of Religion,* 22 (1983): 75–86), calls attention to two groups, Gush Emunim and 'Eda Haredit, the umbrella name for Neturei Karta, as extremists. The general points he makes are valid, but the context to which they relate is Israel as a secular polity. Secularism is the implied center, the privileged norm, for Israel as for other nation-states, and so the word "extremism," unlike fundamentalism, prejudges the character and also the significance, of both Gush Emunim and Neturei Karta as religious movements. "Ultraorthodox" is an apt term to describe Neturei Karta but *not* Gush Emunim. Only "fundamentalism" permits both groups to be framed within a rubric that addresses their paradoxical interrelatedness.

4. See Joseph Dan, "Hasidism," in *The Encyclopedia of Religion,* ed. M. Eliade, (New York: Macmillan, 1987), 6: 208.

5. Jacobs, *Hasidic Thought,* 75.

6. Not only for this quotation but for detailing the complex relationships between traditional rabbis and the emergent *rebbes* I am indebted to the insightful article of Menachem Friedman, "The Changing Role of the Community Rabbinate," *The Jerusalem Quarterly* 25 (Fall 1982): 79–99. The quotation just given is found on p. 82.

7. "Commonwealth" refers to the successive kingdoms that Israel has established in the Holy Land. The first extended from King David to the Babylonian exile (586 B.C.). The second began with the completion of the rebuilt temple (515 B.C.) and lasted till the Roman destruction of Jerusalem in A.D. 70. The "Third Commonwealth" is the most controversial. Many assert that it began in 1948 with the modern state of Israel. Others have argued that it did not begin till 1967, with the reconquest of all Jerusalem, while still others believe that it has yet to come into being.

8. Jacob Katz, "Orthodoxy in Historical Perspective," in *Studies in Contemporary Jewry,* ed. Peter Y. Medding (Bloomington: Indiana University Press, 1986), 2: 3–17, summarizes the origin and variability of the term "Orthodox," with special attention to pre-1948 developments outside Palestine.

9. Gideon Aran, "The Roots of Gush Emunim," in Medding (ed.), *Studies,* 2: 124.

10. See Katz, "Orthodoxy," 8 for this quote. The overlap between these developments and changes in the Hasidic communities of Eastern Europe are brought out in his seminal study, *Tradition and Crisis: Jewish Society at the End of the Middle Ages* (New York: The Free Press, 1961), especially pp. 225–44.

11. The citation from Hazon Ish is provided in Menachem Friedman, "Changing Role," 95.

12. Katz, "Origins," 15.

13. Eliezer Goldman, "Responses to Modernity in Orthodox Jewish Thought," in Medding (ed.), *Studies,* 2: 65. No specific attributions are given, but almost any Neturei Karta spokesman would say something similar about the Zionist "threat."

14. Aran, "Roots," 123. The tense and last phrase have been slightly altered to suit the argument of this paragraph.

15. Katz, "Orthodoxy," 11–12.

16. Ibid., 15.

17. Aran, "Roots," 135. Though Aran uses the expression *rebbe* in a metaphoric sense, others, such as Julien Bauer (see note 18), draw extensive parallels between the loyalty structure of Gush Emunim and traditional Hasidism.

18. Julien Bauer, "A New Approach to Religious-Secular Relationships," in David Newman, *The Import of Gush Emunim* (New York: St. Martin's Press, 1985), 106.

19. We do not make this delineation of two wings *de novo.* Ultimate indebtedness, of course, extends to Karl Mannheim. His analysis in *Ideology and Utopia* has influenced not only ours but numerous other studies of ideology. For instance, Lewis S. Feuer in *Ideology and the Ideologists,* even though scarcely mentioning Mannheim by name, devotes an entire subchapter to "the principle of wings in the ideological use of philosophical ideas" (pp. 20–55). Within studies of Jewish traditionalism, virtually every major scholar has not only relied on a version of the two wings' approach but has also

identified Gush Emunim and Neturei Karta or Agudat Israel as *the* two expressions of Jewish fundamentalism. Jacob Katz in "Orthodoxy" outlines what he calls "the two flanks" of opposition to state authority, one from Agudat, the other from Gush Emunim (pp. 14–16). Gideon Aran traces the dialectical relationship between aggressive Messianism (the Gush) and passive ultra-Orthodoxy, especially in the latter part of his article, "Redemption as a Catastrophe: The Gospel of Gush Emunim," to appear in *Religious Extremism and Politics in the Middle East,* ed. Emmanuel Sivan and Menachem Friedman (Albany: State University of New York Press, forthcoming). Menachem Friedman prefers to draw out the distinction between conservative fundamentalists (Neturei Karta) and innovative fundamentalists (Gush Emunim), according to David Newman's report of an unpublished manuscript titled "Radical Religious Groups in Israel: Conservatism and Innovation"; see D. Newman, "Gush Emunim between Fundamentalism and Pragmatism," *The Jerusalem Quarterly* 39 (Spring 1986): 34. Friedman's further thoughts on the interrelationship of the two wings of Jewish fundamentalism are developed in the essay, "Jewish Zealots: Conservatism vs. Innovation," also to appear in Sivan and Friedman (eds.), *Religious Extremism* (forthcoming). Finally, Ehud Sprinzak, in offering "a balance sheet of Zionist fundamentalism," contrasts the anti-Zionist Neturei Karta, "which preserves a medieval lifestyle," with Gush people who are "modern, well-behaved, and intelligent," many of their members drawn from the professional classes, including "engineers, talented mathematicians, and successful businessmen." See Ehud Sprinzak, *Gush Emunim: The Politics of Zionist Fundamentalism in Israel* (New York: The American Jewish Committee, Institute of Human Relations, 1986), 26. I am particularly grateful to Professors Aran, Friedman, and Sprinzak for providing me with their publications that are either unpublished or not easily available.

20. See Ian S. Lustick, *For the Land and the Lord: Jewish Fundamentalism in Israel* (New York: Council on Foreign Relations, 1988), 20–21. This well researched monograph is replete with insightful observations. Although we challenge the author's basic notion that fundamentalism is ubiquitous, i.e., that it can be located in *any* belief system whose "adherents regard its tenets as uncompromisable and direct transcendental imperatives to political action oriented toward the rapid and comprehensive reconstruction of society" (p. 6), we accept and applaud the accent on religious ideology which he subsequently develops in the heart of his study (pp. 72–90).

21. Ehud Sprinzak, "Kach and Meir Kahane: The Emergence of Jewish Quasi-Fascism," *Patterns of Prejudice* 19 (1985): 9. Only the word order has been changed to fit the sense of our argument. Menachem Friedman also calls attention to the intensified messianism of the Habad Hasidim since 1967. See Friedman's "The State of Israel as a Theological Dilemma," in *The Israeli State and Society: Boundaries and Frontiers,* ed. Baruch Kimmerling (Albany: State University of New York Press, 1988), 211–13.

22. Aviezer Ravitzky, "Roots of Kahanism: Consciousness and Political Reality," *The Jerusalem Quarterly* 39 (Spring 1986): 99. I am indebted to Ravitzky's article for many of the reflections on Kahane that inform this brief excursus on his role in contemporary Israeli religiopolitics.

23. In addition to Sprinzak and Ravitzky, S. Daniel Breslauer has written a monograph (*Meir Kahane: Ideologue, Hero, Thinker*) [Lewiston/Queenstown, New York: The Edwin Mellen Press, 1986] that frames discussion of Kahane as a modern-day zealot prone to use violence and terrorism as valid, necessary weapons for achieving his religious goals. In the last analysis, Kahane will more likely be a footnote to twentieth century fascism than an episode in Jewish fundamentalism, as Sprinzak has already intimated. Among Jewish fundamentalists the closest analogue to Kahane's militant triumphalism is the underground offensive of a splinter group of Gush Emunim. The offensive was directed at the Dome of the Rock, because the thirteen-hundred-year-old Muslim shrine sits astride the Temple Mount, sacred for nearly three thousand years in Jewish history. Yet the vigilante planning of fifteen Jewish ultranationalists took place without the approval of the Gush hierarchy. It was prompted by the psychic shock (what Thomas Kuhn would call "cognitive dissonance") resulting from the Camp David Accord of 1977. By surrendering even some land to Egypt, then Prime Minister Begin seemed to be postponing the messianic redemption that could only take place when

all of *Eretz Yisrael* was brought under Jewish sovereignty. Blowing up the Dome of the Rock was to have been the Gush vigilantes' response to Camp David. The plot became operational in 1982 and was thwarted only by the absence of rabbinical approval. Had Kahane been worthy of consultation, he would likely have given his assent, and the history of Israeli-Arab relations might have entered a new phase of reciprocal violence approaching Armageddonlike proportions.

The emergence of the Gush underground and the stage-by-stage narration of their plot against the Temple Mount have been skillfully depicted by Ehud Sprinzak in "Fundamentalism, Terrorism, and Democracy: The Case of Gush Emunim Underground," Wilson Center Occasional Paper #4 (Washington, DC: The History Culture & Society Program, The Wilson Center, 1986), especially pp. 5–20. The importance of the Gush underground *(machteret)* in connection with the Temple Mount plot has also been discussed at length in Lustick, *For the Land,* 168–76.

Concerning the influence of Kahane on Gush Emunim, it can be illustrated in stark form by the statements of Gush leaders about him. Yoseph Ben-Shlomo, a prominent Gush ideologue, refers to Moshe Levinger, the head of the Gush community in Hebron, as "a leading opponent of Kahane. He understands that if he wants to live in Judea and Samaria, he must relate to his Arab neighbors as human beings and citizens." See *Tikkun* 2 (Spring 1987): 75. Were this any more than a rhetorical aside, Ben-Shlomo would have to specify what he meant by treating "Arab neighbors as human beings and citizens," but since it is a narrow contrast with Kahane, whatever Levinger feels, says, or does is presumed to be at once humane and noble. Even this judgment may have to be tempered by more recent events, however: Rabbi Levinger is now under investigation for having shot to death an unarmed Palestinian shopkeeper in Hebron in fall 1988.

24. Milton Rokeach, *The Open and Closed Mind: Investigations into the Nature of Belief Systems and Personality Systems* (New York: Basic Books, 1960), 65–68. A full decade earlier a similar approach was outlined in T. W. Adorno, D. Frenkel-Brunswick, D. J. Levinson, and R. N. Sanford, *The Authoritarian Personality* (New York: Harper & Row, 1950).

25. Jacob Neusner, *The Way of Torah: An Introduction to Judaism* (Belmont, CA: Dickenson, 1970), 61.

26. Quoted from Gershom G. Scholem, *Major Trends in JewishMysticism* (London: Thames and Hudson, 1955), 29–30, in Jerome R. Mintz, *Legends of the Hasidim* (Chicago: University of Chicago Press, 1968), 129.

27. The argument about *shi'urim,* as also the relatedness of Hazon Ish to the *Shulkhan Arukh* of Hafetz Hayyim on this topic, is cogently summarized by Menachem Friedman, "Life Tradition and Book Tradition in the Development of Ultra-Orthodox Judaism," in Harvey E. Goldberg, ed., *Judaism Viewed From Within and From Without: Anthropological Studies* (Albany: State University of New York Press, 1987), 92–94.

28. Mintz, *Legends,* 130.

29. Quoted in ibid., 28, along with a footnote reference to Simon Dubnow, *Geschichte des Chassidismus,* 2 vols., trans. A. Steinberg, (Berlin: Judischer Verlag, 1931), 1:69–70. Dubnow divides the history of the Hasidic movement into four phases, the last of which is marked by decline. From a modernist perspective, Dubnow is undoubtedly correct, yet the Hasidim themselves do not perceive decline: how can their influence diminish since in the figure of the *rebbe* or *zaddik* they have power equivalent to the living Torah?

30. For much of the above account, and also for the background of this incident, see Marmorstein, Heaven at Bay, 168–69.

31. Menachem Friedman distinguishes Neturei Karta from 'Eda Haredit by noting that the former is "a smaller extremist group" within the latter, though it nonetheless "exercised a decisive influence" on the *haredi* outlook. See Menachem Friedman, "Religious Zealotry in Israeli Society," in *On Ethnic and Religious Diversity in Israel,* ed. Solomon Poll and Ernest Krausz (Ramat-Gan, Israel: Bar-Ilan University Press, 1975), 102–4.

32. Menachem Friedman, "The Haredim Confront the Modern City," in Medding (ed.), *Studies*, 93.

33. The essential article which masterfully charts all the interconnections between the *Gahelet* group and Gush Emunim is Gideon Aran, "The Roots of Gush Emunim," especially pp. 139–40.

34. Liebman, Charles S. and Eliezer Don-Yehiya, *Civil Religion in Israel* (Berkeley and Los Angeles: University of California Press, 1983), have drawn attention to the father-son distinction by quoting from Rav Zvi Yehuda Kook's own writings. Note especially his declaration that "the real Israel is the Israel that has been redeemed: the State of Israel and the army of Israel, a nation which is complete; *not* the exiled Diaspora" (p. 198, my emphasis).

35. On this three-staged model, see Lustick, *For the Land*, 34–35.

36. Ibid., 34.

37. Aran, "Roots," 139–40.

38. In Marmorstein, *Heaven at Bay*, 163, the views of a secular writer, Amos Elon, are cited. In 1954 he argued for the division of Jerusalem into religious and nonreligious districts, "not as a concession to Amram Bloi but to the Torah of Israel, [since] there is no need for traffic to pass through districts populated by people who still believe what they believe."

39. Amnon Rubinstein, *The Zionist Dream Revisited: From Herzl to Gush Emunim and Back* (New York: Schocken, 1984), xii. The tenuous exegetical justifications of Gush Emunim leaders are examined and criticized by Yosseph Shilhav, "Interpretation and Misinterpretation of Jewish Territorialism," in Newman, *Gush Emunim*, 111–24. Despite the reasonableness of the arguments, it is not the written Torah but the living Torah that legitimates the Gush concept of the Land of Israel. Blessed by their own *"rebbes,"* they attempt to produce a ground level reality that will ensure the success of their ideology.

40. Lilly Weissbrod, "Core Values and Revolutionary Change," in Newman, *Gush Emunim*, 74 (with minor changes for contextual clarity). Her interpretation is much less symbolically charged than Schweid, *Israel*, 161: "from an all-inclusive historical viewpoint the War of Independence [1948] was the end of an era, after which there was a decline. But the Six-Day War [1967] was the beginning of an era, which carries with it the opportunity for ascendancy." To those who advocate Zionism as a civil religion, however, 1948 remains the benchmark year for all hope and progress; 1967 accelerates but it does not inaugurate the Zionist nation-state.

41. Weissbrod, "Core Values," 84 criticizes religious Zionism as "a religious doctrine rather than an ideology," since it lacked both a blueprint for the social order and significant popular support until the emergence of the New Zionism, with Gush Emunim as its vanguard, after 1974. Yet the absence of a blueprint for the social order characterizes most ideologies; and it can be argued that religious Zionism did enjoy latent popular support. What sets Gush Emunim apart from prior forms of religious Zionism is their insistent emphasis on action. It is action directed to one goal: expansion and reconsecration of the Land of Israel.

42. Liebman and Don-Yehiya, *Civil Religion*, 16.

43. Rubinstein, *Zionist Dream*, 121.

44. Liebman and Don-Yehiya, *Civil Religion*, 211.

45. Wiessbrod, "Core Values," 72. But others, such as David Newman, see Gush Emunim as having undergone an internal transition to pragmatism that belies their original, religious goals. In an article entitled "Gush Emunim Between Fundamentalism and Pragmatism" (*The Jerusalem Quarterly* 39 (Spring 1986): 33–43), he argues that Gush leaders have become more and more institutionalized within the Israeli political system, with the result that the technocratic, pragmatic approach of current Gush operatives is "a far cry from the fundamentalist divine ideology which provided an initial boost to settlement activities" (p. 41). This approach, however, presupposes that the Gush leadership must be either secular or fundamentalist, and as Aran has skillfully

shown, what exceptionalizes Gush Emunim to date is the ability of its leaders to transcend the dichotomies others impose, and instead to view *all* pragmatic constraints as stages along the path to a fundamentalist utopia, the centerpiece of which will be messianic redemption. The Gush ideology may not dominate in present-day Israel, but that failure is more likely to be caused by factors external to the Gush leadership.

46. The seminal article developing this image to its fullest extent is Ehud Sprinzak, "Gush Emunim: The Tip of the Iceberg," *The Jerusalem Quarterly* 21 (Fall 1981): 28–47. The comments Sprinzak makes about Gush Emunim in general conform to our argument, even though he asserts that "Gush Emunim is not a classical protest movement nor an ideological group nor a counter-culture" (p. 40). We would maintain that they are decidedly a religious ideological cadre, yet we agree with him that "the Gush, unlike Neturei Karta, never created a total counter-culture in Israel, since it never questioned the (potential) legitimacy of the state and the society at large" (p. 40). Instead, Gush Emunim has become inseparable from the "knitted skull cap" *(bnei akiva)* subculture as well as the National Religious Party social and political infrastructures.

47. See Rubinstein, *Zionist Dream*, chapter one for a succinct explanation of the limits to the Herzlian tradition. It appeals to only one group of emigres to Israel—the acculturated, assimilated Jews of Western Europe—precisely those who would be regarded as *maskilim*, or captives of the Enlightenment, by the *haredim* of Eastern Europe. Even the National Religious Party (NRP) in Israel is found wanting: from the retrospect of 1974, and in no small part due to the complaints of Gush Emunim, its objectives seem to have been minimal, its advocates mere epigones. "For the first decades of the State's existence, the NRP concentrated primarily on bringing various aspects of Israeli life under religious control. On matters of foreign policy, security, or economics, the Party was largely docile. . . . The emergence of a new more hawkish generation has necessitated important changes in that stance. Now a comprehensive religious assessment of these matters has been demanded [chiefly by Gush Emunim]." (David Schnall, "An Impact Assessment" in Newman, Gush Emunim, 20).

48. Rubinstein, *Zionist Dream*, 121.

49. This apt phrase occurs in S. Barakat Ahmad's article, "Maududian Concept of Islamic State," *Islam and the Modern Age* 14, (November 1983): 17.

50. Hasidim in the New World do engage technology, imbuing modern consumer goods with religious meaning in order to justify their purchase and use. See Solomon Poll, *The Hasidic Community of Williamsburg* (New York: Shocken 1969), 101–7; quoted in Stephen Sharot, *Messianism, Mysticism, and Magic: A Sociological Analysis of Jewish Religious Movements* (Chapel Hill: University of North Carolina Press, 1982), 194–95.

51. Rubinstein, *Zionist Dream*, 123.

52. Sharot, *Messianism*, 234.

53. A full, though hyperbolic, exposé of Gush Emunim's involvement with secular Israeli politics is set forth in *Middle East Reports in Progress (MERIP)*, February 1982.

54. Rubinstein, *Zionist Dream*, 125–26.

55. For the entire anecdote, as well as the final quotation, I am indebted to ibid., 153. Janet Aviad (*Return to Judaism: Religious Renewal in Israel* [Chicago and London: University of Chicago Press, 1983]) also examines the nature of the *baalei teshuva*, those secular Jews who have "converted" to Orthodoxy. Though she pays minimal attention to either Neturei Karta or Gush Emunim in her book, she deals at length with the significance of Gush Emunim in a subsequent article. See note 72.

56. Rubinstein, *Zionist Dream*, 145.

57. Ibid., 154.

58. The percentage comes from Rabbi Shapira as quoted by Yoseph Ben-Shlomo in *Tikkun* 2 (Spring 1987): 76.

59. The figures cited by Lustick are tantalizingly broad. He gives the range of Gush membership as ten to twenty thousand (*For the Land*, 8), while Meron Benvenisti suggests that the nonurban Gush, i.e., those who live beyond commuting distance to Tel Aviv, Jerusalem, or Hebron, are actually less than six thousand (see *Tikkun* 2 [Spring 1987]: 62).

60. See Lustick, *For the Land*, 53–66 and 162–63.

61. Gwyn Rowley offers a schematic sketch of the eleven stages of the triadic relationship between Y-hweh, the land and the people. The most recent (stage eleven) shows the land and the people linked with only a vague vertical line to Y-hweh. Stage six, by contrast, is marked by a triadic bonding of all three. That unity, said to be characteristic of the Davidic and Solomonic period, becomes the desideratum for Gush Emunim. See Rowley, "The Land of Israel: A Reconstructionist Approach," in Newman, *Gush Emunim*, 134.

62. Rubinstein, *Zionist Dream*, 31. David Ben-Gurion epitomizes the generation of Israeli leaders who were negatively disposed to Jewish existence in the Diaspora. "He was a bitter opponent of Yiddish and among the early advocates of the exclusive use of Hebrew. But he frequently employed symbols drawn from the more distant Biblical past which he associated with Jewish sovereignty in the Land of Israel." Dan Horowitz and Moshe Lissak, *Origins of the Israeli Polity: Palestine under the Mandate* (Chicago and London: University of Chicago Press, 1978), 123.

63. Liebman and Don-Yehiya, *Civil Religion*, 196.

64. Abraham Isaac Kook, *The Lights of Penitence, the Moral Principles, Lights of Holiness, Essays, Letters, and Poems*, trans. Ben Zion Bokser (New York: Paulist Press, 1978), 297–98.

65. On the indifference of recent Gush Emunim settlers to the Rabbis Kook, see David Weisburd and Elin Waring, "Settlement Motivations in the Gush Emunim Movement: Comparing Bonds of Altruism and Self Interest," in Newman, *Gush Emunim*, 187.

66. See Lustick, *For the Land*, 197. Writing in *Nekuda*, a Gush journalist describes Abraham Bar-Ilan, who tried to block the evacuation of Yamit in 1982, as a contemporary *zaddik* (or *tzaddik*). Fittingly, he captions the article: "The *Tzaddik* of Yamit."

67. Jonathan Rosenbaum, "Judaism: Torah and Tradition," in *The Holy Book in Comparative Perspective*, ed. Frederick M. Denny and Rodney L. Taylor, (Columbia: University of South Carolina Press, 1985), 22.

68. Mintz, *Legends*, 122.

69. Friedman, "Haredim," 76–95.

70. Gidon Gottlieb, review of *The Zionist Dream Revisited: From Herzl to Gush Emunim and Back*, by Amnon Rubenstein, *New York Times Book Review* (15 July 1984), 23.

71. Marmorstein details the Neturei Karta interventions against the State for archaeological violations. See also *Middle East Reports in Progress (MERIP)*, February 1982 for another, highly charged account of the "dry bones" fight that American television has subsequently picked up. See *Heaven at Bay*, 185.

72. Janet Aviad, "The Contemporary Israeli Pursuit of the Millennium," *Religion* 14/3 (July 1984): 215. The entire article surveys contemporary Hebrew sources, many written by Gush leaders and/or their supporters, in order to ascertain the most recent thrust of Gush Emunim ideology.

73. The quotations come from an article in *Nekuda* that included reference to the correspondence of Rabbi Zvi Yehuda Kook. See ibid., 215, 222.

74. Ibid., 217.

75. Ibid., 219.

76. Lustick, *For the Land*, 169, comments that "no candidates for . . . [his] . . . leadership position appear to be on the horizon."

77. See ibid., 206. Throughout his monograph Lustick makes more frequent use of *Nekuda* than any other source in offering a ground-level view of Gush policies and relationships.

78. Apart from the journal *Mishereth Homathenu*, secondary literature in Hebrew on Neturei Karta is extremely limited. A review of the major sources is given in Marmorstein, *Heaven at Bay*, 211–12. Other than Marmorstein only two full-length books encapsulate their views: Yerachmiel Domb, *The Transformation: The Case of the Neturei Karta* (London: Mismereth Chomosenu, 1958), an excerpt from which is provided in *Zionism Reconsidered: The Rejection of Jewish Normalcy*, ed. Michael Selzer (London: Macmillan, 1970), 23–48; and Menachem Friedman, *Society and Religion: The Non-Zionist*

Orthodox in Eretz-Israel, 1918–1936 (Hebrew) (Jerusalem: 1977). A fuller exploration of the *haredim* is also set forth in Menachem Friedman's journal articles and book chapters cited above. By contrast, the literature on Gush Emunim in both Hebrew and English is vast and growing. Newman, *Gush Emunim,* provides several references. The Gush self-profile is most strikingly etched by Aran in "Redemption as a Catastrophe: The Gospel of Gush Emunim" and "The Roots of Gush Emunim," while its potential political repercussions are graphically charted by Lustick, *For the Land.*

CHAPTER SEVEN: AMERICAN-STYLE PROTESTANT FUNDAMENTALISTS

Epigraph: Grant Wacker, "The Demise of Biblical Civilization," in *The Bible in America,* ed. Nathan O. Hatch and Mark A. Noll (New York: Oxford University Press, 1982), 126–27.

1. Levy, *War,* 42.
2. See Richard Hofstadter, *Social Darwinism in American Thought* (1944; reprint, Boston: Beacon Press, 1959).
3. This and many other varied interpretations of American religious history are broached by Richard L. Rubinstein, "Religion, Ideology, and Economic Justice," in *The Terrible Meek: Essays on Religion and Revolution,* ed. L. D. Kliever, (New York: Paragon, 1987), especially 175–80.
4. Quoted in several places but cited here from Bryan S. Turner, *Weber and Islam* (London: Routledge and Kegan Paul, 1974), 149.
5. Thomas S. Derr, "The First Amendment as a Guide to Church-State Relations," in A. E. Dick Howard, J. W. Baker, and *Church, State, and Politics* ed. A. E. Dick Howard, J. W. Baker, and T. S. Derr (Washington, DC: Roscoe Pound American Trial Lawyers' Foundation, 1981), 12.
6. Ibid., 84.
7. Ibid.
8. The phrase has become widely known in scholarly circles since the appearance of Elwyn A. Smith, ed., *The Religion of the Republic* (Philadelphia: Fortress Press, 1971).
9. Derr, "First Amendment," 84-85.
10. McLoughlin, *Revivals,* 4.
11. See George M. Marsden, *Fundamentalism and American Culture: The Shaping of Twentieth-Century Evangelicalism, 1870–1925* (New York: Oxford University Press, 1980), 330.
12. See chapter two.
13. See chapter two.
14. Ernest R. Sandeen, *Roots of Fundamentalism,* emphasizes nonsocial sources of millenarian-fundamentalist discontent. Yet he admits that for evangelicals the "three R's"—Romanism, ritualism and rationalism—are the epitome of evil (p. 227). William G. McLoughlin, *Revivals,* finds that the turn-of-the-century influx of Catholic immigrants, in unprecedented numbers, shaped the Protestant upsurge to protect a "pure" vision of the American past (pp. 3–4).
15. George W. Dollar, *A History of Fundamentalism in America* (Greenville, SC: Bob Jones University Press, 1973), xv. This sentence is set out in capital letters, bold type before the introduction to his study.
16. Ibid., 7.
17. Ibid., 80.
18. Ibid., 102.
19. Ibid., 172.
20. Ibid., 85: the order of persons and sentence structure have been changed to anticipate the analysis that follows.
21. The content and consequence of these debates are narrated at length in C. Allyn Russell, *Voices of American Fundamentalism: Seven Biographical Studies* (Philadelphia: Westminster Press, 1976). See also *The Fundamentalist Phenomenon* (New York: Doubleday, 1981), ed. Jerry Falwell, 101–2.

22. Earlier known as *The Fence Rail and the Searchlight*, Norris's journal did not take on the name *The Fundamentalist* till 1927. See Dollar, *History*, 126.
23. Ibid., 135.
24. Falwell, *Listen, America!*, 91–92.
25. Ibid., 91.
26. In addition to A. James Reichley, *Religion*, note the broad-ranging articles in *The New Christian Right: Mobilization and Legitimation*, R. C. Liebman and R. Wuthnow (New York: Aldine Publishing Company, 1983). Collectively the contributors to the Liebman-Wuthnow volume expose the ambiguities that haunt both politicized preachers and pietistic politicians.
27. The varied lists of "fundamentals" is discussed at length in Sandeen, *Roots of Fundamentalism*, chapter eight. It is also critically addressed by K. S. Kantzer, "Unity and Diversity in Evangelical Faith," in *The Evangelicals*, ed. David F. Wells and John D. Woodbridge, (Grand Rapids, MI: Baker, 1977), 73–74.
28. Sandeen, *Roots of Fundamentalism*, xv, xix.
29. Ibid., 246, (my emphases).
30. Kantzer, "Unity," 77.
31. Sandeen, *Roots of Fundamentalism*, 206.
32. Kantzer ("Unity," 79) raises this question about the most recent phase of fundamentalism, but one could generalize his query and apply it to socioreligious movements of all periods, however disquieting its force to social scientific theory and analysis.
33. May, *Ideas*, 166.
34. Sandeen, *Roots of Fundamentalism*, 266. For a full tracing of the relationship between Bryan and the antievolution movement, see Ferenc Morton Szasz, *The Divided Mind of Protestant America, 1880–1930* (University, AL: University of Alabama Press, 1982).
35. Cassirer, *Philosophy*, 159.
36. Numerous authors have argued that it was the embrace of evolution, more than any other indexical shift of Enlightenment thought, which removed the God hypothesis from acceptable intellectual discourse. They differ, however, in how they interpret the theological accommodation to evolution. See, for example, Theodore Dwight Bozeman, *Protestants in an Age of Science: The Baconian Ideal and Antebellum American Religious Thought* (Chapel Hill: University of North Carolina Press, 1977) for the argument that Baconianism, the last attempt of deists to construct and protect a doxological science, was directly routed by evolution, especially among Southern Presbyterians (pp. 166–73). Others maintain that evolution gained the upperhand not by head-on confrontation but through the inadvertent assistance of believers: overreacting to the menace of Darwinism, they shifted referents of belief and emptied religion of its traditional force. James Turner makes this case in *Without God, Without Creed*. "Religion caused unbelief. In trying to adapt their religious beliefs, . . . the defenders of God slowly strangled Him. If anyone is to be arraigned for deicide, it is not Charles Darwin but his adversary Bishop Samuel Wilberforce, not the godless Robert Ingersoll but the godly Beecher family" (p. xiii). The rhetorical appeal of this thesis is greater than its content. The spectrum of choice between God and humans is so collapsed that transcendence becomes immanence, with the result that Turner can conclude about his American subjects, the "godly" Beechers and their sympathizers: "having made God more and more like man—intellectually, morally, emotionally—the shapers of religion made it feasible to abandon God, to believe simply in man!" (p. 261).
37. Chadwick, *Secularization*, 183.
38. See especially Richard Olson (*Science Deified*, 13–14) for a precise review of Hume's stance in his *Enquiry Concerning Human Understanding*. Hume is at once reductive and exclusionary in the narrowness of his vision, yet according to Olson, most scientists share Hume's presupposition.
39. R. C. Lewontin, "Bourgeois Ideology and the Origin of Determinism," in R. C. Lewontin, Steven Rose, and Leon J. Kamin, *Not in Our Genes: Biology, Ideology, and Human Nature* (New York: Pantheon, 1984), 50–51 (my emphases).

40. David L. Hull, *Darwin and His Critics: The Reception of Darwin's Theory of Evolution by the Scientific Community* (Cambridge: Harvard University Press, 1973), 30.

41. Stephen Jay Gould, review of *Not in Our Genes*, by R. C. Lewontin, Steven Rose, and Leon J. Kamin, *New York Review of Books* (16 August 1984), 30.

42. See chapter three.

43. Ernan McMullin ed., *Evolution and Creation* (Notre Dame, IN: University of Notre Dame Press, 1985) lays out the fallacy of creationists' approach to science, and yet demonstrates a sensitive understanding of the "soft" side of scientific hubris (pp. 45–48).

44. The relationship of Peter Berger to theodicy is complex. On the one hand, it can be simply noted (see May, *Ideas*, 164) that in *The Sacred Canopy* it becomes the linchpin for his argument that meaning is more essential to human beings than happiness. On the other hand, one has to consider the idiosyncratic manner in which he tries to wed sociology to theology and his own conservative motives for "justifying" human sacrifices and suffering in the third world (especially in *Pyramids of Sacrifice* and *Facing up to Modernity*). Two essays that shed light on Berger's ambiguous eclecticism are Van A. Harvey and Marie Augusta Neal, "Peter Berger: Retrospect," *Religious Studies Review* 5 (January 1979): 1–15.

45. Marshall D. Sahlins, *The Use and Abuse of Biology: An Anthropological Critique of Sociobiology* (Ann Arbor: University of Michigan Press, 1976), especially pp. 3–16.

46. The controversy sparked by Wilson's work has found echoes in many quarters, but the shrewdest appraisal of his approach to evolution as religion is also the most condemning: "For Wilson the word 'religion' seems to be little more than the banner of an alien tribe, whose assets are to be raided. He seldom mentions any manifestation of religion which is not openly crude and contemptible." (Mary Midgley, *Evolution as a Religion* [London and New York: Methuen, 1958], 113–14)

47. See Hull, *Darwin*, 13–14 for details of the two rejected hypotheses: pangenesis and Darwin's explanation of the parallel "Road of Glen Roy."

48. Ibid., 12.

49. Charles Peirce, *Scientific Metaphysics* (Cambridge: Harvard University Press, 1935), vol. 6 of *Collected Papers*, 297, as quoted in ibid., 33–34.

50. Hull, *Darwin*, which contrasts with the assessment of another Darwin scholar, Peter J. Bowler. See Bowler's *Evolution: The History of an Idea* (Berkeley and Los Angeles: University of California Press, 1984), 289.

51. Bowler, *Evolution*, 182.

52. Ibid., 185.

53. Hull, *Darwin*, 34.

54. Neal C. Gillespie, *Charles Darwin and the Problem of Creation* (Chicago and London: University of Chicago Press, 1979).

55. See Karl Löwith, *Meaning in History* (Chicago: University of Chicago Press, 1949), 67–90 for a superb critique of the limits of Comtian philosophy.

56. Gillespie, *Charles Darwin*, 13.

57. Ibid., 16.

58. Ibid., 18.

59. Ibid., 53.

60. Ibid., 54, quoting an 1861 letter from Darwin to Lyell.

61. Distinguishing the late from the early Darwin is still the subject of debate. Did the shift take place ca. 1840, when his major ideas were formulated, or in 1859, when *Origin of the Species* was published? Bowler (*Evolution*, 164–73) discusses all aspects of the question and leans toward the later date since it was only in 1856 that Darwin advocated the notion of competition for territorial space as the "crucial" economic explanation for the principle of diversity.

62. Mary Midgley, a bit tongue in cheek, dedicates her book "To the Memory of Charles Darwin, Who Did Not Say These Things."

63. Hull, *Darwin*, 6.

64. Ibid., 7.
65. Bowler, *Evolution*, 104, with abbreviations and capital letters to stress the congruence of his argument with that advanced here (my emphases).
66. Hull, *Darwin*, 186–87.
67. Bowler, *Evolution*, 176.
68. Gillespie, *Charles Darwin*, 109.
69. Midgley, *Evolution*, 11.
70. Ibid., 11–12.
71. For a detailed exposition of Darwin's correspondence with Asa Gray, see Gillespie, *Charles Darwin*, 111–18; for a synopsis, see Bowler, *Evolution*, 211–12.
72. See not only Thomas Kuhn's classic, *The Structure of Scientific Revolutions*, but also Gary Gutting, ed., *Paradigms and Revolutions: Appraisals and Applications of Thomas Kuhn's Philosophy of Science* (Notre Dame, IN: University of Notre Dame Press, 1980).
73. Hull, *Darwin*, 25.
74. Gillespie, *Charles Darwin*, 121. Philip Kitcher (*Abusing Science: The Case Against Creationism* [Cambridge: MIT Press, 1982], 168) claims that Kuhn has been misunderstood as an advocate of competing paradigms, yet he himself never offers an alternative interpretation of Kuhn nor does he cite Kuhn's book except as further reading (p. 204)!
75. Kitcher, *Abusing Science*, 191–92.
76. See the still unsurpassed study of Richard Hofstadter, *Social Darwinism*.
77. It is appropriate that sociobiologists are frequently classified as neo-Darwinists. See, e.g., Michael Ruse, *Darwinism Defended: A Guide to the Evolution Controversies* (Menlo Park, CA: Benjamin/Cummings Publishing Co., 1982), chapter eleven.
78. Their perfidy is graphically narrated in C. Allyn Russell, *Voices*, 184–85 and 217.
79. Henry Morris, *The Scientific Case for Creation* (San Diego, CA: CLP Publishers, 1977), chapter one and *The Troubled Waters of Evolution* (San Diego, CA: CLP Publishers, 1975), 82. A complete and also provocative investigation of the major national proponents of scientific creationism, including Henry Morris, is set forth by Christopher Paul Toumey in "The Social Context of Scientific Creationism" (Ph.D. dissertation, Department of Anthropology, University of North Carolina, Chapel Hill, 1987). I am indebted to James Peacock of the UNC Department of Anthropology for this reference.
80. Richard Hofstadter, *Anti-Intellectualism in American Life* (New York: Knopf, 1966), 125, quoted in Frye, *Great Code*, 10.
81. Henry Morris, *The Remarkable Birth of Planet Earth* (San Diego, CA: CLP Publishers, 1976), 75.
82. Richard W. Berry, "The Beginning," in Frye, *Great Code*, 50.
83. Morris, *Troubled Waters*, 61.
84. Frye, *Great Code*, 10.
85. See Ruse, *Darwinism Defended*, but especially Kitcher, *Abusing Science*, chapter two.
86. In establishing innate racial prejudice as a corollary of evolution, Henry Morris quotes from both Darwin and Huxley; see *Troubled Waters*, 164–65. Kitcher (*Abusing Science*, 197) tries to make the counterargument that evolutionary theory can be separated from its evaluative claims. Without blinking, he declares that "evolution did not supply the racist doctrine. It merely played a mediating role, linking two racist claims [!]."
87. Edwin A. Olson treats the case of Jastrow at length to interpret the values of both evolutionary scientists and their creationist opponents. See Olson, "Hidden Agenda Behind the Evolutionist/Creationist Debate," in Frye, *Great Code*, 35–37.
88. A. Bruce Vawter, "Creationism: Creative Misuse of the Bible," in Frye, *Great Code*, 77 (my emphasis).
89. See especially Ruse, *Darwinism Defended*, chapter eleven and p. 279.
90. Ibid., 263–64.
91. One of Ruse's chapters is entitled, "Darwinism as Ideology." Lewontin, Rose, and Kamin, *Not in Our Genes*, chapters nine and ten go even further in stressing ideological considerations.

92. Kitcher, *Abusing Science*, 4, and then later, 164.

93. Ibid., 44 (my emphasis).

94. The crucial category switch is from providence to progress, as if there were no mediating positions. Löwith (*Meaning*, 60–103) exposes the problem with reference to its antecedents and concludes that "the modern[ist] mind is not single-minded: it eliminates from its progressive outlook the Christian implication of creation and consummation, while it assimilates from the ancient world view the idea of an endless continuous movement, discarding its circular structure" (p. 207).

95. Kitcher, *Abusing Science*, 192 (my emphasis).

96. Frye (*Great Code*, 199 and 204) too briefly alludes to the immensely complex history of the two-books metaphor. Both the historian of science Frank Manuel and the philosopher of science A. R. Peacocke have tried to trace the implications of the metaphor for subsequent generations after Bacon. The commonly held view, which Peacocke summarizes, is that the natural sciences provide the necessary framework within which religious reflection must take place. "These fundamental questions (What is there? What goes on? How does it change? Why does it change? etc.) cannot be asked at all without directing them to the world as we best know and understand it, that is, through the sciences." (A. R. Peacocke, *Creation and the World of Science* [Oxford: Oxford University Press, 1979], 47) The implications of this view are inescapably relativist: our theology is only as good as our science; the latter is the index of legitimacy for the former. Albert Einstein was guilty of a similar ranking when he observed that "science without religion is lame, but religion without science is blind!" It is against such a measurement of "the two books" that fundamentalists-creationists raise their hue and cry.

97. Kitcher (*Abusing Science*, 187) and others denounce the public school edition of *Scientific Creationism* because, in its pretense to be science, it omits Biblical citations. That ploy postpones rather than resolves the issues underlying the creationist/evolutionary debate.

98. Marsden, *Fundamentalism*, 228.

99. Edward Harrison, *Masks of the Universe* (New York: Macmillan, 1985), 115–17.

CHAPTER EIGHT: FUNDAMENTALISTS IN PURSUIT OF AN ISLAMIC STATE

The epigraph is my own rendition of the Arabic text of *Al-Farida Al-Gha'iba*, done from a copy that Frank Vogel provided me in Cairo in 1982. Compare with the translation of Johannes J. G. Jansen, *The Neglected Duty: The Creed of Sadat's Assassins and Islamic Resurgence in the Middle East* (New York: Macmillan, 1986), 193. Jansen's translation of the text is literal to the point of stiltedness. It is preceded by a background commentary that is valuable though less satisfying than the detailed study of Emmanuel Sivan, *Radical Islam*. Sivan discusses both 'Abd as-Salam Faraj and his treatise under the title "The Absent Precept"; see pp. 103–4 and 127–9. The variant phrases—"neglected duty," "absent precept," "missing imperative"—all stress a similar theme: some Muslims cling to a sixth canonical obligation (in addition to the well-known "five pillars"). That pillar is *jihad*, the duty to engage in physical warfare against infidels. According to 'Abd as-Salam and his cohorts, when rulers who bear Muslim names fail to wage *jihad*, they themselves become infidels, with the result that true Muslims have the obligation to wage war against them! *Epigraph 2*: Ayatollah Morteza Mutahhari, *Jihad: The Holy War of Islam and Its Legitimacy in the Quran*, (trans. Mohammad Salman Tawheedi, (Albany, CA: Moslem Student Association [Persian Speaking Group], n.d.), 37–38. Mutahhari, one of Imam Khomeini's closest followers, wrote this pamphlet ca. 1960.

1. Marilyn Waldman, review of *Islam in the Modern World* edited by D. MacEoin and A. el-Shahi, in *The Muslim World* (July/October 1986): 238.

2. Jean-Claude Vatin examines how the current Algerian regime adopts this strategy, attempting to institutionalize what he calls a new Islamic vulgate. By coopting Islamic symbols, the thoroughly secular ruling elites claim that they are the true upholders of the Muslim patrimony. In effect, they engage in a masked battle; they do not

pursue a fundamentalist strategy of the kind we have described throughout this book. See Jean-Claude Vatin, "Popular Puritanism versus State Reformism: Islam in Algeria," in *Islam in the Political Process*, ed. J. Piscatori (New York: Cambridge University Press, 1983), 98–121.

3. The crudest elaborations of this approach are to be found in R. Hrair Dekmejian, *Islam In Revolution: Fundamentalism in the Arab World* (Syracuse, NY: Syracuse University Press, 1985) and Fouad Ajami, *Arab Predicament*. More sophisticated and worthy of close scrutiny are the distinctions advanced by Henry Munson, Jr. in his introduction to *The House of Si Abd Allah: The Oral History of a Moroccan Family* (New Haven, CT: Yale University Press, 1984) and Emmanuel Sivan, *Radical Islam*, but also "The Two Faces of Islamic Fundamentalism," *The Jerusalem Quarterly* 27 (Spring 1983): 127–44. Both Munson's "innate fundamentalism" and Sivan's "conservative fundamentalism" are categories that refer to the strict maintenance of traditional Islamic beliefs and practices. In my view, however, the extreme politicization of Islamic loyalty, to the point of advocating *jihad* on several fronts, is the touchstone of Muslim fundamentalists, and that ideology seems to suggest less a shift within categories than a leap into another frame of reference, severing rather than confirming the link to what preceded it. Hence I prefer to separate traditionalism, even warmly embraced, from any form of fundamentalism. On almost all other points, especially the homological perception of modernism/Westernism/Satan that characterizes Muslim fundamentalists of all stripes, I concur with the well-documented analyses of both Munson and Sivan.

4. See Henry Munson, Jr., *Islam and Revolution in the Middle East* (New Haven and London: Yale University Press, 1988), 72–74 for discussion of the dissent of Saudi Shi'is from the ideology of the ruling group.

5. There has never been an official census in the Kingdom of Saudi Arabia. All statistics are extrapolations from other data-gathering surveys, and US government sources at the highest level often put the actual figure of native Saudis as low as four million.

6. Many have claimed that the Saudi regime, oriented as it is to the puritanical preaching of Ibn 'Abd al-Wahhab, is fundamentalist. But, as Piscatori convincingly argues (*Islam*, 70–71), the Saudi ruling elites are not religious ideologues. Rather, there is an inexorable tension between their explicit claims to be a Qur'anic theocracy and their implicit modernizing ideology.

In Morocco all the rhetoric that can be classified as Islamic fundamentalist originates from groups opposed to the monarchy. See especially Henry Munson, Jr., "The Social Base of Islamic Militancy in Morocco," *Middle East Journal* 40 (1986): 267–84. Few, however, doubt King Hassan's attachment to Islamic symbols and the values they embody. I. William Zartman ("Explaining the Nearly Inexplicable: The Absence of Islam in Moroccan Foreign Policy," in *Islam in Foreign Policy*, ed. Adeed Darwish [Cambridge: Cambridge University Press, 1983], 97–111) overstates the case when he suggests that "Moroccan policy is a horse painted green, but it is still a horse," implying that Islam remains only a superficial coloration not a substantive issue in determining Moroccan external alignments. The relationship with Saudi Arabia is especially warm, Zartman admits, precisely because both countries pride themselves as "moderate Muslim Arab monarchies" (p. 102). Muslim Arab monarchism is now a small club, with only three members (including the Hashemite Kingdom of Jordan), and the accent on moderation is thoroughly Islamic, undercutting the oppositional stance of fundamentalists. No one can characterize either the Saudi or the Moroccan ruling elites as fundamentalist, except at the risk of emptying the term of all explanatory force.

7. See Ann Elizabeth Mayer, "Islamic Resurgence or New Prophethood: The Role of Islam in Qadhdhafi's Ideology," in *Islamic Resurgence in the Arab World*, ed. Ali E. Hilal Dessouki (New York: Praeger, 1982), 214.

8. Raymond A. Hinnebusch, "Charisma, Revolution and State Reformation: Qaddafi and Libya," *The Third World Quarterly* 6 (January 1984): 70.

9. Several scholars have made this observation, but the present quote is taken from Ann Elizabeth Mayer, "Islamic Law and Islamic Revival in Libya" in *Islam in the Contempo-*

rary World, ed. Cyriac K. Pullapilly (Notre Dame, IN: Cross Roads Books, 1980), 304. See also the comprehensive study of Mahmoud Ayoub, *Islam and the Third Universal Theory: The Religious Thought of Muammar Al-Qadhdhafi* (London: Routledge & Kegan Paul, 1987).

10. H. A. R. Gibb seems to have coined the term "Islamic fundamentalism" when referring to al-Afghani, even though he stopped short of calling him a fundamentalist. "His [Jamal ad-din's] influence lives on in the more recent popular movements which combine Islamic fundamentalism with an activist political programme." (*Mohammedanism* [New York: Mentor, 1955], 134). Though the term "Islamic fundamentalist" was seldom used in the fifties or sixties, Gibb's appellation stuck, not only for al-Afghani but for a host of other Muslim activists. Gibb's major conceptual oversight was to interpret fundamentalism as solely a scriptural stance; by its very nature as a holistic ideology it had to encompass "an activist political programme," p. 134.

11. Abbas Alnasrawi provides the vital data as well as anyone. "The [OPEC] doubling of oil prices in October and their redoubling in December came to be known as the oil price revolution. . . . For the OPEC countries as a group, the revenue from oil increased from $13.7 million in 1972 to $87.2 billion in 1974. . . . Over $59 billion, or 81% of the total, went to the countries of the Middle East." See Alnasrawi's "Middle East Oil and Economic Development," in *The Middle East: From Transition to Development,* ed. Sami G. Hajjar (Lerden, Netherlands: E. J. Brill, 1985), 21–22. What came to be known as the second oil price shock occurred as direct result of the Iranian Revolution. By 1977 Middle East oil revenue had climbed to $99 billion per year, but by 1980, due to the the fear of a slowdown in Iranian production, the income of these same countries rose to $215.8 billion. The first reduction in OPEC oil prices did not occur till March 1983, and despite further reductions and efforts at conservation and/ or finding alternative sources in the industrialized countries, the significance of oil production and the oil sector for modernizing economies of the Middle East remains as high as ever.

12. Manning Nash, "Fundamentalist Islam: Reservoir for Turbulence," *Journal of Asian and African Studies* 19 (Spring 1984): 74.

13. Ibid., 78.

14. Ira Lapidus, *Contemporary Islamic Movements in Historical Perspective,* Policy Papers in International Affairs, number 18 (University of California, Berkeley: Institute of International Studies, 1983), 64.

15. Mahmoud M. Ayoub, "Islam Between Ideals and Ideologies," in *The Islamic Impulse,* ed. Barbara F. Stowasser (London: Croom Helm, 1987), 36.

16. Bryan Turner, *Marx and the End of Orientalism* (London: George Allen and Unwin, 1983), 67.

17. Levy, *War,* 47.

18. Enayat, *Modern Islamic,* 111.

19. Gellner, *Nations and Nationalism,* 140.

20. Enayat, 121.

21. The best discussion of this issue is Fadwa El Guindi, "Veiling Infitah with Muslim Ethic: Egypt's Contemporary Islamic Movement," *Social Problems* 28 (April 1981): 472–84. Related assessments are to be found in David Waines, "Through a Veil Darkly: The Study of Women in Muslim Societies," *Comparative Studies in Society and History* 24 (October 1982): 642–59; Susan E. Marshall, "Paradoxes of Change: Culture Crisis, Islamic Revival, and the Reactivation of Patriarchy," *Journal of Asian and African Studies* 19 (Spring 1984): 1–17; and Marilyn R. Waldman, "Tradition as a Modality of Change: Islamic Examples," *History of Religions* 25 (May 1986): 318–46, especially 335–37.

22. The relation of Qur'anic passages concerning women to the subsequent codification of Muslim law is complex. I have hinted at the problems attached to any interpretation of the juridical status of Muslim women in my essay, "Human Rights and Islam," in *Religion and Human Rights,* ed. Irene Bloom, (New York: Columbia University Press, forthcoming).

23. The basic study of *mut'a* is Shahla Haeri, "The Institution of *Mut'a* Marriage in Iran: A Formal and Historical Perspective," in *Women and Revolution in Iran,* ed. Guity Nashat, (Boulder, CO: Westview Press, 1983), 231–51. A brief note on its significance for the Islamic Republic of Iran is set forth by Nahid Yeganeh and Nikki R. Keddie, "Sexuality and Shi'i Social Protest in Iran," in *Shi'ism and Social Protest,* ed. Juan R. I. Cole and Nikki R. Keddie (New Haven and London: Yale University Press, 1986), 115–16.

24. Most of these figures are taken from Richard V. Weekes, *Muslim Peoples: A World Ethnographic Survey* (Westport, CT: Greenwood, 1984), even though the percentage of Muslims for India (12 percent) seems to be lower than is actually the case.

25. John A. Armstrong, *Nations Before Nationalism* (Chapel Hill: University of North Carolina Press, 1982), 9.

26. Crawford Young, *Politics,* 88.

27. As Benedict Anderson explains, "A Sukarno's prestige with traditional Javanese might be all the greater to the extent that he could successfully absorb the symbols of Islam into his regalia. A Natsir could not afford to absorb the symbols of non-Islam, for fear of destroying his influence and authority within his own community." Benedict R. O. G. Anderson, "The Idea of Power in Javanese Culture," in *Culture and Politics in Indonesia,* ed. ClaireHolt (Ithaca, NY: Cornell University Press, 1972) 62.

28. Deliar Noer, "Contemporary Political Dimensions of Islam," in *Islam in Southeast Asia,* ed. M. B. Hooker, (Leiden, Netherlands: E. J. Brill, 1983), 198.

29. Julia D. Howell, "Indonesia: Searching for Consensus," in *Religions and Societies: Asia and the Middle East,* ed. Carlo Caldarola (The Hague: Mouton, 1982), 536.

30. Enayat, *Modern Islamic,* 101.

31. While some have criticized Mawdudi for his obsession with the single goal of being both Muslim and modern (see especially Sheila McDonough, *Muslim Ethics and Modernity* [Waterloo, Ontario: Wilfred Laurier University, 1984] 94–96), others have extolled him for providing the model of a fearless intellectual activist; see, e.g., Khurshid Ahmad and Zafar Ishaq Ansari, "Mawlana Sayyid Abul A'la Mawdudi: An Introduction to His Vision of Islam and Islamic Revival," in the volume that they coedited, *Islamic Perspectives: Studies in Honour of Sayyid Abul A'la Mawdudi* (London: The Islamic Foundation, 1979), 359–83.

32. Enayat, *Modern Islamic,* 102.

33. Quoted in S. Barakat Ahmad, "Maududian Concept," 10.

34. Israr Ahmad, *The Rise and Decline of the Muslim Ummah* (Lahore, Pakistan: Markazi Anjuman Khuddam-ul-Quran, 1980), 36.

35. Enayat, *Modern Islamic,* 110.

36. Hodgson, *The Venture of Islam,* vol. 3, chapter four.

37. Daniel Crecelius, "The Course of Secularization in Modern Egypt," in D. E. Smith, *Religion and Political Modernization,* 89.

38. Harold B. Barclay, "Egypt: Struggling with Secularization," in Caldarola, *Religions and Societies,* 135 (my emphasis).

39. Samir Amin, *The Arab Nation,* trans. Michael Pallis, (London: The Zed Press, 1978), 50–64.

40. See Guenter Lewy, "Nasserism and Islam: A Revolution in Search of Ideology," in D. E. Smith, ed., *Religion and Political Modernization,* 266–74.

41. The critique was voiced by the Syrian Ba'th Party ideologue, Yasin al-Hafiz; it has been quoted and interpreted by Bassam Tibi, *Arab Nationalism: A Critical Enquiry,* ed. and trans. Marion Farouk-Sluglett and Peter Sluglett (New York: St. Martin's Press, 1981), 179.

42. John Waterbury, *Hydropolitics of the Nile Valley* (Syracuse, NY: Syracuse University Press, 1979).

43. Morroe Berger, *Islam in Egypt: Social and Political Aspects of Popular Religion* (Cambridge: Cambridge University Press, 1970), 47; quoted by Crecelius in Smith, *Religion and Political Modernization,* 90. The identification of all Egyptian rulers with the Pharaoh as prototypical monarch-dictator has been explored by Gilles Kepel, *Muslim Extre-*

mism in Egypt: The Prophet and the Pharaoh, trans. Jon Rothschild (Berkeley and Los Angeles: University of California Press, 1986).

44. Crecelius advances the crux of this argument in another article, "Nonideological Responses of the Egyptian Ulama to Modernization" in *Sufis, Saints and Scholars*, ed. Nikki R. Keddie (Berkeley and Los Angeles: University of California Press, 1972), 167–210.

45. I am indebted to data provided by Mustapha Kamel El Sayed in a paper titled "The Islamic Movement in Egypt: Social and Political Implications" and delivered at the Georgetown University Conference, "Egypt 88: Critical Decisions," Washington, DC, 14–15 April 1988.

46. See G. Kepel, *Muslim Extremism in Egypt*, 89–90, for an explanation of the two kinds of migration practiced by Society members, one to furnished flats within poor areas of Cairo, the other to jobs outside Egypt from which they earned income that was sent back into the country.

47. Mitchell, *Society*, 237 allows for five hundred law-specific verses in the Qur'an. Barakat Ahmad, "Maududian Concept," 17, places the number at two hundred. Both are correct, depending on how expansive or restrictive is one's concept of "legal."

48. A similar emphasis on direct access to the Qur'an and the reappropriation of its meaning in modern idiom characterized Mawdudi. His Qur'anic commentary, *Comprehending the Qur'an (Tafhim al-Qur'an)*, was begun in 1942. Completed thirty years later, it extended to six volumes.

49. Mitchell, *Society*, 240–41. Hence, according to the Ikhwan, the gruesome *hadd* punishments for theft and adultery could be validly applied only when a true Muslim society existed. Since no contemporary Sunni Muslim nation met the criteria of an Islamic order, the *hadd* punishments were to remain suspended.

50. 'Abd al-'Aziz Khayyat, Minister of Religious Endowments (*Awqaf*), Jordan. Lecture on "Islamic Norms of Conduct" delivered at Duke University, Durham, NC, October 8, 1982.

51. Mitchell, *Society*, 244.

52. *From Nationalism to Revolutionary Islam*, ed. Said Amir Arjomand (Albany: State University of New York Press, 1984), 228.

53. Sayyid Qutb, *Milestones* [an unattributed English translation of *Ma'alim fit-tariq*] (Cedar Rapids, IA: Unity Publishing, n.d.), 126.

54. Enayat, *Modern Islamic*, 109.

55. Mitchell, *Society*, 376.

56. If Mawdudi is guilty of "pathological polysemy" (Ahmad, "Mawdudian Concept," 17), it is due to his ability to pick up a commonly accepted term like *jihad* and exposit it in a singular direction that seems at once holistic and conclusive even though it, in fact, fits his own predetermined understanding of what the term should mean.

57. Sivan, *Radical Islam*, 103.

58. Rudolph Peters, *Islam and Colonialism: The Doctrine of Jihad in Modern History* (The Hague: Mouton, 1979), 134.

59. Fouad Ajami, "In the Pharaoh's Shadow: Religion and Authority in Egypt," in, Piscatori, *Islam*, 33–34.

60. Peters, *Islam and Colonialism*, 131.

61. Ajami, "Pharaoh's Shadow," 32.

62. Abdallah Laroui, *The Crisis of the Arab Intellectual: Traditionalism or Historicism?* trans. Diarmid Cammell (Berkeley and Los Angeles: University of California Press, 1976), 9–10.

63. Both groups are too little studied in works on Islamic fundamentalism. The exceptions are Michael M. J. Fischer, *Iran: From Religious Dispute to Revolution* (Cambridge: Harvard University Press, 1980, 239–41) but more directly "Islam and the Revolt of the Petite Bourgeoisie," *Daedalus* 3 (Winter 1982): 101–25; Henry Munson, Jr., "Islamic Revivalism in Morocco and Tunisia," *The Muslim World* 76 (July-October 1986): 203–18; and the classic socioeconomic investigation of Sadat's assassins by Saad Eddin

Ibrahim, "Anatomy of Egypt's Militant Groups," *International Journal of Middle Eastern Studies* 12 (1980): 423–53.

64. Enayat, *Modern Islamic*, 117.

65. For the unusual circumstances of Southern Lebanon and a preliminary attempt at their analysis, see Fouad Ajami, *The Vanished Imam: Musa al Sadr and the Shia of Lebanon* (Ithaca, NY: Cornell University Press, 1986).

66. Personal communication with Hasan Hanafi in Cairo in June 1982.

67. Reichley, *Religion*, 28.

68. Gellner, *Nations and Nationalism*, 40.

69. See, e.g., Armstrong, *Nations*, 233–34.

70. Said Amir Arjomand, *The Shadow of God and the Hidden Imam: Religion, Political Order, and Societal Change in Shi'ite Iran from the Beginning to 1890* (Chicago: University of Chicago Press, 1984) evaluates the stages of Iranian Shi'i clerical tenacity and its historical legacy through a modified Weberian analysis.

71. Marsden, *Fundamentalism*, 118–23.

72. Ayatullah (Ayatollah) Murtaza (Morteza) Mutahhari, *Fundamentals of Islamic Thought: God, Man, and the Universe*, trans. R. Campbell (Berkeley, CA: Mizan Press, 1985).

73. Ibid., 19.

74. Ibid., 199.

75. Ibid., 207.

76. On the difference between poetry and prose, see ibid., 183-184. On the non-relatedness of the Genesis account to scientific inquiry, see ibid., 215.

77. Tyson, Ruel Jr., James L. Peacock and Daniel W. Patterson, eds. *Diversities to Gifts: Field Studies in Southern Religion* (Urbana & Chicago: University of Illinois Press, 1988), 12.

78. Derived from Karl Mannheim, *Ideology and Utopia*, the two-wings thesis has been recapitulated and extended by Feuer, *Ideology*, chapter two.

79. I am indebted to Hamid Dabashi for sharing with me his thoughts and also his unpublished essay, "Ideology and Utopia in the Islamic Revolution." See also his article, "Islamic Ideology: Perils and Promises of a Neologism," in Amirahmadi, *Post-Revolutionary Iran*.

80. Mutahhari, *Fundamentals*, 53–54.

81. The most perceptive article on this controversial phrase is provided by Hamid Enayat in Piscatori, *Islam*, chapter nine.

82. Variations on the contrast between Arab and Asian expressions of Islamic identity have been detailed in *Islam in Asia: Religion, Politics, and Society*, ed. John Esposito (New York: Oxford University Press, 1987), especially in the comprehensive concluding essay by James P. Piscatori, 230–61.

83. Enid Hill in "Law Courts in Egypt: Recent Issues and Events" (paper delivered at the symposium, "Egypt '88: Critical Decisions," Georgetown University, Washington, DC 14–15 April 1988) details the constant tug-of-war between Islamic interest groups and the Egyptian courts. The courts triumph through juridical compromise and political nonaction.

CONCLUSION

1. Fernand Braudel, *On History*, trans. Sarah Mathews (Chicago: University of Chicago Press, 1980), 15.

2. Anthony Giddens, *The Nation-State and Violence* (Berkeley and Los Angeles: University of California Press, 1987), 254.

3. For instance, on the continuing mystery of that basic function called human speech, see Steiner, *After Babel*, 293–94.

4. Ibid., 462.

5. Douglas R. Hofstadter, *Metamagical Themas: Questing for the Essence of Mind and Pattern* (New York: Basic Books, 1985), xxv, with minor adaptations to clarify the relatedness of the passage to our argument.

6. John U. Nef, *Conquest*, 312 (my emphasis).
7. John Wilson, "Modernity," in *The Encyclopedia of Religion*, ed. M. Eliade, (New York: MacMillan, 1987), 10:21.
8. See chapter eight, note 12.
9. Blumenberg, *The Legitimacy of the Modern Age*, trans. Robert M. Wallace (Cambridge, MA: MIT Press, 1983), 15.
10. Ibid., 74–75.
11. See James Barr, *Beyond Fundamentalism* (Philadelphia: Westminster Press, 1984), 156 and J. Falwell, *The Fundamentalist Phenomenon*, 221–23.
12. See Umar F. Abdallah, *Islamic Struggle*, 26 (my emphasis).
13. The landmark article remains Carl Pletsch, "The Three Worlds," 565–90.
14. In addition to Saad Eddin Ibrahim, "Anatomy," see the extensive study of the Jihad group by Nemat Guenena, "The 'Jihad:' An 'Islamic Alternative' in Egypt," *Cairo Papers in Social Science* 9, monograph 2 (Summer 1986). In Appendix IV (pp. 94-99), she details the professional, often science-related background of those who participated in the movement to purge Sadat. I am indebted to Emmanuel Sivan for reference to this monograph, and to Daniel Brumberg for having provided the actual text.
15. The peculiar constellation of economic forces in Iran is exposed in the insightful but complex article of Homa Katouzian, "The Aridisolatic Society: A Model of Long-term Social and Economic Development in Iran," *International Journal of Middle East Studies* 15 (May 1983): 259–81. For the comparative data from before and after the 1979 revolution, consult Shahrough Akhavi, "Elite Factionalism in the Islamic Republic of Iran," *Middle East Journal* 41 (Spring 1987): 199, and with reference to continuing gender asymmetry in the public sphere, see Val Moghadam, "Women, Work, and Ideology in the Islamic Republic [of Iran]," *International Journal of Middle East Studies* 20 (Fall 1988): 221–43.
16. Ajami, "Pharaoh's Shadow," 34.
17. Mohamed Arkoun, *Rethinking Islam Today*, Occasional Papers Series, Center for Contemporary Arab Studies, (Washington, DC: Georgetown University, 1987), 23.
18. Ibid., 19.
19. Kuhn, quoting Max Planck, in *Structure*, 151.
20. Laroui, *Crisis*, 6 (my emphasis).
21. In addition to Haan, *Social Science*, note the provocative initial three essays in Michelle Rosaldo and Louise Lamphere, eds., *Women, Culture, and Society* (Stanford CA: Stanford University Press, 1974) and also Caroline MacCormack, *Nature, Culture, and Gender* (Cambridge: Cambridge University Press, 1983).
22. Rorty, *Consequences*, 208.
23. See Flo Conway and Jim Siegelman, *Holy Terror: The Fundamentalist War on America's Freedoms in Religion, Politics, and Our Private Lives* (New York: Doubleday, 1982).
24. Wallace Stevens, "Flyer's Fall," cited from *The Mentor Book of Major American Poets* ed. Oscar Williams and Edwin Honig (New York: New American Library, 1962), 286.

Selected Bibliography

Abdallah, Umar F. *The Islamic Struggle in Syria.* Berkeley, CA: Mizan Press, 1983.

Adams, Charles. "The Ideology of Mawlana Mawdudi." In *South Asian Politics and Religion,* edited by Donald E. Smith, 371–97. Princeton, NJ: Princeton University Press, 1966.

Adas, Michael. *Prophets of Rebellion: Millenarian Protest Movements Against the European Colonial Order.* Chapel Hill, NC: University of North Carolina Press, 1979.

Adorno, T. W. et al. *The Authoritarian Personality.* New York: Harper & Row, 1950.

Ahmad, S. Barakat. "Maududian Concept of Islamic State," *Islam and the Modern Age* 14 (November 1983): 10–17.

Ahmad, Israr. *Rise and Decline of the Muslim Ummah.* Lahore, Pakistan: Markazi Anjuman Khudddam al-Quran, 1980.

Ahmad, Khurshid, and Zafar Ishaq Ansari, eds. *Islamic Perspectives: Studies in Honour of Sayyid Abul A'la Mawdudi.* London: The Islamic Foundation, 1979.

Aiken, Henry D., ed. *The Age of Ideology: The 19th Century Philosophers.* Mentor, 1956.

Ajami, Fouad. *The Arab Predicament: Arab Political Thought and Practice Since 1967.* Cambridge: Cambridge University Press, 1981.

———. *The Vanished Imam: Musa al Sadr and the Shia of Lebanon.* Ithaca, NY: Cornell University Press, 1986.

Akhavi, Shahrough. "Elite Fationalism in the Islamic Republic of Iran." *Middle East Journal* 41 (Spring 1979): 184–207.

Alnasrawi, Abbas. "Middle East Oil and Economic Development." In *The Middle East: From Transition to Development,* edited by Sami G. Hajjar, 16–34. Leiden, Netherlands: E. J. Brill, 1985.

Amin, Samir. *The Arab Nation.* Translated by Michael Pallis. London: The Zed Press, 1978.

Amirahmadi, Hooshang and Manoucher Parvin, eds. *Post-Revolutionary Iran.* New York: Westview Press, 1987.

Anderson, Benedict R. O. G. "The Idea of Power in Javanese Culture." In *Culture and Politics in Indonesia,* edited by Claire Holt, 10-75. Ithaca: Cornell University Press, 1972.

Anderson, Perry. "Modernity and Revolution." *In Marxism and the Interpretation of Culture*, edited by Cary Nelson and Lawrence Grossberg, 317–38. Urbana and Chicago: University of Illinois Press, 1988.

Antoun, Richard T., and Mary E. Hegland, eds. *Religious Resurgence: Contemporary Cases in Islam, Christianity and Judaism*. Syracuse, N.Y.: Syracuse University Press, 1987.

Apel, Karl-Otto. *Understanding and Explanation: A Transcendental-Pragmatic Perspective*. Translated by Georgia Warnke. Cambridge: MIT Press, 1984.

Aran, Gideon. "The Roots of Gush Emunim." In *Studies in Contemporary Jewry*, edited by Peter Y. Medding, 2:116–43.

———. "Redemption as a Catastrophe: The Gospel of Gush Emunim." In *Religious Extremism and Politics in the Middle East*, edited by Emmanuel Sivan and Menachem Friedman, forthcoming.

Arjomand, Said Amir, ed. *From Nationalism to Revolutionary Islam*. Albany: State University of New York Press, 1984.

———. *The Shadow of God and the Hidden Imam: Religion, Political Order, and Societal Change in Shi'ite Iran from the Beginning to 1890*. Chicago: University of Chicago Press, 1984.

Arkoun, Mohamed. *Rethinking Islam Today*. Occasional Papers Series, Center for Contemporary Arab Studies. Washington, DC: Georgetown University, 1987.

Armstrong, John A. *Nations Before Nationalism*. Chapel Hill: University of North Carolina Press, 1958.

Aviad, Janet. *Return to Judaism: Religious Renewal in Israel*. Chicago: University of Chicago Press, 1983.

———. "The Contemporary Israeli Pursuit of the Millennium." *Religion* 14 (July 1984): 199–222.

Ayoub, Mahmoud M. "Islam Between Ideals and Ideologies." In *The Islamic Impulse*, edited by Barbara F. Stowasser, 297–319.

———. *Islam and the Third Universal Theory: The Religious Thought of Muammar al-Qadhdhafi*. London: Routledge & Kegan Paul, 1987.

Barr, James. *Biblical Words for Time*. London: SCM Press, 1962.

———. *Fundamentalism*. Philadelphia: Westminster Press, 1978.

———. *Beyond Fundamentalism*. Philadelphia: Westminster Press, 1984.

Barraclough, Geoffrey. *An Introduction to Contemporary History*. Hammondsworth Great Britain: Penguin, 1967.

———. *The Times Atlas of World History* (Maplewood, NJ: Hammond, 1982).

Bellah, Robert. Introduction to *Religion and America: Spirituality in a Secular Age*, edited by Mary Douglas and Steven M. Tipton. Boston: Beacon Press, 1982.

———, with Phillip E. Hammond, eds. *Varieties of Civil Religion*. San Francisco: Harper & Row, 1980.

Bendix, Reinhard. *Max Weber: An Intellectual Portrait*. London: Methuen and Co., 1982.

———, with Guenther Roth, eds. *Scholarship and Partnership: Essays on Weber*. Berkeley and Los Angeles: University of California Press, 1978.

Berger, Morroe. *Islam in Egypt: Social and Political Aspects of Popular Religion*. Cambridge: Cambridge University Press, 1970.

Berger, Peter L. *The Heretical Imperative: Contemporary Possibilities of Religious Affirmation.* Garden City, NY: Doubleday/Anchor, 1979.

——. *The Sacred Canopy: Elements of a Sociological Theory of Religion.* Garden City, NY: Doubleday/Anchor, 1969.

Berlin, Isaiah, ed. *The Age of Enlightenment: The 18th Century Philosophers.* New York: Mentor, 1956.

Berman, Marshall. *All That Is Solid Melts Into Air: The Experience of Modernity.* New York: Simon and Schuster, 1982.

Bloch, Marc. *The Historian's Craft.* Translated by Peter Putnam. New York: Vintage, 1953.

Blumenberg, Hans. *The Legitimacy of the Modern Age.* Translated by Robert M. Wallace. Cambridge, MA: MIT Press, 1983.

Boon, James A. *Other Tribes, Other Scribes: Symbolic Anthropology in the Comparative Study of Cultures, Histories, Religions, and Texts.* Cambridge: Cambridge University Press, 1982.

Bourne, Edmund. See Shweder, Richard.

Bowler, Peter J. *Evolution: The History of an Idea.* Berkeley and Los Angeles: University of California Press, 1984.

Bozeman, Theodore Dwight. *Protestants in an Age of Science: The Baconian Ideal and Antebellum American Religious Thought.* Chapel Hill: University of North Carolina Press, 1977.

Bracher, Karl Dietrich. *The Age of Ideologies.* Translated by Ewald Osers. New York: St. Martin's Press, 1982.

Brass, Paul R. "Ethnic Communities in the Modern State." In *Identity and Division in Cults and Sects in South Asia,* edited by Peter Gaefke and David A. Utz, pp. 12–19. Philadelphia: Department of South Asia Regional Studies, University of Pennsylvania, 1984.

Braudel, Fernand. *Civilization and Capitalism.* 3 vols. Translated by Sian Reynolds. New York: Harper & Row, 1981–84.

——. *On History.* Translated by Sarah Matthews. Chicago: University of Chicago Press, 1980.

Brenner, Louis. *West African Sufi: The Spiritual Heritage of Cerno Bokar Saalif Taal.* Berkeley and Los Angeles: University of California Press, 1985.

Brown, S.C., ed. *Philosophical Disputes in the Social Sciences.* Atlantic Highlands, NJ: Humanities Press, 1977.

Bruce, Stephen. "The Moral Majority: The Politics of Fundamentalism in Secular Society." In *Studies in Religious Fundamentalism,* edited by Lionel Caplan, 177–94.

Bullock, Alan, and R. B. Woodings, eds. *20th Century Culture: A Biographical Companion.* New York: Harper & Row, 1983.

Caldarola, Carlo, ed. *Religions and Societies: Asia and the Middle East.* The Hague: Mouton, 1982.

Caplan, Lionel, ed. *Studies in Religious Fundamentalism.* Albany: State University of New York Press, 1987.

Cassirer, Ernest. *The Philosophy of the Enlightenment.* Princeton: Princeton University Press, 1951.

Chadwick, Owen. *The Secularization of the European Mind in the Nineteenth Century.* Cambridge: Cambridge University Press, 1975.

Clebsch, William. *Christianity in European History.* Oxford: Oxford University Press, 1979.

Cole, Juan R. I., and Nikki R. Keddie, eds. *Shi'ism and Social Protest.* New Haven and London: Yale University Press, 1986.

Cox, Harvey. "Understanding Islam: No More Holy Wars." *The Atlantic Monthly,* January 1981, 73–80.

Cragg, Kenneth. *The House of Islam.* Belmont, CA: Wadsworth, 1976.

Dan, Joseph. "Hasidism." In *The Encyclopedia of Religion,* edited by M. Eliade, 6:203–10. New York: Macmillan, 1987.

Darwish, Adeed, ed. *Islam in Foreign Policy.* Cambridge: Cambridge University Press, 1983.

Davies, Paul. *God and the New Physics.* New York: Simon and Schuster, 1983.

Dekmejian, R. Hrair. *Islam in Revolution: Fundamentalism in the Arab World.* (Syracuse, NY: Syracuse University Press, 1985).

Derr, Thomas S. "The First Amendment as a Guide to Church-State Relations." In *Church, State, and Politics,* edited by A. E. Dick Howard, J. W. Baker and T. S. Derr, Washington, DC: Roscoe Pound American Trial Lawyers' Foundation, 1981).

Devereux, George. *From Anxiety to Method in the Behavioral Sciences.* Paris: Mouton, The Hague, 1976.

Dietrich, Angela. "The *Khalsa* Resurrected: Sikh Fundamentalism in the Punjab." In *Studies in Religious Fundamentalism,* edited by Lionel Caplan, 122–37.

Dollar, George W. *A History of Fundamentalism in America.* Greenville, SC: Bob Jones University, 1973.

Douglas, Mary, and Steven M. Tipton, eds. *Religion and America: Spirituality in a Secular Age.* Boston: Beacon Press, 1983.

Dubnow, Simon. *Geschichte des Chassidismus.* 2 vols. Translated by A. Steinberg. Berlin: Judischer Verlag, 1931.

Durkheim, Emile. *The Elementary Forms of the Religious Life.* 1915. Reprint. New York: Macmillan, 1965.

Eisenstadt, S. N. *Tradition, Change, and Modernity.* New York: John Wiley and Sons, 1973.

———, ed. *Patterns of Modernity.* New York: New York University Press, 1987.

El Guindi, Fadwa. "Veiling Infitah with Muslim Ethic: Egypt's Contemporary Islamic Movement." *Social Problems* 28 (April 1981): 472–84.

Elshtain, Jean Bethke. "On Patriotism." Chancellor's Lecture, University of Massachusetts, Amherst, 18 October 1984.

Enayat, Hamid. *Modern Islamic Political Thought.* London: Macmillan Press, 1982.

Falk, Richard A. *This Endangered Planet: Prospects and Proposals for Human Survival.* New York: Random House, 1972.

Falwell, Jerry, ed. *The Fundamentalist Phenomenon: The Resurgence of Conservative Christianity.* New York: Doubleday, 1981.

Feuer, Lewis S. *Ideology and the Ideologists.* New York: Harper & Row, 1975.

Fischer, Michael M. J. *Iran: From Religious Dispute to Revolution.* Cambridge: Harvard University Press, 1980.

———. "Islam and the Revolt of the Petite Bourgeoisie." *Daedalus* 3 (Winter 1982): 101–25.

Foucault, Michel. *The Order of Things: An Archaeology of the Human Sciences.* Eng. trans. of *Les mots et les choses.* New York: Vintage Books, 1973.

Frederich, Carl J. *Man and His Government.* New York: McGraw-Hill, 1967.

Fremantle, Anne, ed. *Medieval Philosophers: the Age of Belief.* New York: Mentor, 1954.

Friedman, Menachem. "The Changing Role of the Community Rabbinate." *The Jerusalem Quarterly* 25 (Fall 1982): 79–99.

———. "Haredim Confront the Modern City." in *Studies in Contemporary Jewry,* edited by Peter J. Medding, 2:74–96.

———. "Jewish Zealots: Conservatism vs. Innovation." In *Religious Extremism,* edited by Menachem Friedman and Emmanuel Sivan forthcoming.

———. "Life-Tradition and Book Tradition in the Development of Ultra-Orthodox Judaism." In Harvey E. Goldberg, ed. *Judaism Viewed From Within and From Without: Anthropological Studies* (Albany: State University of New York Press, 1987), 90–114.

———. "Religious Zealotry in Israeli Society." In *On Ethnic and Religious Diversity in Israel,* edited by Solomon Poll and Ernest Krausz, 91–111. Ramat-Gan, Israel: Bar-Ilan University, 1975.

———. *Society and Religion: The Non-Zionist Orthodox in Eretz Yisrael, 1918–1936.* Jerusalem: Yad Izhak Ben-Zvi Publications, 1977.

———. "The State of Israel as a Theological Dilemma." In *The Israeli State and Society: Boundaries and Frontiers,* edited by Baruch Kimmerling, 169–219. Albany: State University of New York Press, 1988.

———, and Emmanuel Sivan, eds., *Religious Extremism and Politics in the Middle East* Albany: State University of New York Press, forthcoming.

Fromm, Erich. *Marx's Concept of Man.* London: Ungar, 1935.

Frye, Northrup. *The Great Code: The Bible and Literature.* New York: Harcourt Brace and Jovanovich, 1982.

Gadamer, Hans-George. *Reason and the Age of Science.* Translated by Frederick Lawrence. Cambridge: MIT Press, 1983.

Geertz, Clifford. *The Interpretation of Cultures.* New York: Basic Books, 1973.

———. *Local Knowledge.* New York: Basic Books, 1982.

Gellner, Ernest. *Nations and Nationalism.* Ithaca, New York: Cornell University Press, 1983.

Gibb, Hamilton A. R. *Modern Trends in Islam.* Chicago: University of Chicago Press, 1946.

———. *Mohammedanism: An Historical Survey.* New York: Mentor, 1949 reprinted in 1955.

Giddens, Anthony. *The Nation-State and Violence.* Berkeley and Los Angeles: University of California Press, 1987.

Gillespie, Neal C. *Charles Darwin and the Problem of Creation.* Chicago and London: University of Chicago Press, 1979.

Goldman, Eliezer. "Responses to Modernity in Orthodox Jewish Thought." In *Studies in Contemporary Jewry,* edited by Peter Y. Medding, 2. 52–73.

Gould, Stephen Jay. "Between You and Your Genes." Review of *Not in Our Genes,* edited by R. C. Lewontin et al. *New York Review of Books,* 16 August 1984, 30.

Gouldner, Alvin W. *The Dialectic of Ideology and Technology.* New York: Seabury Press, 1976.

Gran, P. "Political Economy as a Paradigm for the Study of Islamic History." *International Journal of Middle East Studies* 11 (July 1980): 511–526.

Guenena, Nemat. "The 'Jihad:' An 'Islamic Alternative' in Egypt." *Cairo Papers in Social Science* 9 (Summer 1986).

Gutting, Gary, ed. *Paradigms and Revolutions: Appraisals and Applications of Thomas Kuhn's Philosophy of Science.* Notre Dame, IN: Notre Dame University Press, 1980).

Haan, Norma et al., eds. *Social Science As Moral Inquiry.* New York: Columbia University Press, 1983.

Habermas, Jürgen. *Toward a Rational Society.* Translated by Jeremy J. Shapiro. Boston: Beacon Press, 1970.

Haeri, Shahla,"The Institution of *Mut'a* Marriage in Iran: A Formal and Historical Perspective," In *Women and Revolution in Iran,* edited by Guity Nashat, 231–51.

Hajjar, Sami G., ed. *The Middle East: From Transition to Development.* Leiden, Netherlands: E. J Brill, 1985.

Hammond, Phillip E., ed. *The Sacred in a Secular Age: Toward Revision in the Scientific Study of Religion.* Berkeley and Los Angeles: University of California Press, 1985.

Hampshire, Stuart, ed. *The Age of Reason: 17th Century Philosophers.* New York: Mentor, 1956.

Hargrove, Barbara. *The Sociology of Religion: Classical and Contemporary Approaches.* Arlington Heights, IL: AHM Publishing Corporation, 1979.

Harris, Marvin. *Cultural Materialism: The Struggle for a Science of Culture.* New York: Random House, 1976.

Harrison, Edward. *Masks of the Universe.* New York: Macmillan, 1985.

Harvey, Van A. and Marie Augusta Neal. "Peter Berger: Retrospect." *Religious Studies Review* 5 (January 1979): 1–7.

Hatch, Nathan O., and Mark A. Noll. *The Bible in America: Essays in Cultural History.* New York: Oxford University Press, 1982.

Hernadi, Paul. *The Horizon of Literature.* Lincoln and London: University of Nebraska Press, 1982.

Hill, Michael. *A Sociology of Religion.* London: Heinemann Educational Books, 1973.

Hinnebusch, Raymond A. "Charisma, Revolution, and State Formation: Qaddafi and Libya," *The Third World Quarterly* 6 (January 1984): 59–73.

Hobsbawm, E. J. *The Age of Revolution, 1789–1848.* New York: Mentor, 1962.

Hodgson, Marshall G. S. *The Venture of Islam: Conscience and History in a World Civilization* 3 vols. Chicago: University of Chicago Press, 1979.

Hofstadter, Douglas R. *Metamagical Themas: Questing for the Essence of Mind and Pattern.* New York: Basic Books, 1985.

Hofstadter, Richard *Anti-Intellectualism in American Life.* New York: Knopf, 1966.

———. *Social Darwinism in American Thought.* 1944. Reprint. Boston: Beacon Press, 1959.

Honigmann, John J. *The Development of Anthropological Ideas.* Homewood, IL: The Dorsey Press, 1976.

Hooker, M. B., ed. *Islam in Southeast Asia.* Leiden, Netherlands: E. J. Brill, 1983.

Horowitz, Dan, and Moshe Lissak. *Origins of the Israeli Polity: Palestine under the Mandate.* Chicago and London: University of Chicago Press, 1978.

Hull, David L. *Darwin and His Critics: The Reception of Darwin's Theory of Evolution by the Scientific Community.* Cambridge: Harvard University Press, 1973.

Humphreys, R. Stephen. "Islam and Political Values in Saudi Arabia, Egypt and Syria." *Middle East Journal* 33 (Winter 1979): 1–19.

Hutchinson, William R. *The Modernist Impulse in American Protestantism.* Cambridge: Harvard University Press, 1976.

Ibrahim, Saad Eddin. "Anatomy of Egypt's Militant Groups." *International Journal of Middle Eastern Studies* 12 (December 1980): 423–53.

Jacobs, Louis. *Hasidic Prayer.* New York: Schocken, 1973.

Jakobsen, Roman, with M. Halle. *Fundamentals of Language.* The Hague: Mouton, 1966.

Jameson, Fredric. "Theories of Ideologies." Class handout for Duke University course on "Marx and Freud," Comparative Literature 281, Spring 1986.

Jansen, Johannes J. G. *The Neglected Duty: The Creed of Sadat's Assassins and Islamic Resurgence in the Middle East.* New York: Macmillan, 1986.

Jaspers, Karl. *Origin and Goal of History.* Translated by Michael Bullock. London: Routledge & Kegan Paul, 1953.

———. *Truth and Symbol.* Translated by Jean T. Wilde, William Kluback, and William Kimmel. New York: Twayne, 1959.

Kantzer, K. S. "Unity and Diversity in Evangelical Faith." In *The Evangelicals,* edited by David F. Wells and John D. Woodbridge, 65–78. Grand Rapids, MI: Baker, 1977.

Katouzian, Homa. "The Aridisolatic Society: A Model of Long-Term Social and Economic Development in Iran." *International Journal of Middle East Studies* 15 (May 1983): 259–81.

Katz, Jacob. "Gush Emunim in the Light of Jewish Messianic Tradition." In *Religious Extremism,* edited by Menachem Friedman and Emmanuel Sivan.

———. "Orthodoxy in Historical Perspective." In *Studies in Contemporary Jewry,* edited by Peter Y. Medding, 2:3–17.

———. *Tradition and Crisis: Jewish Society at the End of the Middle Ages.* New York: The Free Press, 1961.

Keddie, Nikki R., ed. *Sufis, Saints, and Scholars.* Berkeley and Los Angeles: University of California Press, 1972.

Kepel, Gilles. *Muslim Extremism in Egypt: The Prophet and the Pharaoh.* Translated by Jon Rothschild. Berkeley and Los Angeles: University of California Press, 1986.

Kitcher, Philip. *Abusing Science: The Case Against Creationism.* Cambridge: MIT Press, 1982.

Kliever, Lonnie O., ed. *The Terrible Meek: Essays on Religion and Revolution.* New York: Paragon Press, 1987.

Kline, Morris. *Mathematics in Western Culture.* New York: Oxford University Press, 1953.

Kook, Abraham Isaac. *The Lights of Penitence, the Moral Principles, Lights of Holiness, Essays, Letters, and Poems.* Translated by Ben Zion Bokser. New York: Paulist Press, 1978.

Kritzeck, James. *Sons of Abraham: Jews, Christians, and Moslems.* Baltimore: Helicon, 1965.

Kuhn, Thomas S. *The Structure of Scientific Revolutions.* Chicago: University of Chicago Press, 1962.

Lapidus, Ira. *Contemporary Islamic Movements in Historical Perspective.* Papers in International Affairs, no. 18. Berkeley: Institute of International Affairs, University of California, 1983.

Larain, Jorge. *The Concept of Ideology.* Athens: University of Georgia Press, 1979.

Laroui, Abdallah. *The Crisis of the Arab Intellectual: Traditionalism or Historicism?* Translated by Diarmid Cammell. Berkeley and Los Angeles: University of California Press, 1976.

Lawrence, Bruce B. "The Fundamentalist Response to Islam's Decline: A View from the Asian Periphery." In *Islam in the Modern World: 1983 Paine Lectures in Religion,* edited by Jill Raitt, 11–40. Columbia, MO: University of Missouri, 1983.

———. "Muslim Fundamentalist Movements: Reflections Toward a New Approach." In *The Islamic Impulse,* Barbara F. Stowasser, 15–36. London: Croom Helm, 1987.

———. "Religion, Ideology, and Revolution: The Case of Post-1979 Iran." In *The Terrible Meek,* edited by L. D. Kliever, 60–92. New York: Paragon Press, 1987.

———, ed. *The Rose and the Rock: Mystical and Rational Elements in the Intellectual History of South Asian Islam.* Durham, NC: Duke University South Asia Program, 1979.

Leach, Edmund. *Levi-Strauss.* Glasgow: Fontana/Collins, 1974.

Levy, Jack S. *War in the Modern Great Power System, 1945–1975.* Lexington, University of Kentucky Press, 1983.

Lewontin, R. C. "Bourgeois Ideology and the Origin of Determinism." In *Not in our Genes: Biology, Ideology, and Human Nature,* R. C. Lewontin, Steven Rose, and Leon J. Kamin, 48-72. New York: Pantheon, 1984.

Lewy, Guenter. "Nasserism and Islam: A Revolution in Search of Ideology." In *Religion and Political Modernization,* edited by D. E. Smith 266–74.

Liebman, Charles S. "Extremism as a Religious Norm." *Journal for the Scientific Study of Religion* 22 (Spring 1983) 75–86.

Liebman, Charles S., and Eliezer Don-Yehiya. *Civil Religion in Israel.* Berkeley and Los Angeles: University of California Press, 1983.

Liebman, Robert C. and Robert Wuthnow, eds. *The New Christian Right: Mobilization and Legitimation.* New York: Aldine Publishing Company, 1983.

Lindsey, Hal. *The Late Great Planet Earth.* New York: Bantam, 1981.

Lorenzen, David N. *Religious Change and Cultural Domination.* Mexico City: El Colegio de Mexico, 1981.

Löwith, Karl. *Meaning in History.* Chicago: University of Chicago Press, 1949.

Luckmann, Thomas. "Theories about Religion and Social Change," *Annual Review of the Social Sciences of Religion* 1 (Spring 1977): 1–27.

Lustick, Ian S. *For the Land and the Lord: Jewish Fundamentalism in Israel.* New York: Council on Foreign Relations, 1988.

MacCormack, Caroline. *Nature, Culture, and Gender.* Cambridge: Cambridge University Press, 1983.

Major-Poetzl. P. *Michel Foucault's Archaeology of Western Culture.* Chapel Hill: University of North Carolina Press, 1983.

Mannheim, Karl. *Ideology and Utopia.* Translated by Louis Wirth and Edward Shils. New York: Harcourt Brace and Jovanovich, 1936.

Manuel, Frank, ed. *The Changing of the Gods.* Hanover, NH: University Press of New England, 1983.

———. *The Enlightenment.* Englewood Cliffs, NJ: Prentice-Hall, 1965.

Marmorstein, Emile. *Heaven at Bay: The Jewish Kulturkampf in the Holy Land.* London: Oxford University Press, 1969.

Marsden, George M. *Fundamentalism and American Culture: The Shaping of Twentieth-Century Evangelicalism, 1870–1925.* New York: Oxford University Press, 1980.

Marshall, Susan E. "Paradoxes of Change: Culture Crisis, Islamic Revival, and the Reactivation of Patriarchy." *Journal of Asian and African Studies* 19 (January 1984): 1–17.

Martin, David. *A General Theory of Secularization.* New York: Harper & Row, 1978.

May, Henry F. *Ideas, Faiths, and Feelings: Essays on American Intellectual and Religious History, 1952–1982.* New York: Oxford University Press, 1983.

McDonough, Sheila. *Muslim Ethics and Modernity.* Waterloo: Ontario Wilfred Laurier University Press, 1984.

McLoughlin, William. *Revivals, Awakenings, and Reforms.* Chicago: University of Chicago Press, 1978.

McMullin, Ernan, ed. *Evolution and Creation.* Notre Dame, IN: University of Notre Dame Press, 1985.

McNeill, William H. *The Great Frontier: Freedom and Hierarchy in Modern Times.* Princeton: Princeton University Press, 1983.

———. *The Pursuit of Power: Technology, Armed Forces, and Society.* Chicago: University of Chicago Press, 1982.

———. *The Rise of the West: A History of the Human Community.* Chicago: University of Chicago Press, 1963.

———. *The Shape of European History.* New York: Oxford University Press, 1974.

Medding, Peter Y., ed. *Studies in Contemporary Jewry.* Bloomington: Indiana University Press, 1986.

Megill, Allan. *Prophets of Extremity: Nietzsche, Heidegger, Foucault, Derrida.* Berkeley and Los Angeles: University of California Press, 1985.

Mendes-Flor, Paul R. "Rosenzweig and Kant: Two Views of Ritual and Religion." In *Mystics, Philosophers, and Politicians: Essays in Jewish Intellectual History in Honor of Alexander Altman,* edited by J. Reinharz and C. Swetschinski with K.P. Bland, 315–41. Durham, NC: Duke University Press, 1982.

Michaelson, Robert S. *The American Search for Soul.* Baton Rouge: Louisiana State University Press, 1975.

Midgley, Mary. *Evolution as a Religion.* London and New York: Methuen, 1958.

Minault, Gail. *The Khilafat Movement.* New York: Columbia University Press, 1982.

Mintz, Jerome R. *Legends of the Hasidim.* Chicago: University of Chicago Press, 1968.

Mitchell, Richard P. "The Islamic Movement: Its Current Condition and Future Prospects." In *The Islamic Impulse,* edited by Barbara Stowasser, 75–86.

———. *The Society of Muslim Brothers.* New York: Oxford University Press, 1969.

Moghadam, Val. "Women, Work, and Ideology in the Islamic Republic [of Iran]." *International Journal of Middle East Studies* 20 (1988): 221–43.

Momen, Moojan. *An Introduction to Shi'i Islam: The History and Doctrines of Twelver Shi'ism.* New Haven and London: Yale University Press, 1985.

Moore, Barrington, Jr. *Reflections on the Causes of Human Misery.* Boston: Beacon Press, 1972.

———. *Social Origins of Dictatorship and Democracy.* Boston: Beacon Press, 1958.

Morris, Henry M. *The Remarkable Birth of Planet Earth.* San Diego, CA: CLP Publishers, 1976.

———. *The Scientific Case for Creation.* San Diego, CA: CLP Publishers, 1977.

———. *The Troubled Waters of Evolution.* San Diego, CA: CLP Publishers, 1975.

Munson, Henry, Jr. *The House of Si Abd Allah: The Oral History of a Moroccan Family.* New Haven: Yale University Press, 1984.

———. "Islamic Revivalism in Morocco and Tunisia." *The Muslim World* 76 (July/October 1986): 203–18.

———. *Islam and Revolution in the Middle East.* New Haven and London: Yale University Press, 1988.

Mutahhari, Morteza. *Fundamentals of Islamic Thought: God, Man, and the Universe.* Translated R. Campbell. Berkeley, CA: Mizan Press, 1985.

———. *Jihad: The Holy War of Islam and Its Legitimacy in the Quran.* Translated by Mohammad Salman Tawheedi. Albany, CA: Moslem Student Association [Persian Speaking Group], n.d.

Nash, Manning. "Fundamentalist Islam: Reservoir for Turbulence." *Journal of Asian and African Studies* 19 (Spring 1984): 73–78.

Nashat, Guity, ed. *Women and Revolution in Iran.* Boulder, CO: Westview Press, 1983.

Needham, Joseph. *Science and Civilization in China.* Cambridge: Cambridge University Press, 1954.

Needham, Rodney. *Belief, Language, and Experience.* Chicago: University of Chicago Press, 1972.

Nef, John U. *The Conquest of the Material World.* Chicago: University of Chigaco Press, 1958.

———. *The Cultural Foundations of Industrial Civilization.* Cambridge: Cambridge University Press, 1958.

Neusner, Jacob. *The Way of Torah: An Introduction to Judaism.* Belmont, CA: Dickenson, 1970.

Newman, David "Gush Emunim between Fundamentalism and Pragmatism." *The Jerusalem Quarterly* 39 (Spring 1986): 33–43.

———, ed. *The Impact of Gush Emunim.* New York: St. Martin's Press, 1985.

Norris, R. B. *God, Marx, and the Future: Dialogue with Roger Garaudy.* Philadelphia: Fortress Press, 1979.

Olson, Richard. *Science Deified and Science Defied: The Historical Significance of Science in Western Culture.* Berkeley and Los Angeles: University of California Press, 1982.

Osgood, Charles E., William H. May, and Murray S. Miron. *Cross-cultural Universals of Affective Meaning.* Urbana: University of Illinois Press, 1975.

Parsons, Talcott. *The Social System.* New York: The Free Press, 1951.

Peacocke, A. R. *Creation and the World of Science.* Oxford: Oxford University Press, 1979.

Peirce, Charles. *Scientific Metaphysics.* Cambridge: Harvard University Press, 1935.

Piscatori, James P., ed. *Islam in the Political Process.* Cambridge: Cambridge University Press, 1983.

———, "Asian Islam: International Linkages and Their Impact on International Relations." In *Islam in Asia: Religion, Politics and Society,* edited by John L. Esposito, 230–61. New York: Oxford University Press, 1978.

Pletsch, Carl E. "The Three Worlds, or the Division of Social Scientific Labor, circa 1950–1975." *Comparative Studies in Society and History* 23 (October 1981): 565–90.

Pullapilly, Cyriac K., ed. *Islam in the Contemporary World.* Notre Dame, IN: Cross Roads Books, 1980.

Ravitzky, Aviezer. "Religion and Politics in Contemporary Jewish Thought." In *Religious Extremism,* edited by Menachem Friedman and Emmanuel Sivan.

———. "Roots of Kahanism: Consciousness and Political Reality." *The Jerusalem Quarterly* 39 (Spring) 1986: 90–108.

Reichley, A. James. *Religion in American Public Life.* Washington, DC: The Brookings Institution, 1985.

Ricoeur, Paul. *Hermeneutics and the Human Sciences.* Edited and translated by John B. Thompson. Cambridge: Cambridge University Press, 1981.

———. *Lectures on Ideology and Utopia.* Edited by George H. Taylor. New York: Columbia University Press, 1986.

Rieff, Phillip. *Freud: The Mind of the Moralist.* Garden City, New York: Doubleday, 1961.

Robertson, Roland, ed. *Sociology of Religion.* New York: Penguin, 1969.

Robinson, Francis. "Islam and Muslim Separatism." 26–39. In *Political Identity in South Asia,* edited by David Taylor and Malcolm Yapp, London: Curzon, 1979.

Rokeach, Milton. *The Open and Closed Mind: Investigations into the Nature of Belief Systems and Personality Systems.* New York: Basic Books, 1960.

Rorty, Richard. *Consequences of Pragmatism (Essays: 1972–1980).* Minneapolis: University of Minnesota Press, 1982.

Rosaldo, Michelle, and Louise Lamphere, eds. *Women, Culture, and Society.* Stanford, CA: Stanford University Press, 1974.

Rosenbaum, Jonathan. "Judaism: Torah and Tradition." In *The Holy Book in Comparative Perspective,* edited by Fredrick M. Denny and Rodney L. Taylor, 10–35. Columbia: University of South Carolina Press, 1985.

Rosenthal, E. I. J. *Islam in the Modern Nation-State.* Cambridge: Cambridge University Press, 1965.

Rubinstein, Amnon. *The Zionist Dream Revisited: From Herzl to Gush Emunim and Back.* New York: Schocken, 1984.

Ruse, Michael. *Darwinism Defended: A Guide to the Evolution Controversies.* Menlo Park, CA: Benjamin/Cummings Publishing Co., 1982.

Russell, C. Allyn. *Voices of American Fundamentalism: Seven Biographical Studies.* Philadelphia: Westminster Press, 1976.

Sahlins, Marshall D. *The Use and Abuse of Biology: An Anthropological Critique of Sociobiology.* Ann Arbor: University of Michigan Press, 1976.

Samay, Sebastian. *Reason Revisited: The Philosophy of Karl Jaspers.* Notre Dame, IN: University of Notre Dame Press, 1971.

Sandeen, Ernest R. *The Roots of Fundamentalism: British and American Millenarianism, 1800–1930.* Chicago: University of Chicago Press, 1970.

Schell, Jonathan. *The Fate of the Earth.* New York: Alfred A. Knopf, 1982.

Schluchter, Wolfgang. *The Rise of Western Capitalism.* Berkeley and Los Angeles: University of California Press, 1981.

Schneider, Louis. *Religion, Culture, and Society.* New York: John Wiley and Sons, 1964.

———. *A Sociological Approach to Religion.* New York: John Wiley and Sons, 1970.

Scholem, Gershom G. *Major Trends in Jewish Mysticism.* London: Thames and Hudson, 1955.

Schweid, Eliezer. *Israel at the Crossroads.* Translated by A. M. Winters. Philadelphia: Jewish Publication Society of America, 1973.

Sebok, Thomas A., ed. *A Perfusion of Signs.* Bloomington: University of Indiana Press, 1977.

Selzer, Michael, ed. *Zionism Reconsidered: The Rejection of Jewish Normalcy.* London: Macmillan, 1970.

Sensat, Julius, Jr. *Habermas and Marxism.* Beverley Hills and London: Sage Publishers, 1979.

Sharot, Stephen. *Messianism, Mysticism, and Magic: A Sociological Analysis of Jewish Religious Movements.* Chapel Hill: University of North Carolina Press, 1982.

Sharpe, Eric J. *Understanding Religion.* New York: St. Martin's Press, 1983.

Shepherd, William E. "Fundamentalism: Christian and Islamic." *Religion* 17 (October 1987): 355–78.

———. "Islam and Ideology: Towards a Typology." *International Journal of Middle Eastern Studies* 19 (October 1987): 307–36.

Shils, Edward. "The Concept and Function of Ideology." In *International Encyclopedia of the Social Sciences,* edited by David E. Sills, 7:66–76. New York: Macmillan, 1968.

———. *Tradition.* Chicago: University of Chicago Press, 1981.

Shweder, Richard A., and Edmund J. Bourne. "Does the Concept of the Person Vary Cross-culturally?" In *Cultural Conceptions of Mental Health and Therapy,* edited by Anthony J. Marsella and Geoffrey M. White, 80-115. Dordercht, Holland: D. Reidel Publishing Company, 1975.

———. "Storytelling among The Anthropologists." In the *New York Times Book Review* 21, 1, 38-39.

Siddique, Sharon. "Conceptualizing Contemporary Islam: Religion or Ideology?" *Annual Review of the Social Sciences and Summary Religion* 5 (Summer 1981): 203–23.

Sivan, Emmanuel. *Radical Islam: Medieval Theology and Modern Politics.* New Haven: Yale University Press, 1985.

———. "The Two Faces of Islamic Fundamentalism." *The Jerusalem Quarterly* 27 (Spring 1983): 127–44.

———, and Menachem Friedman, eds. *Religious Extremism and Politics in the Middle East.* Albany: State University of New York Press, forthcoming.

Skocpol, Theda, ed. *Vision and Method in Historical Sociology.* Cambridge: Cambridge University Press, 1984.

Smart, Ninian. *Beyond Ideology: Religion and the Future of Western Civilization.* New York: Harper & Row, 1981.

Smith, Anthony D. S. *Nationalism in the Twentieth Century.* New York: New York University Press, 1979.

Smith, Donald E., ed. *Religion and Political Modernization.* New Haven, CT: Yale University Press, 1974.

Smith, Elwyn A., ed. *The Religion of the Republic.* Philadelphia: Fortress Press, 1971.

Smith, Jonathan Z. *Imagining Religion.* Chicago: University of Chicago Press, 1982.

Smith, Wilfred C. *The Meaning and End of Religion.* New York: MacMillan, 1962.

Sprinzak, Ehud. "Fundamentalism, Terrorism, and Democracy: The Case of Gush Emunim Underground." *Wilson Center Occasional Papers,* No. 9. Washington, DC: The History, Culture, and Society Program, The Wilson Center, 1986.

———. *Gush Emunim: The Politics of Zionist Fundamentalism in Israel.* New York: The Mericon Jewish Committee, Institute of Human Relations, 1986.

———. "Gush Emunim: The Tip of the Iceberg." *The Jerusalem Quarterly* 21 (Fall 1981): 28–47.

———. "Kach and Meir Kahane: The Emergence of Jewish Quasi-Fascism," *Patterns of Prejudice* 19 (1985): 80-105.

Stark, Rodney, and William S. Bainbridge. "Secularization, Revival, and Cult Formation." *Annual Review of the Social Sciences of Religion* 4 (Summer 1980): 85–118.

Stott, John R. W. *Fundamentalism and Evangelism.* Grand Rapids, MI: Eerdmans Publishing Co., 1959.

Stowasser, Barbara F., ed. *The Islamic Impulse.* London: Croom Helm, 1987.

Streng, Frederick. *Understanding Religious Life.* Belmont, CA: Wadsworth, 1985.

Tax, Sol, ed. *Horizons of Anthropology.* Chicago: Aldine Publishing, 1964.

Thompson, John B. *Critical Hermeneutics: A Study in the Thought of Paul Ricoeur and Jürgen Habermas.* Cambridge: Cambridge University Press, 1981.

———. *Studies in the Theory of Ideology.* Berkeley and Los Angeles: University of California Press, 1984.

Tibi, Bassam. *Arab Nationalism: A Critical Enquiry.* Translated and edited by Marion Farouk-Sluglett and Peter Sluglett. New York: St. Martin's Press, 1981.

Toulmin, Stephen. *The Return of Cosmology.* Berkeley and Los Angeles: University of California Press, 1982.

Toumey, Christopher Paul. "The Social Context of Scientific Creationism," Ph.D. diss., Department of Anthropology, University of North Carolina, Chapel Hill, 1987.

Toynbee, Arnold J. *An Historian's Approach to Religion.* New York: Oxford University Press, 1956.

Troll, Christian. *Sayyid Ahmad Khan: A Reinterpretation of Muslim Theology.* New Delhi: Vikas, 1978.

Turner, Bryan. *Marx and the End of Orientalism.* London: George Allen Unwin, 1983.

Turner, James. *Without God, Without Creed: The Origins of Unbelief in America.* Baltimore: Johns Hopkins University Press, 1985.

Tyson, Ruel W., Jr., James L. Peacock, and Daniel W. Patterson, eds. *Diversities of Gifts: Field Studies in Southern Religion.* Urbana and Chicago: University of Illinois Press, 1988.

Vatin, Jean-Claude. "Popular Puritanism versus State Reformism: Islam in Algeria." in *Islam in the Political Process,* edited by James Piscatori, 98–121.

Vergote, Antoine. "Religion after the Critique of Psychoanalysis." *Annual Review of the Social Sciences of Religion* 4 (1980): 1–17.

Voegelin, Eric. *From Enlightenment to Revolution.* Edited by John H. Hallowell. Durham, NC: Duke University Press, 1975.

Wacker, Grant. "The Demise of Biblical Civilization." in *The Bible in America,* edited by Nathan D. Hatch and Mark A. Noll, 121–38.

Waines, David. "Through a Veil Darkly: The Study of Women in Muslim Societies." *Comparative Studies in Society and History* 24 (October 1982) : 642–59.

Waldman, Marilyn R. "Tradition as a Modality of Change: Islamic Examples," *History of Religions* 25 (May 1986): 318–40.

Wallwork, Ernest. *Durkheim: Morality and Milieu.* Cambridge: Harvard University Press, 1972.

Walzer, Michael. *The Revolution of the Saints.* Cambridge: Harvard University Press, 1965.

Waterbury, John. *Hydropolitics of the Nile.* Syracuse, NY: Syracuse University Press, 1979.

Weber, Max. *The Sociology of Religion.* Translated by Talcott Parsons. Boston: Beacon Press, 1963.

Weekes, Richard V. *Muslim Peoples: A World Ethnographic Survey.* Westport, CT: Greenwood Press, 1984.

Wells, David F., and John D. Woodbridge, eds. *The Evangelicals.* Grand Rapids, MI: Baker Book House, 1977.

White, Morton, ed. *The Age of Analysis: 20th Century Philosophers.* New York: Mentor, 1955).

Whitehead, Alfred North. *Science and the Modern World.* 1925. Reprint. New York: Macmillan, 1967.

Wiesel, Elie. *Souls on Fire.* New York: Summit, 1982.

Willner, Ann Ruth. *The Spellbinders: Charismatic Political Leadership.* New Haven and London: Yale University Press, 1984.

Wilson, Bryan R., ed. *Patterns of Sectarianism: Organization and Ideology in Social and Religious Movements.* London: Heinemann, 1967.

———. *Religion in Secular Society: A Sociological Comment.* London: C. A. Watts and Co., 1966.

———. *Religion in a Sociological Perspective.* London: Oxford University Press, 1982.

Wilson, John F. *Religion: A Preface.* Englewood Cliffs, NJ: Prentice-Hall, 1972.

———. "Modernity." In *The Encyclopedia of Religion,* edited by M. Eliade, 10:17–22. New York: Macmillan, 1987.

Wrong, Dennis H., ed. *Max Weber.* Englewood Cliffs, NJ: Prentice-Hall, 1970.

Wuthnow, Robert. "Science and the Sacred." In *The Sacred in a Secular Age,* edited by Phillip E. Hammond, 42-56. Berkeley and Los Angeles: University of California Press, 1985.

———. "Indices of Religious Resurgence in the United States." in *Resurgence,* edited by Richard T. Antoun and Mary E. Hegland, 15–34.

Yeganeh, Nahid and Nikki R. Keddie. "Sexuality and Shi'i Social Protest in Iran." In *Shi'ism and Social Protest,* edited by Juan R. I. Cole and Nikki R. Keddie, 112–34.

Young, Crawford. *The Politics of Cultural Pluralism.* Madison: University of Wisconsin Press, 1976.

Zartman, I. William. "Explaining the Nearly Inexplicable: The Absence of Islam in Moroccan Foreign Policy." In *Islam in Foreign Policy,* edited by Adeed Dawisha, 97–111.

Zucker, Norman L. *The Coming Crisis in Israel: Private Faith and Public Policy.* Cambridge: MIT Press, 1973.

———. "Secularization Conflicts in Israel." In *Religion and Political Modernization,* edited by Donald E. Smith, 88–106.

Zwi-Werblowsky, R. J. *Beyond Tradition and Modernity: Changing Religions in a Changing World.* London: The Athlone Press, 1976.

Index